Susan Hayward

Books *by* BEVERLY LINET

Susan Hayward: Portrait of a Survivor   (1980)

Ladd: The Life, the Legend, the Legacy of Alan Ladd   (1979)

Susan Hayward

Portrait of a Survivor

by Beverly Linet

Atheneum

NEW YORK

1980

Library of Congress Cataloging in Publication Data

Linet, Beverly.
    Susan Hayward, portrait of a survivor.

    1. Hayward, Susan. 2. Moving-picture actors and actresses—United States—Biography. I. Title.
PN2287.H378L5 1980   791.43′028′0924 [B]   80-66003
ISBN 0-689-11079-0

Susan had a very special gift for laying bare the agony of a woman. . . . She had been taught to understand the suffering of others. She learned it the hard way.
ROBERT WISE, Director of *I Want to Live!*

The only thing a woman should ever be afraid of in her life . . . is not having lived it.
SUSAN HAYWARD

$\mathcal{A}$ $\mathcal{P}ersonal$ $\mathcal{N}ote$

THE LAST TIME I saw Susan Hayward in person was on April 6, 1959—the night of her greatest professional triumph—at the Thirty-first Annual Academy Awards Presentation.

I desperately wanted her to win, and was almost as nervous as the nominee. As I sat in my twelfth-row-center seat at Holly-wood's Pantages Theater and heard her name called out, I jumped up screaming in excitement.

After the awards, my press pass admitted me into the back-stage tent erected for the occasion. My attention was focused on Susan. She was like someone before a firing squad. A hundred men and women were waiting to interview her: reporters with notebooks and tape recorders, TV cameramen, press from all over the world. "How did it feel to win an Oscar?" How did it feel, in-deed! It was what she had wanted all her life.

Later, at the Governors' Ball at the Beverly Hilton Hotel, I stopped by her table to congratulate her.

A day earlier we *had* talked. I was vacationing at the Beverly Hills Hotel that spring. She had flown in from Georgia and was staying in an outside bungalow. As we were leaving for the dress rehearsal of the Oscar ceremonies Sunday morning, we bumped into each other in the private garden. I felt compelled to tell her how much I was rooting for her and how I had almost kicked in my television set three years earlier when Anna Magnani had cheated her out of the award she had so richly deserved for *I'll Cry Tomorrow*.

"Win it for Brooklyn," I shouted, as we went our separate ways. At the dress rehearsal, we nodded to one another.

On Oscar night, at the festive Governors' Ball, I was seated at the same table as Sonny Tufts, a former Paramount star whose career had long since faded into oblivion. Sonny had had a great deal of champagne, and he was talking up a storm about "that ambitious little redhead" he knew from the old days. Early in his career Sonny had worked with Susan's former husband Jess Barker but, he told me, "I regret I never had a chance to work with her.

"The big shots didn't care for her. She was about the only starlet they couldn't screw. Now look at her! Someone should do a book about her. Why don't you?"

"Maybe some day I will." I laughed. "But she should really write her own—with Gerold Frank—like Lillian Roth."

From that night on, the idea of a book about Susan never left my thoughts. She had done enough living by that time to have filled a volume. Who could have prophesied what lay ahead?

Susan once said, "Being from Brooklyn is a common denominator among show-business people." Although I was a writer, I always considered myself show biz, and because I was a kid from Brooklyn too, I had followed the career of this local-girl-made-good with intense interest. There was a considerable gap in our ages, and she was a natural beauty—but we had grown up in the same environment. I was eleven when I first saw her in person: she was at the Loews' State, appearing in a vaudeville act with Louella Parsons, and when the show was over I waited outside the stage door to get her autograph. Fourteen years later, as a professional writer, I was a hostess at the *Photoplay* party the night she won their Gold Medal. Living in Hollywood, I frequently visited the sets of the movies she was making: *White Witch Doctor, Demetrius and the Gladiators,* and *I'll Cry Tomorrow* among others. As a writer, I was the first to do stories on many of her leading men, including Don Taylor, Robert Mitchum, Robert Wagner, James Mason, Kirk Douglas, and Charlton Heston, as well as interviews with such men as Jeff Chandler, Stephen Boyd, and John Wayne. Many of them contributed material to this book.

Special heartfelt thanks go to Robert Wagner, who revealed a side of Susan most people did not know—her generosity in helping aspiring young performers.

A Personal Note

I am particularly indebted to Jess Barker, Susan's first husband. Jess had refused all requests for interviews concerning Susan for more than twenty years. His warmth and graciousness in speaking to me is deeply appreciated . . . as is the friendliness and generosity of Jess's and Susan's son Timothy Barker, who phoned me of his own accord, gave me permission to quote him, and assured me that I was the only writer he and his father had spoken to since his mother's death. I hope this book does not disappoint either of them.

Susan's only brother, Wally Marrenner, spent endless hours correcting the myriad errors about Susan's early years that have appeared in print and may continue to do so. He also contributed the only picture in existence of their father. None have ever been seen before. Delightful new material about their childhood, as well as more distressing facts about her final days, came from Wally too.

My acknowledgments to the many others who came to my assistance will be found on page 326.

One final note. The last time I saw Susan Hayward, I was one of millions who watched her present the Oscar to Glenda Jackson on April 2, 1974. I knew the rumors that she was dying were true. That spring I was undergoing a grave personal crisis in my own life. I can truly say that her bravery during her final crisis gave me the will and determination to overcome mine, which was so very small in comparison.

This book does not make Susan Hayward a saint. She wasn't one. I have tried to present her as a human being. And a survivor. And *that* she certainly was.

BEVERLY LINET

New York City
1980

CONTENTS

Prologue   3

Part One: EDYTHE MARRENNER, *Brooklyn, New York,*
June 30, 1917–June 30, 1935   7

Part Two: EDYTHE MARRENER/SUSAN HAYWARD,
Hollywood, December 1937–July 22, 1944   37

Part Three: MRS. JESS BARKER, *Hollywood, July 24,*
1944–April 26, 1955   85

Part Four: SUSAN HAYWARD, *Hollywood, April 26, 1955–*
February 8, 1957   185

Part Five: MRS. FLOYD EATON CHALKLEY, *Carrollton,*
Georgia–Fort Lauderdale, Florida, February 8, 1957–
January 9, 1966   215

Part Six: THE WIDOW CHALKLEY, *Fort Lauderdale,*
Florida, January 9, 1966–January 22, 1971   251

Part Seven: SUSAN HAYWARD, *Beverly Hills, California,*
September 1971–March 14, 1975 (2:25 P.M.)   279

Epilogue   309

Appendix A: *Last Will and Testament of Edythe*
Marrenner Chalkley   315

Appendix B: *Filmography*   318

Acknowledgments   326

Index   329

xi

ILLUSTRATIONS

(FOLLOWING PAGE 82)

Weeks-old Edythe Marrenner and mother, 1917
    INSET: *father, Walter Marrenner, in 1936*

Edythe at six, and pony

Edythe and sister in 1924

Edythe at nine and one-half and eleven

The graduating class of P.S. 181, June 1931

As a Walter Thornton model, 1937

Studio portrait as Susan Hayward

As a Warners starlet

Paramount's "Golden Circle" of promising stars

Susan as Isobel in Beau Geste

In Louella Parsons' "Flying Stars" vaudeville tour

Susan in New York on the Parsons' tour

Near Paramount's DeMille Gate in 1940

Publicity for Adam Had Four Sons, *opening at Radio City Music Hall*

Scene from Adam Had Four Sons

With Robert Preston in Reap the Wild Wind

Susan and Veronica Lake in I Married a Witch

With brother Wally on the set of Hit Parade of 1943

On the set of Jack London

Susan receiving calls on the set of And Now Tomorrow

Marriage for Susan and Jess Barker, 1944

The Barker twins grow up

Twins at six and one-half with Susan and Robert Mitchum

Twins at nine, celebrating Susan's birthday on the set of The Conqueror

At the 1956 Oscars

Lux Radio Theater production of The Petrified Forest, *1945*

xii

Illustrations

First Oscar nomination for portrayal in Smash-Up—The Story of a Woman

Lee Bowman, Susan, and Eddie Albert in Smash-Up

In My Foolish Heart

A 1953 studio portrait

(FOLLOWING PAGE 178)

In David and Bathsheba, with Gregory Peck

With a Song in My Heart, with Robert Wagner

Posing with school buddy Jeff Chandler at Photoplay party

Julio Aparicio dedicates a bull to Susan in Spain

Waiting for court hearings on her divorce to begin

Swimming pool that was alleged to be "scene of the crime"

In 1955, a near-fatal dose of sleeping pills

On her release from the hospital

Scenes from I'll Cry Tomorrow, with Jo Van Fleet

With Lillian Roth and Mike Connolly at I'll Cry Tomorrow premiere

With Ingrid Bergman at Cannes Film Festival in 1956

Secret marriage to Eaton Chalkley in 1957

The Chalkley's farm near Carrollton, Georgia

Breakthrough movie, I Want to Live!

Walter Wanger and Susan in New York for publicity on I Want to Live!

Receiving New York Film Critics' Award for Best Actress

Oscar night, April 9, 1959

Back home in Georgia

Sister Florence in 1960

Bette Davis and Susan

With Patty Duke in Valley of the Dolls

Susan in Mame at Caesar's Palace in Las Vegas

Susan attends son Gregory's graduation from University of Alabama

Saved from fire in her apartment

With Lee J. Cobb in 1972 TV movie

Last public appearance, as an Oscar presenter in 1974

Funeral near Chalkley home

A lasting memorial at Hollywood's "Chinese Theater"

xiii

Susan Hayward

PROLOGUE

THE DATE WAS April 2, 1974; the place, the Dorothy Chandler Pavilion of the Los Angeles Music Center; the event, the Forty-sixth Annual Awards Presentation of the Academy of Motion Picture Arts and Sciences.

That evening, as always, a capacity crowd had endured the preliminaries, awaiting the climax of Oscar night: the winners of the major awards for acting, directing, and Best Picture. Unlike always, however, there was an unusual amount of suspense in the air. Several weeks earlier, the Academy had announced that Susan Hayward would be appearing on stage to present the Best Actress award—but the rumors had been circulating for months that Hayward was gravely ill, even dying, of cancer. Multiple brain tumors, it was said—the words alone were terrifying. She could not possibly appear.

The tension increased as David Niven, who had shared the 1958 acting Oscars with Susan, appeared on stage and announced: "Ladies and gentlemen, Charlton Heston has created many miracles . . . just illusions on the screen. But in presenting our next award, he brings with him, not an illusion, but the real thing—*Miss Susan Hayward.*"

And there she was, on Heston's arm. The audience in the Chandler Pavilion exploded in applause, many rising to their feet to pay their respects. What they didn't know, however, was that that night Susan Hayward *was* an illusion.

A blazing red wig covered her head, now bald from cobalt treatments. Her missing eyebrows had been penciled in and her face carefully made up to hide the ravages of the illness. A dazzling, green, form-fitting, sequined gown with a high neck and long sleeves concealed her emaciated body and withered right arm; within her body a massive dose of Dilantin fought to ward off seizures—and, holding it all together was Susan herself: her

3

determination, her refusal to give in, her desire to go out "looking smashing."

And that's exactly how she did look. What the audience saw that night was not a dying woman but a vision of loveliness; a woman who looked only a few years older than she had when she'd stepped on the stage of the Pantages Theater fifteen years earlier to receive her own Oscar for *I Want to Live!*

Only once did Susan waver—the moment before she was about to step on stage. Charlton Heston took her firmly by the arm, murmured, "Easy, girl," and supported her to the microphones. Later she admitted, "He did it at the right moment. I was shaking so bad."

The eyes of fifty million viewers were focused on Susan Hayward that night. Few now recall the award she gave out, to Glenda Jackson for *A Touch of Class.* It was Susan Hayward in the last year of her life who gave the greatest performance of the year. Flushed and wobbly afterward, Susan admitted to her nurse Carmen Perugini, who had been waiting offstage in case Susan needed her help: "Well, that's the last time I pull that off."

In 1974, the Hollywood establishment was behind Susan with prayers and a fervor she could never have anticipated. Hollywood had always considered Susan Hayward a strange one. During the course of a career that had spanned nearly thirty-seven years and five Oscar nominations, she had been called shy, aggressive, fearful, domineering, brilliant, amateurish, impulsive, calculating, ambitious, gracious, inhibited, explosive, parsimonious, and generous beyond words.

Among her directors, producers, and co-stars, she had evoked intense reactions, both pro and con. Richard Denning, a Paramount contractee in the forties, had called her "ambitious, unscrupulous, and selfish," and Bette Davis had said frankly, "It is with sadness that I tell you that Miss Hayward was utterly unkind to me." Yet John Wayne always admired her, Agnes Moorehead would say, "I was her greatest fan," and Robert Wagner, who became prominent overnight after doing *With a Song in My Heart* with Susan, would affirm: "Susan was marvelous. . . . She was a very big star, and I was just a young kid starting out and didn't know much about what I was doing . . . and she must have realized that, because, my God, she was so helpful."

Perhaps the most significant comment came from Fredric

March, who'd worked with her early in her career. "She was touchy on the set, and it was a rare day she mingled with the cast," he said. "But somewhere along the line she learned to act. Every inch of that woman is an actress. She can portray a lonely, desperate, frustrated woman because she has experienced all those emotions. If you look closely, you'll see they left scars on her heart."

All through her life, Susan Hayward had to battle for happiness. For over three decades, she dazzled audiences and critics with portrayals of tragic, stormy women—a gallery of winners, losers, fighters, and survivors—and she knew them well, because they were all her.

Born to poverty and bred to insecurity, Susan was left with a permanent handicap by an automobile accident at the age of seven that made her the butt of cruel jokes. The defenses she set up to protect herself caused her to be rejected and unpopular in her teens; but she found comfort in the fantasies in which she envisioned herself a great lady, a brilliant actress, a perfect wife; and with fierce determination she struggled to make those fantasies realities. She fought the Hollywood casting-couch system and proved she could make it without cheapening herself. She fought the erosion in her first marriage until it ended in a headlined donnybrook, then battled her way through a calamitous divorce and wrenching custody suit.

She endured four losing tries for an Oscar she desperately wanted before finally grasping the prize; survived a suicide attempt, scandal headlines over a triangle affair, a devastating widowhood in her second marriage (to a man she thought she knew, but didn't), a string of professional disasters, a comeback fiasco in Las Vegas, and a narrow escape from a fire that destroyed her apartment and almost her life. Finally she succumbed to a cancer of suspicious origin—but not before a years-long struggle that doctors called "absolutely extraordinary."

These were the external events and most were played out in the public spotlight. But what was the driving force so deeply buried in the soul of this complex, volatile woman, the elements that both brought her to tragedy and gave her the strength to fight back and triumph—even over death itself?

Tim Barker, one of her twin sons from her first marriage, says today, "My mother was a very private woman. Very private. . . .

No one can get to the heart of my mother unless one knew my grandmother."

He is partly right. To get to the heart of Susan Hayward—born Edythe Marrenner—one has to know not only her mother, but her father too. And the Brooklyn that shaped all three.

PART ONE

Edythe Marrenner
Brooklyn, New York
June 30, 1917 — June 30, 1935

My life is fair game for anybody. I spent an unhappy, penniless childhood in Brooklyn. I had to slug my way up in a town called Hollywood where people love to trample you to death. I don't relax because I don't know how. I don't want to know how. Life is too short to relax.

SUSAN HAYWARD

chapter 1

EDYTHE MARRENNER'S earliest memories were of fear—and of survival.

She could never pinpoint how old she was when she first learned how it felt to be scared, really scared, but the incident remained vivid throughout her life.

She had been visiting her Grandmother Pearson, when an uncle with a sadistic streak warned her that there was a bogey-man at the top of the stairs waiting to get her if she wasn't a good girl. Edythe was not too sure what a bogeyman was, but she had heard of this terrible creature who lurked in the dark ready to pounce on children who weren't obedient or didn't listen to their elders or who spoke out of turn.

After that she never liked the dark or her uncle, and she avoided both whenever possible. More than a half century later, when she was dying, an acquaintance asked if she was afraid of the dark.

"Let's put it this way," she replied, "I feel more comfortable sleeping in the daytime."

When the sun was shining she was fearless. Although she had been warned repeatedly not to cross the street by herself, she was never afraid that a bogeyman might be hiding behind the auto-mobiles that lined the Church Avenue curbs. Until the accident.

Shortly after Edythe turned seven, she bought a three-penny paper parachute at the local candy store. With the help of a warm summer breeze, she glided it through the air until it floated out onto the avenue and she had to retrieve it. She could hear neighbors warning her to be careful, but she didn't see the car swooping down on her: just a blur. Edythe was very myopic—and she didn't own a pair of glasses.

Vaguely she remembered one of the ladies screaming, then felt a terribly sharp pain as she was tossed onto the curb. For a little while, she just lay there, half-conscious, as someone rushed to 3507 Church Avenue and up four flights of stairs to get her mother, Ellen. No one called an ambulance. Edythe never recalled how she was carried there; Ellen never said, but the little girl was taken directly to the office of the neighborhood doctor.

Edythe was lucky. The driver had seen her just in time. Had she been hit a split second sooner, she could have been killed. As it was, no signs of internal injuries were detected: just a broken hip. The physician suggested an ambulance be called and Edythe taken to nearby Kings County Hospital, but her mother was suspicious of hospitals and particularly leery of the city-run Kings County, which had opened a few years earlier. Although it possessed some of the most modern facilities and equipment available at the time, it also carried a reputation among the ill-informed of being a "nut house," and a place where only charity patients went. In fact, the hospital did have a psychiatric wing for the mentally disturbed—one of the most advanced in the country—but mental illness was considered as bad as the plague among the women on Church Avenue. And it did have wards for those unable to pay medical bills, but there were also private and semiprivate rooms for those who could afford it. Ellen Marrenner was aware of none of this. All she knew was that if someone did or said something different in her neighborhood, they were put down with the words, "You should be sent to Kings County." That's how it was in Brooklyn in 1924. Ellen would not have her daughter stigmatized in that way.

Edythe was encased in a plaster-of-Paris cast and carried back to the apartment. Because the doctor insisted she be placed in traction immediately, her father Walter Marrenner set up a makeshift pulley device. Years later, Edythe would relate how Mrs. Robert Emslie, their downstairs neighbor, thinking the contraption barbaric, vainly tried to persuade the family to take the patient to the hospital for proper treatment. Ellen ignored the advice, insisting Edythe would be better cared for and happier at home.

In truth, Edythe *was* happier. She enjoyed being the center of attention and she'd later remember how Deacon Titus of the Baptist church on Nostrand Avenue, where she and her brother and sister, Wally and Florence, attended Sunday School, would visit and bring her jigsaw puzzles and oranges.

Other neighbors brought her presents too: dog-eared copies of *Photoplay* and *Motion Picture* magazines. Edythe would read about Douglas Fairbanks's exploits in *The Thief of Bagdad* and marvel over the costumes worn by Mary Pickford in *Dorothy Vernon of Haddon Hall*, Lon Chaney, Jr., in *He Who Gets Slapped*, John Barrymore in *Beau Brummell*, and Rudolph Valentino in *Monsieur Beaucaire*.

Edythe was old enough to know it was all make-believe, and young enough to be plunged into fantasies of being part of another world in another time. Her months in bed afforded an escape from the ugly world outside. A child of intense feelings, she hated the effect poverty had had on her mother and on her weary, resigned father. She was repelled by the squalor of the streets and the smell of roach-infested garbage cans. Even before her accident she had detached herself from this world, whenever and however possible.

Decades would pass, however, before she'd admit that "as a child you could say I was the world's biggest liar. I would weave tales like you wouldn't believe. I can still remember walking home from school when I was six, telling the other children about all the beautiful dresses I had at home in the closet—lying through my teeth! I guess that's when I first began acting, or at least getting interested in it—pretending, making believe, using my imagination. This I was born with—an imagination and a natural talent for lying. The perfect ingredients for an actor."

Confined to bed for months, Edythe had ample opportunity to let her imagination go wild. She had an Aunt Lillian, whom she adored, who had escaped from Brooklyn when she'd married a handsome Southern gentleman named Walter Scott Meriwether, editor of the *Mississippi Sun*. Her aunt would often write to the family and send snapshots taken in front of her Mississippi home. Edythe often fancied herself in that setting, dressed in green chiffon or white organdie. These fantasies would later have a profound effect on her vision of the ideal marriage.

Katie Harrigan Marrenner would come by often to look in on

Edythe. Grandma Marrenner was shanty Irish down to her finger-tips, but Edythe's imagination, helped by the fiction fed her from the fan magazines, transformed her into Katie Harrigan, the most talented actress in County Cork, who had given up her career to marry the man she loved. In years to come, Edythe would perpetrate that fiction to such an extent that it would become an accepted "fact" of her background. In truth, neither Katie nor grandfather Joseph Marrenner ever got closer to Ireland than the annual Saint Patrick's Day parade.

But when Edythe looked back on those endless weeks in bed, the happiest moments she'd recall would be the ones she spent alone with her father—when Ellen and Florence were out shopping, and Wally was off somewhere playing with his friends. Her father would read to her, or just talk with her. Sensing her pain and her need for love, fearful of the possibility that she might be lame for life, Walter would tell her, time and again, "You must be like a rubber ball. The harder they hit you, the higher you'll bounce. That is, if you are a good ball to begin with. If not, you might as well give up anyway."

His words were repeated often enough for her to accept them as gospel. For the rest of her life, they would provide Edythe with the impetus to bounce right back and fight.

Sara Little, Edythe's only close childhood friend—the friendship would survive for four decades—would describe Walter Marrenner as the single most important influence in his daughter's early life. "He was an extremely sensitive man, and he had a significant effect on her. There was a beautiful rapport between them."

Edythe had ambivalent feelings toward her mother. She wanted Ellen's approval and love, yet she was unhappy that Ellen was so different from the Aunt Lillian whom she admired so much. Edythe wanted to grow up to be like Aunt Lillian; she didn't want to be like the defeated, careworn Ellen Marrenner. And she wondered how two sisters could turn out so differently.

Edythe was unaware of it at the time, but Ellen herself was consumed with envy when she compared her life to Lillian's. In fact, all her brothers and sisters were living in comfort, while she had to content herself with their children's cast-off clothes for her family. Ellen's father had admonished her, however: "You made your bed. . . ." Had Ellen not met Walter Marrenner, everything would have been different.

Ellen F. Pearson's family had migrated to America from Skåne, Sweden. Most of Theodore Pearson's contemporaries had continued west to settle in Minnesota's rich farm belt, but Theodore Pearson was attracted to the possibilities of Brooklyn and nearby Queens. He foresaw a need for housing to accommodate the hordes of immigrants wishing to settle in New York City, and set out to fill that need—and his pockets—by building railroad flats on the undeveloped Carroll and President streets, and tenements on the land facing Saint Anne's church on Front Street in Brooklyn.

He was as prolific in bed as in the building business. In addition to Ellen (born October 10, 1888), he sired three sons, Theodore, Jr., Oscar, and Guy; and six more daughters, Lillian, Alice, Jenny, Emma, and twin girls who died in infancy. He built a large house for himself and his family on Hoyt Street in downtown Brooklyn, and made sure his children were well fed, well dressed, and well disciplined. Pearson instilled in his sons the value of the dollar. His wife instilled in her daughters the same attitudes toward sex that had been instilled in her by her mother, who had, in turn, inherited her values from her mother before.

What the Pearsons had in cash, they lacked in class, but, like others of their kind, they had hopes that their wealth would be instrumental in assuring proper marriages for their children. In spite of this, Theodore Pearson wanted his daughters to be self-sufficient and encouraged their working until they were wed.

Ellen was twenty, and working as a stenographer, when she met twenty-nine-year-old Walter Marrenner, a dashing, red-headed Coney Island barker. The details of their meeting and subsequent courtship would never be discussed with their children, but their son Wally is aware that "the old man never cared much for my father." Pearson, in fact, was so opposed to the match that he threatened to disown Ellen if she persisted in seeing Marrenner. He would not have his daughter marry beneath her. He underestimated the extent of Walter's charm and sex appeal, however—and he underestimated his daughter's strong will.

Pearson's antagonism toward the young man was aggravated by the fact that Walter Marrenner was a Catholic. To Pearson, getting involved with a Catholic was doubtless almost as bad as getting involved with a Jew. Ellen's promise to bring her children up in the Protestant faith failed to budge him an inch.

Walter Marrenner's parents were equally distressed by the match. Brooklyn-born Joseph and Katherine Harrigan Marrenner were staunch Catholics. To them, a marriage outside the church was the same as no marriage at all—but Walter had always been the rebellious one of their five children, the one who would skip church on summer Sunday mornings in order to beat the crowd to Coney Island. Then, when Walter had been old enough to hold down a job, he'd headed for Coney for a different reason and, being a young man of intense glibness and charm, had been hired as a barker for one of the live attractions—a Brooklyn Billy Bigelow from *Carousel*. During the winter, he worked as an usher at the Brooklyn Academy of Music, to keep himself in spending money until summer rolled around again. Marrenner had no worries, no responsibilities, and a multitude of girl friends until Ellen entered his life. How she was able to land him when so many other prettier, sexier girls had failed was a family mystery, but Ellen had an iron will when it came to getting what she wanted, and she wanted Walter Marrenner.

On August 14, 1909, the two ran off and were married. According to their son Wally, there were no wedding pictures taken of his mother and father; if there had been, he would have seen them. In fact, he remembers today, "My father never posed with any members of the family. Not even for a little snapshot." There had never been an engagement ring, either—a fact that would later trouble the young Edythe.

Two weeks after the wedding, Ellen Marrenner conceived. Their first child, a daughter they named Florence, was born on May 29, 1910. Florence, a captivating baby with red hair, a pert nose and expressive eyes, resembled Walter physically and also inherited many of his personality traits. There would be little of the Pearson heritage in her.

When Florence was nine months old, Ellen became pregnant again. She had fallen in love with Walter because of his gaiety, charm, and dashing, irresponsible nature, but now she demanded he put his Coney Island days behind him and find an honest job. "You have responsibilities," she told him firmly.

Totally lacking in practical experience at the age of thirty-one, Walter found it difficult to get a decently paying position with a chance for advancement. He settled, instead, for blue-collar work as a lineman with the Interboro Rapid Transit Company. His hours were long and erratic. Some months he'd be put on the night shift and not return home until the early hours of the morning; other times he'd be up at the crack of dawn.

Walter Marrenner, Jr.'s birth on December 8, 1911, brought additional problems and expenses. Wally was a frail, sickly child with an undiagnosable stomach ailment that weakened his legs. "It wasn't polio or anything like that," Wally says today. "I don't know what they called it. But I had to wear braces for a long time."

Wally didn't look like Walter Marrenner, nor did he resemble the Pearson side of the family, according to his own evaluation. And his infirmity did little to help the rift between his mother and Theodore Pearson.

"I don't remember the old man very well," says Wally. "He died when I was a kid"—but not before cutting Ellen out of his will entirely and expressing a wish to the rest of the family that he didn't want "that Irishman ever laying a hand on a dime of my money." Grandpa Pearson had convinced himself that Walter's interest in his daughter had been motivated by the Pearson wealth, and his admonishment, "You made your bed, now lie in it," would extend to the grave.

Wally was five when his mother became pregnant for the third and final time. His baby sister, given the name Edythe, was delivered by one W. T. Pink of 160 McDonough Street on June 30, 1917, in the family's Church Avenue apartment. Mrs. Emslie, in keeping with Scottish tradition, put a shiny new dime in the baby's hand a few hours after her birth. It would be symbolic.

Like Florence, Edythe was a perfect, red-headed infant, and Florence would proudly wheel the baby carriage around the block showing off her new sister to the neighbors.

Edythe's crib was placed in the Marrenners' bedroom. When she outgrew it, she shared a room with Florence and Ellen. Wally remembers being moved into his father's room—an arrangement that would last for as long as the family lived on Church Avenue. For years, the Marrenners were unable to accumulate enough money to move to larger quarters, although Walter was moving up in his job and would eventually, according to Wally, "become a wire chief up in the telephone department of the company."

Unlike his sisters, Wally took the family's fortunes philosophically. "Sure we were poor," he confirms, "but so were most people in the neighborhood, so there was nothing different about us. We got along good and had enough to eat. . . ."

Wally resents stories that have portrayed Walter as an alcoholic. "My father was never a drinker. He couldn't take more than two drinks at any one time. And he never gambled away his money." Almost sheepishly, though, Wally admits that his father had "extra activities" going on. Trapped in a marriage that restricted him, bound to a wife who was increasingly full of gloom and doom, Walter eventually found someone else to escape to.

Wally says he never knew the woman's name, nor is he able to provide definite information as to when and how she entered Walter's life. However, she was definitely a part of it to the very end. The only time Wally saw her was "when my father's lady friend attended his funeral." He doesn't know if his mother ever became aware of her rival, but concedes that Ellen "was suspicious." The chances are she was more than that; certainly her bitterness would affect both her daughters.

Aware that she had been swept away by a physical attraction for Marrenner, Ellen blamed her loveless, poverty-stricken life on her weakness. She was determined to make certain her children would not fall victim to a similar fate—but she never realized how much damage she'd inflict by her harangues against men. In that respect, Ellen was not that much different from other women of her neighborhood and class—women who talked of menstruation in whispers, and considered girls who petted on front porches "fast" and premarital sex the hallmark of whores. Across the bridge in Manhattan, the Jazz Age was in full swing; buildings were getting taller, skirts shorter, and morals looser every day. Ellen's Brooklyn might as well have been located on a different planet; its residents were that far removed from the times.

Florence, fourteen when Edythe had her accident, was painfully aware of what was going on across the bridge and eager to be part of it. A student at Erasmus Hall High School, popular with the boys—and interested in them in return—Florence laughed off Ellen's dramatic warnings that boys were only interested in one thing, and that girls who let boys touch them were ruined for life. Walter's warm blood flowed through her veins, as did his love of show business.

Florence dreamed of being on Broadway. A natural-born dancer, she managed to get together enough money to take tap and ballet lessons at Miss Edna Simmons's local studio. When she came home from dance class, she'd entertain her mother and her bedridden sister by doing the new steps she had learned that day. Ellen did not discourage Florence's ambitions. She had read of the money paid to show people and perhaps thought that through Florence she'd find a better life. As a result, she tended to favor Florence a bit, without realizing that she was planting the seeds of resentment in Edythe's head. Edythe would grow up always thinking her mother preferred Florence to her.

Florence was possibly unaware of the effect her mother's attentions were having on her baby sister. Florence had always been fussed over as a child. Years later, she'd say, "A lot of people said I was the prettier, but I never agreed with that. When Edythe was run over by the car, I was so scared. I thought I'd die if anything ever happened to her. I guess I always had a protective instinct about her."

Wally was blissfully unaware of the psychological forces at work. Having spent the first nine years of his life in braces, he didn't consider Edythe's temporary cast such a big deal. "I kept outgrowing them," he remembers. "So one day my father just said, 'We can't afford new braces any more. Let the kid go without them.' I was getting a little older and stronger, so out they went. I started running in high school, and when that got too strenuous, I turned to ice-skating. And I haven't had a bit of trouble with my legs since."

Edythe would not be that fortunate.

Ellen Marrenner gave only one magazine interview during her lifetime. Her daughter Edythe had made certain Ellen was off-limits to the press, and the one time she did talk, in March 1957, it was mainly about the automobile accident.

Ellen remembered that "For a year and a half I hauled her three blocks to P.S. 181 in a little wagon, then she hobbled into her room on crutches. In the afternoon, I'd be there waiting with the little wagon. But Edythe never cried. She was full of grit—more so than her brother and sister—and harder to handle. She'd struggle on her legs, making herself walk on pure nerve, stubborn-like. You'd die for her, but you knew she'd do it. She's been like that all her life."

Edythe, however, never told her mother of the humiliations she suffered in her classroom. Young children can be the cruelest of creatures, and Edythe would wince when they'd refer to her as the Gimp. In addition, she was the butt of jokes because of her red hair: redheads were decidedly in the minority at P.S. 181 — they were different, considered freaks. There was also the problem with her eyesight. Young boys and girls who wore glasses were nicknamed Four Eyes and tormented, so, though Edythe could barely see the figures on the blackboard, she never let on.

The situation at school only worsened after her cast was removed. Because of the improper traction, the hip did not heal properly and, according to Wally, Susan was left with "one leg a half inch shorter than the other. That's why she had to wear a lift in her shoe which gave her the strut in her walk. Not a limp—just a different kind of walk, but it was noticeable."

It was a strut that would later be considered "sexy"; at the time, her schoolmates thought it funny. Edythe was determined that no one would know how deeply hurt she was; she merely ignored the other kids at school.

Nor did she partake in the neighborhood's social life.

Wally would remember that whenever he or Edythe or Florence had a birthday, the celebration was strictly a family affair. Their dad would buy a quart of ice cream and a little cake, and that was the extent of it. Edythe once recalled that "We kids never had a birthday party . . . we couldn't afford them. Kids never invited me to their parties, because they knew I couldn't return the invitation. Anyway, I never had a party dress to wear. My Christmas present was hand-me-down clothes from cousins who were living a little higher on the hog. But they didn't fit— always three sizes too big. Our Christmas trees too were castoffs. Wally and I waited until the last minutes on Christmas Eve when the storekeepers threw them out. We'd pick out the least misshapen one and drag it home. How poor was I? When I had a hole in my shoe, I had to slip cardboard into it. I had to pick up second-day bread at the bakery. I had a gray linen dress that meant everything in the world to me because it was a present from my father—not a hand-me-down. When I spilled cocoa on it, there wasn't enough money to have it cleaned."

Eager to have some money of her own, she persuaded Wally to allow her to help him on his paper route on weekends. The two added to their incomes by finding and cashing in milk and soda bottles. Wally remembers going around to the different apartments salvaging old newspapers and selling them to a local junk-man by weight. They'd increase their take by cutting a hole in the middle of the pile and filling it with rocks, until the junk dealer got wise and threw them both out.

Florence detached herself from these kinds of activities. There was always some local boy eager to take her to the picture show and then blow ten cents on an ice cream soda at Mrs. Grossel's candy store. Florence was counting the days until she could quit school and embark on a career as a professional dancer. Wally, by now a whiz on skates, wanted to join an ice show and spent all his extra money going to the Brooklyn Ice Palace.

Edythe, constantly reminded of her slight deformity by her classmates, and abashed by Flo's prettiness, thought all avenues of escape were closed to her. Nonetheless, she'd remember that "Mother believed I could do anything I set my mind to. It was she who always fought our inclinations as youngsters to say, 'I can't do this' or 'I can't do that,' telling us not to say we can't do a thing because, of course, we could do anything anyone else could do."

When Edythe was ten, another world opened up to her. A drama teacher at P.S. 181 named Charlotte Rappaport took an interest in her. Edythe remembered that "Miss Rappaport was tiny and blondish—and she thought it was about time fairy princesses in school plays were brunettes and redheads instead of blondes. She always encouraged me and cast me as the princess in one play after another and took great pride in my performances."

In one such play, *Cinderella in Flowerland,* Ira Grossel, the dark-haired son of the candy-store owner, was cast as Prince Charming. Ira ran into voice trouble during rehearsals, however, and Miss Rappaport reluctantly had to replace him. Edythe was sympathetic, and the two budding performers struck up a friendship that, if not intimate at the time, would be fondly remembered when the two met again in Hollywood a quarter of a century later. He would then be known as Jeff Chandler, and an overromantic press, encouraged by the studio, would conspire to make a big affair of the childhood association and their current dates. Ira and Edythe were not childhood sweethearts. Mrs. Grossel, a religious lady embittered by her husband's desertion, owned a house next door to the local synagogue (at 209 East 37th Street) and would not have had her little Ira mixing with any of the *shiksas* in the predominantly Jewish neighborhood.

Edythe was about to enter sixth grade, when Florence came home one afternoon and informed Ellen and Walter that she was leaving Erasmus. She had been offered seventy-five dollars a week to tour the East Coast with Ned Wayburn's dance troupe and had been promised a ballet specialty act of her own. This was the chance she had been waiting for, and it meant a lot more to her than a high school diploma. Before Ellen had a chance to become too agitated, Florence promised to send home a generous portion of her salary. Ellen sent her off to Philadelphia with her blessings, and Edythe saw her leave with few misgivings. Edythe was still convinced—perhaps unjustifiably—that she had been playing second fiddle to her sister.

Florence, however, saw things in a different light, remembering that, as Edythe grew up, "We all sort of gave in to her. My mother never ordered her to do any chores around the house, but I was always more of a homebody than Susan, and I used to help with the dishes and cleaning and go to the grocery store. Susan never liked doing things like that, and nobody ever made her do it."

Edythe may have had to help with the dishes now, but she was nonetheless probably at her happiest when Florence was on the road with Ned Wayburn. The bedroom wasn't strewn with Florence's possessions, and when Edythe returned from school she had more privacy in which to indulge in her daydreams.

Meanwhile, the domestic situation was not good. Edythe could hear Ellen berating her husband when Florence's checks came in the mail, "Your daughter is making a better living then you are." There would be many such scenes, not totally understood at the time perhaps, but remembered years later when Edythe would describe her mother as "an intensely emotional, dramatic woman who frequently climaxed emotional arguments with my father by extending her arm and wailing, 'Go on, break it, break it.' With Mom, everything was a three-act play. And she wanted to play all the parts herself. I guess I get some of that quality

20

from her. But Dad would just laugh and leave to join his cronies."

Walter would laugh—and leave. But not always to join his cronies.

Ellen's dramatic flair reached a new high when Florence returned to New York. In the spring of 1929, exhilarated by her success with Ned Wayburn, Florence auditioned for and won a job as a chorus replacement in the Broadway musical hit *Follow Thru* starring Eleanor Powell, Jack Haley, and Zelma O'Neill. When Florence hinted that she was considering sharing an apartment in the city with another show girl to avoid the long trip back and forth to Brooklyn every night, Ellen put her foot down, as she warned of the fate that could befall a single girl living on her own.

A compromise of sorts was reached. Florence agreed to live at home; Ellen found a larger and better apartment at 2568 Bedford Avenue, which Florence's earnings would now subsidize.

Edythe celebrated her twelfth birthday by attending a matinee performance of *Follow Thru,* and Florence remembered introducing her to Eleanor Powell, who shook Edythe's hand and told her that she was a beautiful girl. Mrs. Rappaport had told her that too. But Edythe didn't feel beautiful. How could she when the kids at school were still teasing her, and when she knew she couldn't see ten feet ahead of herself?

Visiting Florence at the theater, however, left a very deep impression upon her. The dancing girls were all huddled in a large, crowded basement room, where they were forced to strip naked in front of one another. Eleanor Powell, the lead dancer, had a private room to herself on the main floor, and no one could enter without her permission. Being in a show wasn't all that great, Edythe concluded, unless one was the most important thing in the show: the *best* dancer, the *best* singer, the *best* actor. She never allowed herself to forget that. Somehow Florence wouldn't seem very special to her again.

The Wall Street crash the following October, which heralded the Great Depression, had no immediate effect on the Marrenner family. Florence continued on Broadway, going from *Follow Thru* to *New Moon,* and she remained at home with the family.

According to Wally, the two sisters seemed to be getting along well at the time. He can, in fact, remember only one serious fight between them, though the details escape him. "Florence was real mad when I stuck up for Edythe. She thought I was doing it because Edythe was younger. I thought 'Jesus, I'm in the middle now.' But things like that happen in every family and it was soon forgotten." Or so Wally thought.

Early in 1931, the family was shocked when Florence abruptly quit show business. The source for this fact is Wally Marrenner. "She gave it up," explains Wally, "because she fell in love with some guy, some German. I think she got married. I don't know. I can't say. [Florence never said either.] I guess she threw up whatever her career may have been in the future, and she got a job in a bakery store. Isn't that some comedown?"

Edythe probably felt it and was secretly pleased to be overshadowed by her older sister no longer. Ellen's reaction was probably more of confusion: she had come to depend on Florence's contributions but, more than that, she had hoped that Florence's career would lead her into a marriage with one of the wealthy men who, she read, were drawn to show girls. She wouldn't have known what had gotten into Florence, or considered that her own preaching had likely contributed to Florence's rebellion.

Now Ellen transferred her frustrations to Edythe, pounding into her head the methods men used to lead gullible girls astray— though she never specified exactly what the latter entailed. Mothers couldn't talk openly about sex with their daughters in 1931; they could only hint of the dangers of being "touched." "Advice to the Lovelorn" columns warned: "Boys never marry girls who will tarry."

Ellen did her job well. When Edythe graduated from P.S. 181 in June, she decided against attending Erasmus Hall High School, which most of the kids in her class attended automatically. Edythe had at least three reasons for her decision: She wanted to get away from the schoolmates who had made fun of her. She didn't want to attend a coeducational school. And she felt she could have a whole new life at the school she chose—Girls' Commercial High, located a five-cent trolley ride away on Clausen Avenue in the shadow of the Brooklyn Museum, a few blocks from Prospect Park. It was an exclusive neighborhood, dotted with large private mansions and newly constructed elevator apartment buildings, and Girls' Commercial High was attended by the daughters of professional men—doctors, dentists, and lawyers. Edythe's classmates for the most part were thoroughly upper middle class, majoring in typing and stenography, and hoping to be married before the occasion arose for them to have to use either skill.

In September 1931, Edythe was probably the poorest teen-ager in her freshman class. Once again, pride drove her into herself. Feeling socially inferior, mistrusting a show of affection that could turn to rejection if her background was revealed, she pretended disdain and sprouted porcupine quills. Though some of her classmates may have felt she was stuck up, it was a form of defense, her instinctive way of salvaging her ego. And she would never admit that, outside the classroom, her myopia prevented her from recognizing her schoolmates until she was almost on top of them. It was easier to remain aloof. Only Sara Little was able to penetrate her facade. Sara was bright, independent, and, like Edythe, wanted something more out of life than to be a Brooklyn housewife. Years later, Sara would reminisce: "That was the era of the big dream. But there was no question of our ultimate success. We felt we were destined."

At Girls' Commercial High, Edythe's ambition to act was furthered by a teacher named Florence O'Grady: "We once had to write a composition on any subject and I turned in one called 'I Want to Be an Actress.' Miss Grady said, 'Well, why don't you do something about it?'"

She did. She appeared in all the school plays, and Mrs. Dorothy Yawger, who ran the dramatic club, recalled, "Edythe always chose the parts no one else would take. Usually it was the unpleasant one, like a toothless old woman—any part with dramatic possibilities. She did them well."

She may have done them well because she identified with them. The toothless hag and the girl with one leg shorter than the other were compatible. Princesses represented perfection—and no matter what her father or Sara Little or her teachers said, Edythe knew she was imperfect.

Nevertheless, she still pursued her dream of becoming an actress. She had her idols. Barbara Stanwyck was high on her list, and not just because Miss Stanwyck was a fine actress. Barbara Stanwyck was a Brooklyn girl named Ruby Stevens who had risen above her background and become both a movie star and a great lady, in Edythe's opinion. Among the Marrenners' neighbors were a couple who had been good to the young Ruby when she was struggling. Once a month now, without fail, during these black days of the depression, the couple would receive a check signed "Barbara Stanwyck," which they would bring to Stokes's butcher shop to cash, after, of course, showing it to the rest of their neighbors. Consequently, whenever a Stanwyck film played the Glenwood Theater or the RKO Kenmore, Edythe would prevail upon her father for a dime so she could go and see it. She studied the way Stanwyck walked and talked (without a trace of a Brooklyn accent) and dressed. Edythe was forced to wear middy blouses and skirts at Girls' Commercial. That was the way everyone had to dress so that the poorer teen-agers wouldn't feel inferior. However, Edythe vowed that once she got out of school, she would wear the same smart suits Barbara Stanwyck always wore when her picture appeared in the movie magazines.

Edythe's ambition to become an actress did not go unnoticed by her parents. Ellen, spoiled by the now-lost income she had received from Florence, didn't discourage it, but she reminded Edythe that she would never be able to dance with the same grace and ease as Florence. Ellen equated a theatrical career with dancing. Years later, Edythe would insist: "I can't remember when I didn't want to be an actress, but only my dad and I believed I had any talent."

In her junior year, she found an inspiration to strengthen her belief that she *could* become a great actress in spite of any infirmity she might have. "Edythe," Wally confirms, "could think of nothing except acting. That was her ambition. Not to be a movie star, but to be an actress. Sarah Bernhardt was one of her idols, and she was always carrying around some book about her. She read a lot about Sarah Bernhardt in those days." The reason was simple: here was a woman who had continued to act even after having a leg amputated, who—after countless "farewell tours"—had kept returning to the stage until she died during rehearsals of a new play in Paris . . . at the age of seventy-nine.

Edythe was definitely impressed. She didn't try to emulate Madame Bernhardt's off-stage image, however—the "rouged face and painted lips" that some of Bernhardt's contemporaries had found deplorable. Edythe wore practically no make-up, and her relationships with boys were tenuous at best. Looking back, she'd

24

admit: "In those days boys didn't like me. They thought me too fresh and flip. When a boy asked me to attend a dance, I was sassy, troublesome. I remember once I had a date for a De Molay dance. My friend's date brought her a corsage, but mine didn't. I was burned up and asked him why. He said he had no money. It made me miserable, and I made him miserable. Need I say I never saw him again?"

Nevertheless, during her senior term at Girls' Commercial, she developed a crush on a boy named Eddie Dixon, and she'd remember him fondly for years to come.

"Gosh, he was nice. He was a crackerjack pianist, and he used to encourage me to sing, which he did quite well too." She'd vividly recall going to Oetjen's café with him and having a wonderful time, but that relationship also petered out. Perhaps she sensed that, if they became too serious, they could end up with a life like Ellen's and Walter's.

Edythe wanted to be free to pursue her career as an actress. Although she had no intention of leaving school before receiving a diploma, the way Florence had done, she restlessly looked forward to her graduation in June 1935.

In the class yearbook, the following credits appear beside her picture: "Dramatic Club—V.O.A., Honors in Math, Science and Art, Arista." Arista was the interscholastic honor society of the time. Seventeen years later, as a promotional gimmick for her movie, *With a Song in My Heart,* Edythe returned to Girls' Commercial High—since renamed Prospect Heights High—to address the class of 1952. "I have a confession to make," she said humbly. "The Yearbook says I was in Arista. I never made Arista. Good marks weren't enough. You had to be voted in, and the girls didn't want me."

In that same yearbook, Edythe was proclaimed, "One of our prize actresses." The following fall, with steely determination, she set out to prove those words true.

chapter 2

IN MID-AUGUST 1935, Edythe headed for Manhattan to find an acting job.

Despite the depression, there was a remarkable amount of activity on the boards. Producers were auditioning for *Idiot's Delight,* *Porgy and Bess, Winterset, End of Summer, Dead End, Victoria Regina,* and *Boy Meets Girl.* The Theater Guild, the Playwrights' Company, the Group Theater, and the Mercury Theater Company all had new productions in the works. The 1935–36 season was about to go into full swing—but no matter where Edythe went, she inevitably heard the same three questions:

"Are you a member of Equity? Do you have any experience? Do you have an agent?"

Her negative replies elicited a chilly, "We're only seeing professionals."

It was the show-business Catch–22: Without an agent or an Actors' Equity card, it was almost impossible to get into a show. Without a show, it was almost impossible to get an Equity card or an agent. There were exceptions, but—in 1935, with jobs at a premium—they were rare.

At the time, actors making the rounds often congregated in Walgreen's drugstore at West 44th Street and Broadway to exchange bits of information, casting tips, anything that might help. Edythe seldom joined them—she didn't really feel comfortable among them—but she was not above learning from others' experiences. One of the things she learned was that aspiring actresses could make ends meet by modeling for "confession" magazines—they were always on the lookout for new and pretty faces to illustrate such "true" stories as "I Was Branded Back-Seat-of-a-Car Sal" or "I Dared to Love a Boy Above My Class."

The confession-field jobs were at the bottom of the modeling scale financially, but the work was fun, respectable enough, good training, and no agents were required. Besides, the girls could often obtain free professional photographs—a valuable fringe benefit when every cent mattered.

One of Edythe's first jobs, however, was not for a magazine, but for the *New York Daily News*, which was also on the lookout for fresh young faces to pose for its popular feature "The Correct Thing." Edythe was hired for a series of photos illustrating etiquette on a first date. Example: "The girl should not ask the boy to take her to an expensive night spot. The boy must not ask for a goodnight kiss."

The boy posing with Edythe in those pictures was a former child actor named Dick Clayton, who would later become well known as a Hollywood agent, the representative for Jane Fonda, Angie Dickinson, and Burt Reynolds among others. It was about this time, Clayton recalls, that Edythe made a slight change in her identity: "She dropped the double *n* from her last name. She preferred the way it looked in print—Edythe Marrener. Who cared? She was one of the most beautiful girls I had ever met. I was going steady at the time and didn't ask for a date, but I sure wanted to. We met again years later and always had a laugh about 'The Correct Thing.' She could be the warmest woman there was if she didn't think you were a phony."

Edythe Marrener she would remain—for just about two years more. Then a much larger change would come over her identity.

It was about this time too that Edythe learned of the Feagin Drama School. Feagin's was hardly on a par with the American Academy of Dramatic Art, but its tuition and eligibility requirements were lower, and Edythe could just about manage both. By early 1936, Edythe was studying voice, movement, and improvisation. She was also falling in love with one of her fellow students—or so she thought. Years later, refusing to identify the callow youth, she'd recall:

27

I'd meet him every day after class at a little café. He never worked, but he talked of his well-to-do parents. After dating three months I agreed to marry him . . . that very night. He had no way of supporting me, but I didn't give it a thought. We were headed for Gretna Green, Maryland, where there were no waiting requirements. The elopement fizzled when we reached Grand Central Station and he wired his father, a Pennsylvania dentist, for money, meanwhile leaving me at the YWCA. The next morning when we returned to the Western Union office, there was no cash. His father was waiting instead.

"Do you love this girl?" he asked his son.

"Well . . ." My hero hesitated, looking at the ground.

That did it. I took my suitcase and went home to make some explanations to my parents.

Ellen Marrenner did not take the incident lightly. "I told you he was no good when you brought him home," she wept. "What do you want with those actors anyway? All they care about is themselves."

Her father was more sympathetic. "Consider yourself lucky you found out about his character before you made a serious mistake. Divorce is an ugly business." And then, to calm his fears, he asked, "You didn't make *any mistakes* last night, did you, Edie?"

She assured him she hadn't—and *wouldn't*—and he never brought up the subject again. But she never forgot it. It colored her relationship with men for years—perhaps for the rest of her life.

Edythe survived the breakup of her ill-fated romance, more determined than ever not to lose sight of the goals she had set for herself: fame and fortune—with emphasis on the latter. Sara Little, her friend, insists:

We were the last of the career girls of the Depression. There are no more like us. We were conditioned by hard times and the urgent need to earn a living. It was not a matter of staying around and marrying the grocery boy. You had to be gifted. It was the only way.

That was the era of the big dream. We'd meet every Thursday night in the President Cafeteria on Lexington

Avenue. Afterward we'd window shop and talk endlessly about what we were going to do with our lives. One of our dreams was being able to go home to Brooklyn in a taxi just to avoid the smelly subway.

There was no question of our ultimate success. We felt we were destined.

But destiny needed a push.

Later that year, convinced she had gone as far as possible at Feagin's, and in need of money, Edythe coolly put aside all acting ambitions to concentrate on full-time modeling. By now she was armed with an impressive portfolio, but she still had no agent. And in order to score as a high-priced model, it was not only necessary to have an agent, it was essential to be represented by one of the czars of the field: John Robert Powers or Walter Thornton. Edythe decided to tackle Thornton first.

Through the portals of the Walter Thornton Agency literally passed some of the most beautiful girls in the world. To be chosen by him all but guaranteed a successful career. Thornton dealt only with the top advertising agencies, art directors, and illustrators, and his own taste was impeccable. If a Thornton girl violated the boss's standard, she was quickly and quietly dropped from his "list."

Before an aspiring or even working model could get into the inner sanctum for an interview, however, she had to be carefully screened by Thornton's secretary, who was well schooled in the qualifications necessary to impress her boss. Most applicants never made it past her. When Edythe came in, the woman cast a perfunctory glance at Edythe's portfolio—then a long look at Edythe herself. A few minutes later, the newcomer was being scrutinized by the great man himself.

"A flaming mop of red hair was not to be dismissed without a second or third thought," Thornton would recall later. "Color photography had suddenly produced a loud chorus of calls for redheads and more redheads." He studied her carefully with what he called his "thousand eyes"—his equivalent of a sixth sense. Her dress size wasn't quite right for her height—size 12 to 13 was a bit large for her 5′ 3½″—she'd never be a can-

didate for the high-fashion pages of *Vogue* or *Harper's Bazaar*
. . . but there was something about her. Her smile and natural
animation, when she let her guard down, were very attractive,
and that, with her turned-up nose and expressive hazel eyes,
convinced him she had the quality that could reach out from the
printed page to persuade a ten-dollar-a-week shopgirl that all
her romantic problems would be solved for the price of a new
Tek toothbrush.

"Even then," he recalled, "she revealed a sensitive flair for
self-dramatization." In a letter she wrote in answer to a request
for early biographical file material, she noted the following, in
a discussion of clothes and colors: "In beige I feel like a very
good little girl. Butter melts in my mouth. I've worn a great deal
of beige lately, and I'm tired of being an angel."

To relieve her of this burden, Thornton sent her out on a call
from the advertising company representing Hickory "Luralace"
foundation garments. Although the one-piece "foundation" was
more suitable for a middle-aged matron than a twenty-year-old,
the agency was anxious to attract younger, more nubile buyers
with a campaign that emphasized: "Sweet is the word for you
in Luralace *with that artful uplift.*"

Because most of the top models resisted "intimate apparel"
assignments, no matter how tasteful, the advertising agencies
paid a higher fee to those willing to take them on. Eager for
any extra money, Edythe accepted the job. The result showed
her from the thigh up, her face in profile, her arms stretched
high in the air, and looking sweet indeed in her beige Luralace
foundation, a garment far less risqué than the standard one-
piece swim suit. She wore her share of those too, in group
beach scenes and in one head-and-shoulders ad illustrating how
Noxema brought "Instant Relief" to painful sunburn. In the
first photograph, Edythe wears an expression of intense pain,
with a balloon spelling out, "Oooh, what an awful sunburn!"
In the adjoining picture, her face is lit up in ecstasy as she
applies the magical cream, and the balloon fairly bursts with
the word "AH."

It was in such ads that Edythe's suppressed acting desire
came to the surface, and as the months went by she was frequently commissioned to appear in these little illustrated dramas
—all of which promised instant relief or instant romance.

Away from the photo studios, however, there was no romance in Edythe Marrener's life—instant or lingering. Her
mother was pleased at her daughter's modeling success, but
looked upon it solely as a means to an end—a wealthy husband.
After her abortive elopement, however, Edythe regarded the
young men she met with disdain bordering on contempt. Most
of the art directors she met were either married or more interested in the male models; and the latter she considered vain and
shallow. She had neither the inclination nor the time for casual
partying and was appalled when other girls showed up for a
job bleary-eyed and listless, or when she overheard gossip telling of how past Thornton girls had burned themselves out by
high living before they were twenty-five. She was so distant, in
fact, that one of Thornton's most vivid recollections was that
of Edythe "stoically enduring the status of wallflower for a party
which I gave for all my models. My wife kept saying to me,
'Dance with her. No one's asked her.' "

"She was," Thornton continued, "the quietest girl who ever
worked for me, a real lone wolf—a girl with no time for friends
or a social life. But she was a very fine model."

So fine, in fact, that when Vitaphone decided to do a 1936
short subject about modeling and went looking for girls, Thornton sent her to represent his agency. It was to be Edythe's first
experience before the motion picture cameras, and although her
"role" of "Edythe Marrener of New York" required little his-
trionic ability, the experience was enough to convince her that
given a real opportunity, she could make it in Hollywood, and
that there was where her future lay. But she would have to bide
her time and save her money.

Saving was almost an impossibility. It was easy to resist the
temptation to find a small place of her own in Manhattan, since
a major part of her pay checks was turned over to her family,
but clothes were a necessity: the rest of her money went toward
building the conservative, tasteful wardrobe essential to making
a good impression when she was sent out for a job. By 1937
she was striking an oddly sophisticated note. On East 21st Street
where her family, at her insistence, had moved, neighbors remember her as a beautifully dressed, aloof girl, never without
a hatbox, the trademark of a model.

She was also beginning to make an impression on many

artists and photographers who now specifically demanded her services. Two in particular remembered her.

Jon Whitcomb, the celebrated illustrator and commercial artist, would recall: "She had a kind of self-confidence that made you remember her. The first time I saw her, she swept into the studio as if she owned the place. Long before such catchwords as 'positive thinking' were in vogue, she was using them to propel her way to fame."

Photographer Ivan Dmitri, who remained friendly with Edythe for more than twenty years, remembered the young model as "a nice Brooklyn girl—very, very ambitious. She had that little dynamo going all the time. But she possessed that healthy, unsophisticated look which I felt typified the American beauty at that time."

If Edythe was using positive thinking, she had need of it. She never discussed her personal problems in the studio, but the situation at home was becoming tense and depressing. Walter Marrenner's health was deteriorating. His heart was weak, his kidneys failing, and he was plagued by chronic cystitis. As he was periodically forced to miss work, his morale and his pride were at an all-time low, money was tight, and he and Ellen Marrenner would fight all the time. Edythe learned early how inactivity could affect a man's psyche, behavior, and marriage. It was a lesson she was to remember again much later, to her pain.

Shortly after her twentieth birthday, the break Edythe had been awaiting finally came. She was summoned by Thornton to discuss a very special assignment: the *Saturday Evening Post* had persuaded him to be the "author" of a by-lined piece about the modeling world titled "The Merchant of Venus." Because Thornton's dictum had always been "beauty is not enough," the initial idea of illustrating the piece with a group of Thornton girls had been rejected in favor of a minidrama, "The Day in the Life of a Model." It was essential that a girl with whom the readers could identify be used. Ivan Dmitri had suggested Edythe, arguing that the red hair would be a plus in calling attention to the article.

The script was simple enough:

"A model comes to work. The author [Thornton] looks her over. She's taught to register. Artist [John] LaGotta reads her the script. She poses for him. And another pose—PERFECT! Ready for canvas."

This would not be like any of the clothing ads she was used to: anonymous Edythe in a pretty pose but distinctly secondary to what she was wearing. Not only would her fee be much more substantial, but Thornton would identify her by *name* in the accompanying article. "Edythe Marrener," he would proclaim, "a Brooklyn girl, today is one of the country's most successful models, and her flaming red hair has contributed largely to making her popular."

The early photographs too looked very promising. Ivan Dmitri would recall: "For the first series of pictures she was a rather demure-looking teen-ager wearing sweater and skirt and dainty white gloves. That fabulous red hair was neatly pinned down. For the photographs with LaGotta, we fluffed out her hair, dressed her in a white satin gown with tulle overskirt. Seated before LaGotta, she looked like a vision from another, more innocent century."

"Merchant of Venus" was scheduled for the *Post*'s October 30 issue. Whatever excitement Edythe felt, however, was tempered by her concern about her father. His once ruddy complexion was now a sickly yellow, and he could barely make it to the bathroom.

On October 17, 1937, according to hospital records, Walter Marrenner collapsed on the job and was rushed to the nearby Metropolitan Hospital on Welfare Island. "He was very, very sick," Wally remembers. "There was no time to bring him back home to Brooklyn."

Possibly not, but anything would have been preferable to Metropolitan, which for the most part contained facilities for what the city termed "destitute incurables." Waves of horror and humiliation engulfed Edythe when she learned of her father's whereabouts. "We could have raised the money to send him elsewhere," says Wally, "but he couldn't be moved."

Less than two weeks later, the *Saturday Evening Post* hit the newsstands.

Across the country, thousands of shopgirls were undoubtedly looking at the redhead in the white satin gown and envying her. Pulp fiction and film had portrayed a model's life as one filled with evenings of dancing at the Stork Club, her closets bursting with exquisite gowns and furs in Fifth Avenue apartments furnished with plush carpets, satin settees, and sleek Art Deco mirrors.

That was the fantasy. For Edythe, reality was seeing her adored father helpless and useless at age fifty-eight. Then she received a call from Kay Brown, David O. Selznick's right-hand woman in New York.

In a work of fiction, what followed would be dismissed as plot contrivance. But as one of those confession magazines Edythe had modeled for proclaimed, "Truth is stranger than fiction."

Throughout 1937, an epidemic of what was to be known as "Scarlett Fever" had been sweeping the country, as David O. Selznick launched his much-publicized search to find an "unknown" to portray Margaret Mitchell's celebrated heroine in *Gone with the Wind*. At Selznick's urging, George Cukor, the director, had agreed to make a tour of Southern colleges on the off-chance that a Scarlett might be hidden among the magnolia trees in some obscure Dixie campus or little-theater group. They were hiding there all right; Cukor was hounded by Scarletts of all sizes, shapes, and ages, but every meeting or audition brought Cukor closer to the conclusion that his Southern trek was a waste of time and money. He headed for New York for a respite.

The story of how Edythe Marrener came to audition for *Gone with the Wind* has undergone many revisions over the years. Some studio biographies have even erroneously credited Selznick himself with the discovery. Those stories insist he saw the redhead's picture on the cover of the *Saturday Evening Post*. However, Edythe wasn't *on* the cover of the *Saturday Evening Post;* her first and only cover for that magazine was on October 7, 1939—nearly two years later. A *Post* piece in 1959 merely deepened the false impression when it reprinted the 1939 cover above a caption that read: ". . . this *Post* cover photograph won a Hollywood screen test for Susan Hayward, who was then an unknown Brooklyn model." Plainly wrong.

Other stories claim that Cukor saw the article and rushed to sign her up; others, that Selznick's wife Irene saw some of her ads and showed them to Selznick. Cukor very firmly says today, "I never saw the story in the *Saturday Evening Post*. Irene never saw the girl modeling hats or anything else. All those stories are pure bull." And Irene Selznick, asked whether she or Cukor brought the star to her former husband's attention, frankly admits: "I honestly can't recall whether I did or he did. I do remember being very impressed with the girl and thinking that she had definite possibilities for movies. It's possible we both became aware of her at the same time and suggested her as a potential candidate for the role."

However it happened, it was in Selznick's New York office that Edythe did meet Cukor, talked with him—and, a few days later, having made an excellent impression, was signed to a "test contract" with Selznick Studios.

Ivan Dmitri remembered that "she came bouncing into my office with the good news, joyously announcing, 'Dmitri, I'm in the movies,' and when I congratulated her she said archly, 'Well, it's about time.'"

The Selznick office insisted that Edythe, still under twenty-one, be chaperoned to California for the test; sister Florence was elected—her alliance with Wally's mysterious "German" must have ended—and the office booked train space for them both. On the Chicago to Los Angeles leg, it was even on the same crack streamliner, the *Chief,* that David and Irene Selznick would be riding. George Cukor could have done the test right where he was—there were studio facilities in New York—but the director was feverishly preparing to film *Holiday* with Katharine Hepburn and Cary Grant before becoming exclusively involved with *Gone with the Wind,* and had little free time, to say the least.

The office insisted, as well, that Edythe leave New York immediately. Walter Marrenner was disturbed and pleaded with his wife. "Don't let her leave, Ellen. She's not ready. She'll have her heart broken out there." But Edythe's and Florence's bags were already packed. On November 18, 1937, they boarded the train, with Thornton there to see her off, at Edythe's request. Before leaving, she had signed a contract with him granting him an agent's fee of 10 percent of all her future earnings, and, the day before, autographed a picture crediting him with "whatever success I may be fortunate enough to gain."

There was no thought of discord when Thornton and his wife saw Edythe to the train at Grand Central Station.

"In fact," he said, "that day was the only time I ever saw her

35

express any emotion of any kind. She asked my wife if she could kiss me goodbye. I think my wife said 'Yes.' I don't really remember . . ."

And it really didn't matter. Within two years, Edythe would be kissing him off—for good, referring to him coldly as "the nasty man."

And *that* Thornton would never forget.

PART TWO

Edythe Marrener/
Susan Hayward
Hollywood
December 1937 — July 22, 1944

*I worked harder for Susan than I had on any other girl.
Her Selznick tests were terrible. She couldn't act. Nobody liked her. . . . Her drama coach at Warners told
me, "Benny, this is not a very nice girl." Nobody liked
her at Paramount. Henry Ginsberg said, "Benny, what
are you wasting your time for? She's got nothing."
. . . She was a bitch.*

BEN MEDFORD, *Susan's first agent*
March 1980

*All my life I'd been terribly frightened of people. I
thought everyone was so brilliant. I felt so inadequate.
The only way I knew how to protect myself was to
scare people before they scared me.*

SUSAN HAYWARD

chapter 3

EDYTHE MARRENER was a very frightened young woman when she went through the front door of the Selznick studios for the first time in December of 1937. The entire atmosphere of the bustling Washington Boulevard lot in Culver City overwhelmed her. She had bragged to everyone in New York that her time had finally come, but now that she was actually in California, she wasn't nearly so confident. What if they hated her? Everyone around her looked so . . . professional, and here she was with her few months of acting classes. There was nothing for it but to brazen it through.

Her first test, directed by George Cukor, was slated for the morning of December 6, 1937. Contrary to Hollywood history, however, she was *not* being tested for the role of Scarlett O'Hara.

Aware that he is debunking a forty-three-year-old legend, George Cukor says today, with a chuckle, "We never really thought of her for Scarlett. She was very young and not too experienced, in fact, completely inexperienced. It would have been stupid to get a twenty-year-old girl to play a most demanding part. We thought, David thought, 'This girl may have some possibilities. Let's bring her out and use her for tests and put her under contract.'

"She was very pretty, a very sweet, dignified girl. Very correct. Very nice. At least that was her facade. If she was tough underneath, you couldn't tell it, because she was very, very dignified."

Responding to the stories that have circulated for more than four decades that, when Edythe was asked to do a scene a certain way, she replied, freshly, "Who's playing this scene, you or me?" Cukor protests, "Oh, nonsense. No, no, no. She was a very young girl and very well behaved."

Edythe *did* portray Scarlett, but it was as a vehicle to test other actors for other roles and to see just what she could do. In her first test, she worked opposite Selznick contractee Alan Marshall in what was known as "the Library scene at Twelve Oaks," in which Scarlett declares her love for Ashley Wilkes for the first time, while, unknown to her, Rhett Butler lounges on a couch at the back of the room. For the remainder of her test contract, she was used to assist in the auditioning of potential Melanies, particularly Dorothy Jordan (who would later become the wife of Merian C. Cooper, the director of *King Kong* and one-time vice-president of Selznick International). Seen now, the tests reveal the freshness and intensity that obviously attracted Selznick and Cukor to her in the first place, but they also reveal her great inexperience; her voice clenches, sometimes sinking to barely above a whisper, she seems uncertain of what to do with her body—and she is obviously scared out of her wits. When the director ends the scene, her sigh of relief is audible.

She was painfully aware of her shortcomings. "I looked like a snub-nosed teen-ager," she said later. "What did I know about Southern belles?" The studio executives agreed with her. Though she had potential, they thought, it wasn't enough to keep her on. She was given her release.

In years to come, studio flacks would fabricate a snappy epilogue: "When David O. Selznick broke the sad news to her, he kindly suggested she return home and get some more experience.

"'I like oranges. I'm staying,' was her sassy reply. 'Besides, I've already cashed in my return ticket.'"

That story was repeated often enough to become accepted as fact. David O. Selznick, however, had neither the time nor the inclination to play sympathetic Dutch uncle to any of the hundreds of unknowns he was testing and rejecting. It was one of Selznick's aides who wielded the hatchet, and Edythe's response was not recorded.

There was one element of truth in the flack's story, however. After the test contract with Selznick expired, Edythe did go to the nearest Santa Fe office and cash in her ticket. With that money she rented an inexpensive, furnished bungalow in an unfashionable section of Hollywood and went to look for work. Her worst fears had been realized: they hadn't liked her—but damned if she was going to give up. There was only one way she was going back to Brooklyn: as a famous movie actress. She blocked out the possibility of failure. She also blocked out the fear that she might never see her father again, and dismissed her mother's pessimistic letters as typical Ellen Marrenner gloom and doom. Mother always had dramatized so. Meanwhile, Edythe scrambled for whatever modeling jobs she could find, with the help of a young agent named Ben Medford, who had been introduced to her by George Cukor.

Life wasn't easy. Florence wasn't contributing much and the little money from Edythe's modeling and the ticket refund went for food and local transportation. Dating was a waste of energy, even though "everyone was on the make for her," Medford remembers. "But Mrs. Marrenner was determined to keep her a virgin." The New Year started miserably, and got worse. She received word from home that her father, still hospitalized on Welfare Island, couldn't risk a transfer. On January 2, Walter Marrenner underwent surgery for drainage of a scrotal abscess. Ellen's letter filled in the depressing details.

Medford, meanwhile, was having problems selling her to the studios. Finally, he recalled, "I got permission to show the *Gone with the Wind* test to Max Arnow," a talent executive for Warner Brothers. Arnow agrees that, although Edythe was no Scarlett, "she had an intangible quality worth developing," and continues: "We signed her to a six-month, one-hundred-fifty dollars a week contract. We then got around to the business of changing that dreadful name. It didn't suit her at all. I was doing business with agent Leland Hayward [Margaret Sullavan's husband, Brooke Hayward's father]. I liked the sound of the name 'Hayward.' But I can't remember where the 'Susan' came from. Maybe Cantor was singing "If You Knew Susie" on the radio; maybe I saw some black-eyed Susans that morning at a florist. Who knows?"

After sending the newly named Susan Hayward to the gallery for the standard studio portraits, Arnow placed her in the Warner Brothers' drama school. "She worked every day with a great dramatic coach, Frank Beckwith," he recalled, "but this new girl didn't quite have the heart. She had a wonderful mind, but she didn't have the heart."

Arnow was wrong. She had the heart all right, but Susan was still controlling herself, still keeping her emotions under tight rein. It would be years before she would learn to open herself up on screen—and then the rush of feeling would be stunning.

Peggy Moran (Mrs. Henry) Koster—who married the noted director and gave up her career in 1942—appeared with Susan about then in a thirteen-minute Warner Brothers short subject called *Campus Cinderella*. She also was a student of Beckwith's.

"I remember Susan Hayward well from the days in acting class," she says. "At that time we rehearsed scenes from famous plays and motion picture scripts. She wore no make-up, and sometimes she took pins out of her purse and casually pinned up her flaming red hair without benefit of a mirror. The effect was stunning. It often distracted the rest of us from our work—Diana Lewis [later married to William Powell], Lana Turner, Carole Landis.

"Susan was of great beauty, but she was hard to approach and always seemed aloof [a condition her myopia did not help]. Perhaps she did not want to disclose her private life to others." There Mrs. Koster's impression was right on the mark. There were a great many things Susan didn't want disclosed, her background among them. In a town filled with glamour and exoticism, the poverty of her childhood seemed shameful—and a sure impediment to her success. It also came to represent her greatest dread: "My mother's great fear," Susan's son Timothy Barker reveals today, "was the idea of ever having to return to Brooklyn—the kind of life it represented."

Susan had arrived in Hollywood scared, and she was still scared: scared people would look down on her, scared she wasn't glamourous or talented enough, scared she'd be a total flop. And there was nothing she wanted more than to succeed. Many years later, one of her producers, Walter Wanger, would say, "Susie suffers from one of the strangest and most startling guilt complexes you can imagine. She's embarrassed that she's a beautiful woman. She doesn't think she deserves it. She knows that it is a priceless gift, but she is afraid that on the inside she isn't so beautiful. It causes her to avoid other women on her own level. It's responsible for her fits of temperament. Actually, her beauty makes her miserable. Ironic, isn't it?"

So Susan raised her barricades and arrayed her defenses. She determined never to let anyone get close enough to know what she was feeling—or to wound her. As a result, she sometimes wounded others.

Ben Medford remembers: "George [Cukor] was very helpful to her—and to me. He was a wonderful help to Susan. He got Gertrude Fogler, who was under contract to Metro at the time and was not permitted to teach people off the lot, to work with Susan. It was Gertrude who changed Susan's high-pitched voice to a low-pitched one, and between Gertrude and Frank Beck-with's efforts, she was turned into an actress.

"But after the time Gertrude spent with the girl, do you think Susan ever gave her a little present? Never!

"I got Susan a little automobile so she could get around, taught her how to dress, gave her money. I used to bring her to night clubs with George Montgomery just to have their picture taken, to get her name in the papers. She didn't like him and he didn't like her. . . ."

And just because Susan now had a Warner Brothers contract didn't mean she was getting work. The individual producers and directors on the lot had to be convinced to use her. She was still a hard sell. "Hard to photograph," says Medford. "She had this bulbous nose, and I passed money to the cameramen and lighting guys to make sure she got the proper treatment. Their job was to concentrate only on the stars."

Then something happened that would take Susan's mind off her faltering career. On March 16, 1938, at 2:50 P.M. Walter Marrenner gave up. Metropolitan Hospital on Welfare Island noted the official cause of death: "Uremia and complications of arteriosclerosis with narrowing of the coronary arteries."

Susan was not home that afternoon, and by the time she was notified of his death, Walter Marrenner had already been cremated, just another box of ashes to be disposed of by the Fresh Pond Crematory in Meadow Valley, Queens. That night she cried until she was thoroughly exhausted, until there were no tears left to be shed. Future stories about Marrenner's death would undergo assorted variations: the most oft-repeated one that Susan's father had died without ever learning she had failed her test for Selznick. Certainly, though, Ellen Marrenner would have passed the news to her husband, and Susan obviously wrote her father during the three months prior to his death. But she was still guilt-ridden that she had been incapable of facing the squalid horrors of Welfare Island the month before she'd left for California.

Publicity stories would also dramatize an emotional deathbed farewell between Marrenner and his daughter beside his hospital bed—this too was a fantasy, as Wally Marrenner confirms: "No, Susan never went to see my father at the hospital before he expired, not that I remember."

With nothing to keep her in Brooklyn, Ellen Marrenner decided to join her daughters in Hollywood. "We came out by bus," says Wally, "and moved in with my sisters in a house near Paramount studios—Irving Boulevard, I think it was called at the time." Susan's reaction to having her mother live with her is not recorded—it must have been a mixed blessing at best— but at least it provided some financial relief. Wally remembers Susan saying to him, "Oh, Wal, I wish you had come out with me instead of Flo.' I don't think they were getting on too well because Flo made no effort to help out with the expenses. I had a little money I had saved, but that went in a hurry for food and stuff. Ben Medford helped us a bit. I got a job which didn't pay much, but it was a job to keep us going. . . ."

Susan's salary, added to Wally's, took care of the rent and their necessities. She was certain that if she was given a chance to prove herself in a halfway decent part, Warner Brothers would increase her salary. Posing for publicity shots and studying with Beckwith for $150 a week was hardly her idea of being a movie actress. Medford had told her she had been assigned a good role in an important new movie called *Brother Rat* and urged her to be patient.

Max Arnow, however, was impatient about the progress she was making. "Beckwith gave her heavy dramatic scenes to see if he couldn't get some emotion out of her and get her to cry. It took quite a while." Susan, aware of her difficulties, described them differently in a letter she wrote her former mentor in late April:

Monday

Dear Mr. Cukor,

I passed the Troc the other noon, and there you were! My first glimpse of you in ages. It was you, wasn't it? You were with a group of about six people and evidently the host.

Looking very well and extremely happy. Just as I was about to release a wild scream in greeting, the light changed and a tourist carried me downstream on his bumper.

Life, at present, is not as exciting for your self-appointed protégé as it might be. It will become so tho when "Brother Rat" goes into production. I'm scheduled to play the part of Joyce, the girl who likes boys and a rumpus and not much else. It's going to be a lot of fun! On the other hand "B.R." might not roll for weeks—who knows? In the meantime, the camera and the technical side of motion pictures hold so much of interest. The camera is exceptionally revealing and I've been trying to control my grimacing somewhat. This restraint is causing a studio head no end of anguish. He thinks I'm cold, no feeling. The other day he instructed Frank Beckwith, with whom I've been working, to "Let Hayward overact if she pleases. Let her be a ham—as long as it comes from the heart." . . . Now I ask you . . .

There is so much that must be done. How can I ever thank you for making possible my entry into this world? The only way I can think of is to some day soon win the Academy Award for the finest performance and in return present it to you to whom I owe so much.

I send my love with this and a heart filled with gratitude.

Sincerely,

Edythe Marrener

As things turned out, however, Susan was unceremoniously removed from the cast of *Brother Rat,* and Priscilla Lane installed in the role of Joyce. The explanation: Jack Warner had seen a rough cut of Miss Lane's new movie *Four Daughters.* Astutely aware it would turn her into a major star, he wanted to take immediate advantage of her predictable box-office appeal. He rushed her into *Brother Rat.*

Susan, an unknown quantity, was assigned a tenth-billed role in a sixty-three-minute, soon-forgotten quickie, *Girls on Probation.*

Producer Martin Rackin, one of Susan's close professional friends throughout the years, said, shortly before his death: "Jack Warner used to boast that one actor on his ass was worth two on his feet, and he kept them that way. Susan was very shy and very insecure then. She really got kicked around, and I think it got to her. After the Warner treatment she never let down her guard. It made her a loner, and she never changed."

"Even before her six-month option came due," says Medford, "I heard she was being let go. But I believed in the girl and I didn't want to give up."

The result was an interview with Paramount's head of talent Arthur Jacobson, and there she made a far better impression. Jacobson remembered Susan "entering my office, sedately dressed in a little black suit, wearing sensible medium-heeled shoes and very little make-up." She was a refreshing contrast to the over-made up glamour girls that had been passing through his offices. He felt she would be an important addition to a group of young players Paramount was trying to build into stars. Medford negotiated a seven-year contract with Paramount at a starting salary of $350 a week with guaranteed yearly raises. "That was a lot of money in those days," he notes.

Marvin Houser, a Paramount press agent assigned to her at the time, observed, "Susan Hayward was a lonely rider tilting at windmills even then. She worked day and night to shed her accent—quaint but unmistakable Brooklynese."

A New Yorker himself, Jacobson was confident Susan would succeed. It was vital for him—and the studio—that she do so.

chapter 4

IN 1939, Paramount was having female trouble. A year earlier, two of its most dazzling leading ladies, Marlene Dietrich and Mae West, had had their reputations tarnished, if not permanently damaged. They, together with Katharine Hepburn, W. C. Fields, and others, had been branded "box-office poison" by a powerful group of movie exhibitors who had, not too subtly, indicated that the fewer films these once-towering stars made, the happier the showmen would be.

In addition to this blow, Paramount was being driven to distraction by the irrational behavior of Frances Farmer, for whom it once had had such high hopes. The studio's two newest imports, Franciska Gaal from Norway and Olympe Bradna from France, had simply failed to catch on with either critics or the public. Of the many young actresses Paramount had signed in the early thirties, when the advent of sound had decimated their contract list, only Claudette Colbert had shown she had staying power. Ruth Chatterton, Sylvia Sidney, and Nancy Carroll had diminished in appeal and returned to Broadway. Carole Lombard and Miriam Hopkins had long since departed for greener pastures.

In addition, although there was still a strong stable of male stars, including Crosby, Hope, Cooper, Fred MacMurray, and Ray Milland, many of these contracts were coming up for renewal, and the studio was in desperate need of "leverage." In an effort to obtain it, Paramount originated what it optimistically called its "Golden Circle," consisting of new young performers who were promised a "star build-up" and paid only about $200 a week. It was a no-lose situation, even if only two or three of these hopefuls turned out to have the golden touch. The others could and would be quietly dropped at option time—and a new Circle begun.

Susan was introduced to the other twelve members of the Circle of 1939 during the shooting of group photographs. Coolly, she sized up the female competition: Louise Campbell, Ellen Drew, Betty Field, Judith Barrett, Patricia Morison, Joyce Mathews, Janice Logan, and Evelyn Keyes. None of them seemed like potential threats. Of the four Circle men, she considered William Holden and Robert Preston, newly recruited from the Pasadena Playhouse, "interesting," and Joseph Allen, Jr., and William Henry "too pretty." The way to the top seemed clear.

Susan's first chance to show what she could do came when Paramount cast her in their remake of the stirring Ronald Colman silent film classic of 1926, *Beau Geste*. This time the three brothers who join the French Foreign Legion would be played by Gary Cooper, Ray Milland, and Robert Preston, with Susan cast in the tiny role of ward Isobel Rivers. Susan would later mock her role by quipping, "I waved goodbye to the boys at the beginning and hello to them at the end," but she was given billing directly behind Brian Donlevy, who played the villainous Sergeant Markoff and probably made the biggest impression in the picture; and her final scene with Ray Milland, as the only surviving Geste brother, John, was appealing enough to inspire Paramount to publicize her as "the personal discovery of producer-director William Wellman." (Even though Wellman privately told the Paramount executives, "She'll never get anywhere with that bump on her nose.")

Beau Geste was booked into the New York Paramount on August 2. Hoping to inject some glamour into an essentially male-oriented film, Paramount sent Susan east a few days before the opening. It was her first trip home since settling in Hollywood, but with the exception of Sara Little, there were few friends or relatives she wanted to see. She had never felt she had much in common with her cousins, and saw no reason to subject herself to a barrage of questions about life in the film capital.

The *Saturday Evening Post* editors, elated by the role their magazine had played—or supposedly played—in her new-found eminence, eagerly asked her to pose bare-shouldered for their October 7, 1939, cover (the same cover later mistakenly credited for her "discovery"), which she did with pleasure. Other than that, Paramount's New York publicity office found themselves hard put to get Susan much coverage other than a few beauty and fashion pieces. Entertainment editors who had seen a screening of *Beau Gest* were more interested in male angles, and with an abundance of great pictures vying for space that fall, they were indifferent to "just another young starlet." Still, Susan had come home just as she had wanted—as a star (however small)—and nothing could diminish her pleasure at that.

The reviews, when they appeared, were generally good; the critics mostly ignored Susan; but the picture was a rousing adventure yarn, it did well at the box office and, despite the brevity of her role, audiences seemed to respond to her fresh beauty. Her career seemed *finally* to have gotten off the ground.

Paramount, however, dissipated whatever interest there was in their new discovery by carelessly casting her in two "B" clinkers: *Our Leading Citizen*, with former radio comic Bob Burns, and *$1,000 a Touchdown*, an exercise in mindless lunacy starring an also-faltering Martha Raye and Joe E. Brown.

Susan felt enormously frustrated after such a promising start —and then any hopes she may have had for being cast in a major role at Paramount seemed to be shattered for good when the studio signed Paulette Goddard to a long-term contract. As the first runner-up in the Scarlett O'Hara sweepstakes, and now free of a contractual obligation to her "husband" Charlie Chaplin—no one was sure they had actually been married until they were divorced, and even then there was some doubt—Goddard had suddenly become the hottest property in town.

After losing *Gone with the Wind* to Vivien Leigh, Goddard had been borrowed by MGM for strong co-starring roles in *Dramatic School* and *The Women*, but she had been less than enthusiastic about signing with a studio that already had more queens than Henry VIII. Paramount, with its dearth of leading ladies, offered Goddard more money than MGM and better opportunities, and swiftly lived up to its promise by casting her opposite Bob Hope in *The Cat and the Canary*, which became the comedy success of the year.

A fellow New Yorker, Paulette Goddard was six years older

than Susan, but there was little difference photographically. Nor was her talent or experience much better: as an actress, Goddard would never walk off with any prizes. She had an appealing screen personality, however, was considered an outspoken, shrewd, and worldly woman, and the Chaplin connection commanded respect.

As Susan watched Goddard being escorted grandly to her suite in the stars' dressing-room row, she was overcome by feelings of insecurity . . . and hostility. Here was a woman with whom she knew she couldn't compete and one who could influence whatever future there might be at Paramount. Goddard, on the other hand, was barely aware of Susan's existence. Susan could see her career melting away.

It was then, in mid-October, that Louella Parsons decided to play fairy godmother to the neglected Cinderella. She was planning a coast-to-coast personal appearance tour for later that year—four or five live shows at carefully selected movie houses. Paid $7,500 a week for the package, she planned to allot $4,200 of this to be divided among her "supporting cast" of six young contractees. These hopefuls would do the actual performing while Louella sat imperiously behind a desk trying to decide whether the youngsters deserved a plug in her column. The project was self-aggrandizing and blatantly corny, but audiences lapped it up.

Of Parsons' Flying Stars, as they were called, Susan was perhaps the least familiar to Louella's audiences. Of the others, Warner's Ronald Reagan and Jane Wyman had appeared in fifteen films each; redheaded Arleen Whelan, a Zanuck favorite, had co-starred with Warner Baxter in *Kidnapped* and with Henry Fonda in *Young Mr. Lincoln;* blonde, pert June Preisser, under contract to MGM, had won a substantial fan following after appearing in *Babes in Arms* and *Dancing Co-Ed;* and Joy Hodges had made an impression in eight RKO pictures.

Hodges, who returned to the Broadway stage soon after the tour was over, never forgot those eleven weeks on the road—or Susan's behavior during the engagement.

"Frankly I was a little afraid of her—that directness, that lack of humor. I never thought of Susan as a girl I'd want to know well, one to whom I could say, 'Come on, let's go out and have dinner.' Somehow she seemed uneasy and withdrawn with other performers. It wasn't the usual competitive thing. I just think she felt unsure of herself among people in a profession in which she had so little experience. But she was always extremely open and friendly with doormen and elevator operators.

"There was something so alone about Susan. The rest of us each had something going for us. I was a brand-new bride. Jane and Dutch [Ronald Reagan] had each other. Arleen was very gay, with plenty of beaux. June already had a career on the stage with her sister Cherry. No question, we each had more mileage in show business than Susan, but even then she was special. She'd charge on stage with that bulldog walk, her head bent forward, and plant her feet. The rest of us would sort of float out. Susan—she seemed to have nothing, except talent. And she was so beautiful."

The routines were mainly musical, but Susan had a comedy scene with Reagan that, Hodges remembers, "she played with incredible fervor. I can still see her—the blue velvet dress with that red hair, the spotlight on just the two of them. In the skit, she stabbed Dutch, and every time he'd try to sit up, she'd bop him down again. Susan played it completely straight. The audiences howled, but she never faltered, and not even when Dutch broke up, as he usually did. We all marveled at how she kept her composure."

Jane Wyman, however, found it difficult to keep hers. Then engaged to the actor (they would marry in January 1940) she watched the scene every night from the wings, furious at the "realism" Susan put into her punches.

Susan was equally annoyed by Wyman's presence, and complained to Parsons that it made her very nervous. When Louella passed this on, Wyman exploded: "Too bad about *her!* If I don't stand there and watch, she'll knock Ronnie out. She hits him too hard. She just slaps him that hard because she thinks it makes me mad."

Louella, caught between two warring factions, tried to be conciliatory and, when that failed, took a neutral stand. But despite this infighting, the act played to packed houses throughout the country, and extra shows had to be added when it was booked into the Loews' State in New York for a Christmas week engagement starting December 21. Susan brought the house down when she made her entrance shouting, "Anyone here from

Brooklyn?" Even Parsons herself couldn't compete with that show-stopper.

The columnist developed a deep and lifelong fondness for the girl and would later reminisce:

"When I first asked Susan to join the act, she was her completely honest self when she told me right to my face that she thought being associated with me 'will help my career.'

"You come to know people very well when you travel with them, and I was surprised that with all Susan's sexy beauty, she was at heart a real 'Miss Prim'! She was easily shocked by backstage stories, even when they were mild, and her feelings were so easily hurt she dissolved into tears when anyone even looked at her crossly.

"She seldom went out, even when we hit big towns like Philadelphia and New York. She was an ultra-conventional and moral little thing, a quality that endeared her to me fully as much as her loveliness and sweetness."

When the tour ended on December 27, the other cast members—with the exception of Wyman and Reagan—went their separate ways, relieved to have it over and done with. Susan, however, decided to remain in New York until after the New Year, Louella arranging a special rate for her at the Warwick, where they had all been staying. She told a *Daily News* reporter, happily, that she was up for a leading role in the Group Theater's production of Clifford Odets's *Night Music* with Elia Kazan and Morris Carnovsky, which was about to go into production. Paramount had no new film for her in the immediate future, and she'd never completely abandoned her dream of becoming a Broadway star. Now that the tour had given her the confidence to appear before a live audience, the possibility of doing the play was exciting, and she spent the rest of her time in town going to the theater.

One of the shows she saw was Katharine Hepburn in *The Philadelphia Story*. With Louella's help, she was able to get a ticket for the December 30 Saturday matinee performance. This biographer, not yet in her teens, was seated nearby and, recognizing Susan from the Loews' State show, was as transfixed by her as Susan was by Hepburn.

After the show, Susan was in the crush of matinee women crowding around the Shubert Alley stage entrance. Twice she opened the door, obviously intending to go backstage—and then lost her nerve. Before she tried a third time, Miss Hepburn, in a heavy coat and bandana, dashed by and into a long black limousine. The car sped away, barely missing autograph seekers anxious for a close-up look at the star. The crowds dispersed, leaving just a few stragglers waiting for Van Heflin's and Joseph Cotten's autographs. It had gotten dark, and a freezing wind swept through Shubert Alley as Susan raced across 44th Street and into Sardi's.

She was never signed for *Night Music*. Perhaps Paramount vetoed the idea, blaming the Group Theater for the problems they had been having with Frances Farmer, who had run out on her contract with them to do *Golden Boy* and *Thunder Rock* with the Group Theater, disdainfully declaring herself a *stage* actress. They may not have wanted another of their players "corrupted" by the theater. More likely, the Group had never seriously been interested in Susan in the first place. She was, after all, hardly up to their standards—not yet—and the whole idea may have been just an agent's dream. Susan never discussed what had to have been a bitter disappointment again.

Nor would she discuss what turned out to be an unpleasant reunion with Walter Thornton. Thornton had heard of her success in Hollywood, such as it was, and wanted both the credit and the money for it. Claiming he was responsible for launching her on her career, he promptly announced plans to sue for $100,000, asserting she had walked out on a personal contract with him.

Flaring up, Susan charged that the whole contract had been illegal in the first place and that she had no intention of paying Thornton one penny. "One hundred thousand dollars is a lot of money," she told reporters succinctly. "He's not going to get it." Thornton made more noises about suing, then changed his mind —"it simply wasn't worth the effort," he declared—and the two never spoke again.

It was in this frame of mind that Susan returned to Hollywood after the holidays, only to be sent packing again. The studio, in a less-than-altruistic goodwill gesture, had arranged to send the remaining members of the Golden Circle on a whistle-stop tour of Paramount exhibitors to hype its spring releases. Betty Field was co-starring in *Seventeen*, Ellen Drew in *Buck*

Benny Rides Again, and Robert Preston in *Typhoon;* William Henry had a strong feature role in *The Way of All Flesh,* Judith Barrett was in *Road to Singapore,* and Patricia Morison was Ray Milland's leading lady in *Untamed.* Susan was, in fact, the only member of the group not in a forthcoming Paramount movie. It made her feel a bit odd, but fortunately it made little difference to the exhibitors, who managed to get plenty of local coverage as a result of her appearances.

On tour, Susan was treated like a star. Back home again, however, she was the "invisible" girl once more. When she complained about her lack of work, the studio bluntly told her she should be grateful she was still under salary. Golden Circle hopefuls Janice Logan, Louise Campbell, Joyce Mathews, and Joseph Allen, Jr., all had had their options dropped, they pointed out, while she had received a $100-a-week raise.

It was little consolation to an ambitious young actress, however, and her impatience with the studio grew. Further, it spilled over into her home life. The Marrenner family was now living in a large, if rather unfashionable, two-bedroom bungalow near Paramount. Wally was still bringing in a small salary, but Florence and Ellen continued to contribute nothing to the up-keep, and not only was Susan paying the rent, she was beginning to find the lack of privacy suffocating. Finally, it all got too much for her.

According to Florence, "One day Susan came home and told my brother and me that she didn't want us to live there any more. She said she just wanted my mother to live with her. We asked why, but she wouldn't say why she wanted us to leave. My brother was working as an usher in a theater and took a bachelor apartment. So I went to live with friends—a man, his wife, and daughter." That seemed to defuse the situation. For a while . . .

Except for the mandatory twelve-week layoff (a studio contract guaranteed only forty weeks on salary), Susan earned her pay during most of 1940 by doing despised "cheesecake" lay-outs, either alone or with other young actors on the lot. Richard Webb, who came to Paramount at that time (and was under contract there for nine years) still retains vivid memories of those days:

"For years," says Webb today, "I had an 8 x 10 glossy of

54

Susan and me modeling matching bathing suits around the pool of the Beverly Hills Hotel. In fact, publicity at one time had me engaged to Susan and [actress] Martha O'Driscoll simultaneously. I found Susan very interesting. I dug her.

"Sure, she was disliked by those who didn't have what she had and were jealous of her. They were, in fact, actually afraid of her. She was accused of snubbing people, of being aloof. I noted at times she would get within ten feet of me before saying hello. She would always apologize—but she had bad eyes and didn't want people to know.

"To my knowledge, she never hurt anyone on her climb. If she didn't like someone—or something—she stayed away from them—it. But she had a tremendous will, came on strong. She knew where she was going and wanted it *Now*."

Several years later, after she had left Paramount, Susan would reflect on her behavior at that time:

"When I arrived at the studio, I had preconceived notions and stubbornly clung to the belief that they were right. I was a green kid, fresh at times, and it was probably that quality that made them see possibilities in me as an actress.

"I was pushed around in those years—so I spoke up. The studio kept referring to me as a promising young actress. What I wanted to know was—just *how* long could a girl be promising? I got the reputation of being, to put it politely, a wave-maker.

"People around the studio had told me that I should change, that my attitude was wrong. So, suddenly, overnight, I stopped being myself and tried to copy everyone else. As a result, I got so mixed up and was more confused than ever. Some people did try to straighten me out, but their approach was all wrong. A word of encouragement produced a glow inside—like good, fine wine. But mostly I was criticized. I guess it never occurred to anyone to find out why I behaved the way I did.

"Other girls were going right to the top while I got the parts no one else wanted. I was getting a good salary by then, but being basically an honest person, I felt like a fraud for accepting it.

"Things went from bad to bedlam."

chapter 5

ALTHOUGH her option had been picked up with a substantial pay increase, Susan felt she was languishing at Paramount. Approaching twenty-three, convinced that time was passing her by, she was determined to do something spectacular to make them sit up and take notice.

In mid-1940, as was its annual custom, Paramount invited its exhibitors to the coast for a week of lavish entertainment and screenings of future Paramount products, the whole affair to be climaxed by a gala luncheon attended by top studio brass and spiced by the presence of Paramount's major stars—Hope, Crosby, Goddard, and Colbert—as well as by current hopefuls. Each was to be introduced individually from a stage constructed especially for the occasion. Richard Webb recalls:

"Each speaker had a brief script prepared—the usual bromide thanking exhibitors for their past good work and expressing confidence in their future enthusiasm. Everyone followed the script. Everyone, that is, but Susan Hayward."

Sweetly, Susan made her way to the platform and, after taking a bow, exploded her bomb:

"Most of you gentlemen know me already. When I visited your hometowns you've been good enough to ask why I am not in more pictures. There's somebody here who can answer that question." She turned pointedly to Y. Frank Freeman and demanded:

"Mr. Freeman, will *you* tell these men why I'm not in pictures?"

This display of spunk brought the exhibitors to their feet whooping and hollering for more. Concealing fury and embarrassment with a tone of feigned amusement, Freeman announced, "Don't worry, friends, you'll be seeing Susan Hayward in more movies." But you could tell he was gritting his teeth while he said it.

"That was a stupid thing for Susan to do," Medford insists today. "It only added to the executives' antagonism toward her. However, Paramount was planning some big airplane story, and Susan was perfect for the second female part. I did my best to persuade Freeman to test Susan for the role—she was physically perfect for it—and because there was no one else on the lot the right type, he agreed to the test. I felt sure this would be her big chance."

Unfortunately, according to Medford, "Her work was so amateurish the director suddenly stopped the cameras, snorted in disgust, and stamped off the set, leaving Susan standing there while the crew squirmed in embarrassment. Shortly afterward, Paramount found that other girl—the one with the hair falling all over her face—and she got the part."

The part Medford is referring to was that of Sally Vaughn, the siren of *I Wanted Wings*. It made an overnight star of Veronica Lake, although Lake herself was dismissed by the *New York Times* as a girl who "shows little more than a talent for wearing low-cut dresses." Immediately signed by Paramount, Lake would join Paulette Goddard on Susan's private hate list. She was convinced that both women were the cause of her career impasse. Ben Medford found it difficult to convince her that perhaps she was being her own worst enemy.

Nevertheless, Medford refused to falter in his belief that Susan could be a big star if she could only find the right part and land it. And shortly thereafter, thumbing through the script of *Adam Had Four Sons*, he thought he had found such a part. The story was about a man with—as the title says—four sons, and the beautiful governess who, years later, returns to the household, sure she is in love with the widowed Adam. She runs afoul of Adam's vicious daughter-in-law Hester Stoddard, however, who is married to one son and on the make for another, and it is not until the end that Hester is exposed for the bad lot she is and that Adam and the governess find a new life together. The role of Hester Stoddard seemed to be written with

Susan in mind: "a hard-drinking, faithless little baggage who almost destroys the entire family and its governess . . . malicious and irresponsible. And gorgeous."

"Gregory Ratoff was a client of mine," continues Medford. "I begged him to persuade Harry Cohn to use Susan. I told Susan, 'This is an important part, regardless of who plays it. The part will take care of you. It will stand out because you're playing a first-class bitch.'

"But first I had to convince Ratoff, who had to convince Cohn."

A few blocks up the street, mogul Harry Cohn was planning Columbia's major "class" production of 1941. Under his dictatorial management, the studio mainly turned out profitable potboilers, but Cohn still came through with one prestigious blockbuster a year. Thus the man who brought America *The Shadow, The Lone Wolf Strikes Back,* and *Blondie Goes Latin* was also responsible for such classics as *It Happened One Night, You Can't Take It with You, Lost Horizon, Mr. Deeds Goes to Town, Mr. Smith Goes to Washington,* and *The Awful Truth,* all but the last under the direction of Frank Capra.

Capra and Cohn had parted company after the completion of *Mr. Smith,* and the latter was now finding himself faced with the task of scoring a bull's-eye without his peerless director. Undaunted, he persuaded David O. Selznick to lend him Ingrid Bergman, who had made a spectacular American debut the previous year in *Intermezzo,* for the leading female role in *Adam Had Four Sons.* As Adam, he cast 1931 Oscar winner Warner Baxter, who'd signed with Columbia after a decade-long association with Twentieth Century-Fox. At forty-eight, Baxter had lost much of his early romantic appeal, but Cohn was convinced that one big hit would revive his faltering career. And as Adam's four sons, Cohn chose Richard Denning, Johnny Downs, Robert Shaw, and Cris Lind.

But what to do about the daughter-in-law, Hester Stoddard? The vixenish role seemed tailor-made for Paulette Goddard, but Cohn's bid for her services came too late. Goddard was committed to a loan-out to United Artists for *Pot of Gold.* So Freeman, not too altruistically, agreed to allow Medford to try to get Susan in the film. For Freeman, the loan-out to Columbia would serve a triple purpose: the studio would get good money for her services; if the picture was a hit and her reviews were satisfactory her price for future loan-outs would increase while her salary at Paramount stayed the same—and, most important, he'd have her out of his hair for a few months.

There was another aspect to the deal too, one that amused Freeman vastly. Once Susan had suffered the trauma of working for Harry Cohn, she was certain to return to her home studio in a more compliant mood. Susan was looked upon as "untouchable" at Paramount—a real iceberg. For a girl as career-hungry as Susan, this attitude was incomprehensible to many of the people there. And no one cared enough to try to change it. With sex the cheapest commodity in town, many at Paramount felt a good roll in the hay was just what Susan needed.

Harry Cohn, to say the least, was not a man easily put off by any woman. His sexual exploits were legendary. According to the stories, newly signed starlets supposedly had to go through an "initiation" week of unspeakable physical indignities, not to mention liberal doses of his notoriously profane and abusive language. Dubbed White Fang by author Ben Hecht, Harry Cohn, noted Hedda Hopper caustically, "is a man you have to stand in line to hate."

Cohn reckoned without Susan Hayward, however. And Louella Parsons. Inexplicably, Louella Parsons was a rare Cohn supporter and he, in turn, would do nothing to jeopardize that fearsome lady's affection and friendship. When Louella learned her little Susan was set to work at Columbia, she lost no time informing Cohn of her motherly feelings toward the girl. Swallowing his frustration, Cohn promised to behave, and Susan sailed through the picture as virginal as ever.

Selznick was equally as protective of Ingrid Bergman, both personally and professionally. At first when he was approached by Cohn, Selznick had negative feelings about Bergman's doing *Adam Had Four Sons*—he'd rather have paid her salary himself than have her work for that man—but, as Bergman said, "I wanted to work and since it was the best thing available, I chose to do it." Overruled, Selznick made no bones about warning Cohn: Bergman must be accorded the utmost respect—or else!

Too shrewd to antagonize Selznick for what he politely termed "a piece of ass," Cohn kept his hands off her as well.

In a later interview, Susan would call the role of Hester Stoddard "one of my favorites." For Bergman, only ten months her senior, she had nothing but praise. When asked how the two of them were getting on, Susan replied, "She's been wonderful to me and just as concerned about the quality of my close-ups as she is with her own." For years to come Susan would cite Ingrid Bergman as "one of my favorite actresses." Still, although Susan held her in such high esteem and their professional relationship was always cordial, the two of them never became close. Part of the reason was Susan's natural reserve. Part of it was that Bergman possessed the one quality Susan felt was sorely lacking in herself, no matter how hard she tried to fake it.

Bergman had "class."

Susan was less intimidated, however, by *Adam*'s director Gregory Ratoff, and the association that began with this film would develop into a lasting friendship. ("I don't think," says Ben Medford, "that Susan knew Ratoff wanted to fire her from the picture three times." Medford also scoffs at the legend that Ratoff's actress wife Eugenie Leontovich, who was coaching Susan in the role, threatened, "I will never sleep with you again if you don't use Susan in that part." "If that was true I would have known about it.")

Affectionately dubbed the Mad Russian by his peers, Ratoff's homely, bearlike exterior and heavily accented English was deceptive. Although he is best remembered today as an actor— his portrayal of Bette Davis's producer Max Fabian in *All About Eve*, for instance, is a classic—Ratoff was, in fact, a multi-talented writer, producer, and director as well. After his direction of *Intermezzo*, Bergman trusted him implicitly; within a few days after beginning *Adam*, Susan would too.

Although Ratoff would scream, "Susan, you are the most steenkeengest actress I've ever seen," whenever she muffed a scene, he was equally as emotional in his praise. "You are vunderrr-ful, marvoolooous," he would roar when he obtained the desired results. Susan flourished under his direction and between takes rushed to his side for additional advice and instructions. "She pestered the life out of him," says Medford. Sure she had made enormous strides under Ratoff, she was convinced that, once her bosses at Paramount saw a rough cut of the film, they would follow it up with an important assignment.

She had one particular picture in mind.

Writer Ketti Frings had just completed a beautiful script for Paramount titled *Hold Back the Dawn*, about the plight of European refugees stranded in Mexico while desperately trying to get into the United States. Charles Boyer was scheduled to play the irresistible heel who woos and wins a guileless school teacher for the sole purpose of getting across the border, before reluctantly falling in love with her. Olivia de Havilland was set for the teacher—an ideal choice that would bring her another Oscar nomination.

There was a second feminine lead, however, the role of Boyer's wisecracking former dancing partner Anita Dixon, who gets them all in a pile of trouble. Three women at Paramount would have been perfect for the part: Paulette Goddard, Veronica Lake, and Susan.

Only Susan was readily available.

Sultry Veronica Lake was scheduled to appear in Preston Sturges's *Sullivan's Travels*, and Goddard was set to star with Bob Hope in *Nothing but the Truth*. As she waited for *Adam Had Four Sons* to open, Susan was free and clear. Besides, even though the role of Anita Dixon was a showy one, it was decidedly not of star caliber, and Susan thought it unlikely, not only that it would be offered to Goddard, but that Goddard would even want it.

Writer Cameron Shipp said: "Susan fought and scrounged for parts, but she never begged. She had a certain angry integrity. She demanded."

But when she demanded the role of Anita Dixon, Buddy De Sylva coldly informed her that Goddard's schedule had been rearranged to do this film as well as Hope's. Instead, he arranged another loan-out for Susan. She would be reporting to Republic studios to play Judy Canova's selfish, snotty cousin in *Sis Hopkins*. After getting third billing to Bergman and Baxter, Susan would be demoted to fifth—following Canova, singer Bob Crosby, character actor Charles Butterworth, and comedian Jerry Colonna.

Just the *threat* of being sent to Republic was enough to terrorize any major studio contract player. An actual loan-out to the studio was considered the proverbial kiss of death. Even a suspension or dropped option was preferable. Republic was a "poverty row" studio that had found gold in the North Hollywood hills with Gene Autry, Roy Rogers, and John Wayne westerns, but to the rest of the industry it was a necessary evil, useful only for feeding the tastes of the least discriminating audiences. If Paramount was hell-bent on punishing Susan for arrogance and temperament, they couldn't have chosen a better way. But she went. She was miserable, frustrated, and angry, but she went. To her, as to Medford, her agent, "The most important thing was to keep working."

She reported to Republic, played her scenes under the inept direction of Joseph Santley, remained aloof from the other members of the company, and left the instant the cameras stopped rolling. When her role in the picture was completed, she dismissed the entire episode from her mind.

Adam Had Four Sons was scheduled to open at Radio City Music Hall on March 28, 1941. Cohn was aware that *Adam,* dismissed by preview audiences as dreary domestic drama, needed all the help it could get. (In fact, when Susan finally got a chance to view the completed picture at a sneak preview, she forgot her early estimation of the film and blew up at Medford, "You've ruined my career!") Any excitement engendered by *Adam*'s being Bergman's "eagerly anticipated" second film was also dissipated when MGM rushed Bergman's third film, *Rage in Heaven,* into the New York Capitol exactly one week before the Music Hall opening. Always intimidated by Louis B. Mayer, Cohn could do little more than voice a meek protest.

Bergman, busy completing *Dr. Jekyll and Mr. Hyde,* was unavailable to publicize either film. Media interest in co-star Warner Baxter was nil.

Whatever Cohn's personal feelings toward Susan Hayward, he shrewdly calculated that her combination of Brooklyn background and dazzling looks would prove potent space-grabbers, so, with Paramount's blessings, Cohn made arrangements to fly her, and Florence again as chaperone, to New York. He put them up at the Waldorf, and told the East Coast publicity department to take it from there. In short, she was given star treatment. Susan was elated. Aside from the usual generous distribution of leg art, little had been done for her by Paramount publicity. The fan magazines (which she read secretly) seemed oblivious to her existence. Occasionally a magazine used a pinup shot, but by and large Paramount's fan magazine department made little or no effort to promote her.

The trip to New York for Cohn gave both Susan and *Adam Had Four Sons* some badly needed coverage.

On March 14, 1941, wearing an ill-fitting, rumpled beige suit, she checked into Manhattan's plush Art Deco Waldorf-Astoria. The hotel was just a few blocks from the Lexington Avenue cafeteria where she and Sara Little had once "talked endlessly about what we were going to do with our lives." To spend just one night at the Waldorf—the stopover for millionaires, movie stars, and royalty—had been part of that dream. In 1937, Edythe Marrener would have been ecstatic with a $7-a-night single there. Now she commanded a suite facing Park Avenue.

Once installed, she obediently glided through the itinerary Columbia had carefully planned: one that ranged from the sublime—a sitting for the coveted cover of the *New York Sunday News* Coloroto section—to the highly ridiculous: a carefully rigged competition for "Presidency of the Perfect Legs Institute." Mostly, however, there were meetings with the press. As both a Brooklynite and a rejected Scarlett, Susan made good copy and a fine impression—"a refreshing relief from the dumb broads" usually foisted on them, one of them said—and so both Susan and the movie got plenty of ink.

When the reviews came out, they were encouraging too. Though the critics agreed with the preview audiences' estimation of the picture, they did like Susan. The *Dallas Morning News* noted that "little Susan Hayward, heretofore an also-ran at Paramount, gives it the works as the mischief-maker," and the *Richmond News-Leader* enthused: "Two unusually talented and charming women walk away with the entire picture. Ingrid Bergman as the gentle, loyal, fiercely devoted governess who would stain even her own name to save the honor of Adam's sons, is contrasted with Susan Hayward as the predatory and treacherous wife of one of them. Miss Hayward is stunning in the latter role, making it quite as outstanding as Miss Bergman's exemplary one." Only Bosley Crowther of the *New York Times*—initiating a love-hate relationship with Susan Hayward that would continue for more than a quarter of a century—was decidedly negative, writing that "Susan Hayward so coyly overacts the romantically unlicensed mischief-maker that often she is plain ridiculous."

Susan didn't care, though; she was riding high. Her first major reviews! Only one thing happened to dull her pleasure in the event—but when that came, it was a blockbuster.

Throughout her press sessions, the newsmen saw plenty of

Susan, but never one glimpse of Florence. Whenever an interview was scheduled at the Waldorf, Florence was told to catch a movie or go shopping. Nor, when Susan was invited to an evening on the town, did she ask her host if he could include an extra man for her sister. Susan's resentment of Florence's apparently cavalier attitude toward the expenses had been smouldering for a long time. She felt she was being used, and she could never jibe Flo's active social life with her own "ultraconventional" sensibilities. Besides, Flo was a living reminder of the Brooklyn past Susan was trying so hard to forget (even while she used it to gain hometown support), and on this trip in particular she wanted desperately to impress the press and movie people who were escorting her about—to have them think of her as Susan Hayward, movie star, not as Edythe Marrenner of the second-day bread and cardboard-soled shoes.

The explosion had been building up for a long time, and on the eve of their departure back to California, it broke. Florence later recalled it this way: she had invited people to the suite—relatives, she said—while Susan was out with some of her movie friends. When Susan got back that evening, however, and saw them, "she got very angry and asked them what they were doing there. And then she got mad at me because I had told them they could come over. I didn't see anything wrong in it. 'How can you *do* this to me?' she screamed. 'How can I entertain my friends when you have company? This is supposed to be a *business* trip for me.' She raved on and said a lot of things. I said a lot of things too. It was a terrible scene. I asked her what made her think her friends were so much more wonderful than her relatives. . . . The next morning she told me she was going to leave me in New York. . . . Looking back on it, I just think she asked me to go to New York because she wanted me to leave Hollywood."

Flo checked out of the Waldorf and went to Brooklyn to stay with friends, hoping her mother might be able to make peace in the family. Mrs. Marrenner was heartsick to learn of her daughters' falling-out and Flo's subsequent decision to remain in the East. After a futile attempt to affect a truce, Ellen Marrenner kept her own counsel. Wally, though working, was unmarried, and eligible for the army. Susan was responsible for her mother's support, and Ellen had no intention of jeopardizing that by becoming involved in a personal squabble. She advised

Florence, then thirty-one, to try to find a nice boy and settle down; and a year later, Florence did just that, marrying an old beau named Udo Zaenglin at army headquarters in Spartanburg, South Carolina. As it later turned out, though, Florence's problems were just beginning.

Meanwhile, back in California, Susan was greeted with mild praise for having acquitted herself well on tour, and ordered to report to wardrobe for fittings for *Among the Living*, an insignificant melodrama. Albert Dekker, the nominal star, was cast in the dual role of an upstanding millionaire and his psychotic twin. Susan had second billing as the daughter of the rooming-house owner—a predatory, money-hungry tramp completely taken in by the murderer during his more lucid moments. Frances Farmer, who a few years earlier had been one of Paramount's most promising young stars, was winding up her contract—billed fourth. The role misused her considerable talents and served as an example of how a major studio could destroy an actress who failed to conform to its standard of behavior.

Surprisingly, *Among the Living* won favor with the majority of the critics. The *New York Herald-Tribune*'s Howard Barnes said, "*Among the Living* is head and shoulders above most of the filler shows which are ground out by Hollywood to perpetuate the double feature system. Susan Hayward is especially good." The *New York Times*, *Variety*, and the *New York Post* also singled out Susan for special mention. Frances Farmer was generally ignored.

Susan's performance also won the attention of Cecil B. De-Mille. After considering almost every sweet young thing on the lot, he cast her as Drucilla Alston, the tragic ingenue of his epic sea drama *Reap the Wild Wind*, starring, as luck would have it, Paulette Goddard. Goddard played the spirited owner of a salvage schooner whose hand is being fought over by a ship's company lawyer (Ray Milland) and an embittered sea captain (John Wayne). Convinced he has been double-crossed by Milland and Goddard, Wayne makes a deal with an evil salvage operator to wreck his own ship; but things go awry when Goddard's cousin (Susan)—who is also the girl of the salvage operator's brother—goes down with the ship. At the end, Wayne and Milland descend to the ocean depths, where the conflict is chillingly resolved.

Although it would be one of Cecil B. DeMille's most popular

pictures, the filming left little impression on its huge cast, which also included Robert Preston and Raymond Massey. Even the director's biographer devoted his pages to the giant squid that swam off with most of the reviews. Constructed of bright red sponge rubber, its insides operated by electric motors and its thirty-foot tentacles a complex set of hydraulic, piston-operated cable, the monster deserved the attention it received.

It certainly got a great deal more attention than Susan, who later said, "On the first day of shooting, I approached Mr. De-Mille timidly. 'Excuse me, Mr. DeMille, but do you think that . . .'

"He cut me short, saying, 'I hired you for this film because I want an actress who can think for herself. Do that and you'll take a load of worry off my life and add years to your own.'"

Susan was charming in the picture, her death pivotal to the climax in which Milland and Wayne descend to the wrecked ship and find her shawl . . . just before the giant squid finds them. Seen on television today, it is still a rousing adventure.

Susan's next film encounter with Goddard came when director George Marshall pitted them against one another for the affections of Fred MacMurray in *The Forest Rangers*. Shooting started in March 1942 on location in Santa Cruz, California.

The film, which received mediocre reviews, does not merit description, but one incident does: Susan very nearly drowned during the filming. A log jam on which she was standing broke up, and she was hurled into eight feet of water, among swirling lengths of lumber. Five studio workers plunged in to rescue her and only succeeded in sending her down again, before Roy Mowrer, a thirty-year-old scaler for a lumber company, pulled her out.

She ignored a bad lump on her head and was back on the set the next morning.

In a letter later sent film historian Doug McClelland, Marshall noted how much Susan had impresed him during that hazardous location shooting, and explained why:

Her courage turned up on *The Forest Rangers* in the part where she and Paulette Goddard had to run through some fire. Paulette was frightened, and in spite of our showing her all the safety factors and how impossible it was for her to be injured or burned, she still backed off and started to cry. I really think that she had a date and wanted to get off early. Susan came up to me and whispered, "Get the cameras going." Then she went over to Paulette, as though to comfort her. When I gave her the signal, she grabbed Paulette by the hand and said, "For God's sake, stop being such a baby!" and pulled her through the scene. Ironically, in the story it was Susan who was supposed to become frightened.

As an actress she was one of the best, because her emotions stemmed from the inside and were not just the mouthings of an inadequate actress who reads lines without the slightest idea of what they mean. Susan knew her craft. She had sincerity and courage, and at times would be a bit stubborn, but not to the point of being disagreeable.

Susan was obviously beginning to learn her trade. Nevertheless, her career still seemed to be stalling, her next two films doing little for her: Rene Clair's *I Married a Witch* with Fredric March and Veronica Lake, in which Susan unhappily played yet another nasty role—March's fiancée—and an insignificant "B" film called *Young and Willing*, adapted from a moderate Broadway hit called *Out of the Frying Pan. Young and Willing* mainly served as a showcase for Paramount's young contract players: Susan had billing in a cast that included William Holden, Eddie Bracken, James Brown, Barbara Britton, and, from the Broadway original, Florence MacMichael.

Both films, curiously enough, though shot on the Paramount lot, with Paramount players, were released through United Artists, in a complicated arrangement that confused many at the time. With the war cutting off a steady flow of European-made films, United Artists was in desperate need of products to fulfill contractual obligations to its exhibitors, so Paramount, with a huge backlog of films awaiting release, agreed to sell them *I Married a Witch* and *Young and Willing*. In the latter case, at least, it was apparently with few regrets.

Paramount had even fewer regrets when they shipped Susan back to Republic for the female lead in what that poverty-row studio considered their musical extravaganza of the year, *Hit Parade of 1943.*

chapter 6

It was during the filming of *Hit Parade of 1943*, in November 1942, that Susan became romantically involved with a leading man for the first—and only—time in her life.

Speaking about her shortly before his death from leukemia in April 1979, John Carroll, at age seventy-two, remembered: "She was something, even back then. I knew a great many lovely ladies in my lifetime, and I can safely say I met my match in that determined little redhead."

For Susan, that was no mean accomplishment. Carroll, born in New Orleans with the poetic name of Julian LaFaye, left home at the age of twelve seeking adventure; and presumably he found it as he became, successively, a steeplejack, barnstorming pilot, range rider, and ship's cook, finally ending up in Italy, where, he claimed, he studied voice with a man named Victor Chesnais. No one was ever sure how much of this was the truth.

In the late twenties he obtained free passage back to America by signing on to conduct a luxury liner's band; migrated first to Florida, then to California; then, after knocking around as an extra for a couple of years, got a role in a 1934 "B" quickie called *Hi Gaucho*. By that time he had fallen in love with a fiery Hungarian dancer-actress, Steffi Duna, married her, and fathered a daughter, Julianna. (The marriage was short-lived, and the first Mrs. Carroll went on to a lasting union with actor Dennis

O'Keefe.) Generally disliked in Hollywood social circles, considered a liar, a bounder, and an egomaniac, Carroll still managed to get signed by MGM in 1939. He was convinced he possessed the rugged appeal of Clark Gable, to whom he was frequently compared, plus the strong baritone voice of Nelson Eddy. Eddy's marriage earlier in the year had been looked upon with disfavor in official circles, and Louis B. Mayer felt it expedient to have another masculine singer-actor waiting in the wings. Despite an inglorious MGM debut in *Congo Maisie*, one reporter commented, "It's practically a natural that John Carroll is going to become Hollywood's next BIG star—that is, if Hollywood and John Carroll can stand each other that long. At the moment neither the town nor Carroll are at all sure at this point."

Carroll's career at MGM was similar to Susan's at Paramount. He was cast in romantic leads in "B's" and supporting roles in major films, and was habitually loaned out to lesser studios in an attempt to deflate his gigantic ego and punish him for his transgressions. Neither Gable nor Eddy considered him much of a threat. Although selected as a male "Star of Tomorrow," together with Van Heflin, Eddie Bracken, and Alan Ladd, in the 1941–42 *Motion Picture Herald* poll of movie exhibitors, whatever charisma he may have had was not given the chance to register on screen. Off-screen, however, he knocked women dead. Much to MGM's distress, he was often linked with some "ladies" of rather dubious repute—among them Virginia Hill, alleged to be the former moll of mobster Bugsy Siegel. Studio pressure put an end to that association in record time. In mid-1942, Carroll, at loose ends and awaiting induction into the air force, was sent back to Republic for what they considered their two most important pictures of the year: *Flying Tigers* (in which he was billed second to John Wayne) and *Hit Parade of 1943* (for which he got top billing).

The story of the latter was all fluff and nonsense: a young songwriter (Susan) has had her song stolen by the owner of a minor music publishing company (Carroll), and within the course of some ninety minutes falls in love with the charming heel. So much for plot. The Ray McKinley, Freddy Martin, and Count Basie bands were dragged in to provide most of the music. Carroll's baritone was heard to moderate advantage, and

Susan "mouthed" her songs to the prerecording made by a now-forgotten vocalist.

Wanda Hale in the *New York Daily News* would comment: "In trying so hard to make *Hit Parade of 1943* a gorgeous musical spectacle, the producers have only made a wasteful, trying picture." Second-stringer Tom Pryor of the *New York Times,* though, was less critical, noting, "Republic wisely put forth a modestly backgrounded potpourri of songs, dances, and romance in a comedy vein—in short, a pleasant and unpretentious entertainment . . . a musical package not too gaudy but all right." Pryor, however, rather gullibly added: "but it was a bit surprising to learn that Susan Hayward can include singing among [her] accomplishments."

During most of the shooting, Susan, as usual, kept her relationship with Carroll on an exclusively professional basis. He later reported: "Susan continued to act as if I didn't exist when we were away from the camera. However, I dismissed her as one of those super-serious actresses who had to keep the on-screen emotions going after the director called cut, and the script called for her to dislike me intensely."

Then, however, something happened. The final days of shooting centered around a scene early in the script—a rather intense fight between the two principals, and Carroll remembered: "I was embarrassed to find myself with a perpetual erection. And Susan suddenly was more communicative between takes. When we wound up the picture, I asked if she'd celebrate the occasion with me by having dinner. After that first evening we became what columnists refer to as 'an item.' Few, however, expressed much interest in us at the time, and when we dated, we stayed away from photographer-frequented places, at Susan's insistence. She obviously didn't want anyone to call us a publicity gimmick."

Although uncertain about the depth of his feelings, Carroll could not deny that he was totally fascinated with Susan. The ruthlessly ambitious actress he had worked with on *Hit Parade of 1943* bore little resemblance to the quaintly old-fashioned girl he was dating.

"Susan," he'd later tell a friend, "considered a kiss a commitment and anything beyond that a marriage proposal." He never boasted of going beyond a kiss but, during the Christmas holidays of 1943, a few days before leaving for active duty in the air force, he asked Susan to marry him. ("Susan was a virgin when she was dating Carroll," comments Ben Medford. "And she was a virgin when she broke their engagement. The only way he could get her into bed was to marry her!")

Ellen Marrenner was far from pleased by the news. Carroll was ten years older than Susan, divorced and burdened with the responsibility of supporting both a young child and a mother living in his house. A rumor also had it that Carroll was deeply in debt to Republic's president Herbert Yates. Carroll's mother Emma LaFaye, an attractive, white-haired Southern lady, took an equally dim view. She felt John could do better for himself than a Yankee starlet.

Although she did not break the news to the press, Susan considered herself engaged. Before Carroll took off, Wally remembers, "He told Susan to pick out a ring and send him the bill." On Valentine's Day they'd notify their respective studios. No wedding date was set, however, and if Carroll had any misgivings about his decision, at least there were no immediate pressures.

Susan spent the next few days on a grand tour of the Beverly Hills jewelry establishments, finally settling on a perfect 4½ carat diamond—the most beautiful ring she had ever seen. "My sister was no dummy," Wally adds. "She picked out the most expensive ring she could find. She told me, 'If he really wants to marry me, he'll buy me that ring.'" (Echoes of the young Edythe Marrenner, troubled over her mother's lack of an engagement ring.)

When Carroll called from his base that night, she excitedly described it to him in detail. His reaction was neither excited nor amused. He was, in fact, furious about the size of the ring, and its price—especially the price. Predictably, a heated argument ensued. By the time the phone conversation had ended, so had the engagement.

The next day, Susan returned to the jewelers and paid for the ring herself. She told everyone it was a Christmas present from her mother.

Louella Parsons happily wrote, "I talked with Susan Hayward the other afternoon, and she is all over her John Carroll infatuation. She is wearing a diamond ring—a gift from her mother. I suspect she received it after she said adieu to John as a reward."

Ed Sullivan had his own suspicions when he noted: "Since the Susan Hayward and John Carroll romance is off so quickly, I'm beginning to believe that it was a dream-up by Republic. Susan isn't a bit upset."

In truth, she wasn't.

Ellen Marrenner, convinced that Susan had never been in love with John, told her: "I think you wanted an engagement ring, not an engagement."

Years later when Susan told the "true" story about the ring and the engagement, Carroll would be identified only as "an actor who was in the army." It didn't matter. By that time Carroll was a forgotten man in films. (His name would later make the papers when a court insisted he return $180,000 to an eighty-year-old woman who claimed he had bilked her out of a considerable fortune.)

Buying that diamond herself may have been the best investment Susan ever made, and she had no trouble erasing Carroll completely from her mind. Wally Marrenner does note, however, that in his possession is a photo of the three of them taken on the set of *Hit Parade*. "Susan had a habit of writing little remarks on photos. On the one I have, she put 'the kid' above me, 'dog meat' above John Carroll's head."

Although Paramount had heard good things about Susan's work in *Hit Parade*, they once again refused to consider her for one of their more important pictures of the year, *So Proudly We Hail,* the story of army nurse trapped in the South Pacific during the invasion of Bataan and Corregidor. Claudette Colbert was set for the lead, but there were two other major roles for which Susan could have been considered: the sexy, wise-cracking Joan O'Doul and the brooding Olivia D'Arcy, out to avenge the death of her fiancé at Pearl Harbor. Not surprisingly, the roles went to Paulette Goddard and Veronica Lake.

By now Susan was counting the months until her contract finally ran out. She was no longer mystified by Paramount's practice of regularly renewing her options and raising her salary. One loan-out arranged by Medford would cover her salary for a year—the rest was sheer profit for Paramount. It was a no-lose situation for the studio, a no-win deal for Susan. She felt like an indentured slave. If she screamed, she was labeled "bitch" or worse. If she complied docilely, there were no rewards. All she could do was wait and try to build her name as a personality and, hopefully, as an actress. But at twenty-six, she felt she couldn't wait too long.

With no new pictures scheduled, she boarded a train east and arrived in New York on Washington's Birthday to do advance publicity for *Hit Parade of 1943*. The picture was not due to open until April 16, but Republic, grateful to get her, picked up her tab for the first three weeks. On March 19, she garnered an additional thousand dollars by starring on Charlie Martin's "Phillip Morris Playhouse." More importantly, on March 17, she got the opportunity to attend King Features' Banshee luncheon in honor of Barry Faris and Pat Robinson of International News Service, who had recently returned from the South Pacific fighting fronts.

The invitation from King Features Syndicate was welcome, because leading editors and publishers attended these annual luncheons, and they offered a rich opportunity to get publicity without having to pose in bathing suits labeled "Wild Wind" or endure the indignities of accepting contrived titles such as "Titianette Queen" or, as Susan would later quip, " 'Miss Everything' except 'Miss Take.' "

Beyond that, it meant dignified recognition of her success in her hometown—she thought.

Columnist Leonard Lyons, who attended the Banshee luncheon, commented, "Miss Hayward might just as well have remained in Hollywood. For she was introduced at the luncheon as "Rita Hayward," and the only news photo she posed for—a photo showing her kissing Sgt. Carl Hickman, one of the Marine Corps' heroes of Guadalcanal—was ordered censored by the Marine Corps as being undignified."

Not quite. One photo managed to make it into the *Daily Mirror* the next day; but, more importantly, the impact Susan made on the attending publishers would serve her in good stead in the years to come.

To Susan's astonishment, she was recognized and fussed over wherever she went, despite the dark prescription glasses she wore to enable her to see farther than a foot ahead. Watching a new building under construction on Sixth Avenue, she was besieged by blowtorch operators who wanted her to autograph everything from a helmet to a scrap of paper that had blown onto the site. To a public oblivious of the power plays at Paramount or the punishing demotions and loans, she was a *star*. Autograph hunters waited en masse outside the Phillip Morris broadcast and oohed and aahed when she left the theater. A friend of Charlie Martin's who was there that night recalls:

"Susan's prettiness in films was always obvious. But she was absolutely breathtaking the night Charlie had her on the show. She wore very little make-up—radio didn't require any, of course —and her skin had an almost translucent quality. Now, Charlie was a charmer in those days. He managed to get all the top glamour girls on the program—Turner, Hayworth, you name it. And they were all crazy about him.

"He could have any girl he wanted for the asking, and he usually dated the stars he had on his show—at least once— even if she had a lover back in Hollywood. Hayward, however, was all business. She did the show, returned for the rebroadcast for the West Coast, and went home alone. I guess you can say she was the one who got away."

(A few years later, Charlie Martin was the one who got away when Betty Hutton prematurely shouted the news of their engagement from a stage in Madison Square Garden. Mortified, he never saw her again.)

Since Paramount was in no hurry to have her back, Susan went on a brief war-bond selling tour before returning to Hollywood in early April. After having been treated like a star for the nearly two months she'd been away, she bristled at the indifferent treatment accorded her once she was back on the lot. De Sylva told her she had been penciled in for both the female lead in an implausible thriller called *The Man in Half Moon Street* and the role of Loretta Young's selfish kid sister in *And Now Tomorrow*. Eventually, she was replaced by Helen Walker in the former, and the latter was delayed pending Alan Ladd's return from service. She waited . . . and waited. . . .

Two months later, she was handed the script of *Standing Room Only*. Once again she'd have to appear as a bitchy society girl. Once again she'd have to compete with Paulette Goddard for Fred MacMurray's affections—and come off second best. It was the same old story—but this time she refused to do it. Storming into De Sylva's office, ablaze with anger, she told him what he could do—with his script, Goddard, and the remaining two years of her contract.

As usual, Louella Parsons came to her defense. In her column of August 7, 1943, Louella sympathized: "We don't blame Susan Hayward for walking out of the cast of Paramount's *Standing Room Only*. . . . Her role was much too small for her talent— much of the footage going to Paulette Goddard, Fred MacMurray, and Roland Young. Susan claims the studio had promised her bigger and better roles."

After Parsons's item, bigger but not necessarily better roles *were* forthcoming, though not at Paramount. Happy to get "that ambitious bitch" out of his office, his life, and his now-thinning hair, De Sylva permitted Medford to make a trio of loan-out deals for her services: to United Artists for *Jack London* ("I got her $15,000 under the table for the London film. When Paramount found out, I was almost barred from the lot"), to Republic again for *The Fighting Seabees* (opposite John Wayne), and back to United Artists for a bastardized version of Eugene O'Neill's *The Hairy Ape*, opposite William Bendix.

Susan breezed through the first two films without either incident or notable display of temperament (or notable reviews, for that matter). For the third, she got some of the best notices of her career. Even though the *New York Daily Mirror* commented cattily during the shooting of *The Hairy Ape* that "Susan Hayward is a darling, but couldn't be more unlike Carlotta Monterey O'Neill, who created the femme lead in *The Hairy Ape* on Broadway," when the picture was released the following July, the critics were united in praise.

Said *Time* magazine: "Susan Hayward, as the girl who drives him [Bendix] crazy, is much tougher—too coarsely so for the size of the girl's penthouse or the height of her social standing— but she is more convincing. She is, in fact, Hollywood's ablest bitch-player."

The *New York Herald-Tribune*'s Otis L. Guernsey, Jr., noted: "Susan Hayward is appropriately hateful as the empty-minded rich girl who is frightened by the animalistic world of the stoke-hold. She achieves a good deal of villainy in spite of a wealth of corny dialogue that has been included in her scenes." And even the often-sour *New York Times* commented, "Miss Hayward . . . contributes her full share to the picture."

Susan was understandably delighted—maybe *now* somebody would take notice—but for once, though, she did not have all her attention on her career. Surprising even herself, she found she had far more pressing matters on her mind. . . .

She had just begun work on *The Hairy Ape* in late November when, one Friday night, she decided to drop by the Hollywood Canteen. The canteen was a recreational facility sponsored by Bette Davis to provide a place where lonely servicemen adrift in Los Angeles (usually before embarking for combat in the South Pacific) could spend an evening in the company of lovely, carefully picked hostesses, munch donuts and sandwiches, and be entertained by those top names in Hollywood who felt obliged to do their bit for our fighting men.

Susan was a canteen regular and usually broke up the place with her sure-fire "Anyone here from Brooklyn?" opener. Though she danced with the servicemen, however, she rarely fraternized with her fellow performers and always went home alone.

On this November Friday night, Jess Barker, a twenty-nine-year-old Broadway actor who had just completed two films at Columbia, was serving as master of ceremonies. Impulsively, he asked Susan to join him for coffee after the canteen had closed for the night—and impulsively, she accepted.

When he tried to kiss her goodnight at her door, she slapped him hard across his face.

Three months later, he asked her to marry him.

chapter 7

SOMETHING STRONG pulled Susan and Jess together. Something more powerful pulled them apart. From the beginning, they were a mismatched pair, drawn to one another by an overwhelming physical attraction that blinded them to their psychological incompatibility. It would take them nine long years to find that out.

After her experience with John Carroll, Susan had sworn off actors. "I said over and over," she told friends, "I'd never marry an actor. No woman in her right mind would marry an actor. I didn't even want to date one. But after I met Jess . . ."

That first evening, after playing hard to get, she refused Jess's calls for a week because, she admitted, "I thought he'd be intrigued by such behavior." Susan was nonetheless determined to see him again: "I found out where Jess was likely to be and was there at the same time. Of course, I chased him. Why not? I knew two weeks after I had met Jess that I wanted to marry him."

To her surprise and delight, she learned that her old friend and mentor Gregory Ratoff had been responsible for Jess's return to Hollywood.

Few people were aware that he had even been there before—it was never mentioned in any story or studio biography—but "I came out here in 1935," Barker reveals today. "You know how I got my first screen contract? Leland Hayward, then an agent, signed me, and Walter Wanger brought me to the coast under the name of *Philip* Barker. That's how I got into *The Trail of the Lonesome Pine*, the first outdoor color picture. I played one of the heavies—the youngest son in the Fallin family. Robert Barrett was my father.

"Then I went back to Broadway in *You Can't Take It With You.* I worked a lot of stock. I worked with . . . well, just go down the line."

In September 1942, Mrs. B. P. Schulberg, the producer's wife, saw a performance of *Magic*, starring Eddie Dowling, but she found her attention riveted on Barker. To Mrs. Schulberg, the handsome young blond looked like movie material. She arranged what was known as "an interview test," cameras rolling as Gregory Ratoff chatted informally with Barker.

"Wait and see," Ratoff shouted to everyone within earshot. "Theese is the only one with talent. If Cohn doesn't sign him, I will." He didn't have to. The test was mailed to Harry Cohn on a Friday. By the following Friday, contracts had been drawn up. When *Magic* proved a misnomer at the box office, Jess left for Hollywood.

Due to Alan Ladd's phenomenal success earlier that spring in *This Gun for Hire*, blond actors were now being sought instead of spurned by filmmakers, and "I was called a tall Alan Ladd," Barker laughs. "I never could work with him because I was six inches taller than he was."

Two months after being signed by Columbia, Barker was given a role in *Good Luck, Mr. Yates*, with Claire Trevor, but after that Harry Cohn, more interested in the careers of his leading ladies than in male contractees, let Barker cool his heels for a while. In August 1943, though, RKO borrowed him for the movie, *Government Girl*, with Olivia de Havilland and Sonny Tufts, and Barker acquitted himself so well that Columbia moved to assure him that he had a future with them. The studio cast him in Rita Hayworth's *Cover Girl*. His role, Otto Kruger as a young man, was limited to flashback sequences and offered little opportunity for Jess to prove himself, but he registered sufficiently to evoke a good amount of fan mail, a promise of the male lead in *Jam Session*, and the interest of other studios whose contract lists had been decimated by the draft.

Barker, exempt from service by an overrapid heartbeat, had three brothers serving as sergeants in the army. Self-conscious about his 4-F classification, he spent almost all his free evenings working at the Hollywood Canteen. "It's old hat to some people," he explained, "but it's little enough for me to do."

A profile released at the time noted: "The Greenville, South Carolinian lives alone in a small Hollywood apartment, has all his meals out, drives a little blue roadster, enjoys every kind of music, and keeps up with current books, thinking of them in terms of plays and movies."

The sketch went on to reveal that, although Jess was "blessed with a facile tongue and sense of humor, he never keeps letters or is sentimental about anything. He never kills a fly or a moth and reports that consequently he has never been bothered by them."

"That was true," Barker confirms. "It's still true. When a fly comes in and it drives me crazy, I just open the door and out it goes."

During his first year in Hollywood, Jess Barker was linked with so many starlets that when a friend from New York asked whom he was going out with that week, he replied, "That seems to depend on which newspaper you read." In fact, at the time he met Susan, Jess was reported to be engaged to Nina Foch, a twenty-year-old Columbia contract player.

"*Almost* engaged," Jess corrects.

Despite her intellectual European and theatrical background, though, Foch was outclassed by the Brooklyn redhead ("Susan called Nina 'the toothless wonder,'" Ben Medford recalls), and Foch did not take it lightly. "Nina was a great girl," says Barker. "Yet when I went off with Susan she destroyed all my clippings, ripped them to pieces."

Susan did something similar. Once she started dating Jess, she insisted that his little black book be thrown out with the morning trash. He'd see her exclusively or not at all. He saw her exclusively.

Their names began being paired in gossip columns: "Jess Barker and Susan Hayward a newsome-twosome at Perino's," or "Susan Hayward and Jess Barker cheek-to-cheeking at Mocambo." However—remembering the John Carroll fiasco of the previous year, and Susan's bitter disclaimers about actors—few gave the items any significance. After all, Jess was not only an actor, he was a Southerner, like Carroll—one would have supposed Susan would have been turned off by that combination forever.

It was precisely that Southern background, however, that proved so irresistible to Susan. She had never forgotten her dream of the courtly Southern gentleman, the gracious mansion life. If Carroll had fancied himself the second coming of Rhett Butler and acted accordingly, Barker was in the Ashley Wilkes tradition—passive, gentle, a man with dreams—even if he didn't actually have a mansion.

In fact, the Barkers of Greenville were as poverty-stricken as the Marrenners of Brooklyn had been. Jess's mother Miss Winnie worked as a baby's nurse after the death of his father, a former railroad-yard worker. As with Susan, his genteel poverty was a trap from which Barker was determined to escape. He remembered well being jilted as a youth by a young woman with whom he had fancied himself in love. The girl had told him disdainfully, "Where are you going to get the money to support a wife?"

He had been convinced he'd get it up north. After a few months at the Theodora Irvine School for the Theater and a season in summer stock in New England, he'd made his Broadway debut in *Allure* in 1934. In the next ten years, he'd lost his Southern accent, but not his Southern manner—and, whatever her experiences with Southerners, Susan's affinity with them was almost magnetic.

By the time Susan and Jess started seeing each other on a regular basis, Alan Ladd was out of the army, and Paramount could finally make *And Now Tomorrow*, a pallid film that did neither Ladd nor Hayward any good. By now, Susan's Paramount pact had only a year to go, and she was counting the days until it was over—a feeling that was only intensified by what happened next. The studio informed her that it was loaning her to Benedict Bogeaus, an independent producer working with United Artists, for a highly dramatic role in *Dark Waters*, a chiller-thriller with psychological overtones set in a Louisiana bayou. That seemed promising, until one morning, idly browsing through the Hollywood trade papers, Susan spotted a brief news item in *Variety*: "Merle Oberon was signed yesterday to star in *Dark Waters*."

By noon, ugly rumors had reached her through the grapevine that Buddy De Sylva wanted to teach her a lesson and consequently would not hold Bogeaus to the loan-out agreement. When she finally got to see De Sylva, he didn't bother refuting the gossip. He told her bluntly that she had been rude and snippy to stars and directors and ungrateful to the studio for the opportunities they had given her to earn while learning how to become an actress.

"In short, Susan," he concluded, "you've been a first-class bitch."

Paradoxically, the studio did not want to release her before her contract ran out. They were privately negotiating with her new agent Charles Feldman to keep her on at a considerable increase.

"This was very ironic," says Medford, "because Susan walked out on me when Feldman promised her that if she signed with his agency he'd personally get her a release from the studio. My personal contract with Susan had another year to go. I could have sued, but what the hell, you get to expect these things in this business."

For Susan, her remaining time under the old contract was tantamount to a jail sentence—with no time off for good behavior. The news of Paulette Goddard's supporting Oscar nomination for *So Proudly We Hail* only strengthened Susan's determination to put Paramount and everyone associated with it out of her life . . . for good.

In early February 1944, exhausted by work and the continuing hassles with the studio, Susan fell apart; her doctor ordered four weeks of complete rest. During this period, Jess was a pillar of strength, a comforting shoulder upon which to cry. By the end of the month, he had impulsively proposed marriage.

That was exactly what Susan wanted, though Jess wasn't 100 percent sure it was what *he* wanted. *Cover Girl* was going into release in March, and Columbia was planning a publicity build-up designed around bachelor Barker. Jess was told, not too subtly, that marriage to *anyone* would "damage your popularity with the bobby-soxers." Harry Cohn raged, "Of all the girls in the world, Barker had to get involved with that Hayward bitch."

Still holding a grudge because of his own problems with her during *Adam Had Four Sons*, Cohn's hostilities were aggravated by a paranoid conviction that Hayward was getting a free ride on the Hayworth name. The fact that Barker was coming out in a Hayworth spectacular compounded his annoyance. Unceremoniously, he decided to drop Jess's option and privately cursed Gregory Ratoff, who had now defected to Twentieth Century-Fox, for inflicting Barker upon him.

Only the romantic Russian was genuinely pleased that his

two self-appointed protégés had found one another. He beamed his approval when Susan promised, "We'll name our first son after you."

Ellen Marrenner, relieved when Susan had broken her engagement to Carroll the previous year, had forebodings about Jess. He was an actor. Actors were notorious skirt-chasers, and she feared Susan would endure the same humiliations she had suffered as a young girl with her feckless fellow student at the Feagin Drama School. She was also convinced that Jess was in no financial position for matrimony. With Florence's marriage rocky—Florence was living with her mother again in California with her baby son Larry; Zaenglin's peripatetic army life hadn't agreed with her—Ellen Marrenner was less than ecstatic when Susan told her, "Mom, I'm going to marry Jess Barker."

"I'll believe it when I see the ring," Ellen said. She didn't know Susan had already picked one out—Susan had never been slow with rings—this time in a cocktail-style setting consisting of diamond chips and emeralds.

As it turned out, Ellen Marrenner had some just cause for concern. Within days, the pattern began: the ring was being sized when the engagement was abruptly called off after a quarrel that, Susan claimed, had something to do with Jess's failure to show up for a dinner date. With her mother's warnings echoing in her ears, Susan was convinced that Jess was out with Nina Foch. An explanatory telegram from him placated her, but within a few weeks the fights began again.

The battles were over everything and nothing. One day Susan tossed a gold cigarette lighter—a gift from a former girl friend of his—into the Pacific Ocean. One night he poured all the perfume he had given Susan down the bathroom sink. Another time, the ring went back to the jewelers; by the time the two had made up and Jess had gone to retrieve it, it had been sold. Not being able to find another one either of them liked as much, they decided to forget about a ring. All this time, they continued seeing each other exclusively, but were hesitant about setting a date. Susan came up with a dozen rationalizations for her own temperamental outbursts, but it was Jess's indecisiveness that was at the root of her problems.

In June 1944, uncertain about her professional future and relationship with Jess, Susan was persuaded to attend a mam-

Edythe Marrenner (the spelling would change later) with mother, Ellen Pearson Marrenner, in 1917, just a few weeks after the baby's birth. Inset: the first picture ever published of Walter Marrenner—he disliked having his picture taken—snapped in 1936, two years before his death. (Wally Marrenner)

Edythe at six, and pony, posed on a Brooklyn sidewalk. An itinerant photographer probably took this daguerrotype for a dime. (Author's collection)

Sister Florence, fourteen, with seven-year-old Edythe in 1924. Their relationship would end bitterly in 1941. (Author's collection)

Edythe at nine and a half (left) and eleven (right). An auto accident left her with one leg shorter than the other—carefully concealed in these pictures. (Author)

The graduating class of P.S. 181, June, 1931. Edythe is at the far left (arrow) and a dark-haired boy named Ira Grossel—later Jeff Chandler—at far right. (Eduardo Moreno Collection)

Walter Thornton model Edythe Marrener (new spelling) in a 1937 millinery ad. Shortly after, she went to Hollywood for her screen test for *Gone With the Wind*. (Doug McClelland Collection)

Rejected by Selznick, Edyth was signed by Warners, an renamed Susan Hayward. Thi is the second studio portra: she ever posed for. (Saul Goo man Collection

The starlet frolicking. Susan was waiting to begin *Brother Rat*, but Warners chose Priscilla Lane instead, used Susan in bits, and dropped her at the end of her six-month option. (Author)

As one of Paramount's "Golden Circle" of "promising" stars. Top row, from left: Louise Campbell, Betty Field, Joseph Allen, Ellen Drew, Judith Barrett. Middle: Robert Preston, Patricia Morison, Susan, William Henry. Bottom: Joyce Matthews, Janice Logan, William Holden, Evelyn Keyes. (McClelland)

Back to New York in 1941 for publicity on *Adam Had Four Sons*, opening at the Radio City Music Hall. (American Airlines)

Harry Cohn tried, but the only time he got Susan into bed was for this scene from *Adam Had Four Sons*. (Columbia)

With Robert Preston, as ill-fated lovers in DeMille's
Reap the Wild Wind. (Paramount/MCA)

Bitchy Susan was pitted against witchy Veronica
Lake in *I Married A Witch*, with Frederic March,
Robert Warwick and Robert Benchley. (United Artists)

With brother, Wally, in 1942 on the set of *Hit Parade of 1943*. (Author)

On the set of *Jack London* with Charmian Kittredge London (left), the author's widow. Susan played her, Michael O'Shea, Jack. Also present: Mrs. Sam Bronston, the producer's wife. (Author)

By January, 1944, Susan was receiving daily calls on the set of *And Now Tomorrow*. The caller: actor Jess Barker, whom she had met in November. (Author)

After a stormy courtship, Susan and Barker were married at St. Thomas Episcopal Church on July 23, 1944 (UPI)

The twins grow up: a time compression. Timothy and
Gregory Barker, born February 19, 1945, made their camera
debut fourteen weeks later. (McClelland)

At six and a half, with Susan and Robert Mitchum on the
set of *The Lusty Men*. (Author)

At nine, celebrating Susan's birthday on the set of *The Conqueror*. This was the infamous production, filmed near a former atomic testing site, which some say caused the cancer that eventually killed Susan, co-star John Wayne (center), director Dick Powell (center left) and others. (Author)

At eleven, at the 1956 Oscars (Susan was up for *I'll Cry Tomorrow*). With them was Floyd Eaton Chalkley, a "mysterious" gentleman from Georgia. (Moreno)

Back to the 40's. Susan's first job following the twins' birth was the April 24, 1945 Lux Radio Theater production of *The Petrified Forest*. Ronald Colman and Lawrence Tierney co-starred. (Author)

Susan received the first of her five Oscar nominations for her portrayal of Angelica Evans, the neglected alcoholic wife of "singer" Lee Bowman in 1947's *Smash-Up—The Story of a Woman*. (McClelland)

Lee Bowman, Susan, and Eddie Albert, playing Bowman's
songwriter pal, in *Smash-Up*. (McClelland)

Eloise "was a nice girl" torn between pride and passion when
Dana Andrews made advances in *My Foolish Heart*, a four-
hanky film which won Susan her second nomination. (Samuel
Goldwyn Productions)

A 1953 studio portrait. Susan had just been signed by Darryl Zanuck at Twentieth for $200,000. You can see why. (Moreno)

moth dinner party honoring Clark Gable's return to civilian life. Actress Jan Clayton, Gable's date for the evening, recollects that Gable was attentive and affable to her, but "then Susan Hayward walked in and his attention was gone. Susan had an intense way of looking at men that was universally misinterpreted. It wasn't sex; she was terribly myopic. She was trying to *find* them. When I mentioned after that party that Clark had stared at her all evening, she said, 'He *was*? Why didn't somebody *tell* me?' "

Gable, thinking he had been rebuffed, made no attempt to get Susan's number. If he had, it wouldn't have done him much good. A few weeks after the Gable party, she and Jess finally decided to marry.

This time it was no impulse. Jess had finally decided he was ready, and by now, Susan had endured nine stormy months of their off-again, on-again affair. If she had stuck with it this long, she was convinced, she really was in love with Jess Barker. Convinced too that her mother was dumping her own fixations on her, she dismissed Ellen Marrenner's nagging suspicion that Jess couldn't cope with the responsibilities that went along with marriage. It was time for Susan's dream to come true.

Of course, there might have been another element involved in the decision as well. Ben Medford reveals an astonishing fact: "Ellen Marrenner was violently opposed to the marriage. In fact, she called me and asked me if I could locate an abortionist."

An abortionist! Prim and proper Susan had finally been persuaded into bed—and now she was pregnant. If anyone thought she was going to allow *that* situation to remain without the sanction of marriage, they were mistaken.

At the same time, Susan refused to abort. Jess was the first and only man she had had an affair with in her life. She was sure they could be happy.

Nevertheless, on July 22, Susan did an extraordinary thing for a bride who was neither princess nor heiress (her yearly income was now $26,000). She had an attorney draw up an airtight agreement, attested to by a notary public, irrevocably separating her income and properties from Jess Barker's.

Susan later claimed she did this to make her marriage safe, pointing out that it was usually the man who benefited when the community property clause was waived. Maybe it hadn't occurred to her, or to Jess, that a legal distinction between "thine" and "mine"—or an insistence that they both keep possession of their own apartments "until we find a house big enough for the two of us"—was not the most passionate way to warm a wedding bed.

Indeed, Susan at twenty-seven looked far from radiant after she and Jess exchanged marriage vows on July 24, 1944. Publicists Henry Rogers and Jean Pettebone were the only attendants. "Miss Winnie" Barker was unable to make the trip from Atlanta, where she was working as a nurse, to meet her new daughter-in-law; and although Ellen Marrenner attended the ceremony, she was not identified in the wedding pictures released to the press. Sister Florence would later say, bitterly, "I didn't go, because Susan didn't invite me."

Immediately after the wedding, the Barkers left for a brief honeymoon at Rancho Santa Fe, near San Diego.

Theirs may have been one of the briefest honeymoons on record. Within two months, the pregnant bride was seeing her lawyer.

PART THREE

Mrs. Jess Barker
Hollywood
July 24, 1944 — April 26, 1955

I married for security and love. I didn't get either. I married a man who wasn't in love with me. I did everything I knew to make the marriage work. Then I had to spill my personal life from coast to coast to keep my sons. I'm a divorcée, and I never wanted to be divorced.
SUSAN HAYWARD, 1955

After all, I've only been married once. So I must have been in love with somebody.
JESS BARKER, *January 19, 1980*

chapter 8

As a lover, Jess proved gentle and considerate, undoubtedly a decided contrast to John Carroll who, according to impeccable sources, "treated all women as if they were concubines, out-Flynned Errol, and had a decided appetite for the more erotic and exotic aspects of sex."

Nevertheless, during the initial weeks of Susan's marriage, they had troubles sexually—she was "cold as a polar bear," Jess would later say. Susan felt guilty about the premature pregnancy, which only added to her guilt feelings about sex in general—attitudes that had been deeply instilled in her since childhood. Even wedlock could not shake them. They created an emotional turmoil that prevented her from enjoying sex to its fullest. It wasn't Jess's fault, it wasn't hers. Ellen Marrenner had done her job all too well. It was not an auspicious beginning.

Neither was the house situation: the Barkers spent most of August house-hunting, but could find nothing in their price range. Susan was appalled at the cost of even the most modest dwelling. Consequently, they took turns living in one of their two apartments.

Jess had made few friends—other than female—since coming to Hollywood; Susan felt she had none. The Barkers were given no bridal showers, no dinners, no spate of parties. They lived in a vacuum of their own making. Both insisted they hated big parties. Still, when Ann Rutherford and her husband David May invited them to a Saturday night bash at their home on September 17, they were glad enough to go—unfortunately. For, as it turned out, it was a bash that turned into a headlined brawl.

Lana Turner and her current lover Turhan Bey were on the star-studded guest list, and so was Turner's former husband Steve Crane. Perversely, Turner spent most of the evening dancing with Crane. Noticing that she was wearing the engagement ring he had given her, made from a stone belonging to his mother, Crane demanded that she not wear it while out with someone else. Bey, overhearing this, exchanged insults with Crane, then blows. Crane suffered a bump on the head, Bey several scratches; Turner threw the ring at Crane; the ring fell to the ground, was retrieved by the host and returned to Turner—and she departed, with the ring, Bey, and a badly frayed temper. By that time, everyone's temper, aided by the contents of the well-stocked bar, had reached the breaking point.

In spite of the chaos, Jess Barker was having a marvelous time, but Susan, disgusted with the entire melee, demanded to be taken home immediately. The two left the May house together . . . but Jess returned to his apartment alone.

The following Monday, Susan announced, "I've moved out for good, and I'm planning to see my attorney. My decision is irrevocable."

Jess, unable to reach his bride by phone, tried to explain what had happened. "I wouldn't know about the chances for a reconciliation. The whole thing started as a joke, and the joke turned into something serious. I had a little trouble opening the car door. I thought it was funny—but Susan didn't think so. She tapped her foot for a while and then disappeared. I waited several minutes and then looked for her. I couldn't find her anywhere, so I went home alone. I haven't seen her since."

Susan spent a week alone in her apartment, ignoring the incessant ringing of the telephone. She made calls to her mother; to her attorney, Sidney Justin; to her agent, Charlie Feldman; and, naturally, to Louella Parsons who, on September 25, sadly related: "My heart goes out to Susan Hayward . . . who wanted so to make a go of her marriage. I talked to her the day she made up her mind to marry Barker and again when she came back from her honeymoon. But her marriage didn't work out, and Susie has decided on a separation. I don't know Barker, who had a brief fling at the movies at Columbia, but he lost a mighty fine girl."

Parsons's sympathy was wasted. By the time that article had appeared, Susan's temper had cooled, and she was answering her phone again. When Jess got through, she didn't hang up. Instead, she agreed to meet him for dinner to discuss their problems.

Sitting with Jess in a dim corner of the restaurant, talking quietly with him, she must have realized how ludicrous the incident in the May driveway had been. Had she really been provoked by his delay in opening the car door, or had the whole incident—with an engagement ring as the centerpiece—simply aroused her memories of the disastrous affairs with Carroll and that boy in drama school, and with it the memories of their own stormy courtship? But that was over and done with, wasn't it? She should stop thinking about the past.

In addition, could her mood have had something to do with being with Turner for the first time since they had been kids in Frank Beckwith's class at Warner's? She had been jealous of Turner then, even though they had rarely exchanged more than a couple of words. Now Turner was undisputedly the glamour queen of MGM. She had a beautiful home, a closet filled with furs, gorgeous jewelry—and men making fools of themselves by fighting over her.

In contrast, Susan was the Paramount pest, her career treading water as the years slipped by. She considered herself a better actress than Turner, but Turner had a way with men, a technique Susan couldn't master. Turner had been the star of the May bash—despite the outcome of the evening. And, ironically, Jess had just completed a pallid featured role in Turner's *Keep Your Powder Dry*.

At any rate, when Jess drove Susan home after dinner that night, he stayed. The next morning they prepared a joint statement to the press saying that they realized "our love persisted and we have decided to give our marriage another chance." In the same statement, they announced they "were going house-hunting and were expecting a baby about next April."

Throughout her pregnancy, Susan kept a low profile, avoiding places where photographers and reporters congregated. Although she tried to eat sensibly, she gained an alarming amount of weight and by early winter, X-rays confirmed what her doctor had suspected: she was carrying twins. Financially, things looked grim. She couldn't work, and Jess's agents were trying to find a good deal for him. Finally, after months of agonizing, he signed a term contract at Universal, where he was promised a star build-up. His new salary would enable him to support his family, if not in luxury, then at least in comfort. The Barkers moved into a small house in Beverly Hills.

On February 17, 1945, Timothy Marrenner Barker and then, seven minutes later, Gregory Marrenner Barker were born. Susan kept her promise to Ratoff by naming one of the twins after him, further complimenting him by giving his name to the boy who bore the stronger resemblance to her. Timothy inherited his father's looks. Susan's choice of her maiden name as both boys' middle name was never explained.

The twins' birth, two months earlier than expected, set the press off on the popular game of finger-counting: July, August, September . . . yes, it was only seven months. Anticipating this, Susan and Jess provided the standard Hollywood bromide of "premature birth." She made much of the fact that each boy weighed only four and a half pounds. If anyone had bothered to check, this was an acceptable weight for a twin born full-term.

Another fact that set the gossipers buzzing was that, though both parents needed publicity desperately at this point in their careers, Susan and Jess proceeded to antagonize *Time, Life, Look, Newsweek,* and the newspaper syndicates by refusing to pose for photographs with Timmy and Greg. Bigger stars than Susan had posed with their children soon after birth—was she trying to hide something about the babies? Their size, perhaps? Mindful of the talk—"I think people who repeat tales about other people should have their mouths taped," she was later to say privately—Susan quietly left the hospital on March 8, keeping her departure date a secret from the press.

On April 23, 1945, Susan returned to work for the first time, co-starring with Ronald Colman and Lawrence Tierney in the "Lux Radio Theater" broadcast of *The Petrified Forest*, in the role Bette Davis had played in the 1936 film version. The next month, an RKO murder mystery, *Deadline at Dawn*, marked her return to the screen. Susan had no intention of letting motherhood stand in the way of her movies. She was glad to have the boys, but . . . well, motherhood wasn't quite what she'd pictured it to be.

Later, she admitted to Dutch-aunt Louella about those first months: "When a girl becomes a mother, a whole change is supposed to take place in her. But it hadn't in me. When I came home each night from the studio, things were the same, except we had two babies. There was a nurse who would bring them to me. I would get a full report on their day. I would hold them and cuddle them. Then they would be carried back to the nursery, and I would sit back knowing that there was something wrong. Something was missing, but I didn't know what. One night when I was sitting with Jess after dinner—the babies had been in and were gone again—suddenly, I burst into tears. 'I'm no good around here.' "

Later, she realized she'd been undergoing a standard attack of post-partum depression. To overcome it, she tried her hand at the usual motherly chores before rationalizing, with relief, that changing dirty diapers was not necessarily proof of maternal devotion.

Possibly to provide that proof, however—to herself as well as to the rest of the world—she finally agreed to allow the Universal still photographers into the nursery in late May after the completion of *Deadline at Dawn*. Tim and Gregory were a robust fourteen weeks old by then, and the differences in their looks and personalities made for a very attractive set of pictures. Much to Universal's—and the Barkers'—satisfaction, these were picked up and printed by *Time* magazine, a majority of the country's newspapers, and—of equal importance in 1945—by all the leading fan magazines. The exposure would be welcome since sixteen months were to elapse between Susan's last screen appearance in *And Now Tomorrow* and *Deadline at Dawn*'s release in April 1946.

Of more immediate importance to Universal was the plug for Jess's first film with the studio, *This Love of Ours*. The Merle Oberon–Charles Korvin starrer was their class production in a year that included such schlock as *Frisco Sal*, *Shady Lady*, and *Jungle Captive*. No question, the studio was in serious trouble— barely avoiding bankruptcy only by the grace of a now-fading Deanna Durbin, repetitive Abbott and Costello comedies, and periodic returns from the grave by their *Frankenstein* monster. In desperate need of new blood, the company decided to allow independent producers on the lot for the first time, and to package and release their films. Walter Wanger was one of them. It would turn out—at last—to be the break Susan had been waiting for.

Wanger, married to Joan Bennett, was fifty-one when he

moved onto the Universal lot. By then he had produced some three dozen pictures, among them: *Queen Christina* (with Garbo), *Stage Coach, Foreign Correspondent,* and *Algiers* (for the last he had discovered and made a star of Hedy Lamarr). He was a man of impeccable taste, manners, and sophistication, a refreshing contrast to the grittier De Sylva, and from 1939 to 1944 had even served as president of the Motion Picture Academy of Arts and Sciences.

Now Wanger had a script ready to film called *Canyon Passage,* and he thought Jess Barker might be a possibility for a leading role. Susan and Jess were vacationing in Palm Springs when, Barker confirms, "Walter Wanger sent me the script of *Canyon Passage.* I was up for an important part [that of the second male lead] and I spent five hours coaxing Susan to read it."

Ironically, Jess never got his part, losing it to Brian Donlevy, but Susan got one instead—Wanger not only liked the idea of using her in his picture, he promptly signed her to a long-term contract. Later, the story would go around that Susan signed with Wanger because she was "furious Selznick kept me waiting to see him about a contract," but that had about as much truth in it as the fairy tale about Katie Harrigan and County Cork.

While the studio papers were being drawn up, Susan and Jess quietly celebrated their first wedding anniversary. She looked radiant, and for the first time in years was filled with optimism about the future. A week later, she called Parsons about the Wanger deal: "Life is beautiful," she bubbled. "My career is moving along, and you should see my babies! Jess has been such a good boy, and we believe we are making a success of our marriage."

Louella didn't think it odd that Susan should refer to her husband as "a good boy." In passing along the conversation to her readers, she added, in her most motherly manner: "Susie and Jess are working hard to plan for their babies' future, and the little ones have brought them closer together. Right now, they are getting on but wonderfully."

Susan was also getting along wonderfully with her new boss. Wanger's gentlemanly ways and astute taste were a breath of fresh air to her after the people she'd been dealing with at Paramount, and, reminiscing about Wanger nearly three decades later, Susan said, "I owe *everything* to Walter. He was the guy who had faith in me. We both agreed about the sort of roles I should play on screen and went after them." *Canyon Passage* didn't turn out to be the ideal professional debut for the new relationship—a middling adventure yarn with gorgeous scenery about a girl traveling to Oregon to join her fiancé, and the escort with whom she falls in love, Dana Andrews—but soon better, much better, things were to come.

Meanwhile, however—call it coincidence or bad timing—after Susan's arrival on the Universal lot, Barker's career went into a tailspin. The studio gave him seventh billing in a dismal Abbott and Costello comedy called *The Time of Their Lives* and then unceremoniously let his option drop. Susan would later rationalize that "it was best in a way that Jess wasn't cast in *Canyon Passage* because both of us couldn't have been away from home and leave the twins."

The awkwardness of the Barkers' role reversal, three decades before it would become trendy, did not escape notice by Universal employees.

One of Susan's wardrobe women, Mollie Briggs, reminisces: "Shortly after I married, my husband, who worked for a studio, went on layoff. When I arrived home and discovered he hadn't started dinner, I was a bit peeved. The next day I asked Susan, 'Don't you get a little upset when you come home and find Jess has been sitting around all day?'

"Well, this was the only time Susan ever got mad at me. She really flared up. 'Jess works very hard,' she protested. 'You have no idea of all he does.' She was very loyal and protective of him.

"I thought Susan was wonderful. So did most of the other people who worked with her on a one-to-one basis. Though she was very down-to-earth, she was a private person. And she was a lady. She never swore, never allowed anyone in her dressing room when she was taking her clothes off, like some stars who would perform that act before the mail boys, or whomever!

"I was in her dressing room—she was fully clothed—when Walter Wanger came in. She addressed him as 'Mr. Wanger.' He told her to call him Walter, but she wouldn't. 'As long as your name is on my pay checks, you are Mr. Wanger,' she replied.

"She was extremely conservative with money. She usually didn't discuss money; once, however, she let slip that she was putting $2,000 a month away for the boys because she never wanted them to be poor like she was as a child. I never met her mother, but when she talked family (other than Jess and the twins), it was about her late father. It seemed to me that Susan worshipped him.

"Then, one day—I'll never forget this—Susan was finishing a take when she was given the message that someone was at the gate who kept insisting she was her sister. Susan asked one of the girls to get her and take her directly to her dressing room. 'Tell her to stay there until I'm finished on the set.' Everyone was so surprised! Susan had never mentioned having a sister, though we knew about her brother Wally.

"I was more surprised when I saw the sister. The woman . . . she looked just like a . . . well, a hooker! I'm not saying she was . . . she just looked like one. Susan didn't talk about the visit and I never again saw the sister on the lot." Before long, Mollie Briggs found herself subjected to several more surprises. . . . "One time, Susan called at two o'clock in the morning. Jess was out of town, I think. She told me she was alone in the house and was afraid to be alone. She wanted somebody to talk to. I never thought Susan was afraid of anything."

Even more astonishing to the young wardrobe woman was what she termed "the diamond ring incident."

"We were on location and staying in a motel. I stopped by Susan's room to say goodnight. She was getting ready for bed, and she had a large diamond on her nightstand. I told her that it should be put in a safe; it was dangerous to have it in her room. She interrupted my warning by saying:

" 'What would you do with this ring, if I gave it to you?'

" 'Pay off the loan on my house.'

" 'Then I won't give it to you!'

"Of course, I wouldn't have accepted the ring. And I'm still not sure she was seriously considering giving it to me. But when I got back to my room, I remembered she was always scolding me for spending money on my new home and not saving it.

"As I have said, she was *very* conservative about money. Jess was too. I once heard him bawling her out for spending $7.50 for four director chairs to place around the pool."

As early as March 1946, there were subtle indications that Jess's involuntary idleness was having an effect on Susan. Even her would-be upbeat anecdotes sounded slightly off. Susan told newspaper woman Virginia Tomlinson of Jess's fury as he talked her out of buying a fur coat, adding, "Then he turned around and gave me a *down payment* on a more expensive one."

If the reporter thought it strange that Susan should emphasize "down payment," she didn't pursue the subject, nor did she ask why Susan needed a mink coat during a balmy spring season. The truth was, for Susan, the mink was a tangible symbol of success—of stardom—that had always figured in her fantasies. It was the only fur she had ever wanted—she was contemptuous of the typical starlet's white fox. She felt she was at the plateau in her career where she belonged in mink. And she was too impatient to wait until her husband could afford to make the final payments.

Soon she would be able to afford the payments herself. Sometime earlier in 1946, Wanger had sent her the script of her next picture. Originally titled *Angelica*, it was alleged to be a *film à clef* of the Bing Crosby–Dixie Lee marriage, in which Susan would play a neglected young wife turned alcoholic because her husband's spectacular singing career has left him little time for their marriage. As the story goes, lonely and depressed, unable to compete with the predatory women in her husband's life, Angelica turns to liquor for comfort and eventually loses complete control of herself. After her husband Ken sues for divorce and custody of their daughter, Angelica kidnaps the little girl and almost destroys both of them when she falls into a drunken stupor while smoking. Badly burned rescuing the child, Angelica is given another chance at happiness when her husband, suddenly aware of the problems that led to Angelica's alcoholism, decides to give the marriage another try—a blatant Hollywood "happy ending."

There was no question that it was the strongest role Susan had yet received, and Wanger cast the other parts carefully to show her off, passing over Jess Barker to put the weaker Lee Bowman in the role of the singer husband. Wanger was taking no chances of Susan's being outshone by anyone. With his wife Joan's box-office potential declining, Wanger had a desperate need for a strong female star, and was confident he could turn the girl he had been calling "a Brooklyn Bette Davis" into just that.

With this in mind, he gave Susan top-star billing, retitled the film *Smash-Up, The Story of a Woman*, and issued an ironclad edict to everyone concerned with the production, from director

Stuart Heisler to film editor Milton Carruth: "Favor Susan Hayward in every possible way."

For Susan, the film marked a turning point in her career and in her life. Before filming began, Wanger told Heisler with remarkable insight the lines that have been quoted earlier: "Susie suffers from one of the most startling guilt complexes you can imagine. She's embarrassed that she is a beautiful woman. She doesn't think she deserves it. She knows it's a priceless gift, but she's afraid that on the inside she isn't beautiful."

Then added: "If we can get her to bring that complex to the surface in this role, we'll get a performance worthy of an Oscar from her."

chapter 9

SUSAN HAYWARD, an expert at hiding almost everything, never attempted to conceal her fondness for Scotch. She freely admitted that she enjoyed a stiff drink with Jess when she arrived home from the studio exhausted. When they went to Mocambo or Ciro's, she thought it ridiculous that coffee cups were substituted for liquor glasses whenever a photographer wanted to grab a quick shot. Everyone in Hollywood drank, and everyone knew it—but the edict came from the studios, and heaven help the photographer who violated it.

Strictly a social drinker, however, Susan didn't know what it was like to get drunk. She had gotten giddy at times but never smashed, therefore when filming of *Smash-Up* began, she found it difficult to reach inside herself for the necessary effects. Director Stuart Heisler tried everything he could think of. One afternoon, in desperation, he even sent out for a couple of bottles of booze and persuaded Susan to try to get drunk, but it didn't work. She did manage to get fairly tipsy, but drunk actors can't play drunk scenes—that's an accepted show-business axiom. Finally, Heisler enlisted the aid of Yale University's authority on alcoholism, Dr. Elvin M. Jellinek. Susan spent hours with him and, somehow, whether it was through his help or her own inner resources, between the three of them, Susan's performance began to take shape.

It was different with Lee Bowman, however. Bowman—who would appear in seventy-five movies during his film career, from

1937's *I Met Him in Paris* to 1964's *Youngblood Hawke*—was one of those competent, noncharismatic actors who just never caught on with the public.* Originally signed by Paramount, Bowman had his option dropped in 1939, the same year that studio had put Susan under contract. After two years at RKO, he had again met the same fate.

Bowman was perpetually cast as the guy who lost the girl to the male lead. In fact, coincidentally, he had played the modern socialite who lost Rita Hayworth to dancer Gene Kelly in *Cover Girl*—Jess Barker had played his turn-of-the-century counterpart ditched by "grandma" Rita for "piano player" Johnny Mitchell. Further in the coincidence department, Bowman's wife Helene was the daughter of Victor Fleming, the man who had replaced Susan's first mentor George Cukor as director of *Gone with the Wind*—and the Bowmans were close friends of Steffi Duna, John Carroll's first wife.

One might assume that Susan and Bowman shared enough background for hours of small talk, but between takes they barely exchanged a word. Bowman made no effort to conceal his hostility toward Susan from the day *Smash-Up* started production. "Of the many stars I've worked with," he later said, "she was the only one with whom I ever had any difficulty." A great deal of the difficulty, actually, came from the fact that he was seething with resentment. When he had signed for the film, he had been certain it would make him a major star after ten years as an also-ran. After ten days of shooting, however, he no longer had any such illusions; he felt he was being shafted by Susan, by Heisler, and by Walter Wanger.

Susan, however, was exhilarated. Bowman had been hoping for recognition as a star; Susan wanted to be accepted as a serious *actress*. Grateful for Heisler's professionalism, she responded to his direction with an uncharacteristic obedience, and had little doubt that this time she would reach her goal. Yet when Wanger, after seeing the rushes of some of the more dramatic sequences, suggested that she might just possibly snare an Oscar nomination, she refused to allow her hopes to be built up. That would be *too* much to expect.

---

* He would retire in 1968 to take up teaching camera techniques to GOP politicians and the art of public speaking to corporate executives at Bethlehem Steel. He died in December 1979, at the age of sixty-five.

By the time she had completed *Smash-Up,* however, she felt secure enough to start looking at houses. Since her marriage, she and Jess had been virtual gypsies. They had already been evicted from two homes because the owners had objected to pets and then to children, a commonplace occurrence in southern California. They had felt they would be secure for another year or two in the three-bedroom house they had been leasing in Bel Air, but then in May the owner had returned from Canada and wanted possession as soon as possible. The postwar housing shortage hadn't peaked, and it was a seller's market.

Jess complained bitterly, in an interview, "Sure, we can buy a lot of those Spanish-type houses built in 1925 for $30,000 and up. They're worth maybe $8,000 and most of them are broken-down wrecks. The real estate people all give us the same line: 'You can do wonderful things with this house.' Sure we can do wonderful things with another $10,000.

"We heard of a house near us in Bel Air. The price was $35,000. We went to see it. The real estate people recognized Susan. The price suddenly shot up to $55,000."

"And we can't afford $55,000," Susan chimed in. "Sure, *I* saved a little money. I've been saving it for a rainy day. I can't see putting it all into a house. Especially now when taxes are so high. Sure I make good money, but you should see those checks I write to the Treasury Department."

The Barkers' only alternative was to forget about Bel Air and Beverly Hills, and start house-hunting in the San Fernando Valley. At that time, the suburbs west of Universal City still had a country atmosphere, and homes there were comparatively new, well built, and reasonably priced. After a long search, Susan and Jess found a charming place complete with swimming pool at 3737 Longridge Avenue in Sherman Oaks, well worth the $47,000 asking price. Its value, she was assured, could only increase. Unlike most married women, however, Susan went to the real estate broker alone, wrote the check, and put the house in her name— alone. The family moved in on Christmas Eve, 1946.

Smash-Up was released in April of 1947. The film received mixed reviews, due mostly to the inevitable comparisons with *The Lost Weekend,* but Susan's performance was a revelation to most of the critics.

Variety commented in its inimitable style: "Just as Ray Milland achieved his greatest prominence because of *Weekend,* Susan Hayward gets her biggest break to date in this one. . . . Miss Hayward handles a difficult thesping job with ease and assurance, faltering only where the story bogs down. Pixie quality and her beauteous looks enhance greatly her characterization of a gal who becomes a dipso to overcome an inferiority complex. . . . Cast, though overshadowed by Miss Hayward, does well."

Howard Barnes of the *New York Herald-Tribune* particularly applauded the film's writing, "A female alcoholic takes her place in the gallery of psychiatric cases. *Smash-Up* is a somewhat savage account of dipsomania. . . . John Howard Lawson, Dorothy Parker, and Frank Cavett have written sequences which are literate and terrifying, while Stuart Heisler has staged them with ominous underlining. . . . Since Susan Hayward plays the heroine with considerable power, the production is definitely disturbing."

Of Lee Bowman, *Life* magazine said he played his part "with all the enthusiasm of a stuffed moose." *Variety* simply noted: "Bowman is miscast as the husband."

Susan, encouraged by her exceptional reviews, began taking Wanger's Oscar nomination predictions seriously, and was beginning to regret he had released the film in April, prolonging the suspense for another ten months. However, she had little time to ponder about the future. She was busy enough in the present.

First there was a film called *The Lost Moment,* which had begun shooting on March 12, a bastardized version of Henry James's *Aspern Papers,* which, Susan later admitted, "was a disastrous film. As miserable a failure as you've ever seen. Their name for it may have been *The Lost Moment,* but after I saw it I called it 'The Lost Hour and a Half.' " (The critics later agreed.) Then, in June, she began preparations for *Tap Roots,* from a book that Jess Barker, in fact, had persuaded Wanger to read and buy. Being idle, Barker had immersed himself in Susan's career, though few people were aware of it at the time.

"Yes, I brought that to Mr. Wanger myself," he points out today. "A certain Italian producer on the lot said, 'Jess, did you ever read *Tap Roots* by James Street?' and I said, 'No.'

" 'Well,' he said, 'it's in the library. You should go get it. I think Susan would be great in it, because it's just like from *Gone with the Wind.' "

In *Tap Roots*, Susan played Morna Dabney, the spitfire daughter of the leader of an independent group in Lebanon County, Mississippi, which decides to secede from the state when Mississippi secedes from the Union. With the Confederate army closing in, Morna has her own problems when she becomes paralyzed after a fall from a horse; loses her fiancé to her selfish sister, and finds herself attracted to a "notorious newspaper publisher and duellist," Keith Alexander. In the end, Lebanon County is lost, Keith Alexander is won, and all ends happily.

Wanger was forced to give Van Heflin top billing in order to borrow him from MGM for the Rhett Butlerish character of Alexander—but, as with *Smash-Up*, Susan was favored in every sequence in which she appeared. Aware of this, she occasionally stepped out of bounds. George Marshall was the director on *Tap Roots,* and he later remembered:

"In one scene her reputed stubbornness came to life. The scene, I admit, was rather clichéd, but it played an important part in the plot. Susan was in a wheelchair, since she was not supposed to be able to walk. The character played by Van Heflin thought that she could, and was intent upon proving it. He felt that if he could make her mad enough, she would get up.

"The first take was a real dud. She played it almost to the point of apathy, and here is where our wills clashed for the first time. She felt she should play the scene in this deadened form, while I knew it had to be explosive, to be in contrast to everything she had done before. I told this to her and insisted she loosen up. The director has to be boss or an agreement must be reached. The next take was even worse. She got up from the chair, ran to her dressing room, and slammed the door. I thought, 'Well, that screws up our schedule for the day.'

"But she returned in a little while, after she had fixed her face, to give me a big kiss, and say, 'I'm sorry. I knew in my heart what you wanted. I just didn't want to give in. But I still think you are a miserable so-and-so.'

"I didn't believe those cuss words for a minute. Susan always remained one of my favorite people."

She had another slight problem during the shooting too, a rather curious one. Yvonne Wood, who designed the costumes for *Tap Roots*, remembers, "I had a little trouble with Susan and bust pads. After the censor had passed on all the wardrobe tests,

Walter Wanger called me frantically to say, 'Susan is showing a lot more cleavage in the dailies, and we're going to have to re-shoot some scenes.' I went straight to the set, reached into Susan's dress, and pulled out bust pads and other assorted things she had stuck in there. After that, Susan behaved herself." Miss Wood isn't the only one who recalls Susan's concern about her breasts. Jane Greer, who had worked with her the previous year in *They Won't Believe Me,* laughs. "Even back then, Susan hated to wear bras. She used to tape herself under the arms so her breasts would flow freely. Every night she'd yank off the tape, to the horror of the wardrobe lady."

No bras but bust pads? Extra cleavage from a woman leg-endary for her modesty? Perhaps it was one more way for her to compensate for her fear, as Wanger said, "that on the inside she isn't beautiful." Or maybe she had simply become more deter-mined than ever to make an impact on the screen—even if it meant showing more skin.

As it turned out, she needn't have worried. After her rejection for *Gone with the Wind,* she had said, "What did I know about playing Southern belles?" But in the decade since, she had learned quite a lot. As a movie, *Tap Roots* left much to be desired, but the critics generally admired Susan—"the film owes its effec-tiveness mostly to the expert performances . . . especially Miss Hayward's," wrote *Newsweek*—Susan liked the Scarlett-type role, and working and living on location in Asheville, North Carolina, had been very pleasurable.

While there, she had had the opportunity to visit the famed Vanderbilt estate, a fifty-eight-bedroom mansion on five hundred acres of land situated nearby. A member of the clan in residence had invited the cast to a cocktail party in honor of the movie. Susan had been overwhelmed.

"I'd never seen anything like it. It was all I could do," she grinned, "to keep from standing in the middle of that baronial hall and shouting, 'Anyone here from Brooklyn?'" That's what she said. In reality, the last thing she had wanted to be reminded of that day was Brooklyn. For a few hours, she had been in the kind of home she had always fantasized about—as her own.

Returning to Longridge Avenue, to a house partially furnished with studio rejects and a living room used for storage space, only heightened her sense of the gap between what she longed for and what she had. She loved Jess. There was no question about that. Yet that love was almost overshadowed by his inability to fill her psychological needs—to make the fantasy come true.

Jess Barker's career was "on hold." He didn't want to leave his family, so he made no effort to get jobs in summer stock or to return to Broadway. Maritally, that may have been a fatal mistake. Had he left Susan and gone east, he might have regained his self-respect and put the marriage back on an even keel. He might also have regained the respect of the rumormongers in Hollywood who said he simply did not want to work. Not want to work? He was dying for a role—any role. When Susan suggested he take classes in agriculture and operate a ranch, or go into the jewelry business, he stuck to his guns. "I'm an actor."

The arguments multiplied: About his career. About her career. About money. About everything and nothing. Finally, the conflict proved more than the marriage could endure.

For the second time in three years, Susan walked out on her husband. On October 1, 1947, she had her attorneys draw up divorce papers and brought suit against Jess on the ground of "cruelty and grievous mental anguish." Again, however, the matter went no further than that. Before any definite action was taken, both agreed to consult with Dr. Paul Popenoe of the Institute of Family Relations and, later, with Dr. Maurice Karp, a professional marriage counselor. Soon Susan dropped the divorce proceedings, explaining:

"I've come to the conclusion, as has Jess, that marriage is a contract that should be lived up to. There really isn't very much in life for you when you reach sixty, say, unless you have lived up to it. . . . Now I know that, when I went to see a lawyer, my faith had wavered and that somehow I'd gotten off the track. Working out my marriage problems has made me realize that I am growing up and maturing.

"I've said some things I have regretted, and Jess has done the same thing. But doesn't that apply to *every* married couple? I mean *every* married couple—not just movie people."

Other than an item or two in the gossip columns, little attention was paid to the split and hasty reconciliation. The two top fan magazines of the time didn't even consider it newsworthy.

Through the wartime years, *Modern Screen* and *Photoplay*, with the exception of an occasional candid shot, had ignored Susan with a regularity bordering on insult. Even now, neither her Oscar nomination for *Smash-Up*, nor the short-lived separation and reconciliation with Jess, nor Susan's luminous beauty had inspired either magazine to assign stories about the couple. Nor were Susan and Jess invited to the lavish star-studded parties held annually by each magazine to present awards to the stars whom the public had chosen as their favorites of the year. Susan Hayward fans could read about her in the lesser publications, *Motion Picture, Silver Screen,* and *Movieland,* but never in the two giants of the field.

Asked about this today, Albert Delacorte, then *Modern Screen*'s young editor and later the Dell publisher, replies: "You know the answer! Susan Hayward was always a personal favorite of mine, but my opinion didn't count. We followed our readers' poll to the letter—or should I say to the number! And in 1945, even after the kids were born, Susan Hayward wasn't even able to register in the top fifty. I admired her work on the screen, my staff shared this feeling. We are all amazed that our readers didn't ask for her. I was just the guy who ran the magazine, but the public told me who to run. That policy was too successful to tamper with; we had an estimated readership of anywhere from thirteen million to damn near fifteen million every month."

In June 1948, Delacorte turned over the editorship of *Modern Screen,* and made plans to start another kind of publication (which ultimately never got off the ground), "a *Parents*-type magazine," inspired by his own fascination on the subject. "I wanted a monthly feature on the way movie stars raise their kids. With this in mind, I asked my West Coast rep to visit the Barker house and send back some intimate information on the Barker boys. Nothing like starting with twins." This was the wire he received back:

Timothy much more sensitive than Greg. Needs more affection. Some people think Susan spoils Tim. Susan always aware of this need in him. (STOP) Tim has exceptionally deep voice for small youngster. Likes to sing. Knows tunes and lyrics. Usually croons when sitting on Susan's lap. (STOP) Timothy stomach-happy. Asks nurse, "Dinner ready, Annie?" Looks immediately for meat when he sits at table. Will eat everything, but meat's got to be there. Inherited this from Susan. (STOP) She and Jess extra careful not to show favoritism. No jealousy between boys. If one is patted on the head, the other gets same treatment. When one is spanked, the other becomes quiet. Then protests punishment for his brother. (STOP) Twins love water, don't object to baths, splash around in swimming pool. Will learn to swim next summer, according to Susan. . . . Love of water extends to sailing toy boats in the john. (STOP) Both are helpful around house. Never miss a trick. If Susan asks where baby oil or red shirt, etc., is, one or both can tell her. (STOP) Susan doesn't dress them alike. Exception coats, boots and sailor suits. She says they're different people, besides being fraternal twins, so why try to make them identical. (STOP) Barkers got them through the Don't-touch stage with little difficulty, except for wall sockets. These fascinated them, and they were forever crawling to one to try and find out what makes lamps light. Used to give Susan strokes. (STOP) Kids love to be read to. Timothy has crush on gingerbread man. Has three different versions of book on subject, plus albums and a toy G.B. man. For Christmas cook baking him one, with gumdrops for buttons. (STOP) Twins will be four February 19. Barkers seldom have guests numbering over four. . . . Don't like more because of kids. Incidentally Susan impresses me as being an exceptionally good mother. (STOP)

Nevertheless, despite this picture of domestic bliss and even after four years of motherhood, Susan still had *some* doubts about that. Although she said, "It seems obvious to me what children require is not necessarily the constant presence of their mother, but the constant knowledge that they are loved and cherished," there were subtle indications that she might be wrong.

Later she admitted, "At first when friends visited us and the babies were brought in, I was sometimes hurt because Greg and Timothy would turn away from me when I held them and want to go back to their nurse. Now that we have a new family deal working, things are different."

It was wishful thinking. Anyway, the boys didn't need to run to their nurse: their father was constantly with them.

In February 1948, it was official: Susan had been nominated for her performance in *Smash-Up*. Although she was competing against such heavyweights as odds-on favorite Rosalind Russell

(*Mourning Becomes Electra*); Joan Crawford (*Possessed*); Dorothy McGuire (*Gentleman's Agreement*) and Loretta Young (*The Farmer's Daughter*), Wanger was optimistic about a last-minute upset. As it turned out, Wanger was absolutely correct. There was, indeed, an upset. The award went to the least likely of all of them—Loretta Young—and Hollywood and Miss Russell didn't come out of shock for months. A wag suggested RKO change the name of her movie to "Mourning Becomes Roz Russell."

Susan took the defeat with good humor, although she had splurged on the most expensive gown she had ever bought. "I can always wear the dress again. And I'll be nominated for an Oscar again. Maybe not next year. Maybe I'll have to wait until the fifties. But I intend to win some day. That's my goal."

In 1948, it was also Walter Wanger's goal. He may have been president of the Academy, but he had never produced an Oscar-winning film, a failing he intended to correct with his multi-million dollar production of *Joan of Arc,* starring Ingrid Bergman. He poured all his time and money into it—the film was running way over on both—and as a result, there was little time for Susan. With his permission, Universal used her in the Robert Montgomery starrer *The Saxon Charm.* It was hardly the best follow-up to her Oscar nomination: As John Payne's wife, her part was secondary to the story, and the second female lead, Audrey Totter, stole the film.

Then, after *Joan of Arc* was completed—he thought—Wanger brought Susan and director Stuart Heisler to Eagle-Lion, for which company he was producing the less-than-epic *Tulsa.* Robert Preston and Susan were reunited for the third time in a story about the "black gold" industry, but Wanger came up with a dry well. *Time* magazine commented: "*Tulsa,* like a damp fuse, provides a loud bang at the end of a long sputter. Its plot is so rambling and logy with clichés that its climax—a big fire scene—seems wonderfully good."

Joan of Arc's final fire scene too was spectacular, but much of the rest of the film was disastrous. Desperate for money for additional sequences and for an expensive ad campaign that he thought—erroneously—might save the picture, Wanger sold Susan's contract to Darryl Zanuck for a reported two hundred thousand dollars.

Susan's feeling about the sale were mixed. She regretted losing

Wanger, whom she trusted and respected as a mentor—but the deal he and the Feldman office had negotiated with Zanuck was overwhelmingly in her favor.

"We'll work together again," Wanger predicted sentimentally.

"I know. I'll work for you any time, in anything," she replied.

That would come to pass nearly a decade later. For now, however, her future was tied to that of the lengendary Zanuck himself—and it would be a bumpy ride.

chapter 10

I cannot remember when I first saw her or under what circumstances I engaged her and put her in her first Fox film. This calls for a great deal of thinking. . . . All I can recall is when I last saw her [in 1963] it was not a very pleasant encounter.
DARRYL F. ZANUCK, *shortly before his death*

WHAT HAPPENED during that final encounter will never be known, for Zanuck died in December 1979. What is certain, however, is that, for all Susan's anticipation, the relationship began inauspiciously.

Zanuck could be wildly extravagant in some ways, but notoriously tight-fisted in others. Susan's salary, prorated on the usual forty-week year, came to $5,000 a week. Zanuck wanted maximum value for his studio's money, so he put her to work immediately (on December 22, 1948) in Joseph L. Mankiewicz's production of *House of Strangers*. There was nothing wrong with *House of Strangers*, but it was basically a male-oriented melodrama about a family vendetta, starring Edward G. Robinson and Richard Conte; and Susan's brief role, as Conte's girl friend, was not the kind of studio debut an Oscar-nominated actress might have expected.

Zanuck knew, however, that Susan was next due to report to Samuel Goldwyn on June 19 for *My Foolish Heart*, and he scented a winner in that one. It was easy to project the effect that *Heart* would have on the career of his newest property: he merely had to sit back and let Goldwyn turn her into a potential superstar, while he lined up properties pending her return to Twentieth.

There was nothing male-oriented about *My Foolish Heart*. It was a woman's picture right down to the last haunting strains of its theme song, which would be (and still is) requested nightly in every piano bar in the country:

> The night is like a lovely tune,
> Beware, my foolish heart.
> How white the ever constant moon,
> Take care, my foolish heart.

Adapted from J. D. Salinger's *New Yorker* story, "Uncle Wiggily in Connecticut," Julius J. and Philip G. Epstein's screenplay put alcoholic, unhappy Eloise Winters at the tail end of a disastrous marriage to a man she had married out of expediency. The sight of an old gown arouses memories and takes her back to 1941— when as a nice girl from Boise, Idaho, she had met a charming Greenwich Village wolf (Dana Andrews) at a party and soon found herself madly in love. At first resisting his sexual advances, she'd finally given in right before his leaving for the army, but then kept her subsequent pregnancy a secret, unwilling to trap him into marriage. On his own, he scribbles a proposal—just before his plane crashes in an army training accident. Desperate, she seduces her best friend's fiancé into a marriage that has made them both miserable. . . . Back in the present (1949), Eloise decides to give up her child rather than to tell her husband the truth, but he too has a change of heart and realizes that the child's place is with her mother.

Yes, in 1949, *My Foolish Heart* was *definitely* a woman's picture.

Dana Andrews in the male lead acquitted himself admirably, but pitted against Susan's portrayal of Eloise and the song title, he came off third best.

Here, as in *Canyon Passage*, the intimacy between Susan and Andrews came to a halt the minute the cameras stopped rolling. Commenting today upon their offscreen relationship, Andrews echoes the words of most Hayward leading men. "I could say Susan was self-centered, but almost everyone in our profession is. She was a very strong young woman with a steel will. She was most attractive and always pleasant to me; we worked extremely well together. But we almost never saw each other socially." (There would be one time worth commenting on, but not until a few years later. . . .)

Director Mark Robson observed: "You know, there are times when it is advantageous to a love story if the two leading players are not too close; they save their emotions for the cameras. I've seen enough instances when co-stars were making it in the dressing room. When they were called on the set a few minutes later, the effect on their performances, particularly in a romantic scene, was disastrous. They were so afraid something would come across, especially when one or the other (or both) were married. They subconsciously froze. Take Elizabeth Taylor and Richard Burton. They were madly in love when they did *The V.I.P.'s,* yet their chemistry in the film was nonexistent."

Returning to Susan, Robson continued, "I think she didn't trust actors or actresses. She had a few directors at the beginning of her career who were out-and-out bastards and gave her no help at all, but once she felt she could trust a director, she'd work her ass to the bones for him. She trusted me and the part of Eloise Winters—ranging from sweet innocent to alcoholic young matron—was an actress's dream.

"It had 'Oscar' written all over it, and I can remember the exact moment when I started placing bets that she would cinch a nomination. It was during the scene—just leading to the flashback—when she sobs: 'I was a nice girl, wasn't I?'

"By the time *Foolish Heart* wrapped, we were convinced we'd sweep the Oscar field."

Oozing with optimism, still preening over his *Best Years of Our Lives* triumph the year before, Sam Goldwyn rushed *My Foolish Heart* into Los Angeles theaters early to qualify for the 1949 awards. The reviews only reinforced everyone's optimism. *Look* magazine's review was typical:

"*My Foolish Heart* tells of a simple wartime love story that ended in heartbreak. These are ingredients for a typical soap opera. But *My Foolish Heart* rises above its material every step of the way . . . proves that freshness can be given a much-worn story if it is approached with a light touch, an adult point of view and a warm understanding for the weaknesses of recognizable human beings. It merges a rich, delicious movie that every grown-up moviegoer should cherish. . . . In her best screen job to date, Miss Hayward makes the tragedy of a girl in love in war-time very real indeed."

My Foolish Heart opened in New York at the Radio City Music Hall on January 20, 1950. A few weeks later, although the antici-pated sweep failed to materialize, Academy Award nominations went to the title song—and to Susan Hayward.

"And the winner is . . ."

On March 23, 1950, for the second time in three years, Susan had to sit and watch with a frozen smile as another actress rushed to the stage of the Pantages to accept the coveted Oscar. This time, it was Olivia de Havilland for her portrayal of Catherine Sloper in *The Heiress*. The award was not entirely a surprise. Earlier in the year de Havilland had been chosen Best Actress by the New York Film Critics' Society, and most of the Academy felt that she had deserved an Oscar for her role in the previous year's *The Snake Pit,* as well.

Nevertheless, de Havilland now had two of the statues (the other one for *To Each His Own*), and Susan had none. With her eyes blazing and just a trace of a smile on her lips, Susan re-peated the prediction she had made two years earlier. "There will be other chances. Don't worry, I intend to win one of those things someday." Now, no one scoffed.

Inexplicably, though, Zanuck continued to cast her in less than star-caliber roles. After stifling her resentment at being cast in *House of Strangers,* she finally rebelled when the studio an-nounced its intention to cast her in a foolish comedy called *Stella* about a family of crazy crooks: despite top star billing, her part would have been entirely secondary to the development of the story. Play, or be suspended, the studio warned. Susan opted for suspension. Her replacement was Ann Sheridan, another redhead and one whose star was waning.

Susan was confident Zanuck would not permit her to remain idle for long, and sat back to wait. Jess Barker, however, had no reason to be that optimistic about his own career.

In 1949, he had worked in two minor films—*The Black Book* and *Take One False Step*—but now at the start of the decade, there were no new offers and none on the horizon. He tried to be philosophical.

"I admit frankly," he told a friend, "that when a man isn't working, especially an actor, it can get on his nerves. He begins to brood, becomes jumpy and irritable. It's happened to me. But you've got to snap out of it. It's not fair to you, not fair to your wife, and certainly not fair to your children.

"Susan and I regard our marriage as a partnership. Whatever each of us earns goes into the family bankroll. The very nature of the entertainment business is cyclical. Right now Susan is having a great run. Next year or maybe the year after, it will be my turn. There's no point in becoming neurotic just because your wife is having a big success."

That's what he said. He tried hard to convince outsiders he meant it and tried even harder to convince himself.

To Jess fell the responsibility of running interference between Susan and outsiders making demands on her time. He took all calls—she hated telephone conversations—screened scripts, and talked to fan-magazine reporters clamoring for stories about the idyllic Barkers. To these persistent intruders, Jess always put on a happy face—though the resemblance to Fredric March in the 1937 *A Star Is Born* was not missed by everyone.

In one story for *Motion Picture*, under his by-line and approved by him, Jess wrote, "When Susan is working and I'm not, I take charge of things around the house. I do the shopping, discipline the twins, just take over. She's too busy, naturally, to have time to run a house on top of everything else. Sometimes we disagree about how to bring up the children. Susan feels I am too stern. And I feel the boys would never learn if I didn't show them I meant what I said."

Barker was determined to present a strong masculine image to his five-year-old sons, and so emphasized order and discipline. It was obvious, though, that there was little order in the household. Jess noted:

"Susan spent two years looking for the drapes for the bedroom. In the meantime, we had no drapes—no nothing. Just old shades we pulled down. Our living room also looks very peculiar. We never furnished it. No sofas, no rugs. In it we have a 16-milli-meter projector, a television set, a player piano, and two tables. It is, in a word, empty."

Jess also admitted that "Neither of us is very neat either. We have one of those desert lamps which I generally throw my trousers over. Nobody touches them. And Susan's clothes are hung over the door. Not on the hook—on the door. No one touches anything Susan or I put in a certain place.

"We put our mail down where we open it—on top of the table, under plates, all over the place. Sometimes I go through it to find the bills. I have a little place where I hide them—in back of the philodendron plants. Then when Susan says, 'Whatever happened to such and such a bill?' I just reach behind the plants.

"Whenever we expect company, we both go tearing around putting stuff away."

In this article, and elsewhere, Barker also tried to make light of "silly domestic problems," hoping to convince everyone that the problems the two of them had had in the early years of their marriage were a thing of the past. As it would turn out, though, they were very much a thing of the present.

Meanwhile, Susan had been successful in her war of nerves with Zanuck. Loath to see his high-priced star idle, he had broken down and offered her the co-starring role opposite Tyrone Power in *Rawhide*. The plot: entertainer Vinnie Holt, taking her niece east by stagecoach, is held hostage in a station by a small group of bandits and falls in love with stationmaster Tyrone Power. Susan didn't like the script particularly, despite a fondness for westerns—she would say, many years later, "I enjoy watching westerns more than any other type of film I can think of. I always know how everything is going to turn out—the bad guys are always going to get knocked off, the good guys are always going to win." This time, however, Zanuck was persistent rather than threatening, and finally Susan agreed, telling Zanuck, "I still don't trust this script, but I trust you."

Actually, her trust was not misplaced. Although *Rawhide* was played more for suspense than for action, Thomas Pryor of the *New York Times* conceded: "Director Henry Hathaway has turned out a surprisingly good entertainment," and added that "Miss Hayward, who has more opportunity to express her indignation and gnawing terror . . . does well by her role." Pryor concluded that, although "*Rawhide* may not be a prize addition to the screen's vast western library, it is sufficiently different to warrant attention"—a view that was generally shared by audiences and critics alike.

Much of *Rawhide* was filmed in a chilly location site (shooting started on January 9) at Lone Pine, California, a four-hour drive from Los Angeles, and there was little social contact between

Susan and Tyrone Power. The latter, recently back from Europe with his new bride Linda Christian, was less than happy in a kind of role he could—and did—play better ten years earlier; wanted to get the picture over with as quickly as possible, and made no secret about it. There was little camaraderie between him and the other members of the cast. Susan, for her part, spent much of her free time with forty-nine-year-old character actor George Tobias, an old acquaintance of the Barkers who had originally met Jess when both had been featured in *You Can't Take It with You*. A wise, unpretentious bachelor, Tobias was among the select few Susan would invite to dinner, then or later.

Susan, however, would see little of Tobias—or anyone else—during most of the remaining months of 1950. She had barely finished *Rawhide* when she had to travel to Georgia on May 18 for *I'd Climb the Highest Mountain*, then to New York on October 2 for *I Can Get It for You Wholesale*, a biting, behind-the-scenes look at Manhattan's garment center.

Based loosely on Jerome Weidman's 1937 best seller, *I Can Get It for You Wholesale* presented Susan as Harriet Boyd, a cold, calculating, model-turned-designer-turned dress-manufacturer who ruthlessly claws her way to the top of the rag heap. Although saddled with a conventional Hollywood happy ending—the ruthless career woman is redeemed by "the love of a good man"—the movie was generally well received, the *New York Herald-Tribune*'s James S. Barstow commenting that "Miss Hayward is just right . . . fast and sassy on her double-crossing climb from $10.95 models to Paris creations; she's nasty-nice enough almost to carry the contrived good-girl-after-all conversion of the climax." "To say that Susan was a highly talented and able actress would be merely to state the obvious," director Michael Gordon notes today. "In a word, she was thoroughly professional in the best sense of the word."

The *New York Times*'s Thomas Pryor had some reservations about the metamorphosis the original novel had undergone, but agreed: "Give Susan Hayward some quick recognition for bringing to life a hard-shelled dame who travels as fast and as loose as the screenplay permits her to. . . . Stories about such chameleon-like characters as Miss Hayward plays . . . are difficult to put over with complete success, and that is why this film falters as a character study, though Miss Hayward does nobly." He was carried away, though, by the "freshness the picture has to offer [in] the scenes which reflect the pulse-beat of the dress-industry—the crowds scurrying along Seventh Avenue amidst the traffic of dress carts and the frenetic atmosphere of the show-rooms. . . . The cameras rove excitingly through this fabulous hurly-burly. . . ."

To achieve this realistic effect, the studio had sent Susan, co-star Dan Dailey, and other key personnel to New York, and photographed them in Seventh Avenue dress establishments. Some of the street scenes had even been shot with hidden cameras.

Susan found the experience exhilarating. As in the past, a return to New York had an electrifying effect on her, renewing her energies and elevating her spirits. She was the hometown girl who had made good, the queen returning to her subjects, and she was treated accordingly. Although her eyes were usually hidden by large tinted glasses with prescription lenses, her long flaming hair made her easily identifiable. Yet she wasn't mobbed in public places—just admired from a discreet distance—and she loved every minute of it. To a *New York Post* reporter who visited a location site one afternoon, she freely admitted: "It's *wonderful* being a movie star, being able to go to the best Fifth Avenue shops and buy the toys for your children you never could have."

But the movie star still couldn't shake some of the "little girl from Brooklyn" ways.

After her scenes for *Wholesale* were completed, Susan stayed on at the Hampshire House with Jess for a few additional days to catch a few shows and do some shopping. A young movie-buff photographer, with whom she had become acquainted during the Parsons' tour, was invited to her suite to say goodbye, and recalls that afternoon as being "absolutely chaotic, frantic. Susan wanted to take some of the hotel's soap back to California with her and asked the maid to get her some additional bars. The maid came back with about a dozen of the guest-size packages. Susan looked at them and told the girl, 'No, this isn't the right kind.' Obviously, the hotel had two different brands covered by their own wrapper, and Susan favored a particular one. The maid disappeared and returned with the proper brand. It was all very strange, since the large economy size could have been picked up at any grocery or drugstore in California at the time for about a dime. I could have understood her doing this if she was traveling about Europe, where good soap was still hard to come by in 1950, or if the Hampshire House soap was made from some special formula. But this was plain Lux or Ivory or Cashmere Bouquet.

"The madness continued when she went downstairs to check out. Jess was busy seeing to the luggage, as I recall. The hotel had charged her for certain meals which Susan insisted the studio should be absorbing. There was quite a to-do about it, and finally the hotel agreed to make an adjustment. I teasingly told Susan that she should consider herself lucky she wasn't charged for all that soap. She was not amused."

By this time, thanks to *My Foolish Heart, Rawhide,* and *I Can Get It for You Wholesale,* Susan's career was accelerating rapidly. Shortly after her return from New York, she was selected as "Queen of Glamour" by the Motion Picture Photographers' Association, and with that lofty though somewhat gaudy title, a siege of calls and letters began, from portrait painters asking her to sit for them, and cosmetic firms wanting endorsement of their products. Dress manufacturers wanted to produce a Hayward gown for the following fall, and a florist announced that he had created a Susan Hayward–Queen of Glamour Rose.

Susan would have none of these projects, but there was no doubt that the glamour build-up had finally begun in earnest. Even as she was stocking up on free soap, Zanuck was mulling over her next project, a rather elaborate rewrite of the Bible that would, as the good book says, "come to pass" and usher in Susan's reign as the queen of Twentieth Century-Fox.

Back on March 26, 1947, James Mason and his wife, Pamela Mason, had made their American stage debuts in *Bathsheba,* "a comedy-drama based on the Old Testament" written by Jacques Deval. Despite Mason's overwhelming personal appeal, the play had lasted a limp twenty-nine performances. Zanuck, who owned the film rights, blamed this in part on the writing, in part on the casting—Mrs. Mason lacked the sexuality to make the steamy affair convincing, he thought—and in 1950, set out to right both wrongs.

First, he threw out the Deval play, and hired prolific writer Philip Dunne to flesh out a two-hour screenplay on the bare bones of the Book of Samuel. The story in the Bible begins,

"And it came to pass that David arose from his bed and . . . from the roof he saw a woman washing herself," and ends tersely, "But the thing David had done displeased the Lord." That was about as much of the Bible as could be found in the finished screenplay too. Dunne's final product owed considerably more to Hollywood than to the Old Testament and, to top it off, it was largely written in blank verse.

"Bathsheba has sinned," Raymond Massey would proclaim sonorously as the prophet Nathan. "She has brought adultery and murder. She has brought the drought and the famine. She has brought the wrath of God upon Israel." And so on.

For the casting, Zanuck was convinced that Gregory Peck, who had so admirably "passed for Jewish" in the Oscar-winning *Gentleman's Agreement,* would be the perfect choice as the Lion of Judea. And Susan Hayward, in spite of her flaming red hair and less-than-Semitic features, was just the one to generate the fire that would justify David's defiance of his God.

Susan didn't exactly fall over with gratitude. She let it be known that she'd be happier if the stage title was retained or if it were called "Bathsheba and David." Then, told that Zanuck was toying with the possibility of filming in Europe or Palestine, she had her agent insist upon a clause in her contract guaranteeing transportation for her twins to either place.

As it turned out, Zanuck had a change of heart about a journey to Jerusalem, and built the holy city on his spacious back lot. And in November, Susan took her famous Biblical bath on a "closed set" behind an opaque screen.

Zanuck called upon Henry King to serve as Susan's director. King had guided Susan through *I'd Climb the Highest Mountain,* a leisurely, presumably inspirational little story about a rural Methodist parson and his perky, city-bred wife, just a few months before, but Susan had not cared for it or him. Known as a "man's director" who had previously helped Tyrone Power achieve stardom, King had directed Peck in such powerhouses as *Twelve O'Clock High* and *The Gunfighter,* and obviously favored his male star. There is no other explanation for his allowing Susan to come across like a 1950 lovesick cheerleader admiring the college football hero. After a suggestive romp on a knoll, she breathlessly inquires:

"David, did you *really* kill Goliath? *Was he as big as they say?*"

To which Peck modestly replies, *"I admit he grows a little bigger every year."*

For all his idiotic lines, Peck's portrayal of King David was unanimously applauded. Susan's Bathsheba and the film itself drew mixed notices. *Time* magazine's review was possibly the most definitive.

It comes dangerously close to serving as a sleeping potion. . . . Peck's performance carried surprising authority. But the script is more notable for words than action, and its pretensions toward serious drama are undermined by a plot that never quite overcomes its resemblance to boudoir farce. . . . Disappointing as a spectacle, *David and Bathsheba* is no more successful in its frank tale of adultery. Even the most sensational episodes are weighed down with portentous airs and long-winded prattle. And while the picture gathers an ever-loftier mood of religiosity, David and Bathsheba spend nearly as much time suffering and repenting their sins as committing them.

Despite its objections to the film, though, *Time* conceded that Susan's performance was thorough. The *New York Times*'s A. H. Weiler, however, while blessing the epic for its "reverential and sometimes majestic treatment," found the cast "entirely overshadowed" by Peck's performance and damned Susan's Bathsheba as "a Titian-tressed charmer who seems closer to Hollywood than to the Bible." Perhaps the most appropriate middle ground was found by *Newsweek,* which allowed that "under the trying circumstances in which they find themselves, both Peck and Miss Hayward bring considerable dignity and conviction to their roles."

The reviews would not appear until the following August, but when the picture wound up its shooting in early February, Susan, still smarting at what she called her "starlet treatment" by King, flippantly told Zanuck, "Well, I'm not counting on any Oscar nominations this year."

"Maybe not," replied Zanuck, "but you'll feel differently after completing your next one." Beaming, he handed her a script tentatively titled *The Jane Froman Story.*

chapter 11

She's my twelve-million-dollar baby.

DARRYL F. ZANUCK

SUSAN'S LOOKING GLASS confirmed what Darryl F. Zanuck had benevolently proclaimed: that among his leading ladies, she was unequivocally the fairest of them all. Approaching her thirty-fourth birthday, she still photographed like a woman in her midtwenties. Furthermore, prompting Zanuck's comment, she was now the star of twelve million dollars' worth of Twentieth Century-Fox's films. In the first four months of 1951, three of them would be released.

With a Song in My Heart was not scheduled to go into production until late spring of that year, but in the interval the movie-going public was deluged with Susan Hayward pictures. Susan had hoped to take a prolonged vacation trip to Ireland with Jess during that time, but the studio wasn't about to let her go away, with so much at stake. Among other duties, it insisted that she (together with Henry King) attend the gala premiere of *I'd Climb the Highest Mountain,* set to take place at Atlanta's Paramount Theater on February 17. Georgia's Governor Herman Talmadge agreed to be on hand to accept an engraved copy of the script. Despite a driving rain, several thousand fans jammed the theater. The picture received some needed publicity, and spurred on by the Twentieth Century-Fox publicity department, the state senate passed a resolution officially naming Susan "an adopted daughter of Georgia." It was an honor that would prove prophetic.

I'd Climb the Highest Mountain did not reach New York until May. However, with *Rawhide* opening at the Rivoli in late March and *I Can Get It for You Wholesale* set for the Roxy in early April, Susan was, without exception, the screen's most visible star that spring.

She began work on *The Jane Froman Story*, now retitled *With a Song in My Heart*, on June 15, 1951.

As produced and written by Lamar Trotti, *With a Song in My Heart* follows the life and career of Jane Froman, beginning with her rise from young radio singer in 1936 to nationally popular radio, recording, and nightclub star. Her career triumphs, however, are counterpointed by domestic discord, as her songwriter husband (David Wayne) fails to become successful. With the advent of World War II, Froman volunteers to entertain the troops in Europe—when tragedy intervenes. The plane crashes, many aboard are killed, but Jane and pilot John Burn (Rory Calhoun), who later falls in love with her, are among the survivors. Not without cost, however: Froman's left knee is shattered, her right leg almost severed, and there is doubt she'll ever walk again—but after a long series of operations, she returns to the stage, to nightclubs, and eventually to her interrupted USO tour: still on crutches, and a shining example of courage both to the wounded GIs and the general public. Her romantic crisis is resolved when her husband gives her up, enabling her to find happiness with John Burn.*

It was a strong script, possibly strong enough to stand alone without benefit of songs, but Twentieth was taking no chances and stuffed the film full of such popular standards as "Blue Moon," "Tea for Two," "That Old Feeling," "I'll Walk Alone," "Get Happy," and the title song. That song, the especially written "Montparnasse," and "Jim's Toasted Peanuts" provided three dazzling production numbers, as did the rousing "American Medley," comprised of songs with state titles: "Deep in the Heart of Texas," and so forth.

Susan was working on her strenuous dance routines with

---

* Burn and Froman were later divorced, and in 1962, Froman married Roland H. Smith, a childhood friend. Froman died on April 22, 1980.

choreographer Billy Daniel when Jane Froman arrived in Los Angeles in May to act as technical advisor and record the songs for the movie. Later, she would remember her time on the set as "one of the greatest emotional experiences of my life."

Susan had been Froman's personal choice for the role, not because of any physical resemblance—there was none between her and the olive-skinned, dark-haired singer—but because "her heart and spirit were right."

"All the time Susan was doing the picture," Froman would recall in a *Photoplay* article, "off the set as well as on, she lived me and breathed me. And so similar to mine was the quality of her speaking voice that it seemed perfectly natural when my songs seemingly came from her lips.

"When I recorded my songs for the picture, Susan was always around. She sat on the set day after day, three and four hours at a time, watching every move I made as I sang, watching, always watching. Susan struck me as being a strange girl, so sensational in appearance, so quiet of voice and manner.

"Then ten days before we went before the cameras, she came up to me in the commissary and said, 'I'd like to have a long talk with you.'

"Half an hour later we met in Susan's dressing room and spent the whole afternoon and far into the night discussing my life. She asked about my childhood, my mother, my father, my grandmother. She wanted to know what my drives were, my tastes, interests, and hobbies.

"We went over the script scene for scene. I can't, of course, recall our conversation word for word.

"But in essence she wanted to know my exact feelings when I was in the water after the clipper went down, what I talked to the pilot about as he held me up in the water, the exact nature of my injuries, and my exact emotional condition before and after my many operations.

"Susan would, in fact, go to director Walter Lang and demand, 'Look, make me ugly—a girl can't go through all this and come out looking beautiful.' And so in this sequence she looked and sounded as I used to—gray, grim, hair messy, tongue thick."

One of the scenes in the picture portrayed a deeply moving true experience: the time when Froman, on crutches and back again with the USO in May 1945, managed to bring a "hopelessly" shell-shocked young soldier out of his trance for the first time. "It was so stirring," Froman remembered, "to be able to make a shell-shocked boy walk and talk when the doctors couldn't, when the nurses couldn't. Oh, brother!"

In recreating the incident, Walter Lang and Zanuck agreed that the proper casting of the boy's role was crucial. Both wanted a comparative unknown, to lend reality to one of the picture's most touching episodes. Zanuck was also shrewd enough to realize that the role could turn that unknown into a valuable property for the studio if, of course, the boy was able to deliver.

After a search, twenty-one-year-old Robert (R. J.) Wagner was the unanimous choice to play the boy, a role listed in the cast sheets as simply "GI Paratrooper." Wagner—who had come to Los Angeles from Detroit and caddied for the stars at the Bel Air Country Club—had had no formal acting training when Twentieth had signed him to a "stock" contract. Up to now, his main achievement had been a fourth-billed role in the Richard Widmark starrer *The Halls of Montezuma*. Now the stunning impact he'd make in *With a Song in My Heart* would set him on the road to stardom.

Bob credits Susan for his success. "When Zanuck put me in that picture," he recalls, "he said it would be the greatest thing I'd ever do, because people would walk out of the theater and ask, 'Who is that guy?' That's true, you know, but when I did it, I had no idea of how it all worked or what was going to happen. And Susan was marvelous to me.

"Before I did the picture, I used to see Susan Hayward on the lot all the time. She was a very big star, and I was just a young kid starting out, but even before we worked together I remember her being so very nice to me—so very, very gracious.

"The Jane Froman role was a very difficult and demanding role for her—to have to 'sing' with all those playbacks, and act a living person. Because Walter Lang, the director, liked me, I was permitted to watch the recordings and be around the music department and all, to get the feeling of things.

"Everything I did in the picture was with Susan. Our first scene together was at the theater where she is appearing in *Artists and Models*, and she calls me to the stage and sings 'Embraceable You.' Then, later on, she recognizes me, a shell-shocked victim in one of the hospitals at which she's performing. It was a very moving thing, because the guy was real and the scene a real incident.

"The thing about that moment was, I didn't know very much what I was doing. You know, they say that young actors or child stars who don't know much about what they're doing are sometimes better. Well, Walter Lang said to me, 'Just watch her. . . .' There's an old saying in our business—one I've often used—that goes, 'It's like working with Rin Tin Tin . . . you just pull the cat out of the bag and the ears will go up.' That's what they used to do with Rin Tin Tin. When they wanted his ears to go up, they'd have a guy standing offstage with a cat in a bag . . . and then let the cat out at the crucial moment. For me, Susan was the best 'cat' I could possibly have had, because when she started to work, I automatically responded. I didn't know how to put the proper emotions across. What she did was produce a whole reaction in me.

"I didn't go home and start to rehearse the part and say to myself, 'Now I have to get tears in my eyes,' because I didn't know how to do that. She must have realized that because, my God, she was so helpful, and it was such a marvelous real moment. When she sang 'I'll Walk Alone' to me in the hospital scene, I got so caught up in the moment that the tears just came. It got to her too—because after it was over, she ran to her dressing room and just came apart.

"Whenever I saw her after that—at the premiere of *The Robe*, for example—she couldn't have been nicer. She was terrific to me always. A few years later, a couple of gossip columnists decided to link our names—but that's a lot of bull. I had a lot of respect for her—always—but it was a totally professional relationship."

Robert Wagner also remembers meeting Ellen Marrenner during the filming—one of the few times Susan ever invited her mother to the lot. And Jane Froman recalls the twins being brought to the set during the big production number featuring the title song: "Susan's attitude toward them was so adult. She treated them like little men . . . with courtesy, charm, and humor."

Over the years, many of the directors who had worked with Susan had admired her ability to lose herself in a role, to actually become the character she was portraying in the film. On the testimony of Wagner, Froman, and others, it is apparent that for the first time in her career, Susan was projecting a *behind-the-scenes* warmth that endeared her to everyone connected with the picture.

She was a model of cooperation. Although she had a clause in her contract forbidding the studio to cut her hair for any role, she herself suggested it be done for this film.

Director Walter Lang would say, shortly before his death in 1972, "I found Susan to be a most dedicated actress, one with great talent—wonderful to work with—one of the screen's greatest stars."

Rory Calhoun, cast as airline pilot John Burn, the man who became Froman's second husband, had admired Susan when he co-starred with her in *I'd Climb the Highest Mountain*. By *With a Song in My Heart*, admiration had turned to adoration. When asked by Merv Griffin in 1972 if there were any players he remembered with special fondness, Rory quickly replied: "Yes, Susan Hayward." As with Wagner, however, the relationship did not extend beyond the studio walls. Only one member of the cast would become a close friend and dinner guest: Brooklyn-born Thelma Ritter, who played her nurse.

On August 10, coinciding with the national release of *David and Bathsheba*, Susan left the set early to get to Hollywood in time to place her footprints in cement in the forecourt of Grauman's Chinese Theater. For the first and only time, the cement was sprinkled with gold dust, in anticipation of the profits the studio expected to make on Hayward pictures.

When *With a Song in My Heart* was released in April of 1952, the accolades Susan received were as lavish as the film itself.

Look magazine praised: "In *With a Song in My Heart*, Susan Hayward steps into the character of singer—World War II heroine Jane Froman and makes her so alive that from now on the two women will be one in the public's mind. . . . All in all, Susan Hayward, with the warmth and range of the artist she has become, makes the Froman story a convincing experience."

David Hanna of the *Hollywood Reporter* applauded: "*With a Song in My Heart* is a picture with everything—great stories, great songs, and great performances. Susan Hayward is warm and lovely as Jane Froman." And *Variety* echoed: "Susan Hayward responds to the [Walter] Lang direction in first-rate fashion.

She punches over the vocal simulation and deftly handles the dramatic phases." In all, in critic Helen Bower's words, the role was "far and away the best role Miss Hayward has ever done—and she had plenty to challenge her talents."

Only Bosley Crowther of the *New York Times* struck a discordant note: "We have to report that Lamar Trotti, who wrote and produced the film, Walter Lang, who directed, and Susan Hayward, who plays the leading role—have combined to do a job that is just about as grandiose and mawkish as Hollywood homage can be. . . . Miss Hayward makes it unmistakably clear that chin-up and eyes-on-the-horizon are the attitudes she wants to get across. One would not call her performance either subtle or restrained. And in her pantomiming of the heroine's delivery of songs, she does it as though she was conscious of performing for posterity."

Mr. Crowther was definitely a minority of one. Had his eyes been as sharp as his tongue, however, he would have really had something to write about.

Bob Wagner laughs as he recalls: "One of the theater owners wrote in, terribly shocked, saying that one of Susan's breasts fell out of her dress in one of the numbers. Now, in 1952, that was pretty heady stuff. I went with Walter Lang and Lamar Trotti to the projection room, and we looked at it over and over and over again—and couldn't find it.

"Finally, in the Movieola, you could see it in just a couple of frames—in a number in which she was dancing with Dick Allen."

With hundreds of prints in distribution and the film breaking house records throughout the country, the studio was faced with a dilemma. Apart from the expense of recalling and reediting the film, the attendant publicity would not have been the kind Zanuck wanted associated with an inspirational family film. So the eagle-eyed exhibitor got a new print, and the studio gambled on no one else's being able to spot the offending frame. No one did—not even the Hays office, that notorious protector of moviegoers' morality.

In April of 1952, Susan was riding high. Between the shooting and the screening of the film, however, a great many things had occurred—not all of them pleasant.

chapter 12

I introduced Susan to Howard Hughes in 1938. She cooked him a chicken dinner. He disliked her intensely. She disliked him. That was that.

BEN MEDFORD

HOWARD HUGHES had been aware of Susan Hayward's development for years, but it wasn't until she had signed with Zanuck and starred as the sensuous Bathsheba that his interest became truly aroused. Maybe it was time for another chicken dinner.

In addition, Hughes, and producer Jerry Wald—who would later become the head of Twentieth Century-Fox—had seen a rough cut of *With a Song in My Heart*. Both were acutely aware of Hayward's box-office lure, particularly with women, and that's exactly what an upcoming production of theirs, *This Man Is Mine*, sorely needed. So, mixing business with pleasure, Hughes resolved to "borrow" Susan.

This involved a little horse trading. Hughes owned Jane Russell's contract, and Zanuck wanted *her* for a projected musical of *Gentlemen Prefer Blondes*, which would co-star Marilyn Monroe, whom Zanuck was building toward stardom. If I can have Russell, Zanuck told Hughes, you can have your pick of the Twentieth Century-Fox ladies. Done, said Hughes. In point of fact, he had had his pick of Twentieth's women for some time. He had already made a minicareer of romancing such Zanuck stars as Gene Tierney, Jean Peters, and Linda Darnell, among others. There was, in fact, an industrywide joke that Hughes

126

didn't need a little black book, he merely had to check the obliging Zanuck's contract list.

In any case, Hughes promptly selected Susan, and Susan found herself perplexed as to why she was being exiled to RKO for *This Man Is Mine*. Any one of a dozen starlets could have played the part of Arthur Kennedy's wife in what was essentially a man's picture. In fact, its rodeo sequences would so far outshine the picture's rather tame domestic triangle that, when the film was released in late October, it would be more suitably titled *The Lusty Men*. Susan felt misused, even though guaranteed top billing.

She also did not get along at all with her chief co-star, Robert Mitchum. The script called for a great deal of antagonism between her character, Louise, and Mitchum's Jeff, and the emotion required no great acting ability on either part. Although respectful of his professionalism, Susan was turned off by Bob's boisterous behavior and off-color language. She was not amused when, seeing her walk by on the way to the set, he'd bellow, "There goes the old gray mare." She was even less amused when Mitchum tried to liven up their working hours by eating garlic before their intimate scenes. Soon her complaints reached to the top.

Hughes was sorry. He couldn't control Mitchum's mischievous behavior—nobody could at that time—but he could and did make certain that both on the lot and on location Susan was otherwise accorded a treatment usually reserved for visiting royalty. The courtesies mollified Susan—and piqued her curiosity.

The details of Susan's first private meeting with Howard Hughes are unrecorded, and it is highly unlikely that their affair began during the filming of *The Lusty Men*. For all his bizarre behavior and varied sexual exploits, Hughes had an almost prudish morality in some ways, which included a self-imposed proviso against bedding another man's wife. However, he was well aware of the problems in her marriage, and he probably concluded it was only a matter of time until she was free. Meanwhile, he made himself agreeable, exercising his not inconsiderable charm in her presence, and let matters take their course.

Before long, word of Hughes's interest in Susan leaked out, and came to the attention of the formidable Hedda Hopper, who requested (demanded) that Susan come to tea at her house.

Susan resisted. Although there was no open hostility between her and Hopper, Susan was still extremely loyal to her friend Louella Parsons—anything important was said to Louella first—and, besides, she resented being summoned to Hopper's house as if she were still a schoolgirl or struggling starlet. She agreed to meet Hopper for lunch at the studio if it was absolutely necessary, but she had no intention of making house calls. Hopper, for her part, was equally adamant that the interview be conducted in the privacy of her own den—without publicity people or interruptions. And she knew how to get her way.

Hopper promptly called Harry Brand at Twentieth Century-Fox publicity and promised him a spread on Susan in the king-size *Graphic* magazine of the *Chicago Tribune*, with subsequent syndication by the Chicago Tribune Syndicate, if he would get Susan to her house. They'd talk at length about *With a Song in My Heart,* she indicated. Aware this could mean a million dollars' worth of free publicity for the forthcoming film, Brand guaranteed Susan would be at Hopper's door at the appointed time even if Zanuck himself had to carry her over his shoulder. Fortunately, such drastic measures were not necessary.

Susan appeared at Hopper's manse looking and acting every inch the star. True to her word, Hopper did talk to Susan at length about Jane Froman, *With a Song in My Heart,* and other career matters (all of which were dutifully recorded in print), but with that out of the way she was free to zero in on more personal topics. Hopper would write:

> Susan Hayward is one of the most gorgeous girls in the star line-up. And when high frequency sex is needed in a starring role, Hayward is the girl who can deliver it. This redhead, whose perfect profile runs clear to the ankles, epitomizes everything a man looks for in a woman. . . . Susan's the perfect location for a mink coat. If you toss in a sky-blue scarf, four diamond wedding rings, a huge mirror-cut solitaire . . . she looked like wolf bait, and we promptly got into the subject.

Miss Hopper, of course, had one particular wolf on her mind. Too shrewd to name names, however, she hoped that Susan could be led unwarily into the trap. But Hopper, it seems, had met her match.

"Wolves," countered Susan. "Do we have any wolves in this

town? I wouldn't know! I'm a happily married woman and the mother of large and active twins who manage to keep very much in evidence. What wolf wouldn't be very much discouraged with such a setup!

"A woman gets back what she invites, largely. Remember, the woman is always the aggressor, although it is her wily way to make the man believe he has thought of the whole thing. That is part of nature's plan. I happen to be a very happy woman, and I'm not naturally the flirtatious type."

Susan was letting Hopper have it with both barrels.

"My husband is one of the most interesting men I've ever met. That's why he and I are seen so seldom in nightclubs. We find we have better Scotch at home, and if we feel like talking we don't like to be interrupted. It's not unusual for us to sit in our own living room and discuss books, plays, pictures, and life in general all night long if I don't happen to be working the following day. Jess is not only a good actor. He's one of the best. He has humor along with intelligence, and I'm in love with him."

And when Hopper tactlessly referred to the slump in Jess's career and the huge gap in their earnings (Susan had reported $374,000 that year; Jess $665), Susan rushed to his defense, calling it just one of those arid spots that come to all Hollywood actors.

"I could have been one who had to ride it out," she explained. "That would have been more serious as I have less to offer than he. It will be over one of these days when the right part comes up, the part he just has to do. The important thing is not to take a lot of little unimportant things in the interim just to say you're busy. This is harder by far for the one who isn't working than for the one who is; if my turn ever comes, I am certain of Jess's backing and loyalty. Marriage is so many things—it's decency and honor and love and respect. It's hanging onto the solid thing."

So there! Any more questions, Hedda? No? Then I must be leaving. But Susan couldn't quite resist going a little too far. "Money doesn't mean too terribly much to me," she concluded. "Perhaps that's because we have everything we want." But then she made a revealing slip, when she added, regarding a new, jeweled wedding ring Jess was getting for her: "An actress should pick larger stones; you get more for them in a pawn shop if you get into trouble."

Hopper didn't catch it, though, having been snowed under

by the rest of Susan's performance. Hedda Hopper was neither sentimental nor gullible nor prone to show partiality to one of Parsons's pets, but by the time Susan had finished, the columnist had become convinced that all was rosy with the Barkers and that the gossip about Hughes was just rumor. It may have been one of the greatest performances in Susan's life. And there the matter lay—for a while . . .

Actually, Hopper didn't realize what it took to get Susan to come to her house. Susan rarely went *to* anyone, usually they came to *her*. And where they came to was the Twentieth lot. Although her living room was finally livable, she refused to permit reporters, photographers, or press agents into the house. Family photographs, when she allowed them, could be taken only in the garden or at poolside.

Other than that, Fox publicity woman Sonia Wolfson remembers, "Susan Hayward was one of the most cooperative stars I've worked with," and Miss Wolfson, now in retirement, has worked with a great many of them. She has other things to add too about that period in the star's life:

"I was assigned to her when she did *David and Bathsheba* and *With a Song in My Heart* and a couple of other films. I never had any fault to find with her. Susan was very warm to me; she never tried to postpone an interview. I met Jess Barker just once, but I was never in her home. However, she told me that she was a silk sleeper. She only slept on satin sheets and pillowcases. But once a week she'd cream herself all over and put old cotton sheets on her bed. Funny, the odd things you remember . . .

"I don't think Susan ever told me an untruth. When she was in the mood she could be sharp—I mean with a quip, not with a fib. She was very quick on the uptake."

Miss Wolfson would usually ask the stars in her charge to expound about kissing. "Susan had a good sense of humor, and when you got her in the right mood, she would love to be provocative." The essence of Susan's dissertation on kissing was hardly one to endear her to any of her leading men. She insisted that the men who had kissed her for the magazine ads when she was a Thornton model had performed their assignments with more mastery than Gregory Peck, Dana Andrews, Rory Calhoun,

Robert Mitchum, or any of the others with whom she had worked.

"I had a new man in every ad," she told Sonia Wolfson. "And we kissed harder and longer for those stills than was ever permitted for a movie. That was my education. I kissed more guys and never saw them again. I remember some of those poses got my back out of whack a couple of times—once so severely that the doctor bill was bigger than my modeling fee. It's interesting, but none of those male models I worked with made it to Hollywood. I guess I must have ruined them."

Susan made sure to add that none of the male models ever "made it" with *her,* either.

Sonia Wolfson has no idea of what caused the friction between Susan Hayward and Darryl Zanuck. She does speculate, though, from her many years at Twentieth Century-Fox:

"Maybe she kept turning him down. He was the one who tried to get every girl on the lot to sleep with him. Some of the gals told me things they wouldn't tell anyone else. And what they said and what he said—well, they're totally different stories.

"Maybe Zanuck kept trying to make passes at Susan, and she wouldn't respond to his advances. That would certainly leave him with an unpleasant feeling about her . . .

"But the wardrobe girls, the make-up men, the crew—they all seemed to like her very much. I never heard any of them say an unkind thing about her."

Something else stands out in Sonia Wolfson's mind: Shortly after Susan checked back at Fox after her loan-out to RKO for *The Lusty Men,* Susan said ambiguously: "You know, Sonia, there are times when the grass looks greener. . . ."

And there was one other portent of the future: about that time, Dana Andrews's business manager, who was also Susan's, came to him and said, according to Andrews, "I don't know what I'm going to do about that girl. She insists on filing an income tax return separate from Jess Barker's and, even though I've yelled until I'm sick that she could save a *lot* of money by filing a joint return, she's too damn stubborn to do it. . . . Dana, she always liked you, and she'll listen to you even if she won't listen to me. *Try* to persuade her to file joint returns from now on."

Andrews said he'd try. He called the studio and made a date to see her for lunch. He then launched into every argument he could think of to get her to file jointly with Jess Barker. She finally stopped him and said something like: "But Jess and I are having problems, and if I file jointly and then subsequently divorce him, he can lay claim to half of everything I've got— which he doesn't deserve."

"Then," Andrews said, "I gave what may be the worst advice I ever gave to anyone. I took her hand and kindly but firmly told her: 'Susie . . . you and Jess have had problems for years, but you've always weathered them, and there's *no* reason to believe you won't again. It's wrong for you to waste so much money on a separate return when it's so unnecessary. You know I'm thinking of what's best for you. Won't you do as I ask?'

"She hesitated, then smiled and said: 'Of course, Dana. You're right, I know.' "

Andrews laughed. "It wasn't long after that that the Barkers were telling it to the judge. . . ."

chapter 13

BY THE START of 1953, Susan was on the verge of a nervous collapse, although she wouldn't face up to it. Since signing with Zanuck, she had made nine films nonstop. Irritable and exhausted—"Whatever it is you want, the answer is *no!*" a studio aide remembers her snapping—she now found falling asleep impossible without the aid of pills, and was smoking up to four packs of cigarettes a day to relieve the tension.

Yet on the surface everything seemed to be going her way. Joseph Schenck, controlling the fortunes of Twentieth Century-Fox from New York, boasted, "On the basis of our investment alone, Susan Hayward is our most valuable player. We've tied up nearly one quarter of our studio budget on her." And the investment was earning out. In 1952 alone, Susan's films returned a then-outstanding eleven million dollars. The reports on *The Snows of Kilimanjaro*, released in September, were still coming in, and *The President's Lady* (with Charlton Heston) and *White Witch Doctor* (with Robert Mitchum) were being readied for distribution. Zanuck was a happy man.

Throughout January and February of 1953, Susan was showered with honors.

The magnetic power of Hayward's box-office appeal had carried her from nineteenth place in the 1951 *Motion Picture Herald* Poll of American Theater Owners to ninth in 1952; Doris Day, in seventh position, was the only other woman on the list. *Box Office* magazine chose Susan as the most popular star of 1952.

At Twentieth Century-Fox, she soared ahead of Betty Grable as the Number One fan-mail draw, although Susan rarely looked at her fan mail and almost never answered it. She let studio secretaries take care of paid requests for photographs. The idea of paying a private secretary out of her own salary appalled her.

Her public took no offense.

With a Song in My Heart and her performance as Jane Froman were overwhelmingly voted *Photoplay*'s Gold Medal winners, coveted awards in the film community. Gary Cooper, with whom she had worked as an obscure ingenue in *Beau Geste,* won the award for most popular male star for *High Noon.* Only one thing spoiled her enjoyment. *Photoplay* always featured its winners on the cover of its announcement issue, but this year, its editors inexplicably chose to use Jane Powell instead. For fifteen years Susan had wanted to appear on the covers of *Photoplay, Modern Screen,* and *Life* magazine. All ran and would run articles on her, and she would appear on the front of other magazines, yet she was consistently passed over as "cover material" by these three giants. Not even her box-office appeal could alter the situation. And now, when she should have had the cover of *Photoplay* guaranteed, she had been passed over. What she considered a deliberate slight understandably diminished her appreciation of the award.

Nevertheless, when *Photoplay* held its awards party in the Crystal Room of the Beverly Hills Hotel on February 9, she was there. Sylvia (Mrs. Irving) Wallace, West Coast editor of the magazine, buzzed about, making sure everything was running smoothly. This biographer, covering the story, was recruited as an official hostess; greeting the guests and assigning them to their table, in Susan's case the dais.

Magnificently gowned in an egg-shell lace gown with tight bodice and bouffant skirt, wearing elbow-length white gloves and large diamond clips, Susan was breathtakingly beautiful. Zanuck escorted her into the reception room, where the photographers were waiting. Jess hovered uncomfortably in the background.

The photographers' attention, however, was abruptly diverted by the late arrival of Marilyn Monroe (who had been voted the most popular newcomer of the year), escorted by the diminutive gossip columnist Sidney Skolsky. Marilyn was shrewdly attired in a skin-tight gold lamé gown—which, to everyone's amusement and delight, fell apart at the seams before she even got to the table. The proceedings were delayed and flash bulbs popped as Marilyn was sewn back into her dress in full view of everyone: producers, stars, and the press.

Susan never got their attention back. Monroe, whose first starring picture *Niagara* had opened a few weeks earlier, was the evening's sensation, all the while innocently protesting embarrassment about the dress. Furious, Susan was overheard voicing her conviction that Zanuck had been a co-conspirator in the stunt. Indeed, had he wished, Zanuck could have insisted that Marilyn be decently dressed for the occasion—but he was wise to the ways of building a new sex symbol. Susan received her gold medal, then left the party as quickly and quietly as possible.

A week later, on February 15, she gracefully accepted another award, this time with no disruption: the gold "Henrietta" given by the Foreign Press Association as the World's Favorite Screen Star of 1952. Appropriately, she took the occasion happily to tell the assembled journalists that she soon would be realizing a lifelong dream—her first trip abroad.

In 1951, she and Jess had made plans for a European holiday, but then had had them cancelled when Zanuck wouldn't allow her sufficient time away from the studio. Now she felt secure enough to turn a deaf ear to his pleas to stay home and represent the studio at the Academy Awards.

For the first time in their history, on March 19, 1953, the awards were going to be seen on nationwide television, and to Zanuck's chagrin no Twentieth Century-Fox production was in competition for Best Picture. Only three times before during his reign—1936, 1939, and 1945—had there been such an oversight. He had been certain that one of his three blockbusters that year—*Viva Zapata, My Cousin Rachel,* and *With a Song in My Heart*—would be one of the top five, and to be passed over in favor of *The Greatest Show on Earth* (the ultimate winner), *High Noon, Ivanhoe, Moulin Rouge,* and Republic's *The Quiet Man* was galling. He concluded (probably accurately) that his three films had split the Twentieth vote and thereby cancelled one another out.

If Zanuck couldn't be a factor in the Best Picture category, however, he could at least be represented at the ceremonies by his stars. The problem was that he couldn't depend on Brando, still steaming over the injustice of being the only member of *A Streetcar Named Desire* cast snubbed the previous year. Newcomer Burton and old-timer Quinn had promised to be there, but neither could be relied on, and the studio needed coverage. Susan was his best hope.

All his efforts to persuade her to change her mind, however, failed.

"Look," she said adamantly, "I attended twice, and lost twice. And had to explain to some of those vultures who had been dying for me to lose, how 'there'll always be a next day.' Well, I'm not going to make a television spectacle of myself in front of a few million viewers, and that's that!"

Susan's attitude was based, not only on a need for a vacation, but on some cold calculation. The previous December, Shirley Booth had won the New York Film Critics' Award on the first ballot, and none of the other Oscar nominees had received a single vote, herself included. For all Zanuck's optimism, and the other awards Susan had won that year, she knew that that vote would influence the Academy. "Uncommercial," Booth might be, but she was the one with the edge for the Oscar. So she might as well go ahead with the trip as planned, Susan figured.

On February 23, Zanuck grumpily wished Susan bon voyage, though he couldn't help adding that she still would have had three weeks abroad if she should change her mind and return for the Oscars. Susan smiled.

In New York, the Barkers boarded separate planes for Paris. To a perplexed reporter, she said, matter-of-factly, "We always travel on separate planes as protection for the boys. After all, if one plane crashes, there would still be someone to look after Tim and Greg." (While they were away, they planned to have Ellen Marrenner look after the boys.)

The flight to Paris in those pre-jet days took twelve hours, and Susan had much to think about—most particularly her marriage. In five months she and Jess would be celebrating their ninth wedding anniversary, practically a record according to Hollywood standards—Lana Turner had already gone through four husbands and God knew how many lovers. No matter how angry Susan had become at Jess over the years, it had never led her to seek vengeance by being unfaithful. And, unlike her father, Jess had never sought outside feminine companionship as balm for his bruised ego. Had he done so, word would have reached Louella—and "well-meaning" Louella would certainly have passed the information to Susan. There were times, to her own amazement, when Susan almost did wish that Jess were seeing someone else. Then she could at least justify a divorce— even if she still wasn't totally sure that was what she wanted.

What she did want, undeniably, was a working husband. And Jess hadn't had a job in over thirty months. In November he had been up for a lead on television—it had seemed like such a certainty that she had told Louella about it, prompting Parsons to comment in her destructive motherly way: "Susan Hayward may find things a lot less strained around her house now that hubby Jess Barker has been lined up to star in a new TV series." The series, however, had gone down the drain.

A great many jobs Jess was up for had done likewise. Susan wanted a working husband, but her relationship to Jess Barker often was the reason for his *not* working. Later an unattributed friend of his would say in a *Motion Picture* article, "Producers looked at him oddly when he tried to get work. 'So he wants a job and his wife makes $400,000 a year?' They'd give the part to someone else who needed the work to pay the rent.

"Or he'd be sent a script that someone wanted Susie for and tell him if he could interest her in it, there might be a part in the picture for him. It was like throwing a bone to a hungry dog. And Jess wasn't interested in getting a job that way."

Prior to their leaving for Europe, Jess had told a writer friend of his, "I'd give my life for Susan." The friend had used that line in another *Motion Picture* story and added a tag line: "In a way he has."

"Susan was burned up about that story," Jess remembers. "My friend denied writing it, and it didn't have his by-line, but I know who did it."

Jess doesn't elaborate as to why Susan was so angry. Perhaps she hated to face that realization on a printed page: *"In a way he has."* Or perhaps she was guilt-ridden about her own ambivalent feelings at the time—guilt feelings that were intensified by an indirect pitch from Howard Hughes.

It was about then that one of Hughes's "aides," by-passing Susan's agent Ned Marin, as well as the mighty Zanuck, had let Susan know that Hughes had been so impressed with her work in *The Lusty Men* that he was considering her for the lead in an upcoming multimillion-dollar epic. The aide, notorious for being one of Hughes's prolific procurers, had also hinted that his boss's interest went beyond her talent, adding, not too subtly, "Too bad you're tied up."

It was a great temptation. Both Hughes's charm and wealth held a powerful fascination for Susan and, of all the opportunities she had had since marrying Jess, this was the only one that gave her pause. She was well aware of his reputation as a ladies' man—his well-reported liaisons with Billie Dove, Katharine Hepburn, Ida Lupino, Olivia de Havilland, Lana Turner, Ava Gardner, and the current Jean Peters, among many others, had provided ample evidence of that. But still . . . what if she were to accept?

It was in that state of mind that Susan approached Orly Airport. Still, it could not have occupied all of her attention. This was, after all, a vacation she had dreamed about all her life. A war, then motherhood, then a career had made it an impossibility. Perhaps that was a blessing. She was coming to Paris not as a green kid or a wide-eyed tourist to be shoved around, but as a glamourous star, newly chosen the world's favorite actress.

Exhausted from the long trip, and concerned as always about her appearance, Susan spent a long time in the ladies' room upon arrival, repairing her make-up and hair, in order to make a dazzling entrance into Paris. Jess's flight had set down an hour earlier, and he was there to meet her. They were pleased to learn that Twentieth Century-Fox's Paris branch had assigned affable, twenty-three-year-old Jean Papote to serve as a combination guide, chauffeur, translator, and press secretary for their stay abroad, also that a low-slung Jaguar had been placed at their disposal. Although Zanuck was annoyed at Susan for not remaining in Hollywood for the Oscar presentations, he was not vindictive.

He was also aware that a good impression abroad would add to the European grosses of her movies, and he had some plans for Europe himself. Studio assets abroad were still being frozen by many countries in desperate need of postwar funds—all monies had to be spent in their countries of origin—but Darryl Zanuck had definite ideas about their eventual use. Because of his passion for his new CinemaScope process, he was planning to produce many films in their actual locales—a sure-fire way of luring viewers away from their tiny black and white television screens.

The Barkers remained at the Lancaster Hotel three days. Paris in February offered little enjoyment. Planning to return in April, they headed for Spain with Papote. "He was a funny little man," Jess recalls today. "Whenever we approached a town, he increased our speed so we'd get through it as quickly as possible. He was in Paris during the Nazi occupation and that had something to do with it." Equipped with Rollei and Stereo cameras, they toured the château country and southern France, photographing all the historic sights enroute, then crossed the border into Spain.

Susan's postcard to her mother read: "Cased every castle in the country. Looking forward to the bullfights."

In mid-March, Susan and Jess arrived in Valencia, where they were the honored guests of the mayor and were escorted by a protective if rather sinister-looking man named Señor La Fuente —"an eighteen-dollars-a-month branch manager for Twentieth," says Jess—to the *corrida*. The weather in Valencia was as chilly and penetrating as it had been in Paris, and Susan had wrapped herself in her full-length mink, with wrist-length white gloves and dark glasses—highly noticeable, to say the least. Toreador Julio Aparicio dedicated his first bull to her as she watched the fights from her front-row seat, and La Fuente explained the finer points of the action as Jess, ignored, and nauseated by the slaughter, regretted not remaining at the hotel. After the fights, Susan was photographed between La Fuente and toreador Antonete. Jess Barker was unceremoniously shoved into the background. Totally unknown in Spain, Jess was inevitably addressed as "Señor Hayward" and treated with even more indifference than Jean Papote.

A few days later, the Barkers ran into Betsy Blair and Gene Kelly touring the peninsula with their little girl Kerry, which stimulated thoughts of their own two boys. That night they put in a call to Tim and Greg in California and were reassured both were happy and in good health.

Leaving Spain soon after, the Barkers, still with Papote in tow, toured the Mediterranean before heading for Italy. Checking into the Grand Hotel in Rome, Susan was handed a wire informing her that Shirley Booth had, as anticipated, won the best-actress Oscar.

"So much for that," she commented, shrugging. "Thank God I didn't listen to Zanuck."

Rome was chaotic. Susan couldn't leave her suite without being besieged by reporters. Photographers dogged her every move, rudely pushing Jess aside, shouting, screaming, and generally behaving in a manner unique to the Italian press. Their American counterparts weren't much better. Those who couldn't get interviews let their imaginations go wild inventing such fantasies as:

There were moonlight nights with Jess, near the Colosseum; love-filled nights on the banks of the Arno, that picturesque river which snakes its winding paths from the Apennines in Central Italy west to Pisa. The Barkers are truly one of Hollywood's few happily married young couples. When two people are as ecstatically happy as Susan and Jess are here in Italy, they've reached the perfect pattern for life!

The night before this idyllic portrait appeared, Susan, according to testimony given two years later by Jess, had taken an overdose of sleeping pills. News of the incident was miraculously kept from the press, however, and an Italian doctor bribed to maintain his silence and attribute his visit to an upset stomach due to exotic food.

It is not known why Susan took the overdose. It might well have been an accident, though it ominously foreshadowed future events, and certainly her insistence on staying in Rome for a full ten days indicates a quick recovery. The next day she was up and about. But it was evident that she was becoming overly dependent on the dangerous yellow capsules.

By now Susan had become enervated by the tedium of motoring, Papote's incessant conversation—he was invaluable for arranging hotel accommodations and negotiating purchases, but his presence could get wearing—and the variables of spring weather. Instructing Papote to drive the Jaguar back to France, they took a flight to Paris, where they again checked into the Lancaster.

April in Paris was not quite the way the song had described it. The hotel provided all the luxurious little touches befitting a movie queen, but Jess was still frequently addressed as "Monsieur Hayward," which nettled. Susan, for her part, found her spirits in a state of fluctuation. She became totally enraged, for instance, by the hotel's telephone system, which turned her attempts to contact the twins in North Hollywood into the Battle of Waterloo. Used to her behavior by now, Jess explained to a reporter: "She seldom keeps any of her problems to herself. When she gets into a mood, I don't barge in and break the spell because I know within a short time she would bring up the subject herself. Not that I cater to the moods. I just consider them."

One of the moods he had to consider was her reluctance to spend money, a hangover from Brooklyn. ("Susan always seemed to have a fixation about money," her sister Florence later said. "She said to me once that she was going to keep working and working and making money because maybe something would happen some day . . . she would lose some of it or she wouldn't be able to make as much as she has now.") One afternoon she and Jess went shopping on the Rue de Rivoli. She had planned to buy a dozen pairs of gloves all in different lengths, but the prices appalled her. When the saleswoman translated the francs into dollars, she stomped out of the salon muttering, "I can get them for half the price at Robinson's [a Beverly Hills department store]."

Since Susan also felt children's clothing and toys were selling at ridiculous prices, she decided to pick up the boys' gifts in New York. Explaining her thriftiness, she frankly admitted: "When you're traveling on studio expense, it's one thing. When you're vacationing on your own, it's blood money." "Spends it like molasses," Jess wisecracked. She did find a couple of antique fans in an out-of-the-way shop, but other than those, and a singing bird in a miniature gold-plated cage, she bought nothing.

Because she was not required to be back in Hollywood for several weeks, she toyed with the possibility of flying to London and then on to Ireland for a few days, but rejected that idea. She also rejected an invitation from the Cannes Film Festival, explaining how anxious she was to get back to her boys. That was probably true. What was even more true, however, was that being with Jess day and night was beginning to get on her nerves. The trip abroad had solved nothing. As far as she was concerned, she was just going through the motions. She didn't know how or when things would finally come to an end, but her emotions now told her that the end would not be long in coming.

chapter 14

ON APRIL 18, Susan boarded a Pan Am Clipper for her flight back to the States, with Jess following a few hours behind on a TWA Constellation. Instead of flying straight to California, however, she stayed in New York to promote *The President's Lady,* a film about the romance between Andrew Jackson and his wife Rachel Donelsen Jackson made from the Irving Stone best seller, and due to open at the Astor Theater in May.

Charlton Heston, who played Jackson, today recalls their relationship as being "very easy" and "a cordial working ambiance." "Cordial" was about the best that many of the critics could say about their performances as well, the *New York Times*'s Crowther noting that "the stars make sincere and energetic but hardly memorable protagonists," and *Time* magazine finding that "in its writing, direction and acting, it comes out as a too-slick biography film."

Fortunately for Susan, the West Coast trade papers were kinder—the *Hollywood Reporter* gushing, "Miss Hayward is nothing less than wonderful as Rachel. She draws out all the tragedy of a woman who gallantly showed forbearance under the most unbelievable of insults and skillfully she imbues the role with a gaiety and fire that is captivating"—and the grosses looked promising. By and large, audiences ignored the criticisms and flocked to the box office.

Susan was in no mood to look at the grosses, however. Not only were her marital problems weighing on her mind, but she'd just heard some very disturbing news. Whenever she came to New York, she spent time with Sara Little, who'd remained her very close friend throughout all those years. On this trip, Sara confided that her sister Martha had contracted cancer and the doctors had given her just a few more months to live.

Susan, who'd known Martha since their teens, was devastated by the news and by Martha's appearance. "The doctors here aren't gods," she insisted. "I've heard of doctors in California who have had remarkable results with your kind of malignancy. Get packed. I'm taking you back to the coast."

When Martha protested that she was able to afford neither the trip nor the high-priced specialists, Susan cut her off with, "Let me worry about that."

Martha finally agreed to be a houseguest in Sherman Oaks; she was desperate for any chance of survival. In the following months, Susan spent a minimum of five thousand dollars on medical expenses for her, but whenever Martha protested about being a bother, Susan told her, "Believe me, Martha, you're the least of my burdens." And even though she had been informed by the specialists that Martha's chances were exceedingly slim, she continued to radiate optimism about Martha's recovery in her presence, doing everything in her power to make her feel better.

Susan, in fact, was so preoccupied with her friend that she was oblivious to the changes that had taken place at Twentieth Century-Fox.

No longer was she queen of the lot. Despite her film successes, the meteoric rise of Marilyn Monroe under the careful on- and off-screen grooming of Darryl Zanuck, had put her in the shade, and now, in a stunningly short period of time, she had been dethroned. It was but another example of the mercurialness of Hollywood. Zanuck still valued her, but he had found a new toy, and Susan's remaining movies under contract to him were, to put it politely, second-rate.

In early May, Susan reported to the studio to portray the wicked Messalina, wife of the Roman senator Claudius in *The Story of Demetrius*. In 1953, Zanuck had announced, with much fanfare, the introduction of wide-screen CinemaScope projection, and with it the first-ever CinemaScope production, an epic called *The Robe* about the aftermath of the Crucifixion. Imperiously, Zanuck had proclaimed, "Hollywood will rise and fall on the success of *The Robe*" and, as an incentive to theater owners to undergo the expensive conversion process, promised a steady flow of CinemaScope films.

As it turned out, though *The Robe* did not actually shake Hollywood to its foundations, it was promising enough to encourage Zanuck to immediately begin making a sequel, even before the first movie was released—and *The Story of Demetrius* was it. Actually, it was a no-lose situation for Zanuck. Since *Demetrius* picked up exactly where *The Robe* left off—the last few minutes of the film were even replayed in *Demetrius*'s pre-credit sequence—producer Frank Ross was able to keep his budget down by utilizing many of the expensive sets of *The Robe* and the costumes that had been created for the proverbial cast of thousands were simply recycled: when you've seen one toga or Roman breastplate, you've seen them all.

Casting Susan as the sadistic, sinful Messalina, however, was hardly the right move to endear the film to a public who had adored her as the courageous Jane Froman and the gentle, loving Rachel Jackson. In an abortive attempt to soften audience reaction, scriptwriter Philip Dunne hoked up a climax where, after the assassination of Caligula, Messalina emerges a reformed woman and devoted wife to the newly crowned Emperor Claudius. It is all supposedly very heart-warming, and hardly authentic—as best as we can tell today, Messalina was a trollop who lived and died without a twinge of guilt—and the audience, when the film was released in September, would not buy it.

During the filming itself, Susan was, even for her, abnormally quiet and withdrawn. Before the cameras, her scenes with Victor Mature were as torrid as the censor would allow, but, Mature recalls, "After director Delmer Daves yelled 'cut,' she just wandered forlornly back to her dressing room.

"Susan acted like someone a hundred years old. I didn't know what the trouble was. We were practically on a 'Mr. Mature' and 'Miss Hayward' basis, but it was obvious something was worrying her. We all wished we could help her, but we didn't know how to go about trying."

Costume designer Charles LeMaire agrees: "There was a haunting sadness in her eyes," he says. Not even her sexy wardrobe excited her, all "richly embroidered and jeweled . . . and hand-woven of the most clinging, gossamer fabric," says LeMaire.

At the party on the last day of shooting, Susan sat alone,

surrounded with her own little coterie—hairdresser, wardrobe woman, make-up man. She was so withdrawn that Johnny Cook, head of the studio's photo-publicity division, instructed his photographers not to bother her. "I couldn't get near her. I sensed it would be better to keep my distance."

There was indeed a great deal disturbing Susan throughout May and June. She was offended by Zanuck's indifference and his apparent disinterest in her performance in the film. Everyone from Zanuck down to the boys in the mailroom were falling all over themselves to get into Marilyn Monroe's good graces. It was a generally accepted perception, true or not, that Marilyn's explosive rise at Twentieth was the result more of her sexual than her screen performance.

One former employee insisted, "Every afternoon Zanuck had to have his virility assured. It was a compulsive thing." And a director who preferred to remain nameless said, "The single most important thing in Zanuck's life, bigger than movies or success, is sex."

Zanuck, of course, flatly and angrily denied all this, adding, many years later, to his biographer Mel Gussow, "Not even Marilyn Monroe. I hated her. I wouldn't have slept with her if she paid me." Nevertheless, he was hardly blind to her appeal and to her potential for dynamite at the box office. Therefore, while Susan brooded through *Demetrius* (released as *Demetrius and the Gladiators*), Zanuck devoted a lion's share of his attention to the promotion and production of *Gentlemen Prefer Blondes* and *How to Marry a Millionaire*. Whatever free time Zanuck had was spent with a Polish adventuress renamed Bella Darvi, whom he was obstinately determined to turn into the new Garbo. So inept was her acting talent, however, that studio wags referred to her as the "new Garbage."

Generally ignored by Zanuck, Susan's confidence was further eroded with the release of *White Witch Doctor* on July 1, 1953. Edited to a meager ninety-five minutes, this story of a dedicated missionary nurse, circa 1907, and a cynical white hunter, played by Robert Mitchum, was generally labeled a "jungle soap opera." Acerbic Bosley Crowther of the *New York Times*, though intrigued by the Equatorial African atmosphere provided by the second unit, dismissed it as "an amazingly unsurprising romantic adventure moving methodically along well beaten film paths."

The script of her next projected film, Charles Brackett's production of *Garden of Evil,* seemed equally trite. An aging Gary Cooper was cast as the leader of three men hired by Hayward to ride with her through dangerous Indian country to rescue her husband buried in a gold mine cave-in. Shooting was scheduled to begin on location in Uruapan, Mexico, at the end of November, with the wrap planned for early February. Already, the studio, more infatuated with the CinemaScope process they were using than with story credibility, was pouring much of its budget into the shooting site.

The only thing that looked good about the film was the enormous luxury of having all summer and most of the fall off. For the first time since signing with Twentieth Century-Fox, Susan would be able to spend the entire summer with Tim and Gregory. She promised to take them on a long fishing trip. She had been hooked on fishing from the day she had caught her first trout and often remarked that, apart from acting, nothing gave her more pleasure "than spending a day on a stream or river and going after a big one." She had even toyed with the possibility of investing in a cabin cruiser—she certainly could afford one now—but the cost of the upkeep went against her grain. It was a great deal more economical to rent a boat for the day or fish from a public pier.

She planned to do a great deal of fishing that summer. It was the one thing that could help her unwind, and she needed to unwind desperately. Her sleeplessness was leaving her irascible and lethargic. The pressures kept building.

The climax came on July 16, 1953, six days short of her ninth wedding anniversary.

At 11 P.M. all hell broke loose.

After that night there was no turning back.

chapter 15

UNTIL the following February 25, the unsavory details of that nightmarish evening of July 16 would not become public knowledge. During those seven months, gossip, innuendo, and half-truths would keep the local columnists feverishly grinding out copy about the forthcoming Hayward-Barker divorce. Susan would receive the lion's share of sympathy, but several members of the press, led by Sheilah Graham, whom Susan detested, would be on Jess's side.

The morning of July 17, Susan packed a couple of bags and, together with Martha Little and the twins, temporarily moved in with friends. The phone at the Barker house rang incessantly. It remained unanswered.

On July 23, Susan celebrated her ninth wedding anniversary by issuing a terse announcement to the press: "I plan to file for a divorce as soon as possible. I'll leave shortly for a Nevada ranch to establish residence. My brother Walter will accompany me and so will my sons. Reconciliation *seems highly unlikely*. I'm only worried about the pain this will inflict on our two boys, Gregory and Timothy."

From Jess, there was total silence; columnist Erskine Johnson reported that, "Jess Barker is still refusing to make any statements on Susan Hayward's decision to divorce him and refers all question-askers to her."

Susan, however, was unavailable to answer any questions. With her twins in tow, she took off to parts unknown, and on

August 10 Sheilah Graham mysteriously noted, "Not even Twentieth Century-Fox knows where Susan Hayward is."

Two days later, Susan and her sons were back at 3737 Longridge Avenue, surprised there'd been any mystery regarding her whereabouts. "Everybody in Bishop [Nevada] knew we were there. We went fishing every day and to the movies every night." She phoned Darryl Zanuck, assuring him she had changed her mind about setting up residence in Nevada and would file for divorce in Burbank, California, on September 9 instead. This would give them enough time to get proceedings started before she had to leave for Mexico to shoot *Garden of Evil*.

The press still clamored for interviews. Anxious to get Hopper and Graham off her back, Susan paid a private visit to Louella Parsons. As always, Louella proved to be a warm and sympathetic friend. The article she wrote was a four-hankie tearjerker:

> When she came in [wrote Louella], I noticed she was trying to keep one side of her face away from me. "Susie darling, don't do that," I said. "I already know about that black eye Jess gave you. Don't you know by now that I am your friend?"
>
> Suddenly she was in my arms, not crying or sobbing, but holding me tight, just as she used to do when she was one of my little starlets on our stage tour and someone had hurt her feelings. No, she was not crying. The tears had dried up a long time before this or else they were dropping back inside instead of spilling down her face.
>
> That poor eye. So discolored and swollen. The whole side of her face was puffed, distorting one of the loveliest faces in the world.
>
> In a voice so low I had to lean close to hear her, she told me how he [Jess] had beaten her unmercifully, blacking both eyes and bruising her body.
>
> "We had been quarreling," Susan whispered, "and I saw that he was going to slap me. He had slapped me many times, but this time I knew it was going to be worse. His face was distorted with rage. I knew he had lost control of himself. I knew I was in great physical danger." Her lovely red hair was moist against her forehead as she sat talking with me across a table in my playroom. I had ordered coffee,

and she sipped it gratefully. This girl, I realized, was exhausted, not only physically, after the beating she'd taken, but *emotionally* and *spiritually as well*.

Her voice was calmer as she said, "I don't have to tell you that Jess has never contributed any money to my support or to the support of Timothy and Gregory. You know all about that.

"And I know you realize that I was deeply sympathetic with him, at first. I believed him when he said he was an actor and couldn't do anything else. But there must come an end to the unnatural way of living in which the woman is the wage earner and the man sits home with the children. The little boys couldn't understand why I got up early every morning and went to work and Daddy stayed home. It was not that way in the homes of the children they played with. Children can be cruel. I'm sure their playmates often taunted Greg and Timmy about their father's going to the market and driving them to school, when in their homes it was the mother who did these tasks.

"A mother can give her children love and tenderness, but she cannot set the example of a father, a leader—a man who is head of his home. Boys need to respect their fathers, and Jess was letting things ride to the point where he didn't even try to get work—as an actor or anything.

"I was not only terrified when I saw Jess's fury—but I realized he was trying to ruin my face, the very means by which I earn my living." Susan paused, then sadly added, "My reputation is highly valuable to me, or I would not be telling these things against the man I have loved for so many years.

"But I am shocked about some of the terrible stories being circulated about why we separated. What I have told you is the truth.

"Since I first met Jess, there has never been any other man for me, and I really believe there has never been any other woman in his life."

A little sigh escaped Susan; she leaned back against the wall and closed her eyes, as though she were consciously remembering Jess as he was when they first met and fell in love.

"Jess can be so charming. He is handsome and young,

and no one has insisted louder than I that he has real ability as an actor.

"Recently, he has been getting some offers. I hope they keep coming for him. If so, I'm sure Jess will be himself again. He is easily discouraged and he had only three days work in his new picture."*

"If Jess does change, is there any chance of your taking him back, Susan?" I asked. "Perhaps he has learned his lesson."

"No, no," she cried. "Never. It's too late. There have been too many 'lessons,' too many 'new' starts, too many times to forgive. When I could keep things to *myself and no one else knew* about it, I could take it. But this time, no.

"Now that the end has come, I want it over as soon as possible." She picked up her bag and prepared to leave.

She had talked as fully and as much as she could. The wounds were literally so fresh that she could go no further.

But as she rose, she said, "There's just one thing, Louella. Despite the sad memory of what brought on our final break, don't be too bitter against Jess in the future. In every marriage breakup, there are two sides, and I'm not pretending to paint myself as an angel and Jess as a devil.

"I have a temper and a hot tongue, and I work so hard I'm frequently tired and almost sick with nerves. Movie stars are never easy to live with, and no one knows that better than I."

I said, "I suppose a psychiatrist might say that Jess's sudden violence was a defense mechanism against living in a set of circumstances intolerable to a man's pride, or perhaps a guilt complex from doing nothing about the situation.

"Perhaps, Susie," I added as I walked with her to the door, "Jess's violence was not really directed so much against you as it was against himself."

"Maybe," she replied softly. "I don't know. I just know that my marriage is finished and done with—a sorry, shabby ending to many moments of happiness. My heart aches very much, but it is closed forever on the past."

* Unidentified. Perhaps *Marry Me Again* or *Dragonfly Squadron*, both released in 1954.

150

Louella was so unraveled by Susan's story that she was unable to make it to her typewriter without the help of a double Scotch. No matter how ruthless she could be to those she felt had cheated her out of a scoop or had done her any real or imagined wrong, Miss Parsons was enormously gullible when it came to her special pets.

Therefore, it is quite possible that she neither asked—nor was told—about Susan's then-current dinner companion. By then, a thin, dark-headed gentleman was making frequent visits to the little house on Longridge Avenue.

chapter 16

AT FIRST, Susan introduced the "stranger" to Timothy and Gregory as "Mr. Magic."*

Eventually he'd be properly referred to as Mr. Hughes.

Every day, a profusion of fresh-cut flowers would arrive at her doorstep. No card was necessary. Howard Hughes had an extravagant romantic compulsion for smothering his ladies with expensive floral arrangements. These would often be followed by trifles of more tangible value: a diamond ring, an emerald bracelet, an automobile. In some instances, after a romance had run its course, Hughes would even bestow an apartment building or small house on the broken-hearted woman.

Just as eccentric was his alleged habit of bedding only once a beauty he admired, even though their dates might continue for weeks or even months more. Perhaps, for Hughes, it was the pursuit that was all-important, the knowledge that he could go after what he wanted—and get it. Certainly, by all accounts, the women pursued did not mind. Paradoxically, no lady linked with Hughes has ever had an unkind word to say about him— not even after his death.

It would be impossible to try to pinpoint the exact moment Howard Hughes and Susan Hayward became intimate. Throughout his courtship of Susan, Hughes was still being linked publicly with his long-time interest Jean Peters, and starlet Debra Paget was coyly flashing a large diamond ring that Walter

* According to later court testimony.

Winchell, among other columnists, insisted was a trinket from the billionaire. However, knowing Hughes's predilections and Susan's vulnerability at the time—particularly for a man like Hughes—it seems certain that intimate they were, and it was probably during the latter part of 1953.

Certainly Susan's mood improved considerably. That August, less than a few weeks after the dramatic recitation that had so destroyed Louella, Susan was back on the phone to Parsons feeling full of fire and newly returned from an Hawaiian vacation with the boys. "You needn't worry about me," she said. "I'm not running from anything, and I'm not going to cry on anyone's shoulder. All that is over. There have been so many false stories, and I'm not even taking the trouble to deny them. Why should I? I'm going ahead with my career, and I'm going to see that my boys are brought up right. I don't even see Jess anymore."

"There's not a chance in the whole wide world" that she and Jess would get together again, she said. "I know that I should have left Jess a long time ago. He'll be better off without me to depend upon, and I'll be better off not having to worry about him."

Although Louella was too tactful or too fearful to bring up Howard Hughes's name, the tycoon was on her mind when she asked: "Will you marry again?"

Susan kept her cool, replying, "Well, that depends on whether I meet the right person. I think it is silly for any person to say he won't remarry. In the first bitterness of a separation, many people say that they will never remarry, but I don't think that's right. If you'll pardon my being bromidic, time heals everything, and I don't see any reason not to marry again."

Louella, in the mother-hen mood that seemed to overcome her whenever Susan was involved, concluded: "I personally hope that Susan will find happiness. She is an unusual girl—sensitive, high strung, and very proud. She says she is not easily hurt, but that I don't believe. I know how deeply hurt she was when the storm of her broken marriage broke over her head."

Another storm was about to break over Susan's head as well. Just back from her vacation, she was entertaining a few friends on Labor Day weekend when Jess stopped by to spend some time with his sons. It started mildly enough, but the events that followed were of hurricane proportions. As with the night of July 16, the details miraculously remained a private affair until February 25, when it all came out in court.

In the meantime, because of the pending divorce and because the Howard Hughes rumors were too loud to ignore, Zanuck demanded that Susan get out and around with a variety of men to provide a more conventional romantic life, on the surface at least. For instance, she was escorted to the star-studded premiere of *The Robe* at Grauman's Chinese Theater by her agent Ned Marin, a white-haired bear of a bachelor. Marin was often used as a decoy to divert attention from an actress's closet lover.

No one was deceived.

Throughout October, Susan had what columnists alternately referred to as "a strong shoulder to cry on," "a constant companion," "a new romantic interest," or simply, "a new beau." Then, on October 19, Sidney Skolsky revealed that "Jeff Chandler and Susie Hayward don't even go to the hideaway spots, but he does drop in and visit Susie at her valley house." Hedda Hopper observed, "Susan Hayward and Jeff Chandler are a mighty handsome couple." The same day, Erskine Johnson wrote that Susan Hayward and Jeff Chandler "no longer keep it a secret that they are in a romantic whirl"; then, forgetting himself, said in his October 24 column: "Susan Hayward and Jeff Chandler are having secret dates."

Sheilah Graham added her two bits as well, noting in her syndicated bulletin on November 11, "Jeff Chandler's dates with Susan Hayward are getting numerous enough to be serious."

Only Louella Parsons failed to jump on the bandwagon. Unable to dismiss the gossip, she allotted it only two brief lines: "Again Susan Hayward and Jeff Chandler were at the Bandbox. They say they are old friends from Brooklyn and it's nothing serious."

She was right. It wasn't.

Chandler had recently separated from his wife Marjorie, but no divorce was imminent; he still had hopes of saving his marriage: "We have a great rapport still in so many things." The friendship with Susan—started when they were children at P.S. 181—had casually resumed when both were under contract at Universal. Chandler had also worked at Twentieth Century-Fox in *Broken Arrow* (as Cochise), *Two Flags West* and *Bird of Paradise,* after Susan had moved to that lot. Although the Chandlers and the Barkers had never become close friends, a good feeling had always existed between the "two kids from Brooklyn." Their brief reunion in early February at the *Photoplay* Gold Medal Awards had been warm and cordial.

While tactfully advising his wife not to be disturbed by the publicity linking him with Susan, Chandler was, at the same time, astutely aware of the value of this manufactured romance. Until now, his "private" image had been painfully mundane. Susan, in turn, was genuinely fond of Chandler, whom she considered a very understanding friend—and their dates did divert the press from her association with Hughes and even, temporarily, from the fireworks that were about to explode.

Because of complicated California divorce laws (since changed), Susan and Jess were required to appear in Children's Court of Conciliation on November 17. A week earlier, reporter Harrison Carroll had written: "Jess Barker won't file a cross complaint for divorce, but he will fight. All he wants is a reconciliation. He won't even talk about a property settlement. His attorney insists that Susan is worth $400,000 in real estate and investments. All in her name."

When November 17 came, the Barkers spent two agonizing hours with Court Conciliator Margaret C. Harpbrite. Unyielding, Susan insisted she "didn't believe continuance of the marriage would be best for our twin sons, since I no longer love Mr. Barker. You can't revive what's dead."

The following day, Jess denied Susan's allegations of cruelty. His lawyer asked the Superior Court to deny her a divorce and requested a legal ruling that would prohibit her from taking the twins out of the country on a movie-making trip. The latter request was granted, and the divorce hearing was put on the court's calendar for January 19, 1954, pending Susan's return from Mexico. Furious that she had been prevented from taking Timothy and Gregory along on location, especially with the Christmas holidays approaching, Susan retaliated by obtaining a court order preventing Jess, who had been living in a motel in nearby Encino, from staying with the twins on Longridge Avenue while she was out of the country.

After spending Thangsgiving with her sons, Susan, together with Gary Cooper, Richard Widmark, Cameron Mitchell, and

Hugh Marlowe, boarded a plane for Uruapan to begin *Garden of Evil.*

On Monday, December 7, Jess, anxious to spend as much time as possible with his sons, moved back to his former home. Two days later, Susan started a long-distance contempt action against him, charging that "he not only kept the twins up past their bedtime, but had moved back into the home in violation of the court order." Even from hundreds of miles away, the bitterness raged.

Meanwhile, life for the cast and the crew of *Garden of Evil* was fairly unpleasant itself. Director Henry Hathaway was more concerned with catching the exquisite vistas of Uruapan in CinemaScope and Technicolor than with the creature comforts of his high-priced company. The cast was dragged through banana tree jungles, ancient deserted villages, and the black volcanic sands surrounding Paricutin Mountain. When shooting was completed for the day, everyone just wanted to take a bath and fall into bed. Studio hopes that a minor romance between Susan and Gary Cooper would provide provocative copy were quickly dashed. Cooper, soon to reconcile with his wife Rocky after his abortive romance with Patricia Neal, chose instead to have a brief fling with a local girl.

The company even had its share of disaster, or at least potential disaster, in which Susan was personally involved. On December 10, in a driving rainstorm, a seven-year-old Indian boy slipped from a lava ledge on Paricutin Mountain during filming and fell five feet to another ledge. He was about to tumble another fifteen feet when Susan jumped down and caught him, risking the same fall herself. The boy was unhurt, but Susan required medical treatment for a sprained ankle.

To top it all off, due to political red tape involving work permits for foreigners, the cast was prohibited from leaving Mexico until the filming there was finished—which meant nobody could go home for Christmas. On December 21, however, Louella proudly proclaimed, "All by herself, Susan Hayward managed to get a waiver on her work permit from the Mexican government, and she is the only person in the *Garden of Evil* company who will be allowed to return to Hollywood for the holidays. She'll make the seven-hour flight Christmas Eve."

All by herself? Doubtful. If Gary Cooper, who had tremendous clout, couldn't get the precious waiver, then the request had to have come from someone far more powerful than a movie star, or a congressman, for that matter. It was not difficult to surmise who had pulled the strings. Howard Hughes had a date with Susan on New Year's Eve.

Actually, if the story in Richard Matheson's 1977 book *His Weird and Wanton Ways: The Secret Life of Howard Hughes* is true, Hughes actually had *three* dates that evening—simultaneously. With the maître d' of the Beverly Hills Hotel in collusion, Hughes supposedly had Susan, Jean Peters, and an unnamed starlet, each in a different dining room in the hotel, each unaware of the others. Hughes bobbed back and forth among the three of them, making excuses, until finally Susan, suspicious, cornered him in the same room as Jean Peters. Denouncing him for his duplicity (actually, triplicity), Susan left the hotel in a huff, while Peters, only vaguely aware of what was going on, made her exit. There is no report of what happened to the third girl.

Whether that story—which sounds too much like a situation comedy to be real—is true or not, one thing is certain. Shortly thereafter Jean Peters walked out on Howard Hughes. On May 29, 1954, she suddenly married Stuart W. Cramer III, a native of Charlottesville, North Carolina, described by her studio as a "civilian in Army Intelligence in Washington, D.C."

As for Susan, she enjoyed her holidays with Tim and Gregory, if not with Hughes. However, she had a contract to do a movie for Hughes that summer—the multimillion-dollar epic had finally gotten off the drawing board and been given a name, *The Conqueror*—and she had no intention of damaging the relationship.

On January 2, she flew back to Mexico in a pensive mood. In spite of its professional honors and financial rewards, 1953 had been a nightmarish year, and she was glad to see it end.

Nonetheless, she was apprehensive about 1954.

Her apprehensions were well founded.

chapter 17

Garden of Evil, plagued by foul weather, ran overtime and over budget, requiring another delay in the divorce hearing. Because Susan could not leave Mexico before the weekend of February 4, she was frantic over the possibility that the judge might refuse a continuance. Twentieth Century-Fox and Susan's attorneys struggled through the maze of legal maneuvers and, to everyone's relief, the court hearing was pushed back to February 25.

In the meantime, the columnists were having a field day. Dorothy Kilgallen commented on February 1, "When the Susan Hayward–Jess Barker divorce comes to trial, the big rhubarb will be over their children. Barker will claim he's closer to the boys than Susan is because he was home with them while she was making movies." Louella Parsons countered on February 15: "Susan Hayward was escorted to Jack Warner's party by Jeff Chandler. I've never seen her look as pretty or as happy. She says she feels free as a bird . . . for the first time in years she's able to spend her money just as she pleases."

Ten days later, court proceedings finally began. Demurely attired in a simple dress, flowing beige jersey coat ("In beige I feel like a very good little girl," she had told Walter Thornton) and dainty gloves, Susan obligingly posed for photographers before the hearing officially opened. The first few minutes of testimony dealt with the Barkers' premarital financial agreement. This was followed by a morning of startling revelations.

Milton Rudin and Martin Gang represented Hayward. S. S.

(Sammy) Hahn represented Barker. Judge Herbert Y. Walker presided. The testimony here is taken directly from the transcript of the Superior Court. Susan was on the stand.

Q   What time of the day or night was it?

A   Well, it was late at night, because my husband had gone out to get the late editions of the newspapers; it was on his return.

Q   Who was at home on that night, July 16, 1953?

A   My husband and myself and my house guest.

Q   Where were the boys?

A   And my children were upstairs.

Q   All right. And it was after dinner then, late at night, about eleven or twelve at night?

A   Yes. We had been talking before this.

Q   What were you doing on that occasion?

A   I had been studying and Mr. Barker had been watching television.

Q   Studying what?

A   My script, or a script. I can't remember right now whether I was working on something at the time or preparing.

Q   When Mr. Barker went out for the late editions of the newspapers, where were you at the time he came back?

A   In the living room.

Q   Can you describe what happened on that occasion?

A   Yes. As I said before, we started to argue. We argued about most of things we've argued about in the past. I remember one thing, that I asked Mr. Barker for a divorce, because I said to him, under the circumstances, that I felt a divorce might be the only solution to these problems. He said I would never get a divorce.

Q   Did you discuss the question of employment or his not working?

A   Yes, this was part of our argument.

Q   And the effect on the children?

A   Yes.

Q   Give the conversation, please.

A   As well as I can remember, it wound up in the fact that he said to me I'd never get a divorce. And I said, "If you don't love me, and don't want to do what I consider right, why do you want to hang on?" And he said, "Well, you're a good meal ticket."

Well, when he said that, I didn't understand, and I looked at him, and I said, "I don't understand you. I think you're very queer."

Q   What did he do?

A   And he walked over to where I was sitting and he slapped me.

Q   In the face, Mrs. Barker?

A   Yes.

Q   Go ahead; proceed.

A   He slapped me again. I tried for him not to hit me. He threw me on the floor, and pulled off my robe, and proceeded to beat me. . . .

Well, when my husband was beating me, I tried to get loose from him, first of all, because it hurt; secondly, because there were children in the house, and Martha Little, who is not well. I didn't want to disturb them. But when he beat me, it hurt, and I was crying.

So finally I got loose and ran out of the house into the back garden. I just wanted to get away. Mr. Barker caught up with me; he forced me back into the house. I was struggling with him, and he hit me again.

Q   Where did he hit you, do you remember? I know it's tough, but we've got to do it.

A   I don't remember where he hit me; he hit me wherever he could.

Q   What were you wearing, by the way, Mrs. Barker?

A   I was wearing a terry-cloth bathrobe.

Q   And what underneath that?

A   Nothing. I sleep in the raw.

Q   All right. Then he was dragging you back in the house. Continue the story.

A   When he continued to beat me, I had to get help. I ran to the telephone. I was going to dial the operator, call the police, or anything I could.

Q   What happened?

A   He came after me and knocked the telephone out of my hand, and he said, "I'll cool you off," whereupon he yanked me by the arm, and dragged me out again, back through the garden and up the steps to the swimming pool.

Q   And what did he do then?

A   He threw me in.

Q   And will you relate what happened after he threw you in?

A   Well, as I said, I was wearing this terry-cloth robe, and it's pretty full. It's a big, pink, voluminous thing, and when I hit the water, the water soaked it up, and I went down. It's hard to get up because there are many folds in a garment. I got up to the top, and I started screaming again, because I was afraid, whereupon he pushed my head under the water.

Q   Were you in fear of your life?

A   Of course I was.

Q   And what did you do after he held your head under the water—pushed it under?

A   I suddenly realized that I was not dealing with a person who was quite himself. I knew that he was so highly enraged that he wasn't responsible for his actions that night.

Q   So what did you do?

A   So when I came up the second time, I kept my mouth shut, and didn't make any noise. He said, "Now get back into the house." So I went quietly.

Q   What happened to the terry-cloth bathrobe?

A   That was soaking wet; and as I said, it was very heavy. It was left by the pool side.

Q   And you therefore had to go into the house without any clothes at all?

A   Yes.

Q   What happened then? Proceed. You walked in with Mr. Barker behind you?

A   Yes. I walked into the house with Mr. Barker. He pushed me into the bedroom, and he said, "Now stay there." Naturally, by this time I was pretty scared, and I knew I had to get out and get help somehow, because I didn't want to stay in the same house with him. So I went to the closet and threw on whatever clothes I could find. . . . There's a little door that leads out of the bedroom, a side door, so I didn't have to go out around again through the den where I thought he might be. I opened the door quietly and walked through the garden, and then, as I remember it, around by the kitchen door, because that leads out into the driveway, and freedom. I got as far as the kitchen door, and it was suddenly—I hate to tell these things.

MR. GANG: I don't know what else we can do. . . .

A   It was suddenly opened by Mr. Barker. He said, "Where do you think you're going? Get back in there." At least I think that's what he said; it's hard to remember.

THE COURT: You can't remember exactly. The Court wouldn't believe you if you gave me the exact wording. Give it as near as you can recollect.

THE WITNESS: He grabbed me and threw me into the kitchen ahead of him, and that was lucky, because he threw me with such momentum that I could race to the front door. You go through the kitchen and the dining room and the hallway to the front door. And I opened it, and I ran out, and I ran down the driveway, and he caught up with me and started to hit me again. He said, "You're not going anywhere." . . .

At this point, of course, again I was screaming for help. I was screaming the man's name next door. It was dark outside, and I was screaming for help from the man across the street, anybody.

The next thing I remember, he tried to get me into the house, and I refused to go, and I was struggling with him, and he threw me over the hedge and I was down on the ground, and he still kept beating me. And that's all I can remember until Martha came out the front door, and she yelled, "What's going on?" because—

Q   "Martha" was Martha Little, your house guest?

A   That's right. She came out the front door, and she ran over and said, "Stop it; stop it." Well, when she said that to him, he stopped momentarily, and I ran back into the house and grabbed the telephone, because I was going to call the police. He ran back in after me, and again knocked it out of my hand. And then suddenly, I don't know, there was a commotion outside, and I ran out, and the police were there. I said, "Would you please call me a taxi?" I told the policeman—

Q   By the way, do you know who called the police?

A   No, I don't; I never reached them.

Q   Proceed. What happened?

A   So, when I asked the policeman to call me a taxi, I must have looked a mess. I said I wanted to go to my mother's house. So they called me a taxi. They offered to drive me in their squad car, but I said that wasn't necessary. So they called a cab, and

I got in it, and Miss Little came with me, and we went over to my mother's house . . .

Q   You spent the night at your mother's house?

A   Yes. And then I tried to reach your office in the morning but I wasn't successful, so I called Mr. Wood, my business manager, at his home, and asked him would he go back to the house with me, and ask Mr. Barker please to leave. Also, my brother came with me.

Q   And you went back to the house the next morning?

A   Yes.

Q   With Mr. Wood and your brother?

A   Yes, and Miss Little.

Q   And Mr. Barker left the house that day?

A   Yes, he left the house that day.

Q   It was after that you filed your complaint for divorce, and asked for a restraining order?

A   As soon as I could reach your office, one of your attorneys came to my home; I explained to him what happened. . . .

Q   And did you secure medical treatment for your injuries?

A   Yes. I was X-rayed, and taken care of.

Q   And can you describe what your injuries consisted of as a result of what had happened the night before?

A   You want a description of how I looked?

Q   Yes. What were your bruises, contusions?

Q   Well, I had a black eye, I guess you call it; bruises on the the left side of my face, on the temple, the jaw, the nose. I thought my jaw was broken. The eyeball was injured—it was all bloody. My body was covered with bruises, mostly on my "fanny" [indicating], and my feet and legs were scratched and bleeding.

Q   What was that from?

A   From being dragged up the steps and down the steps and being knocked against things.

Q   And how long a period of time did it take before the visible evidences of your injuries cleared up?

A   Well, that black eye lasted quite a while . . .

Q   About a week, or two weeks?

A   Two weeks.

Q   Now, Mr. Barker did not live at the home from that time on, did he?

A   He did not.

Q   Did he come to take the children with him on occasion?

A   Yes, he did.

Q   Would you, on those occasions, see him?

A   Yes, sometimes I would.

Q   And he could not stay at the house, however?

A   No.

Q   Just come and get the children, and bring them back?

A   That's right. Or if he wanted to pick up any of his clothes, or things like that.

That's most of what Susan Hayward remembered in court about the fight on July 16. But this is the way Jess Barker remembered the same evening.

After dinner I was sitting in front of the television set for a while, and the programs were dull, and I left it. Mrs. Barker wasn't studying a script, because she wasn't working at the time, and there were no scripts, to my knowledge, that had been sent to her. . . .

Q   You know about scripts?

A   I should know; I have worked with them enough.

Q   You studied the scripts with her?

A   Always.

Q   And you advised her?

A   Yes, I did.

Q   And what else do you do helping prepare for the work as a star?

A   To give her every bit of knowledge I have had in the years in the theater, and what I have had in the motion picture business.

Q   Did you attend interviews with her?

A   I was frequently present in interviews with magazines and newspaper people. Quite frequently Mrs. Barker would ask me to join, as she termed it, for the "light touch."

Q   Did you have to advise her about costumes at the studios?

A   I was with Mrs. Barker on practically every picture she started on the costumes and I saw the tests made, suggested camera angles, anything connected with her work.

Q   In addition to that, you bought the groceries for the house?

A   I bought the groceries for the house.

Q   And you bought the supplies, and maintenance for the house?

A   I did to the best of my ability.

Q   And raise the children?

A   That I did to the best of my ability.

Q   All right. Now, tell us what happened from there on. You say she was not working?

A   Mrs. Barker was sitting in front of the television set when I went to get the newspapers. . . . Mrs. Barker . . . started reading . . . I had a newspaper. . . .

Q   What happened? What was done by you or her?

A   There was a discussion about families in general in Hollywood—not gossip—just in general, about this person, which is the way many of our conversations started out. During the course of our conversation something was said where a remark about my mother was brought into the conversation. Why it was there, I don't know.

Q   What remark did she make about your mother?

A   Well, it isn't very pleasant. It was about an incident I told her about when I was a child. "Possibly," she said, "that's what's wrong with you . . ." . . . after the mention of my mother, I sat in complete stunned silence; Mrs. Barker gave me all of the bad things that she could think about me . . .

Q   What did you do then?

A   I sat on the couch. I stayed right there wondering why a woman that I had all the respect for in the world should say that to me, the father of her children. Mrs. Barker leaned across to me to get a cigarette, and said right in my face, "Besides, I think you're queer." And with that, I think I said, "You're not going to get away with that." And I slapped her, and the struggle was on from then on. . . . She struggled back. I tried to quiet her down, and by this time Mrs. Barker got hold of me, and bit me very hard in the left arm, in the muscle. . . .

Q   Then what happened? How did you get to the swimming pool?

A   Mrs. Barker ran outside; I brought her back inside. I let her back inside; and I gave Mrs. Barker a spanking. . . . I asked her to please keep quiet, the children were upstairs, and I picked her up, carried her and put her into bed, and covered her. . . . And Mrs. Barker got up again, and ran outside, and I said, "If you don't keep quiet, I'm going to cool you off."

Q   What did you do to cool her off?

A   I picked Mrs. Barker up, carried her to the pool, and dropped her in.

Q   Which side of the pool did you drop her in, the nine feet deep or the three feet deep?

A   It's approximately four feet deep. . . . The robe, by the way, that she was wearing, slipped right off. . . . And I said, "Now are you cooled off?" And Mrs. Barker was still screaming, and I helped her out of the pool, and took her back in the house. Mrs. Barker never entered the parkway area gate in the nude— never . . .

Q   Did you ever drag her?

A   I never dragged Mrs. Barker. Mrs. Barker fell a couple of occasions pulling away from me, yes . . .

Q   You did not try to drown her as she says?

A   No, Mr. Hahn. I helped Mrs. Barker out of the pool . . .

Q   Then you went back in the house, and what happened then?

A   Mrs. Barker was in the room for quite some time, and I was in the den, and in the state I was in, I decided to take a walk in front of the home. . . . I was sitting outside by the driveway which has the drain, and Mrs. Barker came out fully dressed with a coat on; I mean fully dressed apparently to the eye, with a scarf over her head. She had the dog in her arm, and she was going down the street in the dark. . . . I tried to get her back, and there was a struggle. . . . I took her to the front door, and asked Mrs. Little to please put Mrs. Barker to bed, and she said, "I will."

Q   That's the first time you saw Mrs. Little that night?

A   That's the first and only time I saw Mrs. Little until she left shortly after that with Mrs. Barker. . . . Mrs. Little opened the door and was waiting.

Q   And then the police arrived?

A   . . . I sat on the front doorstep, or stoop, and sat there until a gentleman walked up to me in uniform and said, "What's the trouble here?" And the only word I spoke to the gentleman was, "Domestic." . . .

Q   Did you at any time throw her over a fence of some sort?

A   I did not.

Q   Did you at any time hear her scream loud and long, "Don't kill me, don't kill me?" . . .

A   I don't remember that.

Q   Did you try to kill her?

A   No, sir, I did not.

Q   Did you try to do her any physical harm other than what you say you considered she deserved, a spanking?

A   I did nothing else, Mr. Hahn. . . . I left the home in the hopes that the home would be reunited and perpetuated. . . . I was back on a Tuesday with flowers. This is the first occasion. . . .

Q   You brought her flowers for your and her anniversary.

A   I did.

Q   She accepted them?

A   Yes.

Q   She appreciated them?

A   She thought they were lovely . . . .

A third witness was called to describe the same incident. Her testimony came between Susan Hayward's and Jess Barker's. Her name was Dodee Hazel Swain, and she had been a maid at the house next door to the Barkers. And she had a room with a view.

Q   . . . you could see from your bedroom into the area in which the pool is located?

A   Yes.

Q   All right. Now, on the night of July 16–17 of 1953, did anything occur which you remember at this time? . . .

A   In the early morning of July 17, I was awakened with a loud scream—a lady's voice. . . . And then I got up out of bed with the loud scream still on. Then I went back to my bathroom and I went straight to the back kitchen door, and I stood in the doorway looking and listening.

Q   At this time of the morning were there lights on in the yard of the Barker home?

A   There was two lights, big headlights, in the back way.

Q   And did you see anything at the time?

A   I saw a lady run by out of the gateway, the back of the house, and she didn't have on anything. If she did, it was very sheer to me. . . . A few minutes after she was in the house, I heard a loud scream, then they ran outside in the backway, direction of the pool, and I heard screaming real loudly, and she was screaming, "Don't kill me; don't kill me," and "Somebody help me; somebody help me; please don't kill me." I heard a man mumbling, said, "You're going to sign that deal." She said, "No, no." And I heard a big splash as if something bumped in the water, and she was screaming and struggling. And then, I heard conversation out near the pool, but I couldn't see, so I just heard mumbling. I couldn't understand what they were saying otherwise . . .

Q   And did you go back to bed?

A   I stood there for a little while, and then I laid back down. And later, in the early morning, I heard a man in the back way, two men, talking. I didn't even get up to see who it was.

Q   Now, did you recognize any distinctive part of the person you saw running—the lady; was her hair noticeable to you in the light?

A   It was kind of reddish-like . . .

Q   Was the person you saw Mrs. Barker?

A   I would say she was.

MR. GANG: Thank you very much. You may cross-examine. . . .

MR. HAHN: Did you notice the naked lady again? . . .

A   I saw her twice.

Q   All right. Now, after you saw her run into the door, when did you see her again?

A   When she ran out the back door next to where I am. . . .

Q   Did you notice her for just about a second again?

A   It was running so fast I guess it was a second.

Q   And that lady was still naked?

A   Yes. . . .

Q   Where did the naked lady run after she got to the driveway?

A   In the direction of the pool. I don't know where she ran after that.

Q   That's the last you saw of the naked lady?

A   That's right. . . .

Q   When did you hear somebody yell, "Don't kill me, don't kill me," after she ran to the swimming pool, or when the naked lady ran through the door the first time?

A   When she ran back to the swimming pool.

Q   That's the first time you heard a lady say, "Don't kill me?"

A   No. She was just hollering when I was awake. I was awakened with a scream; that's what I told you.

Q   Yes, and with screams, "Don't kill me?"

A   Yes, when she ran back to the pool, and there was some slaps like that. . . . Then I heard her hollering, "Don't kill me . . . somebody help me. . . ." Then I heard a man's voice say, "You're going to sign that deal," and she said no, and splash, he throwed her in the pool, and there was a scrambling, and scrambling, and that's the way it was. . . .

Q   A scrambling over a deal?

A   In the water.

Q   Did you go over there and look?

A   No, I didn't go over, because I didn't want to interfere.

Q   Did you call the police?

A   I didn't call the police, because I didn't want to interfere . . .

Q   . . . When you saw the naked lady run in the house, and when you saw the naked lady run out of the house in the swimming pool, you didn't see a man follow her?

A   Yes, there was a man following her, but I didn't look at that second. He was sure following. . . .

Q   Now, when the man's voice said, "Sign the deal," where was that?

A   That was outside.

Q   Outside, when she ran out the first time or second time?

A   The second time.

Q   Well, how soon after she ran out towards the swimming pool did you hear a man say, "You'll have to sign this deal"?

A   It wasn't long afterwards, because that's when the most screaming was.

Q   About how long?

A   About a few seconds. I don't know just how long it was, but it wasn't very long.

Q   How long did this yelling, "Save me, don't let him kill me," go on?

A   It went on quite a while, because I don't see why somebody in the neighborhood didn't hear beside me. . . .

Q   How long did they talk quietly in the swimming pool, in that direction, after the screaming stopped?

A   Quite a while, I guess, because I went and laid down.

The Barkers were the only witnesses who appeared to describe their next struggle. Their disagreement about what happened on Labor Day was even greater than their disagreement on the other night. Susan was examined first.

Q   What occurred on the Labor Day weekend of 1953? . . .

A   I had taken the children and gone to Hawaii, and we had a sort of vacation, and I hadn't seen Mr. Barker, and he called and asked if he might take them out on Labor Day. And I said, "Of course." And they came back, and they were happy together. They were all, you know, laughing—stuff like that. I had guests, Mr. and Mrs. Dorsen.

We were up by the pool. I guess Jesse brought the children back about around six o'clock, and as is the custom in our home, we dine early, usually six-thirty, latest a quarter of seven, because of the children. The children always eat with me.

As Mr. Barker came in, he knew Mr. and Mrs. Dorsen, and I felt it would be embarrassing for me not to ask him up at least to say hello, because the children would wonder why I didn't ask him. So I asked him would he come up and join us in cocktails. We had just started. He said he'd like to, and he came up by the pool side, and he poured himself a drink.

We discussed this and that, social conversation, and then he said he'd like to talk to me. I said, "All right." Mr. and Mrs. Dorsen left, and went down into the house. I said, "Please, Jesse, will you please be sort of quick about it, because dinner is almost ready and I don't want any delay." He started to talk about reconciliation. . . .

Q   What did you say?

A   I said it was impossible, and I didn't want a reconciliation. I felt it would be better for both of us to be apart. He is sort of insistent, and, well, to make a long story short, he didn't want to leave. This caused delays in the kitchen, in my guests, and the children wondering why dinner wasn't there, and why their mother wasn't ready to sit down.

I asked him again and again to please leave—"Let's talk about it some other time, not tonight." It was a holiday; I had guests; it was time for dinner.

Mr. Barker said he would leave when he was good and ready to leave.

Q   Did the guests come in at any time?

A   Yes, they did. They came in to see what was wrong, and tried to persuade him to leave. They were unsuccessful.

Q   Then what happened?

A   Well, I was furious, because I tried to get him to leave peaceably, because I didn't want there to be any disturbance. . . . The children were there, and I had guests, and besides, it's not good. I was quite furious. He was sort of standing near me, and I had a cigarette in my hand; it was lit; and I have a temper, and I said, "I would like to push this cigarette right in your eye."

Q   What did he say?

A   He said, "You haven't got the guts."

Q   What did he do?

A   He put up his hand [indicating] and then smacked me.

Q   You did not succeed in getting the cigarette in his face?

A   This I can't remember.

Q   But you remember—

A   I aimed.

Q   And did you get smacked?

A   Yes, I got smacked.

Q   What happened then?

A   Well, I yelled, and Thelma came running.

Q   Who is Thelma?

A   She's Mrs. Dorsen.

Q   All right; continue.

A   Oh, I forgot when they came in before they tried to calm down the argument, and said, "Well, have another drink, and then leave." So Thelma went out into the kitchen to make this drink, and as she ran back into the room, when I screamed, she had the drink in her hand, and I grabbed the drink and threw the contents of the glass in Mr. Barker's face.

Q   And where were the children?

A   They were in the dining room. Mr. Dorsen, as I understand it, was talking with them about various things trying not to let them hear the commotion going on in the house; but it was pretty loud. Mr. Barker said that he didn't hit me, and that I was a liar.

Q   In whose presence did he make that statement?

A   Mrs. Dorsen, although other people could hear him because he said it pretty loud. I just wanted him to get out of there; and I ran into the kitchen, and he ran after me; and I ran into the den, and he ran after me, and insisting I didn't tell the truth, and that I was a liar.

Q   Did the children hear this?

A   Yes, of course; they must have heard it, although they didn't say anything to me about it.

Q   All right; proceed.

A   Well, finally he was prevailed upon to leave. He left. That's all.

Q   What happened after that?

A   I called you the next day. I said it was impossible, that I want a divorce, and I want it fast . . .

But Jess's report is quite different.

Q   Let's go to . . . the Labor Day incident. Tell us exactly what happened there, briefly, when you came over . . .

A   . . . I said, "Do you mind if I take the boys down to Studio City and see your picture, *White Witch Doctor?*" because they had been promised to see it. And I said, "Would you join us?" Naturally, I was refused; however, I did take the boys to see their mother. . . . We returned home afterward in a very happy frame of mind. The boys talked about the picture, and I felt that they liked it very much, which I was very proud that they had seen their mother and enjoyed her performance.

I was invited up to the pool, and Mr. and Mrs. Dorsen were present. . . . I asked Mrs. Barker if I could speak to her, and Mrs. Dorsen left the pool and we chatted quite a while; and Mrs. Barker informed me that: "How did it feel to know I'd be the recipient of $100,000 at the end of the week?" I thought it was rather a large amount. My remark was, "Is that all?" I didn't know what she was talking about.

She told me—she informed me she was going ahead and get a divorce.

At this point Barker testified that he had been going to the marriage counselor under the impression that he was a psychiatrist and that their visits to him were for the purpose of working out a reconciliation.

172

We were going for a reconciliation, but Mrs. Barker told me since then that she was going merely for the children, which she said, about how the children should be handled.

Q Go ahead and tell us the rest of it.

A Well, we went into the home. I sat on a chair and Mrs. Barker sat on a small love-seat, and we discussed at length about various things. And Mrs. Barker wanted a quick divorce—go to Nevada right away—give a settlement.

So I continued talking about the home, and about the children, and our obligations to the children. Mrs. Barker walked away from me to the table, lit a cigarette, came back, and during the course of the conversation (I was standing beside her), looked at the end of the cigarette and said, "I ought to push this right in your eye."

I said, "Well, I don't think you've got the guts to do it." I thought she was joking. With that, Mrs. Barker reached up and pushed the cigarette towards my face, and with my left hand I knocked the cigarette out of her hand, put my foot on it, and what turned me around was Mrs. Barker yelling and screaming that she had been hit.

I grabbed Mrs. Barker by the shoulder, sat her on the couch and said, "What is the matter with you?" With this, Mr. and Mrs. Dorsen came in, and I said, "This girl claims she's been hit. Would you please take a look and see if she has a mark on her? She's got very sensitive skin; it would show." Mr. and Mrs. Dorsen answered me.

Q Did you hit her?

A I did not.

Q Proceed. What happened next?

A The next thing I know, I was getting a drink in my face.

Q A drink of what, water or whiskey?

A Well, the part that came down my face tasted very much like whiskey.

Q All right. What happened next?

A I said to Mrs. Barker, "Will you please tell the truth?" Mrs. Barker kept yelling that, "You hit me, you hit me," and started moving around, and I moved with her, and I said, "Please tell the truth. I'll not leave the house until you tell the truth."

By this time I knew the children had heard it, and I wanted the children to know the truth too. And after several minutes of this I decided to leave, because I wasn't getting any place, and might have made matters worse. And I left, and the divorce was filed the following day.

In spite of their concern for the welfare of the children, the testimony of both the Barkers implied that their only worry, besides protecting them from the knowledge of their parents' disagreements, was protecting themselves from each other in the eyes of their sons.

Susan told about the questioning of their children about the separation.

THE WITNESS: They didn't quite understand why their mother and father didn't live together anymore.

Q What did they say, and what did you say?

A Why don't their daddy live here any more? And I said, "Sometimes when people grow up, and they can't get along together in happiness, it's better for them to live apart."

Q You started to say something about putting Gregory to bed one night. What did he say?

A He said, "Wouldn't you like it if daddy lived here?"

Q All right. Did you answer him?

A Well—

Q Or did you evade the answering?

A I answered him.

Q What did you say?

A I said, "It's too bad, but sometimes grown-ups can't get along together." . . .

Q With reference to visitation rights, Mrs. Barker, will you relate to the Court the observations on the children when they leave for weekends, and when they come back?

A Yes. During the week they're pretty much relaxed, except for, well, boys will be boys, and once in a while they'll get out of line. But they're nice kids, normal, happy, and they have, well, the best way I can describe it is a rather relaxed and free relationship with me. I do notice when they come back over the weekend with me, they're tense, and it takes a day or two, for the tenseness to leave. I don't know why. I'd like to be able to talk with Mr. Barker and discuss with him how we can work this thing out so that we can work together and not against each other. . . . I told him it was wrong for two people to be in conflict, and try to outdo each other.

Q   What did Mr. Barker say?

A   May I give an incident that's just come to my mind?

Q   Yes. Go ahead.

A   Mr. Barker came to the home after we came back from Hawaii . . . I said, "Tell Daddy how you were surfboard riding, and deep sea fishing, and so forth, and so on." And Mr. Barker said, "Were they very good boys?" I said, "Yes, they were very good boys, but once in a while I'd have to give them a little crack on the behind." So he looked at the children, and he said, "Oh, you've got a very bad mommy."

Well, it wasn't the kind of thing that you say in front of kids, because then, you know, they get confused.

And Jess Barker told the Court why he wanted to keep his wife from permitting her mother to live in the home with the children.

Q   You don't want your mother-in-law to be in the house with you, your wife and your children?

A   I do not.

Q   Tell the Court why.

A   The children told me, during the time I had them at Christmas, that they couldn't understand something. I said, "What are you talking about?" They said, "Something that Grandma said right after you left home." I said, "What do you mean?" The child said, "Grandma said she would kill you." And the child said, "Grandma said to Mommy, 'Get rid of Daddy.'"

It wasn't until that afternoon that Howard Hughes's name and his visit to the house on Longridge Avenue came up in Jess's testimony. Susan admitted that Hughes had been in her home and met her sons, but she insisted he had been there for the sole purpose of picking them up before going out to dinner; they had had business to discuss; she was doing a movie for him in June. Outside the courtroom, cornered by a local reporter, she added that she was "also trying to get work from Hughes for her jobless husband."

On March 15, 1954, relief finally came for Susan. Pending the divorce, the Court awarded her custody of the twins, with Jess receiving permission to take them on Wednesdays and alternate weekends. She was also ordered to pay his legal fees of three thousand dollars, which stung a bit. What stung more was Judge Walker's stern admonitions that both parents watch their language when talking about each other in front of the boys.

For Tim and Greg, not having their father home every day was bewildering. "Wouldn't you like it if daddy lived here?" Greg had asked, and all Susan could say was, "Sometimes when people grow up, and they can't get along together in happiness, it's better for them to live apart." But the boys were only nine at the time, and they loved their father very much. Now, more than twenty-six years later, Tim says tenderly of Jess Barker, "He's a good guy."

chapter 18

SUSAN WAS ANXIOUS as the month of June approached. Her suit for divorce coincided with the starting date of *The Conqueror,* and neither could be put off any longer. Hughes, however, promised she'd be given a few days off for the trial, and made arrangements for Susan to film a couple of her scenes in Hollywood, so she'd be close by.

On June 14 Susan was back in the Burbank court. The testimony over the next few days was a prolonged replay of the February hearing. There were no startling new revelations: Susan stuck to her story, Jess to his. Jess even contested the trial, insisting that he still wanted a reconciliation with his wife.

For reasons never fully explained, the court adjourned to the house on Longridge Avenue for a closer look at "the scene of the crime." Susan avoided Jess's gaze as, wearing a curiously inappropriate large picture hat and black taffeta cocktail dress, she showed the judge around the house. Soon after, the divorce was granted; Jess's lawyers said they'd appeal.

On August 18, the court ruled that Susan could keep the more than a quarter-million dollars she owned in nine savings accounts, her house, her future earnings, and her car. Jess Barker was given their 1952 Ford station wagon and was awarded visitation rights to the boys on alternate weekends. And with that, the case was over. Once and for all, the Barkers were dissolved.

Meanwhile, Susan had received court permission to take the

twins on location with her, and on June 30, a photograph was released from the set of *The Conqueror* showing the boys in Saint George, Utah, together with John Wayne, Dick Powell, and the rest of the cast and crew, watching their mother cut a giant birthday cake, a present from the cast. Susan was thirty-seven that year.

The Conqueror was a rather silly Wild East show about Genghis Khan, played by John Wayne, of all people, and a beautiful Tartar princess, played by Susan. She would later say, "I had hysterics all through that one. Every time we did a scene I dissolved in laughter . . . . Me, a red-haired Tartar princess. It looked like some wild Irishman had stopped off on the road to old Cathay."

During the course of the film, she would develop a lasting affection for Wayne, perhaps the only leading man for whom she would feel that way. "He was tough and strong, just like his screen image, but there was tremendous gentleness about him. Of all my leading men, he was my favorite."

Although Wayne was too tactful ever to name his own favorite leading lady, he was always complimentary about Susan as well. Not long before his death he reminisced: "I have had the good fortune to work with Susan in several pictures, in a variety of backgrounds from the sea to war to world conquest. At no time does her magnetism ever let you forget that she is a woman."

Studio efforts to fabricate a romance between Susan and Wayne during the filming of *The Conqueror* came to nothing, however. Wayne had just gone through a divorce that was in most respects even messier than Susan's, and needed time for a breather. More importantly, despite their liking for each other, the two simply weren't each other's romantic type. Wayne had a passion for fiery Latin ladies, and Susan couldn't shake her obsession with Southerners. Besides, there was always the shadowy figure of bossman Howard Hughes lurking in the background—though he seemed to be getting even shadowier than usual these days, at least when it came to Susan. She put it down as his reluctance to be seen while the divorce action was still pending.

Besides Wayne, though, her relationship with most of the rest of the cast was about the same as usual: reserved and private. Actor Thomas Gomez, who played the sybaritic Chinese

David and Bathsheba, a story of lust, God's wrath, and repentance, took liberties with the Bible and made millions for Twentieth. Gregory Peck was the covetous King David. (Twentieth Century-Fox)

Susan won a Golden Globe and the *Photoplay* Gold Medal for her portrayal of courageous Jane Froman in 1952's *With A Song in My Heart.* Robert Wagner credits Susan for his overnight stardom in the film. (McClelland)

Posing with school buddy Jeff Chandler at the
Photoplay party. She adamantly refused, however,
to pose with the "most popular new star," Marilyn
Monroe, who came in skin-tight lamé. (Moreno)

Bullfighter Julio Aparicio dedicates a bull to Susan
in Valencia, Spain, during a European trip in 1953.
Jess, seated behind her, was ignored the whole time.
Their marriage would end four months later. (Author)

February 25, 1954: Susan looking demure as she waits for the first court hearings on her divorce petition to begin. (Author)

The court adjourns to the "scene of the crime" to see the swimming pool in which Jess (background) allegedly tossed his naked wife after physically abusing her. (AP)

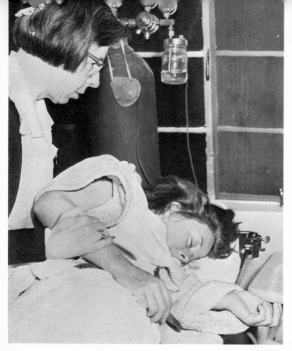

On April 26, 1955, Susan took a near-fatal overdose of sleeping pills. Alerted by Ellen Marrenner, police broke down the door and rushed her to the hospital. (Author)

She was released April 29, "joyously looking forward" to returning to work and her sons—but refusing to discuss why she took the pills. (Author)

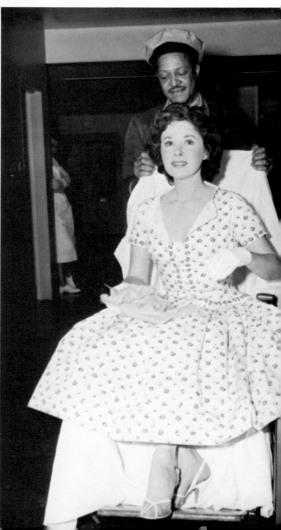

Above, the confrontation between alcoholic Lillian Roth and her mother, played by Jo Van Fleet, was among the scenes in 1955's *I'll Cry Tomorrow* that won Susan her fourth Oscar nomination. Below, the jaunty "I'm Sittin' On Top of the World" number was cut from the final version, but can be heard on the movie soundtrack. (McClelland)

Susan attended the *I'll Cry Tomorrow* premier with Lillian
Roth and columnist Mike Connolly, who assisted on the best-
selling book. (Author)

Taken just before Susan was named Best Actress at the
Cannes Film Festival, 1956. Old acquaintance Ingrid Bergman
was about to film *Anastasia*, the film that would bring her
back into public favor. (UPI)

On February 8, 1957, Susan and Eaton Chalkley secretly eloped to Phoenix, Arizona, and were wed. "I expect this marriage to be *it*, or I wouldn't have married," she said. (Wide World Photos)

The Chalkleys' 450-acre farm near Carrollton, Georgia, where Susan took a year's sabbatical, entertained Eaton's friends and helped remodel the ranch house. (Author)

In 1958, Walter Wanger interested her in the story of Barbara Graham, the fast-living "party girl" executed for murder. With a script based on "Bloody Babs'" letters, and articles by Ed Montgomery, *I Want To Live!* was Susan's final breakthrough. (United Artists)

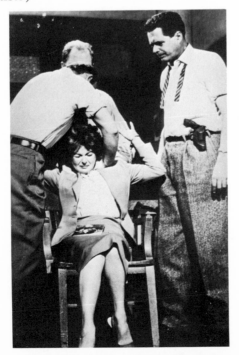

Wanger with Susan in New York, November, 1958, for publicity on *I Want To Live!* (Author)

Receiving the New York Film Critics' Award for Best Actress from *Daily Mirror* critic Justin Gilbert; Elia Kazan and Frederic March standing in for Stanley Kramer, David Niven for himself. Next step: Oscar? (McClelland)

Back home in Georgia. "How could a
fellow ever feel he's playing a minor role,"
said Eaton, "when he's playing the role
for real of Susan's husband." (Author)

Sister Florence in 1960. The
years had not been kind—
at age fifty, she went on
public assistance and wrote
scathing "exposés" about
her sister. (Author)

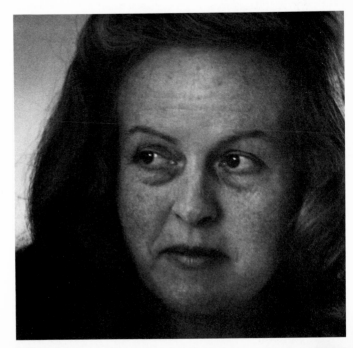

Oscar night, April 9, 1959!
Said Wanger, "Thank heav-
ens! Now we can all relax.
Susie's got what she's been
chasing for twenty years."
(Author)

Bette Davis and Susan meet for the first time ever for their film *Where Love Has Gone*. There was no love lost between them. (Moreno)

As a favor to pal Mark Robson, Susan, now widowed, replaced Judy Garland in 1967's *Valley of the Dolls*, here in a climactic battle with Patty Duke. (20th Century-Fox)

Marty Rackin persuaded her to appear in his Las Vegas production of *Mame* at Caesar's Palace. She opened on December 27, 1968. By March her voice gave out. (McClelland)

Though living in near-seclusion now, Susan emerged in 1969 to attend Gregory's graduation from the University of Alabama—but she refused to finance Tim's UCLA film-making course. (McClelland)

In 1971, she was miraculously
saved when fire swept her apartment after she had fallen asleep
while smoking. Here she stands
on a neighbor's balcony (below)
while repairs are made to her
apartment, above. (UPI)

With Lee J. Cobb in the 1972 TV movie *In the Heat of Anger.*
This was her next-to-last film. Soon doctors would diagnose
cancer. (Metromedia Producers Corp.)

In a chilly drizzle, Susan was buried beside Eaton
in a plot facing the Chalkley home. A neighbor tried
to console Timothy as Gregory looked on. (UPI)

A lasting memorial: Susan's
footprints and handprints in
front of Hollywood's "Chinese
Theater." (Moreno)

prince Wang Khan, recalled: "Susan had a house and a cook. One night she invited several of us, including John Wayne and the Dick Powells, for dinner. Once she greeted us, she disappeared into the kitchen, and despite the fact that she had a cook, we scarcely saw her again until dinner was served. In an evening after work, she may be so cordial that you think you've finally broken through the barriers and made a friend of her, but that wasn't usually the case!"

Susan did, however, stay close to Agnes Moorehead, with whom she had worked twice in the past. Miss Moorehead had been one of Susan's few supporters when both had been making *The Lost Moment* in 1947, and would remain so until the end of her life, telling everyone, "I was one of her greatest fans." Later, Miss Moorehead would remember the day during the filming of *The Conqueror* when Susan showed quite another side of her personality altogether. Saint George, the town in which the film company stayed, was trying to raise money to pay off the debt on a local playground, and the RKO moviemakers had obligingly agreed to play the local chapter of Elks in a benefit softball game. Susan took her sons to the affair, but had no intention of participating, until hecklers got the best of her. She then kicked off her shoes, went to bat, got a hit, and stole two bases in her stocking feet, to the delight of the twins as well as the onlookers.

Another aspect of *The Conqueror* was less amusing. Occasionally wind storms would halt production, giving both cast and crew a breather. It was an ill wind that blew into their lungs, however. Though they did not know it, working in Utah was hazardous to their health. In fact, it might have been fatal.

On May 19, 1953, an atom bomb had been exploded in Nevada, and a freak wind had swept the radioactive fallout across the Utah desert, leaving in its wake an atomic cloud that would later become known as "Dirty Harry."

No one thought much about it then, nor did they in the summer of 1954 on the set of *The Conqueror*. It was not until 1979 that the effects of "Dirty Harry" would finally be known, and become nationwide news, to the accompaniment of lawsuits and banner headlines. But that would not be until twenty-five years later . . . and by then it would be too late.

With *The Conqueror* completed, Susan reported back to Twentieth Century-Fox in early September to appear with Tyrone Power in a movie called *Untamed.* The studio was touting it as a South African *Gone with the Wind,* and, if the columnists are to be believed, the production certainly had as many mishaps. On September 16, Sheilah Graham reported: "During a fire on the *Untamed* set, Susan Hayward rushed in to extinguish the flames while all the men ran to a safe distance. And when hornets invaded the set, Tyrone Power and Richard Egan fled while Susan fought them off with a prop corset."

Susan wouldn't have minded if the whole set burned down, but at least there was one bright spot. She and Richard Egan had first met casually during *Demetrius and the Gladiators,* in which he had had a featured role. An emotional wreck then, she had not talked to him much, but now, to their studio's delight, they began to see each other. In early October, they attended the premiere of Judy Garland's *A Star Is Born* together; and Susan started crying so violently during the film they had to leave before it was over. Obviously it had hit home—reminding her again of her situation with Jess. She later admitted that she returned to see it again—alone. Egan also escorted her to a large party at the Beverly Hills Hotel, and they had several dinner dates, which, needless to say, excited the columnists' imaginations.

The two made a handsome couple, but no one was foolhardy enough to predict marriage. Egan's brother was a priest, and Egan himself a devout Catholic: under no circumstances would he have considered taking a divorced woman as his wife. Still the two had fun together, their dates helped hype *Untamed,* and he diverted Susan's mind from her problems.

The rest of the making of *Untamed* was unmemorable, and with it not due to open until the next March, Susan had time to make another quickie called *Soldier of Fortune.*

On October 13, Susan was back in court asking Superior Court Judge Herbert Walker's permission to take Timothy and Gregory to Hong Kong, where she was scheduled to start work on the film. "I don't think a mother should be away from her children for long, and the trip would help broaden the boys' education."

Studio officials testified the twins would be given first-class accommodations if allowed to go. Judge Walker, however, sustained Jess Barker's contention that Hong Kong was not a safe place for children.

The studio had two choices: replace Susan in the role or film her exterior scenes before a process screen. Co-star Clark Gable had no objection to a replacement: he had originally requested Grace Kelly as his leading lady anyway. It was only when Miss Kelly had wisely turned the role down that Susan was cast. Informed of this, Gable, who had stared at Susan throughout that party a decade earlier, couldn't remember who Susan Hayward was.

In the end, Twentieth Century-Fox decided to send Gable and several other members of the cast to the Orient to shoot what they could, keep Susan in the part, rewrite the script to require very few of the glaring, obvious process shots, and shoot her scenes at home. Once again the studio tried to spread rumors of a real-life romance between the co-stars. Some columnists picked up on such fictional items as: "Clark Gable has started driving Susan Hayward home from work"; "Kay Spreckels and Clark Gable have had some sort of misunderstanding and lately Clark is finding comfort with Susan Hayward"; "On February 2, Clark Gable celebrated his 54th birthday with Susan Hayward." The photograph of the two of them cutting a cake with one candle on the occasion of that birthday was reprinted in newspapers across the country, to the delight of the publicity department. It meant nothing, however, and the reviews this dull little melodrama received are not worth repeating. Gable and Hayward together for the first and last time received about as much enthusiasm as the Hong Kong Flu.

Susan had been aware that *Soldier of Fortune* was a bomb from the beginning. The only reason she'd agreed to do it was for the free trip to the Orient for herself and family. When that fell through, she considered her assignment nothing more than marking time.

In late February, Susan agreed to help publicize *Untamed* by attending its multiple premieres in the Miami area, on the condition she'd be permitted to go on to the Bahamas for a few days' rest. The studio's motivation for choosing Miami as the site of a premiere of a movie about South Africa and Zulu uprisings was never clear. It was a typical media event, long before that expression had been coined. Twentieth's Miami office hired the 110-piece Greater Miami Boys Drum and Bugle Corps to serenade her, and on premiere night, March 1, the corps picked up Susan at the Algiers Hotel, where she was staying, escorted her first to the Lincoln Theater, then down Lincoln Road to the Capri. Miami's mayor Harold Shapiro met Susan on a specially constructed podium and presented her with the key to the city. The whole affair was filmed by Fox-Movietone News for replay in theaters across the country. It was a smashing success—which didn't help the reviews much, unfortunately.

Mocking the studio's attempt to come up with another *Gone with the Wind*, the *Philadelphia Inquirer*'s Mildred Martin wrote: "Compared with Katie O'Neill, Scarlett O'Hara was a little sit-by-the-fire. For Katie, to whom the film's title refers, is just as conniving and several times as active as Scarlett ever dreamed of being. She is, as played by fiery Susan Hayward . . . quite a collector of masculine scalps, acquiring a couple of husbands, a lover, and two sons before screen time and the authentic South African backgrounds run out.

"While Scarlett only had the Civil War to worry her on a grand scale, poor Katie meets hoards of howling spear-throwing Zulus face to face on the South African veldt. . . . But the result unfortunately is just a combination of *Gone with the Wind*, parody style, with South African-flavored horse opera."

Variety also observed that, "Miss Hayward struggles somewhat grimly with a part that would defy any actress. However, she's easy on the eye, wears some attractive period dresses and is emotional when the occasion demands."

And *Time* magazine, calling the entire cast "*Gone with the Wind* machines," dealt the final blow when it quoted Tyrone Power's immortal line when he is reunited with his lost love: "You . . . here in Africa fighting Zulus . . . I can hardly believe it." Neither could anyone else.

Back in Miami, Susan had stayed around to do a little fishing, she said. "I hear Miami has the most magnificent fishing facilities anywhere," she told reporters. What she *didn't* say was that Howard Hughes was floating around in the area and that he was the fish she was interested in catching.

Hughes, however, was the one that got away. Ever since the divorce action, when his name had been dragged through the court, he had been noticeably cool toward Susan and, in fact,

Susan had hardly seen him at all. She was ready to make another stab at it, but it was too late. The only reason he was in Miami now was to be with Jean Peters; she had established residence there to obtain a divorce from Stuart Cramer. By now Hughes had decided he cared enough for Peters to marry her, and didn't even bother to return Susan's frequent phone calls. With a deflated ego, Susan left Miami for the Bahamas.

Back home, things were even more depressing. She received a wire informing her that Martha Little had succumbed to cancer, and, tearfully, she booked the next flight east to attend Miss Little's funeral. While she was in New York, columnists, unaware of her affection for the Little family, blamed Susan's melancholy on Hughes's reconciliation with Jean Peters, but it was much more than that. She had been jilted, true, but also a good friend had died. She had just been through several emotionally exhausting months of personal turmoil, and her career, once so bright, seemed to be on the downswing. The final straw came on the weekend of April 23.

That weekend, Susan agreed to meet Jess in a bungalow at the Ambassador Hotel. Jess later called it "a peace meeting to stop this tug-of-war over the twins. Susan never talks to me when I call to see the boys. She won't even let the servants talk to me. The children see this, and it is bad for them.

"I admit I blew up at the finish of this meeting. We got absolutely nowhere. I said some unpleasant things, but they had been on my chest for two years."

On Monday afternoon, Susan issued a reply: "I have my reasons for not seeing him alone. . . . Moreover, I have an interlocutory degree, and I don't want to jeopardize it. I'm a good mother. I don't believe the boys have ever been so well."

During her eighteen years on the Hollywood scene, there had been many who had compared Susan to a machine—a piece of steel without a heart.

At three o'clock Tuesday morning, the machine broke down.

PART FOUR

Susan Hayward
Hollywood
April 26, 1955 — February 8, 1957

You aim for all the things you have been told stardom means—the rich life, the applause, the parties cluttered with celebrities, the awards. Then it is nothing, really nothing. It is like a drug that lasts just a few hours, a sleeping pill. When it wears off you have to live without its help.

SUSAN HAYWARD

chapter 19

THERE WAS SOMETHING she had forgotten to do . . .

What was it?

The pills were beginning to take effect, and her thoughts and memory were confused.

Oh, yes. She had forgotten to call her mother. She didn't want Ellen Marrenner to feel she was being left destitute. Losing her sole means of support would disturb Ellen more than a loss of a child. There were other children. Susan had always felt the least loved; in fact, sometimes she had felt Ellen would have been happier if Florence had become the star. Ellen wouldn't grieve long for Edythe. It was the money that mattered. It was always the money that mattered. Throughout Susan's girlhood, Ellen had made that quite clear: reminding Walter Marrenner that Florence made more money than he did; fawning over Florence because of her earnings.

Susan dialed Ellen's number by rote. It was unlikely she could see the letters on the dial or the time on the living-room clock. It was 3:15 A.M., and Susan had taken far too many pills.

Mrs. Marrenner was awakened by the phone. There were seconds of silence. Then she heard a slurred voice mumble, *"Don't worry, mother, you'll be taken care of."* And a click.

Aware of her daughter's depression, Ellen Marrenner phoned the North Hollywood police. She was hysterical as she told them: "I think there is something wrong with my daughter, my daughter is Susan Hayward. I'm afraid she's going to commit suicide."

Police detective G. W. Wilkerson and another officer sped to Longridge Avenue in nearby Sherman Oaks. Unable to get in the front door, the detective yelled repeatedly, "Susan, this is Wilkerson of the detective bureau. Let us in."

The two officers went around to the patio, kicked in a door, and found Susan sprawled unconscious on the living-room floor in a white quilted housecoat and pajamas.

After speaking to the police, Ellen Marrenner had called Wally, who rushed to Sherman Oaks. By the time he arrived, photographers were already on the scene. Remarkably, the chaos hadn't disturbed Tim and Gregory, peacefully asleep in their upstairs bedroom.

The police couldn't prevent cameras clicking as they carried the unconscious woman from the house to the police car: Wilkerson couldn't risk waiting for an ambulance. They sped Susan to North Hollywood Receiving Hospital to have her stomach pumped. After the emergency treatment, her condition was described as fair, and the attending doctor said, "It's just a matter of sleeping it off. It was a close one. We acted on the premise that it was an overdose of sleeping pills."

Executives at Twentieth Century-Fox and MGM (to whom Susan was about to be loaned for Lillian Roth's *I'll Cry Tomorrow*), as concerned about the adverse publicity upon their upcoming movies as about Susan, made arrangements to have her removed to Cedars of Lebanon Hospital where, fooling no one, she was registered under the name of Mary Brennen.

Dr. Stanley Imerman, whose name was on one of the two bottles of sleeping pills found in the house, took charge. Someone had to talk to the reporters gathered in the hospital's vast lobby.

Imerman, protective of his patient, had his statement carefully prepared. "Miss Hayward has been despondent for some time because of marital problems. She has also been working very hard in film productions. She took some sedatives to enable her to sleep and find relief from tension, and I am sure the overdose was mainly accidental.

"Her condition is satisfactory and she should be home in a couple of days."

Lillian Roth, questioned at the same time and protective of *I'll Cry Tomorrow*, echoed Dr. Imerman's sentiments, adding, "Susan is too vital, too eager and ambitious a girl to want to

end her life. No, I think she was highly nervous about the filming of the picture and might have had a few cocktails. The
alcohol and the sleeping pills fought each other, slowing her
pulse, making her respiration very shallow, lowering her skin
temperature. When your nerves are a little off-the-beam, this can
happen to you. It happened to me." Neither Miss Roth nor
Dr. Imerman made any reference to Susan's phone call to her
mother.

Susan had barely emerged from her coma when Jess Barker,
in New Orleans on a personal appearance tour for his movie
Kentucky Rifles—since the divorce, he had found some work—
boarded a plane to Los Angeles. Just before take-off, he wired:
COMING HOME AS FAST AS I CAN. LOVE, DADDY. At first he had
signed the wire "Jess," then changed it to "Daddy," remembering
her pet name for him during their marriage. Chill Wills, also in
New Orleans for the picture, told reporters who hadn't been able
to get to Jess before he'd left town, "It's a shame that people in
love have to have this happen to them. He's been carrying the
torch for her for so long, and she's still in love with him."

She loved him. She hated him. She loved him.

But she would not give in to him. The money had been a
weapon. The children had been weapons. Perhaps the suicide
attempt had been one too: another manifestation of the tremendous need she still had to punish him. And herself.

More obvious was the No Visitors sign she had posted outside
her hospital room after receiving Jess's wire.

On the evening of April 26, Jess drove to Cedars of Lebanon,
and was told by night supervisor Jane Allen that Susan was
"resting well," but that Dr. Imerman had left instructions that
no one was to see her. After a ten-minute phone conversation
with Dr. Imerman, Jess told reporters waiting for him:

"Dr. Imerman said that Mrs. Barker is not to see anyone—
not even her mother—until she is fully recovered. He said that
my visiting her would bring emotional stress. I took Stanley's
advice in this matter. He's always been a good friend of mine."

Jess had nothing more to say that night but, frustrated by
evasive studio comments, suspicious of Imerman's statements,
the Hollywood press wouldn't give up. Besieged for interviews,
Jess Barker relented and agreed to a press conference on April
27 at the home of close friends in Reseda.

Discussing the blaring headlines of the previous afternoon,

Jess denied that he had collapsed in New Orleans when informed of his estranged wife's suicide attempt or that he had said, "My God, I love her," as had been attributed to him. So when reporters asked why, then, he was so eager to see her at all, he replied quietly: "Ten years together and two children mean something. Or maybe it should be the other way around—two children and ten years."

When he had not been able to gain admittance to the hospital, Jess had driven to the house on Longridge Avenue to spend some time with his sons. "The boys asked if I had been to see their mother, and they wanted to know if we had made up. I told them I had been to the hospital and she was asleep. The boys know there is something wrong with their mother without knowing the full details. I plan to see them after school today and play basketball or baseball with them. We usually go to a public park or to the home of friends."

As to using the incident as grounds for regaining custody of his sons, he said, "That's a bridge to be crossed later. The important thing now is her recovery and that the children are properly supervised." Jess concluded that he "had no idea" why Susan had taken the pills.

"I know of no other romance in her life. Her family may have an explanation of this, not me. She's the type to let emotions stir up over a period of years. I've said numerous times that it might build up to a sort of breakdown. But in moments of depression she never dwelt on suicide. But remember, I've hardly seen the lady in a year and eight or nine months." He did not mention the meeting the two of them had had the weekend before. Two days later, Jess returned to New Orleans, the orders to bar him from the hospital unrescinded.

While Susan was recovering from the effects of her ordeal, the Hollywood press was having a field day, and the local TV stations built up huge ratings replaying all her old films. Newspapers dug into their files and reprinted whatever pictures they had, supplemented by the grotesque candids taken on the night of the attempt; and, horrified by the pictures that were appearing, Susan finally granted photographers the privilege she had denied Jess Barker. They were allowed into her hospital room.

On April 28, the public was relieved to see a radiant Susan, beautifully coiffured and attired, smiling at them from the front page of their afternoon dailies. The following morning, wearing a white linen strawberry print, and the inevitable white gloves, Susan departed Cedars of Lebanon Hospital looking as if she had never heard of sleeping pills. Hospital rules required that all departing patients be taken out in wheelchairs, but the minute she hit the door she jumped to her feet.

Surrounded by studio press agents and greeted by an army of photographers and reporters, Susan submitted to a few minutes of questioning. She firmly stated that there wasn't a chance in the world of a reconciliation with Jess. She was joyfully looking forward to a reunion with the twins. "They're at school now, but I'll be there waiting for them when they return home." She refuted the rumors that she wanted to get out of her MGM commitment. "Nonsense, I'm starting rehearsals for *I'll Cry Tomorrow* next week!"

She wanted the press on her side—completely. But when one reporter asked the question on everyone's mind—"Why did you take the pills?"—she just shook her head and replied, "That's something that's between me and God." Then, reaching for the young man's hand, she added, "And don't let anyone ever tell you that there is no God. There is."

That was her exit line. She got into the limousine the studio had had waiting and drove home. There Susan called Louella, her protectress, who cheerfully told her readers: "Susan sounded so wonderful—so happy and full of pep—when she told me she was home and rarin' to go. She'll be back at MGM on Monday, and she's having lunch tomorrow with Danny Mann to discuss the script."

On May 2, as scheduled, Susan checked into MGM to begin dancing and voice lessons. She was not expected to sing in *I'll Cry Tomorrow*, merely to record her pronunciation and range for dubbing, but to her astonishment, when she got there, MGM musical supervisor Johnny Green said her voice might be good enough to sing the Lillian Roth songs herself. It required weeks of persuasion and a number of tape-recording sessions with Charles Henderson, the movie's musical arranger and conductor, before Susan was convinced she could do it; but when she was, she threw herself into the sessions with enthusiasm. Soon, all the songs were on tape, recorded in her own deep, resonant contralto.

Everyone, from producer Larry Weingarten to Danny Mann to Johnny Green, was excited. Green immediately called a show-wise group of the Hollywood press to the studio and played them two reels of Susan's songs: "Sing You Sinners," "When the Red, Red Robin Comes Bob, Bob, Bobbin' Along," "Happiness Is a Thing Called Joe," "I'm Sittin' on Top of the World," and the waltz from *Vagabond King.*

The Hollywood press heard a new, fresh voice and liked what they heard.

Johnny Green's eyes lit up. "She's a female bass, isn't she, boys?" he said. "Did you ever hear such timbre?"

Susan herself admitted, "It was a big surprise gift, a new career to be explored."

Donald Pippin, then a young musician, now a leading Broadway musical director, insists, "Green got all of the publicity and credit for Susan's singing, but it was Chuck Henderson who did all the work. I know, I was there. I met Susan at a vocal session at Chuck's for the first time. If it weren't for him, she could never have come through as well as she did."

There is no argument, however, as to who was responsible for Susan's dazzling performance in *I'll Cry Tomorrow.* For the balance of her life, she credited Danny Mann for that achievement.

"Danny checked every detail. He wouldn't let me cheat with lipstick or even a curl. If he thought my hair wasn't mussed up enough, he put water on his hands and mashed it down. Danny and I went to A.A. meetings, hospitals and even jails because I had to know that woman's life and what it had become."

The best source Susan could go to, of course, was Lillian Roth, herself, and Miss Roth served as "technical adviser" on the film.

I'll Cry Tomorrow, based on Roth's autobiographical best seller, was the story of a beautiful and talented young girl, deprived of a normal childhood by an ambitious mother, who first achieves Broadway and Hollywood stardom before she is twenty and then endures sixteen years of alcoholic degradation before she is able to overcome her illness and start a new life. In the film, Roth takes her first drink to help her recover from the death of the first man she loved. From then on, it is a one-way downhill slide: drinking to help her to forget; then drinking to enable her to face her fast-dwindling audiences; finally drinking in remorse and self-pity.

In an alcoholic haze, she finds herself married to an immature aviation officer and, when that fails, to a physically attractive but brutal sadist (Richard Conte). Kept a virtual prisoner and tormented by the man, Roth hits bottom and attempts suicide. Finally, with the help of Alcoholics Anonymous and a former alcoholic (Eddie Albert), she makes the climb back to sobriety and happiness. In the final scene, she tells her story on television, in the hope it will help others who feel beaten by the bottle.

After meeting Lillian Roth for the first time, Susan told International News Service reporter Emily Belser: "It's a man's world, and women must make their way in it the best way they can. Miss Roth went into alcoholism and despair, but her spirit never completely flickered out, and she found a way to restore it. I think this is something worth saying to women, and I think women will understand what it means. . . . This is not fiction. . . . It is the story of a life—a real life. It should have a tremendous impact on people, especially women who have experienced or are experiencing the damnation of alcoholism. It should prove to them once and for all that a person can return to normal with sufficient courage and with the help of God. For me, this film will be a work of love."

Although Miss Roth was thrilled that MGM was able to get Susan to portray her life, she admitted later,* "I was very shocked when I was told that I wasn't going to do my own singing, but she had made her mind up that *she* was going to sing. And that's one thing you find out about Susie—that when she makes her mind up to do something, that's it. I thought she did a good job, but I was so disappointed. . . . I was heartbroken they didn't use my *voice*. Eventually there were two record albums on the film. I did one for Coral, and then there was the sound-track recording which got all the publicity.

"I never found out an awful lot about Susie except that she was a very *forceful* person. We had talked for hours and hours, days, but she never allowed me to get to know *her*. But she wanted to know everything about me. Everything!

"There was so much in my life that was left out of that movie because they were so nervous about the subject of alcoholism!

* In an interview with this writer just two months before Miss Roth's death on May 12, 1980.

And they were afraid to touch the subject of the nut house I was in. But even if it wasn't in the script, Susie wanted to know about it. . . .

"And whenever I came to the set she'd keep staring at me and staring. Things eventually got to the stage where I didn't know if I was me or Susie was me, and vice versa.

"But I thought she was wonderful in the part—real wonderful! Later, when it was all over, they had us attend a lot of the premieres together, but, as I said, I never really got to know her, and she didn't keep in touch. Then maybe fifteen years later I get this beautiful Christmas card from her.

"But I don't think Susie remained close or got close to anyone on the picture except Danny Mann and that Barry guy."

More about "that Barry guy" presently.

A relative newcomer to the Hollywood scene at that time, Mann had a quiet but forceful way of handling the most difficult personalities. Susan, however, presented a different kind of problem. Mann knew that if the picture was to be a success, Susan had to trust him completely—at no time could he seem to be a threat or a problem to her. To convince her that he sincerely wanted to be a friend, he avoided the usual Dutch-uncle talks, and instead invited her to his home to meet his wife and children, to show her how he lived. They discussed the picture very little. They talked about their kids.

"Susan's ability," says Mann, "was matched only by her courage. She reached for the ultimate, and had an enormous capacity for digging into herself emotionally while playing a role. Her ability to concentrate in areas where it is required was remarkable. When an actress goes through the emotional wringer as Susan did in *I'll Cry Tomorrow*, it can't help but be a great strain. The director must be indulgent. But Susan neither required nor wanted indulgence while making the picture. She gave her utmost to the scenes, but when they were over, she stepped out with no bleeding."

When a reporter visiting the set remarked that it took guts to play in that story, Susan, with her usual directness, shot back, "It took guts to live it."

An example of her coolness under fire was demonstrated in a particularly harrowing scene during which Susan had to writhe in bed in the grip of violent delirium tremens, while several members of Alcoholics Anonymous tried to sober her up. The acting was so real that it caused hardened drinkers in the crew to shake in their boots. Yet when the scene was cut, Susan crawled out of the bed and calmly retired to her dressing room to run through the lines for her next scene. Between takes, she cheerfully posed for poster art. If there were any aftereffects of the suicide attempt, she did not show them.

Throughout the filming of *I'll Cry Tomorrow,* Susan and Danny Mann continued to grow closer. On Susan's thirty-eighth birthday, he held a surprise party for her on the set. In turn, when Mann celebrated his forty-third birthday on August 8, Susan, aware that Danny considered nine his lucky number, had ninety-nine roses delivered to him. No one suggested the relationship was anything deeper, however. By now, Susan was extremely interested in someone else.

It was yet another gentleman from the South, from Houston, Texas, this time, whom she had met when he had played a small part in an Alcoholic Anonymous sequence early in *I'll Cry Tomorrow.* He had been born Donald Barry de Acosta. He was better known in Hollywood circles as Don "Red" Barry. And he had already built up quite a reputation for himself as a cowboy star—and as a great lover. Later, one of his former lady friends would say: "I can't define what Don Barry *has,* but whatever it is, he should bottle it."

Susan probably would have been better off if he had.

chapter 20

"SUSAN HAYWARD," Don Barry reflects today, at seventy. "Every man alive should experience one Susan Hayward in his lifetime. I wrote that in a poem about her called 'Portrait of a Lady.' That's what I think. She was to me one of the most wonderful and exciting experiences of my life."

It was an experience that started almost casually, rapidly developed into an affair, then exploded into violent headlines across the country. In the end, it would cause Susan humiliation, contribute to her losing an Oscar—and come close to costing her custody of her sons.

From the beginning, however, the two made no secret of their interest in each other. In August, prior to her leaving for New York for special location shooting on *I'll Cry Tomorrow,* Susan and Don were seen having dinner together at the Captain's Table, a popular seafood spot. Later, after the movie was wrapped, the two resumed dating. Their frequent meetings caused Louella Parsons to report reluctantly in early September, "Just before Susan took off for Honolulu with her twins, she had dinner with Don "Red" Barry at Holiday House. She's been seen quite a lot with him lately, but Susie has had so much trouble with the opposite sex that I don't look to see her getting involved again."

Miss Parsons's crystal ball was decidedly muddy. Barry was at the airport to see Susan off to Hawaii. He would be there when she returned.

In Honolulu, Susan checked in at the Royal Hawaiian Hotel

and looked up old acquaintances and beach boys who had been particularly helpful in the past—Chick Daniels of the Outrigger Canoe Club, Philip at the Princess Kaiulani. The latter promised to keep an eye on the twins when they went surfing.

On rare days when the weather failed to live up to expectations, Susan went on shopping expeditions. The afternoon before leaving Honolulu for Hana-Maui, she took her sons to some native boutiques. Although she never believed in dressing them identically for school or for parties, she bought them swim trunks with matching beach coats, and found several swim suits with paké coats for herself.

It was on this expedition that Timothy spotted an antique hand-carved ivory chess set in a window, which he dearly wanted. Susan was pleased by her son's good taste, but not by the price tag, which read $395. She explained her resistance to the purchase by rationalizing, "This is the sort of set that a person owns after he has become a very great chess player. It is a sort of reward. I'd like to have you own it, but it will have to be earned. When you become a champion, I'll buy this one or one like it for you."

The next morning Susan, Timothy, and Gregory flew over to Hana-Maui. It was then a quiet, elegant, native resort. There was little to do except eat, sleep, rest, and swim. Some nights, the three of them attended the hula shows. These were the sights Susan wanted to share with her sons. More importantly, the ten days away from Hollywood afforded her the privacy to more completely win their affection. Jess was as anxious as ever to obtain full custody of the boys; Susan was determined to fight it with every ounce of her energy.

Back on the mainland, she resumed her relationship with Don Barry. When she was invited to attend a rough cut of *I'll Cry Tomorrow* on September 28, she asked Don to share it with her— but frustrated photographers by leaving through a private door.

Column items appeared regularly:

Parsons, 10/2/55: "Hollywood is talking about Susan Hayward's frequent appearances with Don 'Red' Barry, who had practically disappeared from the public scene since he once escorted Joan Crawford about town."

Skolsky, 10/5/55: "Don 'Red' Barry and Susan Hayward are solid regardless of what you might have read elsewhere."

Kilgallen, 10/10/55: "Susan Hayward, whose marriage to Jess Barker caused her such bitter unhappiness, is feeling optimistic enough to consider trying matrimony again. The chap who looks like Mr. Right is Don 'Red' Barry, the actor."

Nonetheless, Hollywood's army of press photographers were still unable to catch the two together anywhere. When the two of them *were* "caught," it was in his bedroom one Friday morning, and it wasn't by a photographer.

Later, Susan would say: "Why do these things happen? The answer is a question. Have you ever been lonely?" And it was loneliness rather than love which led Susan to spend the night at Don Barry's apartment. She trusted his discretion. What she couldn't have anticipated was Jil Jarmyn's jealousy.

Before he had met Susan, Barry had been going steady with a sexy starlet whom he had met the previous June, when both had been working in a film called *A Twinkle in God's Eye.* As late as October 14, Army Archerd, the columnist for *Variety,* reported, "Don Barry, who'd been dating Susan Hayward, now calling Jil Jarmyn from the Lone Pine location of *Seven Men from Now.*"

He had been calling Susan too. As a footloose bachelor, that was his prerogative. It seemed obvious that he preferred Susan's company, but Jarmyn wasn't about to admit defeat that easily. In fact, she may have been encouraged by an item in Hedda Hopper's October 31 column: "Hal Hayes sure gets around. This time with Susan Hayward at L'Escoffier at the Beverly Hilton." Maybe Hayward was finally about to ditch Barry in favor of the handsome builder columnists had described as a "zillionaire."

Unable to reach Barry on the phone early in the morning of November 4, 1955, Jil Jarmyn drove to his home in North Hollywood. Finding the door open, she entered the house and headed for Barry's bedroom. What happened next depends on whose version one wants to believe—Hayward's or Jarmyn's.

Don Barry, now a happily married family man and churchgoer, still won't say any more today than he did a quarter of a century ago: "Look, I'm in the middle of this." Jarmyn's version, however, is the juicier one:

"I had barely gotten into the room when—pow! Susan pushed Don out of the way and yelled, 'Who is this girl?' Before Don could say anything, she socked me in the jaw.

"Don tried to tell her who I was, she wouldn't listen. She picked

up a wooden clothes brush and hit me over the head. I kept saying, 'If you'll get out of my way, I'll leave.' Don kept saying,
'Susan, will you let her by?'

"Susan calmed down, but then she lunged at me again and the
furniture went all over the place. She quieted down and wanted
some coffee. Then she came back at me with a lighted cigarette.
She threw me down . . . ripped the buttons off my blouse and
socked me.

"I finally got out of there!"

Displaying a sore left jaw, a badly bruised arm and a bitten
thumb, Miss Jarmyn told reporters, "Twentieth Century-Fox studios was on the phone all day pleading with me to hush up the
story."

Miss Jarmyn, in turn, was on the phone with Jess Barker's
attorney Sammy Hahn and the Van Nuys police department.
Contacted, Hahn coolly said: "This incident will help Jess's appeal to get back his children."

That's what terrified Susan. Rather than antagonize the press
clamoring for more of her side of the story, Susan revised her
original statement, which claimed that she and Barry had been
having "a casual cup of coffee" when Miss Jarmyn came bursting in.

"I could say I was in the dining room at the time, but I wasn't.
I was in the bedroom in my pajamas. Miss Jarmyn walked into
the bedroom and made an insulting remark. It was nasty.

"Being Irish, this infuriated me, and I went toward her and a
wrestling match ensued. . . . I don't know who swung the first
blow. I struck her. . . . It wasn't over Don Barry. My anger was
at this woman whom I never saw before daring to use such
language—so insulting that I cannot even repeat it. I don't take
that kind of talk from anyone."

Whoever story was true, the next sequence of events must
have been slightly confusing to the outside world. Jil Jarmyn
entered a signed complaint with Deputy City Attorney Stephen R.
Powers, Jr., of Van Nuys. Then, just as abruptly, on November 7,
she announced she was dropping all charges against Susan Hayward because "Susan's children might suffer." Plainly, Susan's
attorneys had done a bit of talking with the starlet.

Don Barry too broke his silence by asking, "What's the fuss? I
just happened to invite both girls to drop in for coffee some time."

After that, it was left to Marlene Dietrich to make the definitive comment on the whole mess: "That Red Barry must make *some* cup of coffee!"

Despite the embarrassment, Susan continued to see Barry. Early in December, she moved to a new house on Longridge Avenue, just two doors away from her former residence, and Sidney Skolsky noted, "Her first guest was Don Barry, who came over to see the place and have a cup of coffee with Susan." (Apparently Susan's coffee too was pretty good.) Mike Connolly of the *Hollywood Reporter* spotted the twosome "strolling on Longridge Avenue at 1:30 A.M., arm in arm."

Shortly before Christmas, Jess Barker filed a special appeal with the California State District Court, still fighting to have the divorce, which had become final in August, nullified. Susan was advised he didn't stand a chance of having the appeal granted, and gave the matter no more thought. She was in a wonderful mood and refused to allow anything to interfere with the upcoming holidays.

Only Louella knew who really had Susan smiling again: "Now it's Hal Hayes who has been taking Susan Hayward out to dinner. . . ." One needed a score card to keep up with the action.

chapter 21

SUSAN JUBILANTLY waltzed into the New Year in the arms of charming, wealthy businessman Hal Hayes, her date at socialite Cobina Wright's elegant holiday soirée. Noted character actress Lurene Tuttle (mother-in-law of composer-conductor John Williams) recalls: "It was kept quite a secret, but Susan was madly in love with Hal. So were a number of other Hollywood women. He was considered the most eligible bachelor in Hollywood."

A week later Susan left for New York, Philadelphia, and Washington for ten days' publicity on *I'll Cry Tomorrow*, due to open on January 12, 1956, at Radio City Music Hall. Hayes followed her east to—as Dorothy Kilgallen cattily noted—"bask in the stardust," but the stardust must have faded suddenly. On January 13, Susan provoked a mystery by leaving New York in the middle of the night to return to California. "It was too cold," said Susan. "Too hot," said Earl Wilson, chuckling. "Hal Hayes is wearing some scratches on his nose given to him by Susan Hayward during a little disagreement they had. . . ." Wilson didn't go into specifics. Hayes, always the gentleman, refused to discuss his injuries.

Susan's depression following the quarrel with Hayes, however, must have disappeared when she read the reviews accorded her performance as Lillian Roth.

Look magazine devoted a cover story to her: "She gives a performance that does the industry great credit—a many-sided and poignant dissolution of a human being and her right to be re-

habilitated. . . . The story's emotional power is vividly com-
municated by Susan Hayward in a shattering, intense performance that may win her the Academy Award." (It would win
her the *Look* award for the Best Actress of the Year in 1955.)

Edward Schallert of the *Los Angeles Times* let out all stops:
"Susan Hayward becomes an indisputable candidate for the
Academy of Arts and Sciences because of her performance. Her
acting effect is likely even to be more appreciated than the
film. . . . The story is basically repellent, but . . . Miss Hayward deserves all the praise that can and will be bestowed for
this, her major screen effort. She had one prior alcoholic role to
play in *Smash-Up,* which gained her Academy recognition. But
that was pygmy-like by comparison to this fearfully demanding
assignment which seemed to require the utmost, both mentally
and physically, from the star."

With less verbosity, Kate Cameron of the *New York Daily
News,* giving the picture four stars, wrote: "Susan Hayward tears
the heart out of you."

Even the usually critical *Time* magazine conceded that "Susan
Hayward plays her part right up to the cork: she can make the
audience see not only the horror of the heroine's life but the wry
humor of it." And *Life,* devoting a three-page spread to the film,
summarized: "Susan Hayward does a superb portrayal of Lillian
Roth from the spotlight to blackout—including some fine, unexpected throaty singing."

Only the hard-hearted Bosley Crowther of the *New York Times*
had some reservations: "The vaudeville singer that Miss Hayward
puts on the screen . . . gives little signs of being neurotic, un-
stable, or perverse. However, once her baleful lady gets into her
cups, she is thoroughly authentic and convincing, shattering and
sad. . . . The strong part is when Miss Hayward indicates the
actual agonies of Miss Roth."

Heady stuff, indeed. In spite of these raves, though, the New
York Film Critics failed to give Susan a single nod when they
cast their ballots for Best Actress of 1955. Instead, Anna Magnani
scored a first-ballot victory with thirteen votes for her performance in *The Rose Tattoo.* Susan concealed her disappointment
and prayed that, come Oscar time, the often-chauvinistic Academy would ignore a foreign actress.

Meanwhile, her social life was showing a marked improvement. Early in February 1956, columnists dismissed Hal Hayes and Red Barry and began linking Susan to men anonymously identified as "an F.B.I. agent," "a tall, balding fellow," "a Virginia attorney," "a handsome Washington lawyer," and "an Atlanta used-car dealer." It wasn't until Susan introduced Floyd Eaton Chalkley to the press at a *Redbook* party that the newshawks (and the public) became aware that her flurry of dates were all the same man. She didn't let him out of her sight all evening.

But who and what exactly was Floyd Eaton Chalkley? Where did he come from? And what did he have that Susan found so fascinating?

First of all, it was his Southern background. Chalkley was a native Virginian now living in Georgia, and he was quiet, charming, gentlemanly. He had been an FBI agent before and during the war, he said, then allegedly made a fortune as a used-car dealer. Now he dabbled in projects that interested him. He had a hint of mystery, flashed a pile of money, and seemed ready-made for Susan.

If she had wanted to check a little deeper, however, she would have found more than just a hint of mystery. FBI records checked on March 3, 1980, reveal that he was born on June 19, 1909, but give no place of birth. He started working for their offices in Washington, D.C., as a file clerk-typist on June 29, 1934; on October 11, 1937, he was promoted to a position listed as "Special Agent," and he resigned from the bureau on February 16, 1940— six years before he later claimed J. Edgar Hoover dismissed him for budgetary reasons. His salary at the time was $3,200 a year. The reason for his resignation is not recorded in the FBI's files.

The FBI also has no statistics about Eaton Chalkley's personal life, education, army record (if any), or marital life. Regarding the latter, shortly after Eaton became interested in Susan, his sister Mrs. Peggy Irwin of Carrollton, Georgia, where Eaton still had a car dealership and forty acres of choice property, let slip that Eaton had been divorced twice and had three teen-age children then living with their mother nearby. This was later changed to one divorce.

Curious discrepancies. There would be more later.

Right now, however, it was December 1955, and Chalkley, together with his buddy, restaurateur Harvey Hestor, had arrived in Los Angeles, where they contacted another mutual friend,

Vincent X. Flaherty, the author of *Jim Thorpe—All American*. Flaherty invited both men to his gala Christmas bash. Hestor invited Susan, whom he had known for some time, to be his date. Since Hal Hayes had other plans that evening, Susan thought it would be fun to spend some time with—as she called him— Uncle Harvey.

Early in the evening, Hestor introduced Chalkley, who had brought his own date, to Susan, and the two made small talk for a while, but there was little opportunity for private conversation. When the crowd thinned out, Flaherty remembered, "I suggested a small group of us continue the party at the Mocambo." Noticing that Chalkley, a shy man, did not seem to be enjoying the festivities, Flaherty said, "Hey, Eaton, why don't you dance with Susan? Mix in, pal. Mix in."

"That did it," Flaherty boasted. "For the first time I saw my cool and collected pal beset with shakes."

He must have calmed them, however, because Eaton Chalkley invited Susan out before he returned to Georgia, and they agreed to keep in touch. When business brought him back to Hollywood a little later, they had a pleasant dinner at the Sportsman's Lodge. They began seeing each other regularly.

Asked if it was a serious romance, Susan laughed it off. Imitating Scarlett O'Hara, she drawled, "Oh fiddle-de-dee, Mr. Chalkley and I have fun going out together, but that's all there is to it."

Meantime, in the midst of what appeared to be a pleasant social life, Susan was still embroiled in legal controversies, as Jess's lawyer filed yet another divorce appeal. In addition, a series of nasty little items began appearing in the columns, attributed not to Jess, but to rival studios attempting to sabotage Susan's Oscar chances: items about Hughes, Don Barry, the suicide attempt. Preview scuttlebutt about *The Conqueror*, scheduled for release ten days after the awards, was also devastating.

Although she had originally planned to have only the twins as her date for the Academy Awards evening, Susan got a fourth ticket for Chalkley, stirring up further speculation. Uncharacteristically, the woman who never gave parties made arrangements for a "win or lose" bash immediately following the presentations.

When the five nominees were announced that evening in alphabetical order, they were: Susan Hayward for *I'll Cry Tomorrow*, Katharine Hepburn for *Summertime*, Jennifer Jones for

Love Is a Many Splendored Thing, Anna Magnani for *The Rose Tattoo,* and Eleanor Parker for *Interrupted Melody.* Susan Hayward's name was greeted by sustained applause.

A hush filled the Pantages Theatre as the celebrated envelope was opened.

"And the winner is . . . Anna Magnani for *The Rose Tattoo.*" The presenter visibly found it difficult to conceal his disappointment, and the groans from the audience were clearly audible.

Nevertheless, Susan's party went on as scheduled. Louella, who left the party for the winning picture, *Marty,* early, so as not to disappoint her pet, wrote: "Susan Hayward would never give a better performance in her life than she did when the Oscar went to Anna Magnani. Sitting in front of me at the Academy Awards with her twin sons when the announcement was made, she turned to me and said, 'We'll have to try harder next year.' At her party, Susan sang song after song and was the gayest of the few friends who gathered at her home. Her two boys looked more downcast than Susan. I hear it was very close between her and Magnani."

Commenting on that night, Susan confided, "I managed not to shed any tears until everything was over. Then I sat down and had a good cry and decided that losing was just part of the game." Her real feelings were probably unprintable.

Eaton, who remained after the other guests had gone home, provided a strong shoulder for Susan to cry on . . . until the wee hours of the morning. It is possible he provided a great deal more. Harvey Hestor remembered his returning to Georgia behaving like a love-sick kid. For her part, although she admitted to being very fond of him, Susan remained uncommitted. She didn't want to mess up things with Chalkley—but she didn't want to be tied down, either.

Shortly afterward, she was due in Cannes for the film festival, where *I'll Cry Tomorrow* was in competition. Although she still wasn't friendly with Sheilah Graham, she agreed to have dinner with the columnist and was surprisingly talkative under the circumstances.

"The monkey's off my back," she said cryptically, a remark Graham attributed to the divorce from Jess. "My seven-year contract with Twentieth Century-Fox ends in August, and I'll be a free woman not only in my private life but with my career.

205

"I believe my troubles have been beneficial. You must have problems to be able to understand others. Now that it's almost over, and I pray it is, I realize it is better for the children to have a home that is peaceful, and I aim to keep it that way. I can't take the boys with me to the film festival—they're in school, and besides there's always such a bother with Jess when I want to take them out of the country. But one thing I promised them, and this they will get. They love to travel, and when they're 14 years old we're going on a tramp steamer around the world. I have put this money away already for them. The three of us are very close, the twins are different shapes and sizes, but we all love the same things. When I took them to Sun Valley, we all had a great time."

To Graham's surprise, Susan talked frankly of remarriage. "You can be sure I'll be very careful before I marry again, but I'd hate to think I'd live alone for the rest of my life. I'm not the type who can live alone and like it." Reiterating that her marital problems had not soured her on the subject, she added wistfully, "I'd like to marry again. But for now I'm feeling free and wonderful, thank you, and I aim to have a great time at the festival."

Throughout the evening she never mentioned Eaton Chalkley's name.

On April 27 Susan arrived in Cannes. Surrounded by hundreds of reporters and photographers, she yelled out: "Where are the men around here? I don't mean actors, I mean men!"

They'd find her quickly enough.

chapter 22

SUSAN ALWAYS CLAIMED redheads had to be the center of attention. At Cannes, she was just that.

During the film festival, the sleepy Côte d'Azur town turns into Babylon—crowded, noisy, every event a mélange of foreign tongues; men and women shouting, pushing, and generally causing chaos. Everyone wants to be number one—and, in 1956, the competition for the position was particularly formidable.

Kim Novak, then rivaling Marilyn Monroe on the top of the American popularity polls, was undoubtedly the photographers' favorite subject. Ginger Rogers and Ingrid Bergman, the latter still *persona non grata* in America because of her open affair with Roberto Rossellini, were treated respectfully, like grand dames.

On April 29, 1956, however, columnist Bernard Valery cabled New York: "There's murder in the air, and the objects of the looks that can kill are Susan Hayward and Kim Novak. The conspirators: Many other stars of both sexes gathered for the annual film festival. Motive: The other stars have just about been abandoned by the 600 reporters and photographers who have eyes, ears, and lenses only for the two Americans. When Susan Hayward hit the Carlton Hotel, British actor Richard Todd left Cannes and Martine Carol cancelled her reservations. Susan is expected to get the award for the best female acting for her role in *I'll Cry Tomorrow*, which got rave reviews."

Valery called the shot correctly. At the gala held on May 10, with Ingrid Bergman seated at the same table, Susan was awarded the prize for the year's best performance. *Adam Had Four Sons* seemed light years away for both of them, and theirs was a warm and genuinely happy reunion. Soon, Bergman would make the film that would put her too back in America's good graces: *Anastasia.* As for Kim Novak, she was nowhere to be seen.

Susan had planned to be gone two weeks, but she remained in Europe two months. She wrote Tim and Gregory and phoned home to find out how the twins were getting along; scribbled a few post cards to Louella, to her agent, to Eaton Chalkley, and to her mother, frivolously signing them, "Susie Magnani."

Chalkley phoned several times when she was in Cannes. She promised to have dinner with him when she returned, but it was quite obvious that she was in no rush to get back—she was having the time of her life. Besides, abroad, free of her mother, away from her family, relieved of the Hollywood pressures, it was inevitable that she'd become involved with someone, and she did: an attractive, attentive British publisher named Gordon White, whom she met at the festival. White, who had previously been linked with Grace Kelly, knew how to treat a lady, and their romance was the talk of Cannes. As an intimate gift, White presented Susan with a Yorkshire terrier. She adored Sukeh, but British airline officials prevented her from taking him on the plane en route to the Cork Film Festival in Ireland. A scene at the airport ensued, with Susan screaming, "The dog needs me," but the airline won the argument. White promised to take care of the dog. He also promised to see her again in Hollywood that June.

On May 25, to no one's surprise, Susan's performance in *I'll Cry Tomorrow* took the Cork Film Festival's best-acting award. A couple of days later, Susan flew into Idlewild Airport and left immediately on the next plane to Hollywood. When she arrived home, the studio announced her for the starring role in *Three Faces of Eve*, but for some reason, the casting fell through, and Joanne Woodward eventually played the part.

Gordon White's trip in June fell through too. He called Susan to say he couldn't get to California that month, but would try for July. Sorry. Deeply hurt by White's casual attitude, Susan was particularly vulnerable when the persistent Chalkley phoned from Georgia: he would like to fly to Hollywood and help celebrate her upcoming birthday. She was just a year short of forty, though Chalkley didn't know it then, nor did most other people. For years, her birth date had been listed as 1918 on the studio biographies, instead of the actual 1917, but even that statistic depressed her. She ordered the studio to remove her birthdate entirely from all further handouts, with the result that, over the next two decades, her birth would be cited anywhere from 1919 to 1922. In Hollywood, this was standard operational procedure, but in Susan's case, it distorted chronology to such a degree that in future stories she'd be referred to as a child model and a teenage Scarlett contender.

Eaton Chalkley couldn't have cared less about Susan's age. As the father of three—two girls and a boy—he was indifferent to the possibility of starting a new family. When Susan was in Europe, he had read up on her past and asked a great many questions about her personality. The *Barker* v. *Barker* divorce testimony was on public record; anyone could obtain a copy. By this time, Chalkley was well-schooled on Susan's background and temperament. His friends had warned him that she would never give up her career and that Barker would never allow Susan to take their sons out of California permanently, so it was up to Chalkley to convince Susan that, as his wife, not only could she have the best of both worlds, but that, with his legal background, he could find a way for her to have total custody of Timothy and Gregory.

He was patient and persuasive; Susan was evasive. Eaton remained in California until mid-July, telling pals he was there on business. No one could pinpoint its exact nature, however.

At the end of the month, Susan signed an unusual six-picture deal with Twentieth Century-Fox, guaranteeing her $300,000 a year over a twenty-year period, and allowing her to work for other studios. That certainly didn't seem the act of a woman preparing to throw away her career in favor of domesticity in Georgia—or anywhere else. Chalkley was in no mood to admit defeat, however; he wanted Susan and he was a man who always got what he wanted.

On August 1, Susan took off from Idlewild Airport in New York for a holiday in Brazil, as the guest of the Jockey Club of Rio de Janeiro. The club's chairman Jorge Guinele met her at the airport and escorted her to the club's annual Sweepstakes Ball. She was back in New York on August 10, and spent a few days on the town before returning home to begin work on her next film.

In Burbank, a chauffeur drove her to Warner Brothers for pre-production meetings on *Melville Goodwin, U.S.A.* The appearance of the studio had not changed too much from the way she remembered it in her starlet-student days. The old New York street was still standing; the sound stages were humming, though for the most part, it was with pilots for future television productions.

Warner made certain his former one-fifty-dollar-a-week contractee was treated like a queen. The man hadn't softened—but he needed Susan a great deal more than she needed him or his films. The John Marquand novel had been slated originally for Humphrey Bogart and Lauren Bacall. With Bogart stricken with cancer, though, Bacall had backed out. Susan and Kirk Douglas were the only suitable substitutes available, and Warners had already sunk a considerable amount of money into the project, so, retitled *Top Secret Affair*, the script was retailored and pruned to suit the Hayward and Douglas personalities; and even when Susan insisted that Charles LeMaire design her wardrobe, Warner quietly acquiesced. As it turned out, he should have shelved the project completely. The story of an aggressive lady publisher out to discredit a distinguished war hero was a box-office bust.

Susan was winding up *Top Secret Affair* when Gordon White finally found time to visit her in Hollywood. The man, who had seemed so romantic under a Riviera moon, now left her cold. They dined together a couple of times, but it was plain Susan was merely returning the hospitality he had shown her when she was in Europe. Not that she was committed to Chalkley. In fact, Susan continued to play the field, and on November 17, 1956, we have this surprising scoop from surrogate-mother Louella:

"The friendship of Susan Hayward and brilliant Dr. Frederick Meyer, a young professor of philosophy at the University of Redlands, has been a great thing for Susan. She's reading books on philosophy and her whole outlook on life is different. . . . He may be the man she's been looking for all these years. He is certainly in love with her and they are together practically every night." The mysterious Dr. Meyer, however, was never mentioned again.

Jorge Guinele too popped up again, flying in from Rio to spend the Thanksgiving holidays with Susan, but apparently, as with Gordon White, the reunion was a letdown.

In November too, according to Sidney Skolsky, Susan and Jess Barker had a private and friendly meeting and "agreed on new and equal visitation rights concerning their sons, who have just been enrolled in an out-of-town private school."

Throughout all this, Floyd Eaton Chalkley had been hanging in there. Like a Southern summer cold, he simply wouldn't go away. If Susan wanted to date ten, a hundred, or a thousand different men, that was fine with him. He'd give her enough time, wait for the right moment, and then step in.

On November 28, Susan entered a hospital to "undergo surgery." Her physician reported her in good condition, but would not reveal the nature of the operation, saying only "it was to correct a minor ailment." Such vague announcements were commonplace in Hollywood in the 1950s, and they usually meant only one thing—an abortion. The whispers began immediately, the most vicious being that she had done it because she had no idea as to the father's identity. It was ironic, because, a month later, a court declared that, in spite of his denials, Jess had fathered a daughter, Morgana Ruth, by a twenty-five-year-old actress named Yvonne Dougherty. The two had had a casual affair after his divorce from Susan.

It was time to take stock of the life Susan had led in the nineteen months since her suicide attempt. Always contemptuous of girls who "slept around," she realized she had been guilty of promiscuous behavior. She had never stooped to between-take "quickies" in her dressing room, or to sleeping with men just to advance her career, but though she had romanticized the affairs to make them respectable, they were still basically sex-without-love relationships. After the Don Barry scandal, she had tried to be more discreet, but there was no such thing as being discreet enough in a town filled with gossipers. She was running the risk of being branded an unfit mother.

With the New Year approaching, Susan promised herself her future life would be different. She decided to end the old year with a blast. Although she wasn't much of a hostess, she made plans to hold what she tagged a "Point of No Return" party at her home on December 29. Floyd Eaton Chalkley received the first invitation. He didn't have to be asked twice. A few days later he arrived in Los Angeles carrying Susan's Christmas presents.

Mike Connolly, unaware of the turmoil Susan had been going through, romanticized: "It was a wonderful party. Looking back,

I believe this was the time when the actual marriage plans were made by the happy couple. Why do I think so? Because immediately after Christmas, Eaton went back to Georgia, and Susan stopped reading the scripts submitted to her. And the two began acting very mysteriously."

Nevertheless, on January 3, Susan resumed song coaching, with Bobby Tucker, hoping to persuade Fox to cast her as Nellie Forbush in the film version of *South Pacific*. Her hopes were dashed, though, when twenty-six-year-old Mitzi Gaynor got the nod. Susan looked young, but not young enough to make the May-September romance between the French planter and hick nurse credible.

On January 11, Mike Connolly noted that Susan had quietly slipped out of town. For a week, no one knew her whereabouts. Then, on January 18, in a mishmash of misinformation, Sheilah Graham noted: "I'm assured that wedding bells for Susan Hayward and Eaton Chalkley, handsome Washington D.C. attorney, are unlikely. Though he is legally divorced, his religion prevents a second marriage."

Four days later, Connolly let slip that Susan's mystery trip had been to Carrollton, Georgia, to see Eaton's home and meet his family. Mike Connolly's earlier romantic theory had been slightly off. Eaton may have proposed to Susan during the Christmas holidays and invited her to visit his home in Georgia, but she hadn't consented to become his wife—until that final week down South. By the time the two flew back to Hollywood on February 1, Susan had called Charles LeMaire and asked him to whip up a pretty blue dress and matching stole for an afternoon wedding she was planning to attend. She avoided mentioning whose wedding it was going to be.

When Susan and Eaton Chalkley eloped to Phoenix, Arizona, on Friday, February 8, 1957, almost everyone was caught off guard. Neither Ellen Marrenner, the twins (attending school outside Los Angeles), brother Wally, Twentieth Century-Fox nor the doting Louella Parsons suspected that the wedding was to be so imminent.

Even during Chalkley's FBI days, it's doubtful that he had ever pulled off an operation with such secrecy and efficiency. Chalkley had arrived in Hollywood the week before, the houseguest of Vincent X. Flaherty and his wife, and it was during that week that Chalkley and Susan had made their plans. In order to marry as quickly as possible, though, Chalkley realized he would need help. Two days before the wedding, he returned to the Flaherty home after an evening with Susan and took his friend into his confidence.

"Don't tell anybody," he cautioned Flaherty, "but Susan and I are getting married—right away. Do you know anybody in Phoenix who can help us have a quiet wedding?"

Flaherty called Neil McCarthy, an attorney friend in Phoenix, only to find him en route to his ranch. Nervous and impatient, Chalkley wanted faster action. Flaherty next called Frank Brophy, a banker in Phoenix and friend of McCarthy's. After being sworn to secrecy, Brophy agreed to arrange everything for a Saturday ceremony.

The plan was for Susan and Chalkley to leave Friday, with Flaherty following on Saturday to act as best man. On Friday morning, however, Chalkley suddenly made an alarming discovery: he had forgotten the ring! He rushed nervously into Beverly Hills and bought a diamond wedding band, came back and packed his bags, then took off to collect Susan.

"Please be there," he urged Flaherty at the door. "I'll call you as soon as we arrive."

Meanwhile, Susan had risen early and packed two bags, confiding in no one where she was going. Even when Chalkley arrived to take her to the airport, the servants were told only that she wouldn't be back until around Easter. Wearing dark glasses, Susan walked unrecognized through the busy air terminal, and soon they were flying to Arizona.

When they reached Phoenix, their well-laid plans ran into a hitch, though. Applying for the license at city hall, Susan managed to escape recognition with her dark glasses and by using her real legal name, but there they were reminded of a detail that everyone had apparently overlooked in the excitement: Arizona law required a forty-eight hour wait before the license could be used. That meant a Sunday marriage instead of Saturday, as planned. Chalkley called Flaherty to tell him to cancel his flight and make later reservations.

There the matter rested uncertainly for several hours. Susan and Chalkley were disappointed over the delay but resigned to it, when something unusual occurred. That same afternoon, the governor of Arizona provided them with a special writ waiving the usual waiting period. The incident is still unexplained. Rather than wait for the revised arrival date of their best man, Susan and Chalkley decided to be married on the spot, unattended.

Susan had been a divorcee for exactly two years, five months, and twenty-two days when she became Mrs. Eaton Chalkley in a civil ceremony performed by Justice of the Peace Stanley Kimball. Even Kimball had been kept in the dark. He had received a phone call at 4 P.M. asking if he would be available to perform a wedding at 5 P.M., but not until Susan and Chalkley appeared at his door had he learned the identity of the couple.

The newlyweds left immediately for a New Orleans honeymoon. They were still honeymooning there when the Appellate Court in California ruled that she didn't have to pay Barker's attorney's fee ($7,500), and once again affirmed her divorce and her rights of property.

Curiously enough, New Orleans was also the city where Scarlett O'Hara and Rhett Butler had gone after they were married. Maybe it was more than just a coincidence. Timothy remembers teasing his mother after the family had settled down in Georgia: "Well, mom, you finally got what you wanted. You are playing Scarlett O'Hara in real life."

Susan's fantasy life had begun to take shape.

PART FIVE

Mrs. Floyd Eaton Chalkley
Carrollton, Georgia — Fort Lauderdale, Florida
February 8, 1957 — January 9, 1966

Eaton was the first man I had ever met that I felt I could lean on completely. He was the strongest male I ever knew. He had the greatest amount of gentleness and a totally even temperament. I wanted to be with him all the time for the rest of our lives.

SUSAN HAYWARD CHALKLEY

chapter 23

Her marriage to Chalkley turned her into a totally happy woman. She deserved all the happiness she could get. . . .

ROBERT WAGNER, *1980*

WITH ALL HER HEART, Susan planned to be the perfect wife to Chalkley, to devote herself totally to the new life she envisioned—that of a gracious lady, one who'd entertain her husband's friends in the true tradition of Southern hospitality. She had always called her first husband Jess. Chalkley, she would refer to as *my husband* or, in the more Southern tradition, *Mr. Chalkley*. Scarlett would never go hungry again.

The house they returned to from New Orleans was a seventy-five-year-old red and white farmhouse in Carrollton, Georgia. Susan fell so much in love with the house and its surroundings that, though the two of them pored over blueprints for a new and larger home, they finally decided to add on to the original building instead.

"Until now," Susan confided to Harvey Hestor, "I've always lived in places meant for other people. This is the first that will be built for me. Fixing it up has been a tremendous joy to us."

The house occupied her days throughout most of 1957. At night, for the first time in years, she could fall asleep without the aid of sleeping pills. Perhaps, at some point, she thought of the lines she had spoken in *Smash-Up*:

> To Lie in Bed and Sleep Not
> To Wait for One Who Comes Not
> To Try to Please and Please Not . . .

They no longer applied to her; she was certain they never would again.

Over the Christmas holidays, she invited Sara Little to Carrollton and proudly showed her every inch of her home.

Roofed with crushed marble and nestled in a pine grove overlooking a fifteen-acre lake, facing Stone Mountain, the house could be reached by a long driveway that stretched from the entrance gate. The wide entrance hall was a miniature art gallery of original oils—no longer would she settle for reproductions, as she had in Sherman Oaks. The kitchen, located next to the glass-enclosed breakfast room, contained ultramodern appliances, but her greatest pride there was the double-duty fireplace, which served the master bedroom on the other side of the wall as well. The bedroom, decorated in yellow and white, faced the lake. Susan's adjoining dressing room was pink, with matching marble-top counters. "Finally I have enough closets for all my clothes," she said.

Susan took pleasure too in her spacious living room, a startling contrast to the mess in Sherman Oaks. The interior was built of tongue-and-groove logs painted white, with a floor of black slate. Susan did most of her entertaining in this immaculately kept, comfortably furnished room.

Outside was a small glass-walled playhouse for informal entertaining, which also faced the lake. One of its two rooms was a dressing room for swimming parties, the other contained all of Susan's awards, trophies, a player piano, and an indoor barbecue. A pile of scripts, unopened and neglected, were stacked in a corner—a reminder that producers were still clamoring for her services.

Harvey Hestor was considered a member of the family. "The other guests at intimate dinner parties were old friends of Eaton's whom she hoped to make her friends as well. For the most part, they were professional people: Dr. Hadley Allen, the Chalkleys' family physician, and his wife Betty; pharmacist T. R. Griffin, Jr., and his wife; attorney A. B. Parker; Mr. and Mrs. Joseph Kane, Sr., residents of Atlanta.

Mrs. Kane later recalled, "When we got together, the conversation was always interesting and stimulating, and covered practically everything from current events to plumbing. Susan's career seldom entered into our conversation."

In fact, it seldom entered into anyone's conversation. Once the initial excitement of having a movie star in their midst abated, the townspeople took Mrs. Chalkley's presence in stride, though they did ask for her autograph every once in a while when she shopped in town. She graciously agreed.

She tactfully rejected most invitations to join local civic groups, explaining, ingenuously, "I want to do my share, but if I answer all requests, I wouldn't have a chance to be a good wife and mother and that comes first." She did participate in enough activities, however, to inspire goodwill. She served as chairman of the Muscular Dystrophy compaign; attended a performance of *Ondine* at West Georgia College and visited the budding young actors backstage; christened a boat, opening a private lake in nearby Jonesboro; and threw out the first ball on opening day for the local Georgia Crackers baseball team.

The girl who had identified with Scarlett now cast herself as a genteel Melanie Wilkes, a shadow presence beside her husband. Eaton's children lived with their mother, and Susan made no effort to usurp their affections. She described her mother-in-law, Mrs. Alma Chalkley, as "a wonderful person with a terrific sense of humor and an amazing amount of energy that must be put to use," then paused and added: "But I don't want to make her responsible for my decisions. I'm a naturally moody person and always have been. My nerves are very close to the surface. My husband realized how moody I am before we were married. He's so calm and patient and understanding that I'm on a more even keel now than ever before. I love my husband, and I want to be a full-time wife."

One night when Eaton was occupied with some business affairs, Susan sat outside with Harvey Hestor. He said softly, "Tell me, Susan, don't you ever miss Hollywood even a smidgen?"

"Not even a smidgen," she echoed. "All I can ever want is here. I used to make pictures for Academy Awards—but no more."

That state of affairs lasted for exactly nine months, until October of 1957. Then her old friend Walter Wanger made her an offer that, as they say, she couldn't refuse.

chapter 24

IN LATE 1957, Walter Wanger's career looked to be a gigantic question mark. He had trouble putting deals together; people he had valued as friends turned away. The reason for it: the once-distinguished producer was now an ex-convict.

On December 13, 1951, suspecting his wife Joan Bennett of adultery and, in a jealous rage, Wanger had shot Bennett's agent Jennings Lang. Lang had survived the bloody assault; Wanger, mortified, had waived trial; and on April 22, 1952, he was sentenced to four months at the Wayside Honor Farm in Castiac, California.

While at Wayside, Wanger became fascinated by the injustices of the California penal system. Working in the prison library, he read everything he could on the subject and, in 1953, after his release, he managed to get backing for a low-budget film made at Folsom Prison called *Riot in Cell Block 11*. Released in New York the following February, it prompted the *Times* to comment: ". . . [It] is a sincere and adult plea for a captive male society revolting against penal injustices. . . . [It] attains an almost documentary quality . . . in short punches, and preaches with authority."

Riot in Cell Block 11 was only a warm-up, however, to the major project Wanger had in mind—the picture he was gambling on to restore his fortunes.

On March 3, 1953, an eighty-year-old, crippled woman named Mabel Monahan was found murdered—pistol-whipped—in her

Burbank home; the motivation, robbery—the widow had reputedly hidden $100,000 somewhere in her house. One month later, a "B-girl" named Barbara Graham was apprehended by the police in Inwood, a suburb of Los Angeles, together with three male accomplices, Emmett Perkins, Jack Santo, and Bruce King, and charged with the murder.

"Bloody Babs," as the press immediately tagged her, had been in and out of reform school and prisons since the age of thirteen for prostitution, narcotics possession, forgery—and now murder. Despite her protestations that she had been at home with her husband Henry on the night of the murder (he had disappeared in the meantime—police never did find him), she was put on trial in California State Superior Court in Los Angeles in the fall of 1953. Persecuted in the press more for her sordid past than on the basis of any tangible evidence, unable to discredit the men's story that she had been with them, not her husband—their trial was tied to hers and they were certain the Court would not send a woman to the gas chamber—Graham was found guilty and sentenced to death.

Curious discrepancies had come out in the trial, however: testimony showed that Mabel Monahan had been murdered by a right-handed person—and Graham was left-handed. Psychiatrists testified that she was temperamentally opposed to violence. A "confession" she had supposedly made was found to have been tricked out of her by a hired alibi—actually a police officer. Buoyed by a wave of sympathy for Graham and a growing national furor over capital punishment, her lawyers launched a two-year-long campaign of appeals to overturn the verdict, but in the end the appeals and the temporary reprieves only prolonged the agony. On August 3, 1955, Bloody Babs was put to death in San Quentin's gas chamber.

It was a highly dramatic story, and one particularly meaningful to a man who had just gotten out of prison himself for assault, and on March 22, 1957, after three years of research and planning, Wanger set the wheels in motion for the picture that would become *I Want to Live!*

Based on public accounts, letters written by Barbara Graham prior to her execution, and articles written for the *San Francisco Examiner* by Pulitzer Prize–winning journalist Ed Montgomery—who had been one of the first to attack Graham, then changed his mind and helped lead the fight for her acquittal—*I Want to Live!* was not an objective movie. In fact, the script by Nelson Gidding and Don Mankiewicz was designed to show, not only her innocence, but the impossible dilemma into which people with a less than impeccable past could be plunged by newspaper and legal pressures. That it was stacked in favor of Graham's innocence could be discerned when, near the beginning of the film, Babs was, indeed, shown to be at home with her husband on the night she was supposed to be bludgeoning Mrs. Monahan to death.

Susan's attitude toward the verdict was more ambivalent. Before accepting the part, she read all the available material on the trial, talked to some of the people involved, and even visited women's prisons. "I was fascinated by the contradictory traits of personality in this strangely controversial woman who had had an extraordinary effect on everyone she met," she said. "She was first a juvenile, then an adult, delinquent, arrested on bad check charges, perjury, soliciting, and a flood of misdemeanors. But somewhere along the line she was a good wife and mother. I read her letters, sometimes literate, often profound. She loved poetry and music, both jazz and classical. None of this seemed to square with the picture drawn of her at the time of the trial. I studied the final transcript. I became so fascinated by the woman I simply had to play her."

After all her research, Susan finally decided for herself that Graham had been innocent of the murder—but that she also had been present when the widow was killed by one of the men. It made no difference to her portrayal, however—the Graham role was just the kind of part to take her back up to the top, and she plunged into it with all the intensity at her command.

She had other incentives as well. Wanger judged Susan so important to the success of his movie that he had also agreed to give her 37 percent of the profits, sole star billing—and casting approval. The cast would eventually include Simon Oakland, Theodore Bikel, and Alice Backes. The director would be Robert Wise, who had made a name for himself with *Somebody up There Likes Me* and *Executive Suite*, and would go on to direct *The Sound of Music* and *West Side Story*.

The only other female role of any importance was that of Barbara Graham's girlhood friend Peg—third-billed in the film.

A sensitive young character actress named Virginia Vincent remembers being tested and personally chosen by Susan. "She was so beautiful. Oh, that nose, that sweet chin, those eyes, and yet she had a lot of strength though there was something fragile. She was small-boned, everything was in the right place . . . a sweetness and yet such strength."

Later, they met at the old Sam Goldwyn studios, where both were being fitted for wardrobes. "I went over to Goldwyn for my costume calls and my fittings, and we took publicity pictures. Susan and I had to put on these short dresses. They came above our knees, and I felt naked.

"Susan's body was adorable, everything was perfect. She was about 5′ 3″, very feminine-looking . . . soft and trim. Her body was in great shape, not an ounce of fat on her, but not scrawny. She felt her legs were 'terrible,' but they were adorable, and I thought if she's complaining, what am I doing here?

"In the party scene, my dresses were a little too skimpy. Robert Wise said, 'Oh, we ought to put a little more material around it because I don't think Susan would okay it as it is.' I was surprised when I saw the dress she wore, because it seemed very modest for a girl who was a hooker. She was sedate, but you know a lot of people once tore her over the coals. She was very nice to everybody. She was working on scenes in the party, doing all those crazy drills with the sailors and soldiers. She was right there with us, having a good time and enjoying it. She was very professional and just very involved in her work. From what I could see the important thing was the work. She gave it 100 percent.

"Susan was basically very private. She didn't joke, but she laughed a lot when we were doing that rowdy scene. And she just seemed to be enjoying that very much, just as I was and everybody else. You know when you're working on a good movie, it's incredible, it's a real high. Everybody's in a great mood. . . . I saw no temperament from Susan, and I was there when she was talking to Bob Wise and others.

"She was a lady. I never heard her curse, not even an 'Oh damn!' In fact, the only time I ever heard her complain about anything was when she returned to the studio on March 31st, after an awful bout with the measles that she had probably picked up from the twins in Georgia." [Her illness had delayed the start of the shooting.]

" 'My room was kept dark for a week,' she said. 'I couldn't read or watch television or do anything. It was driving me up the wall. And I kept worrying about the cost mounting up till I was well enough to return. How could I have predicted that? A woman of my age getting the measles!' "

Her illness had also prevented her from attending the Academy Awards on March 26th. She hadn't been nominated for anything, but she had still looked forward to the evening. "After her return," Virginia Vincent continues, "we worked on a few scenes, when suddenly in mid-April, Susan's mother died. A couple of days later, Susan told me, 'My mother seemed tired and the doctor put her in the hospital for a little rest—so we wouldn't have anything to think about. It was just for a little rest, that was about it. I visited her at the hospital. Then without warning she had a coronary thrombosis attack and passed away.

" 'It was so unexpected!' Susan said. She was so broken up and was crying at home. Wanger insisted, 'She's got to come to work.' They all talked it out, and she agreed it was the best thing for her. Next time I saw her was when Bob Wise called me. He said, 'Susan would like you to go over the lines of the prison scene.'

"I told her I'd recently lost my mother too, of a heart attack, and we established a rapport. I have something about me that makes people want to open up. Maybe she felt that with me. We went over the lines—it was the scene where I'd come to visit Babs in the prison after they'd laid the murder rap on her. We hadn't seen each other for many years, and Peg, my character, had gone straight, but she'd still come to visit Barbara. Peg was plain and sweet now. She wasn't the B-girl anymore. At first, Barbara doesn't recognize me, and then she tells me I shouldn't be there because of our past association. I say, 'No, my husband knows all about me, I told him everything about my life.' It's a very touching episode. I think it made the audience feel that Barbara was totally innocent, that she couldn't have committed murder. During this crucial scene, Susan had to say, 'If only I could have seen the handwriting on the wall.' And that's when she broke into tears. The scene was filmed when she was so affected by her mother's death. She was using that, you see. *'If only I had seen the handwriting on the wall.'* She just broke up."

Regarding Barbara Graham's guilt, Virginia said, "I remember

224

when Walter Wanger invited the lady I played to visit the set. She was living in San Pedro, married, and had four children. She had a sweet face, but very fat. She had been brought to Hollywood to see Susan. Then she talked to me afterwards. She said, 'I'm telling you the same thing I told Miss Hayward. I knew Barbara, and we did a lot of crazy things, but she could never do a thing like that. She never could hurt anybody. Couldn't! I know her like I know myself. Barbara Graham was innocent. We could tell each other everything.' She said, '*No way.*' This woman convinced me."

Virginia Vincent also met Eaton Chalkley:

"Susan introduced him to me on the set of *I Want to Live!* He was, oh God, he was lovely! Good looking, charming, a gentleman, you know? He was very warm, very sweet. And they were so, so happy. I guess she figured she was pretty lucky having a guy like that. He wasn't hanging around, but he was in and out. I think he was aware she needed time to be alone, to work on the part. There was a lot of work, long, long days and nights. You shoot all those scenes from every angle; it can be very, very tedious."

For all Susan's involvement with the part of Barbara Graham and her breakdown in the scene with Virginia Vincent, she was still, however, the same cool, detached actress she'd always been. As in *I'll Cry Tomorrow,* her ability to shake herself out of the mood of the scene was remarkable. Roman Freulich, a still photographer assigned to shoot action shots of Susan on the set, recalls weeping during the scene in which Barbara Graham goes to her death in the gas chamber. He expected Susan too to be shattered by the sequence. Still wiping away his tears, Freulich went to Susan's dressing room and "found her dry-eyed and humming a little tune!"

I Want to Live! finally concluded shooting in early June, with Robert Wise letting out all the stops: "In motion pictures Susan Hayward is as important a figure as Sarah Bernhardt was on the stage. [How Susan must have delighted in that comparison!] Somewhere within her is a chemical combination that can excite and hold audiences as surely as could Garbo and very few other greats of the screen. Susan is one of two or three actresses who can hold up a picture all by herself. . . . As a performer, so far as I know, she is the only one who completely dominates female audiences. Why? Except for the fact that she is a natural actress,

225

a powerful and honest actress, I don't know. Certainly she has debunked every theory on the necessity of coming to the movies from some outside activity, such as the stage, television, or the serious and dedicated 'method' schools of acting.

"Susan never had a drama lesson in her life. But she can give a few."

Walter Wanger was just as excited. To his good friend Ben Hecht, he proclaimed: "If Susan were a European actress, she'd sweep the world."

They were not alone in their estimation. The reviews, when the film was released in November, made even their enthusiasm sound like understatement.

Bosley Crowther of the *New York Times*, who had never been particularly partial to Susan in the past, was overwhelemed by her performance:

> Susan Hayward has done some vivid acting in a number of sordid roles that have called for professional stimulation of personal ordeals of the most upsetting sort. But she's never done anything so vivid or so shattering to an audience's nerves as she does in Walter Wanger's sensational new drama, *I Want To Live!* Based on the actual experience of a West Coast woman named Barbara Graham, Hayward plays it superbly. From a loose and wise-cracking B-girl she moves onto levels of cold disdain and then plunges down to the depths of terror and bleak surrunder as she reaches the end. Except that the role does not present us a precisely pretty character, its performance merits for Miss Hayward our most respectful applause.

Paul V. Beckley's Sunday feature in the *New York Herald-Tribune* was a solid gold valentine:

> Susan Hayward's performance in *I Want to Live!* is probably her finest. She was excellent in *I'll Cry Tomorrow* a couple of years ago, setting a pace for honest portrayal of hard roles, but I feel she has inched up above the peak in this current hard-bitten dramatization of the trial and execution of the late Barbara Graham.
>
> The performance has balance. One has only to consider how easily it would have been to slip off into the raptures of

hysteria or tear-drenched self-pity or melodramatic heroics of defiance to realize how sensitively she has walked the knife-edge story line. Her style here is naturalistic, but it is a naturalism with depths that indicate how perceptive an insight she has brought to the role. Although it is by no means a one-woman picture, it is focused so intimately and so continuously on her life that its success is largely hers.

Miss Hayward's Barbara has courage, humility and an affectionate nature, qualities which could have led her into a satisfactory life had they not been oriented by an unpleasant childhood toward entirely antisocial habits. So oriented, they helped to bring her to her dread finish, for most of her mistakes were the result of a distrust of society and an unreasonable trust in the criminals with whom she early cast her lot.

Although no footage in this film is given over to her early life, it is there implicitly and unmistakably in Miss Hayward's performance, which has the strength and sharpness of a master drawing—one might say that she exhibits a talent for the incisive dramatic line. Not even at the end, when the details of preparation for her execution become a kind of throb in our nerve ends as we watch, does her performance crack to let the emotions spread out in indefinite pools of misery. Watching it we may feel a misery, but she holds things together in such a way that our vicarious suffering takes on a kind of intellectual focus, almost abstract and certainly aimed at capital punishment itself rather than the guilt or innocence of this particular woman.

There was no question about her receiving an Oscar nomination, but Susan was far from convinced that the Academy, which had already rebuffed her four times, would finally let her have the prize she had wanted for so long. Eaton, however, told her to buy the most gorgeous new dress she could find. Not only were they going to nominate her, he said, this time she was going to win.

chapter 25

MR. AND MRS. EATON CHALKLEY, together with their friend Vincent Flaherty, were driving home from the Santa Anita race track on February 24, 1959, when the nominations for the 1958 Academy Awards were announced.

After what seemed like an eternity, the newscaster got to the Best Actress nominees. As expected, Susan's name was among them, but Susan remained calm. She had been through this before. And the competition was formidable: Deborah Kerr for *Separate Tables*, Shirley MacLaine for *Some Came Running*, Rosalind Russell for *Auntie Mame*, and Elizabeth Taylor for *Cat on a Hot Tin Roof*. It was Kerr's fifth nomination, Russell's fourth and Taylor's second. MacLaine was considered the dark horse.

Flaherty recalled Susan turning to him and saying, "Oh, I don't give a darn about that thing. But I'd like to get it, just once, for this guy sitting here."

Winning the Oscar would put a perfect cap on a new year that was already award-filled. Exactly one month earlier Susan had flown into New York to receive a plaque from the New York Film Critics for *I Want to Live!* Although nine women had been in competition, Susan had won on the fourth ballot—her counterpart David Niven had not been chosen Best Actor, for *Separate Tables*, until the sixth time around. Years later, she would say of her awards, "The big treat was winning the New York Film Critics Award. That's a tough one to win, not because they know so much, but because they're such rats and they don't like to give anyone a prize, especially anybody from Hollywood."

At the party following the presentation at Sardi's, Susan's cup flowed over with gratitude, even for the "rats." "To think that this could happen to a girl from Brooklyn!" she kept saying throughout the evening. Not only was the award itself an honor, but she was acutely aware that Academy members were influenced by the New York Film Critics' choices—no matter how vehemently they denied it. More and more in recent years, the Oscars had been playing follow-the-leader.

Then, on February 13, the Foreign Press Association announced that Susan and David Niven would be the recipients of their Golden Globe Awards as well. Everything was falling into place. The awards were presented at a banquet, on March 5, two days before Susan was due to complete a picture called *A Woman Obsessed* at Twentieth. Then Susan returned to Georgia on March 9 for a few weeks of rest before the festivities. She promised that she'd be on hand April 5 for the Sunday afternoon Oscar dress rehearsal. But not before.

Her timing was carefully calculated. Ingrid Bergman had won an Oscar in absentia the previous year for *Anastasia* (Cary Grant had accepted for her), and for this year's ceremonies was setting foot in Hollywood for the first time in more than a decade. To prove her sins had been forgiven and forgotten, the industry had laid out a red carpet welcome for her. Bergman would present the Best Actor award on Oscar night, serve as an honored guest at the Governors' Ball, and, most prominently of all, receive a gala dinner in her honor to be held in the Crystal Room of the Beverly Hills Hotel on Saturday night, April 4. Stars who had turned down requests to appear at the Oscar ceremonies themselves scrambled for invitations to the Bergman party, to be hosted by Twentieth Century-Fox, the producers of *Anastasia*. Sir Laurence Olivier, Cary Grant, Lucille Ball, Louis Jourdan, and hundreds of others crowded into the room to greet Bergman and her husband Lars Schmidt.

It was the party of the year, but Susan Hayward Chalkley avoided it. She still needed to be the center of attention, and this was Ingrid Bergman's night. Susan felt she could wait.

At the Oscar rehearsal there were rumors of a surprise upset: Susan Hayward was considered a sure thing, but Rosalind Russell might just steal the award. Twenty-four hours to go . . .

Early on Monday, Walter Wanger gave Susan a gold medal, roughly the size of a quarter. On one side was the figure and message: "St. Genesius—Please Guide My Destiny." On the other, "To Susan—Best Friend. W.W."

For this Oscar night, Susan chose a simple black satin gown with a tight bodice setting off a full skirt. The only jewelry noticeable were diamond-and-pearl drop earrings. Her usual white gloves hid her wedding band.

Ingrid Bergman appeared as a presenter wearing an elaborately jeweled gown and looking like a crown princess.

Susan Hayward looked like a lady.

". . . and the winner is . . ."

"The winner is Susan Hayward in I Want to Live!*"* There was a roar of approval as Susan rushed to the stage. She kept her speech short and simple, first expressing her gratitude to Wanger, then thanking the members of the Academy "for making me so happy." Later she admitted, "I'm in shock. After being up for it so many times, I didn't expect to win. . . . This industry has been so good to me I don't know what to do in return." But when photographers asked her to kiss the statue just presented to her, she demurred: "I only kiss my husband." It was a great line, but Walter Wanger delivered an even better one, one that would be quoted often in the following weeks: "Thank heavens, now we can all relax. Susie got what she's been chasing for twenty years."

The most relaxed person in Beverly Hills the morning after was Susan Hayward. She had danced and drunk champagne until the wee hours, yet she was still fresh and bursting with energy. The chase was over; she had emerged victorious. Enthusiastically she greeted the press for the post-Oscar interview ritual. As always, Susan managed to steer the conversation to subjects she wanted to talk about. She refused to rehash the past, choosing instead to speculate about her future, as she sat curled up on a couch in her Beverly Hills bungalow.

She startled James Bacon by declaring: "I'd like to quit now when I am ahead. . . . I don't want this bit where I have to have my face lifted and have the wrinkles painted out in order to play leading ladies. I'd prefer to quit now. Then, if I felt like it, come back after a time and play character roles. You know me. I love to act. The heavier the better. . . . I used to be the girl who could play all night and work all the next day, but I wasn't happy. My sleepless nights and nervous days are all behind me."

Susan's other interviews that morning were all variations on the same theme: A gold-plated Oscar would make a lovely sight in her trophy room back on the ranch, but it came in a poor second to the heart-of-gold guy she had at her side.

Syndicated columnist Joe Hyams was told, "I love my husband. I want to be a full-time wife. I want to be with him all the time. My husband would be happier if his wife was there when he came home. That's my job and I want to be with him all the time."

Eaton's buddy, Vincent Flaherty, speaking for the couple, said: "Susan's marriage to Eaton is a great one. He's a wonderful guy. A little swept over now, perhaps by being a kind of prince consort, which he dislikes, and when he's here he can't get out of town fast enough. But the same goes for Susan. Their lives are wrapped up in their new home. Eaton wanted Susan to get out of films. Perhaps she will make two or three more, then quit."

But was that true? Eaton appeared to be dancing to the sound of a different drummer. He told columnist Paul Denis, "Susan was an actress when I married her, and I accepted that. So why would I want to change her now?"

At the Governors' Ball, a *New York Daily News* reporter asked Chalkley how he felt being married to a celebrity. Did he feel he was playing a minor role?

"How can a fellow ever feel he's playing a minor role when he's playing the role for real of Susan's husband? I love to stand around and watch people rave over her."

He certainly did. By all indications, Eaton was basking in the reflected glory—and the fuss made over Susan by his associates in Atlanta and Carrollton wasn't hurting business either. The money she was bringing in helped too—a later remark by Susan would show just how much. Contrary to Flaherty's view, he seemed in no hurry to get back—who could blame him?

And when they did return to Carrollton, there was a surprise waiting for them. A delegation met the Chalkleys at the Atlanta airport and escorted them home for a ticker-tape parade. Susan had described her new-found Southern friends as people who "didn't eat, drink, and sleep pictures. They have a lot of other things to think about and to talk about." For the next few days, however, all they were thinking and talking about was Susan, and by her side always, beaming, accepting congratulations, was Eaton.

One of the things their friends probably avoided mentioning, though, was the reception being accorded the two films Susan had made immediately upon completion of *I Want to Live!*

Paramount and Twentieth Century-Fox, aware they had two bombs in the can, had held up the release of *Thunder in the Sun* and *A Woman Obsessed* until after the ceremonies, anticipating that, after an Oscar win, the public would flock to see Susan Hayward in anything. They were wrong, however; the box-office takes were bad, and the critics were appalled by Susan's lack of discrimination. Of *Thunder in the Sun,* an eighty-one-minute-long western co-starring Jeff Chandler, the *New York Herald-Tribune*'s Paul V. Beckley moaned on April 9: "Miss Hayward's performance last year in *I Want to Live!* makes the waste here more than usually obvious."

A Woman Obsessed, showcased in May, caused equal distress. The perplexed Bosley Crowther complained, "It's hard to say what goes with Miss Hayward when she gets into these rugged outdoor films. Her good sense and concern as a dramatic actress appear to go by the boards. . . . Fresh air seems to unhinge her. She behaves more reasonably in jail."

Susan seemed indifferent to the pans. "I already have far more offers than I can fulfill," she said with a shrug.

Having sold her property in the valley a few months earlier for $2 million (according to Louella Parsons), Susan also seemed to have more money than she could spend. Paradoxically, she said: "I'm not concerned about winning Oscars any more. Too many disappointments. I'm not retiring, but now I'll act for the joy of it and for the money!" Always the money.

She spent the rest of the spring in Georgia with Eaton and her sons. On July 20 she and Eaton arrived at Idlewild Airport in New York; that evening they left for a three-week vacation in Europe that included stops in Paris, Athens, and Italy. In Taormina, Susan added the David di Donatello Award, the prestigious Italian movie industry prize, to the others received for *I Want to Live!*

The walls and tables in the playroom were running out of space. "I don't think there's an inch left for another award," Susan said, laughing.

As it turned out, her concern was unwarranted. There would be no others.

The 1950s had been a decade filled with traumas and transitions for her, but she was sure she'd never have to look back. Susan welcomed the new decade with a deceptive sense of well-being, convinced that she now had everything she had ever wanted in life. She ignored the warning signs—and they were there.

By the time the 1960s had ended, she'd never be sure of anything again.

chapter 26

ON MAY 16, 1960, Susan returned to Twentieth Century-Fox for a spin on a movie called *The Marriage-Go-Round*. She had had an offer to return under more glittering circumstances, but later she'd thank God she hadn't accepted.

After his triumph with *I Want to Live!*, Walter Wanger had opened discussions with Twentieth Century-Fox about the possibility of producing several pictures for them. Susan was delighted, until he told her what he had in mind for the first movie: an epic based on *The Life and Times of Cleopatra* by the Italian historian Carlo Maria Franzero. Enthusiastically, Wanger painted Susan as the new Queen of the Nile. Affectionately, she told him to buy new glasses.

At the age of seventeen, Susan had seen Claudette Colbert in the role in Cecil B. DeMille's spectacular, and in 1945 had been enchanted by Vivien Leigh's portrayal of the Egyptian queen in George Bernard Shaw's *Caesar and Cleopatra*. Nevertheless, she was aware of what had happened to one of Broadway's most respected talents who'd tackled the part in 1937. John Mason Brown had reported: "Tallulah Bankhead sailed down the Nile in a barge last night and sank." Susan shuddered to think what the critics would have to say about her in the role. "They'll probably change *sank* to *stank*." She laughed. She persuaded Wanger to find someone more appropriate. So it was that Elizabeth Taylor sailed down the Nile in a multimillion-dollar extravaganza that almost sank that studio in a river of red ink.

Not that *The Marriage-Go-Round* was all that much better—just less spectacular in its shortcomings. As her final role under contract to Fox, Susan chose a part that had been created on Broadway in 1958 by Claudette Colbert, co-starring with Charles Boyer. At fifty-five, Colbert was considered too old for the movie version, as was Boyer, and so Susan was cast in the part of a professor's wife determined to protect her husband from the wiles of a predatory younger woman. James Mason was the professor of cultural anthropology. Julie Newmar, the Bo Derek of her day, was recruited from the Broadway cast, as the Swedish siren who wants to mate with the professor because she insists that, with his mind and her body, "they could produce the ideal child."

Due to censorship restrictions, the film adaptation had to sacrifice much of the bawdier humor, and *Time* magazine complained about the casting of Mason, "an actor who could not crack a joke if it was a lichee nut, and Susan Hayward, a bargain basement Bette Davis, whose lightest touch as a comedienne would stun a horse." The *New York Times*, however, disagreed. "Mr. Mason is excellent. Susan Hayward is likewise excellent. Being a dandy with poison-tipped sarcasm and plenty of a looker herself, she easily holds her own against the menace and makes the standard moral ending bearable."

Though Susan was glad to be wrapping up her relationship with Fox, and anxious to part company with them as fast as she could, Sonia Wolfson remembers that during the filming, "She was as obliging as she had been a decade earlier. She was delighted that Charles LeMaire had designed her wardrobe, and she told me how pleased she was to have all her old crew assigned her for a final reunion—Emmy Eckhardt, her hair stylist; Tommy Tuttle, her make-up man; Margie Fletcher, her wardrobe gal. 'It's like old home stuff!'

"She talked about her trip to Ireland the previous year and confided that she and Mr. Chalkley had loved it so much they were thinking of buying one of those inland islands near Galway Bay and building another home there.

"Susan had brought the boys to California with her while she was making the picture; Mr. Chalkley kept commuting back and forth on business. I did meet him on the set one day. He was very friendly, an awfully nice man. I think that was the day I asked Susan what she would do if she and Eaton were ever faced with

235

the situation that was the basis of the plot of her movie. She blurted out, 'In this situation, the girl wouldn't have lasted in my house two seconds.' " The production under Walter Lang's direction went smoothly; the general consensus was that domestic bliss had turned the tiger into a pussy-cat.

Hedda Hopper wasn't buying, however. Hedda confided in her old friend Adele Fletcher that she found "something highly suspicious about Chalkley. Everyone says he's such a nice guy, but that's all you ever hear, such a nice guy. You don't go from a minor F.B.I. man to millionaire in a few years by being a nice guy. And he seems to wear more hats than I own—automobile dealer, rancher, attorney, baseball stadium promoter. Now I hear he's planning to get into movie production with Susan! What in tarnation does that guy know about movie making? And just where is all his money suddenly coming from?" It was the first public rumbling that perhaps the famous "ideal marriage" had something less than ideal about it, after all.

As it turned out, Hedda's suspicions that the money was coming from Susan were dead on target. Wally Marrenner confides today, "Susan did tell me that her money went into a lot of her husband's promotion deals. My mother was still alive when she married Chalkley, and she said to me, 'All of a sudden she's investing a lot of her money in Georgia. Building this and that and building a beautiful lake. Why is she doing this?'

"Later, Susan admitted to me that it was most of her money that was going into these estates. Like my mother I often wondered, 'Why would she go back to Carrollton where Chalkley had a family and buy property?' It didn't make sense to me." If Chalkley was the much-bruited "Georgia millionaire," why wasn't his own money going into these projects?

Wally also remembers one afternoon when the Chalkleys came to the race track where he was working as an usher—Hollywood Park—and "Eaton only played at the hundred-dollar window. I asked Susan where she was betting, and she replied, 'On paper.' Then she handed me twenty dollars and said, 'Pick a horse for us, Wal, and if it comes in, I'll split it with you.' That was the extent of her gambling. But Chalkley—he never bet under a hundred dollars and he didn't win all that much."

Timothy Barker also confirms that Chalkley's personal financial situation was far from what it seemed. "If anyone knew what their incomes were . . . the comparison of their incomes over the years . . . they simply wouldn't have believed it."

Nevertheless, Susan held fast to her faith in Eaton. Only once, when she had had a few stiff drinks, did she discuss her husband's financial wheeling and dealing with an outsider and, even then, she maintained the illusion that all was well. "My husband was a shrewd businessman, a horse trader, as they might say in the South, and he took charge of the finances and advised me wisely and I paid attention."

Not so wisely, as it turned out. Chalkley's grandiose $15-million sports stadium and hotel-complex project never reached fruition, and by then, a substantial amount of money had already gone into the planning. According to Chalkley, "There was an impasse as to whether the city of Atlanta, the state of Georgia, or private monies [Susan's?] would finance it." Susan may have been paying attention, but not to the right signals.

Old friend Louella Parsons hustled in to dispel any notion of difficulties. On August 12, 1960, she noted that with *The Marriage-Go-Round* completed, "Susan Hayward takes off today for Georgia. She says she's eager to get home to see the new mare her colt dropped and . . . has to get the twins, who are now fifteen, ready for Georgia Military Academy. She'll be back in September and has rented a house in Beverly Hills where she and her husband will live while she's making *Back Street*." Of more interest to Louella was the fact that "Susan is wearing a new diamond ring and baguette diamond earrings—not her birthday or anything like it, just that her husband loves her. . . ." By now, one has to wonder who paid for the trinkets.

A month later, after losing fifteen pounds on a strict liquid diet, Susan checked in with producer Ross Hunter for wardrobe fittings on *Back Street*. Hunter, a glamour buff, provided Susan with a $112,000 Jean Louis wardrobe, thirty-nine gowns in all, and magnificent sets by Jacques Mapes but, unfortunately, what he failed to provide was an intelligent script. Hunter's version of *Back Street* marked the third time around for the classic Fannie Hurst tearjerker about a married man and the woman who sacrifices all for him, and for all its opulence, it was distinctly the worst of the three. Both the Irene Dunne–John Boles 1932 original and the Margaret Sullavan–Charles Boyer 1941 remake held more conviction. In addition, the Ross Hunter–Carrollton Production

237

was updated in period, and the locale switched to Paris, and the modernization proved to be ineffective.

Upon its release in 1961, Bosley Crowther of the *New York Times* blasted Susan's portrayal of Rae:

> Behind her make-up and her burlesque stripteaser's drag-foot strut, this little woman of Miss Hayward's is just the figment of someone's cheap and tacky dreams. The square-jawed gentleman of Mr. Gavin's is right out of the Sears, Roebuck catalogue, the other characters are flabby fictions and the film itself is a moral and emotional fraud.

Fortunately for Susan, the Fannie Hurst story worked its usual magic anyway, and *Back Street* became one of 1961's top grossers, but she could not have been comforted by the reviews. Nor could she have been pleased by the reception accorded *Ada,* an implausibility directed by Danny Mann about a celebrated former whore appointed governor of an unspecified Southern state, which had actually been shot after *Back Street* but was released six weeks before it. Dean Martin, who had co-starred as a guitar-playing politician, had been heard muttering that "the experience was enough to drive a man to drink."

It hadn't helped Susan, either. Because of her work in *Ada* and *Back Street*, the Harvard *Lampoon* voted Susan its annual award of "the worst actress of the year." It was quite a turn-around from 1959.

While Susan had been working in *Ada*, Eaton had commuted regularly between Beverly Hills and Georgia. On their fourth wedding anniversary, he had sent six dozen roses to the set. Susan certainly deserved them. Just a short time earlier, she and her husband had invested in a six-hundred-acre ranch near Heflin, Alabama, a short drive from Carrollton, and called it Chalkmar.

The Chalkleys' publicized spending did not escape the attention of Susan's former Beverly Hills lawyers—Gang, Tyre, Rudin, and Brown. On April 25, 1961, they filed suit for $240,000 for unpaid legal fees against Edythe Chalkley and Carrollton Productions.

The lawsuit did little to enhance Susan's public image, which had already been damaged by a couple of magazine articles that month. A few weeks earlier the slipping but still sensation-seeking *Confidential* magazine had come out with a cover headlined: "My Sister Susan Hayward Has Millions—BUT I'M ON RELIEF," written under Florence Marrenner's by-line by a professional writer.

Confidential paid well for these kinds of "confessions," and from the story's content it was evident that Florence was badly in need of money. She claimed that Susan had allowed her mother's ashes to remain in a cardboard box at the Chapel of the Pines instead of buying an urn and sending it back to New York, accused Susan of being selfish and a thief as a child and ungrateful to her mother as an adult, and ended by hinting that Susan's suicide attempt had been over Howard Hughes. The story mixed some truths with many more half-truths and enough misinformation to make the piece suspect.

Florence also revealed some facts about herself in *Confidential*. Apparently, she had finally obtained a divorce from Udo Zaenglin (or, as she put it, "Udo got his divorce from me") shortly after Ellen Marrenner's death. Then, only a little while later, she had met a mining engineer named John Dietrich. "He seemed like a fine man and all his friends were nice people. He asked me to marry him . . . so I agreed. I thought how nice it would be to have a home for Larry, and I thought John would make Larry a good father. But things didn't work out that way. He went off and left me right after I became pregnant." It seemed Florence wasn't destined for marital happiness.

That same month, *Modern Screen* also came out with a Susan-Florence story entitled, more modestly, "The Sisters." It too used inaccurate information about Susan mixed with quotes from Florence, but it did provide some interesting sidelights on what had happened to Florence after being abandoned by Dietrich.

> I happened to have an exercycle. I sold it for $175 and came back to Hollywood with my son, Larry. When we arrived I didn't have a dime. And I discovered I was going to have a baby. I was desperate. I took the only job I could . . . working in somebody else's home. When I was in my seventh month, I could no longer do the heavy work. I went to the Bureau of Public Assistance for help. I took charity. . . . It was either that or seeing my boy go hungry. I was given $40 a month for rent money and $8 food check every week.

I was able to get a one-room place in downtown Los Angeles, and I could manage with a hot plate. It was terrible, but at least we weren't starving. . . . They took me to the City Hospital to have my baby. They put Larry in Juvenile Hall while I was in the hospital.

This took place in late December 1960. Florence had a daughter, Moira. She concluded the interview by saying:

She was such a beautiful baby. . . . She had such a beautiful face with a turned-up nose and red hair like Susan when she was a baby. I don't know if they'll let me keep my baby. I've got to give my baby a home and provide for her . . . otherwise they'll give her out for adoption. I'm at the end of my rope. When Susan and I used to talk in our bedroom about what we wanted to be when we grew up, whoever dreamed that Susan would go so high and I would end up as I have. . . .

Susan Hayward never made a comment on the stories, but it is unlikely she forgave or forgot.

She had other things to worry about, as well. Her dear friend Ira Grossel—Jeff Chandler—had been operated on for a ruptured spinal disc in May and suffered severe abdominal bleeding. Susan sent a large arrangement of yellow roses, but the hospital informed her that only the immediate family would be allowed to visit. She phoned almost daily for news of his condition. Another seven-and-a-half-hour operation followed, during which fifty-five pints of blood were administered, and then another operation on May 27, when the bleeding started again. On June 17 Susan learned that Ira, who was just forty-two, had passed away.

His friends started a petition to investigate, and court permission was granted to Chandler's family for a damage suit against the hospital where he had died. Although hospital officials denied any negligence, Chandler's pal Clint Walker insisted, "Nobody is satisfied about the explanations given about Jeff's death."

Susan certainly wasn't; her lifelong distrust of hospitals was only intensified.

In July, her own lawsuit over unpaid legal fees was still pending when the Chalkleys flew to London. The opportunity to work there and in Ireland may have been the only motivation for

Susan's involvement in *I Thank a Fool,* a murky melodrama. Director Robert Stevens and Susan were at odds from the start, the on-screen chemistry between her and Peter Finch was tepid, the Karl Tunberg screenplay turgid, the reviews dreadful, and the box-office receipts nonexistent.

Susan pretended indifference, but she was hurting inside. She could have accepted bad notices ("I don't like critics very much," she said at one point. "I have much more respect for my own opinions."), but now the critics and public were actually laughing at her. Her own opinion couldn't have been too high, either. Susan had a strong streak of vanity ("If we all weren't vain about certain things, we'd just let ourselves go," she said), and it was beginning to rebel against all the knocks she was receiving.

It was time to take a breather.

She lost herself in the operations at the Chalkmar ranch in Heflin. She and Eaton remodeled the main farmhouse, making it airy and comfortable, and designed a new $25,000 air-conditioned barn with special loading doors that protected the feed from the weather. Eaton modernized a small studio house on the property for Susan to indulge in her current hobby—mosaics. The money continued to flow.

In the spring of 1962, there were 225 head of cattle roaming the ranch, under the experienced eye of a manager named Guy Carrington. Susan told friends, "We plan to turn out a hundred head every hundred days when we get into high gear." Shortly thereafter she casually spent $30,000 on a whiteface bull with the official handle of CMR Perfectionrol. His son, a four-month-old bull calf dubbed Susan's Pride, and a thoroughbred palomino named Texas Sunset, were Susan's personal pets.

In June, Timothy and Gregory, seventeen, graduated from Georgia Military Academy and joined the Chalkleys in Heflin.

"It's wonderful for them in Heflin," Susan told *Atlanta Constitution* reporter William Hammack. "There are horses to ride, woods to explore, streams and lakes to fish." Gregory, though, seemed more taken with the life than Tim. The former told his mother he was seriously considering going to veterinary college, which pleased her—it was such a suitable thing for a rancher's son to be doing. Timothy, however, was interested in moviemaking. When he asked his mother for a loan to pay tuition for a film course at UCLA, she turned him down, telling him to go out and earn the money himself. The reason was never made clear.

Life at Chalkmar never particularly suited Tim. While Susan went on for paragraphs to the press about the number of good friends the twins had made and how much they enjoyed the country life, she never allowed the press to talk to the twins themselves, nor, interestingly enough, did she ever mention their relationship with Chalkley or with their stepsisters and stepbrother. Maybe she didn't dare.

Today, Timothy says rather ominously: "Nobody can talk about those years in Georgia. Even my father doesn't know about them—because he wasn't there. Other than my brother and I, there was only one person who was physically there [the Chalkley maid, Curlie Crowder] and that woman won't talk!"

Of Chalkley, Timothy says: "There was a public image, and there was a private image. I *know* what his background was. I'd rather not discuss that now. My stepbrother, Joseph, and I became great friends when I was living in Georgia, and we were in concert about the man.

"To be honest about it, I didn't get along well with Eaton Chalkley. I didn't like him. He was a pontificating . . . well, he was a jerk!"

Bitterness over some slight? Jealousy of the man who had replaced Jess Barker? (The twins had remained in contact with Barker all through this time and once even hitchhiked north to visit him in Chicago, where, Barker says today, he had become "a disc jockey and TV personality for a while—from 1957 to 1961.") Or was it something more? Only Timothy and Gregory know—and they don't care to tell. One thing is sure, though—there was trouble in paradise.

Susan divided her time between Heflin and Carrollton until the late spring of 1962. Asked if she ever got bored, she told Hammack, "I like to sit quietly in all this solitude and peace and look at the trees and the little creatures." In truth, she was getting restless again.

Unwilling to risk another dud like *Ada* or *I Thank a Fool*, she accepted the Mirisch Films, Ltd., offer to star in *Stolen Hours*, an updated and relocated version (from Long Island to England) of the 1939 Bette Davis classic *Dark Victory*, about a woman slowly dying of a brain tumor. As with *Back Street*, however, the

242

remake failed to live up to the original. Reviewing the film on October 17, 1963, Bosley Crowther, with mixed emotions, said:

> What's wrong, you may ask, with Miss Hayward? Why isn't she able to give as strong a performance as Miss Davis memorably gave?
>
> Well, for one thing, she postures. She strikes dramatic attitudes. She acts like an old opera singer delivering a thundering aria. When she gets the first word from a physician that she may have this trouble in her head, she flashes a rush of resentment that might suffuse a Miss America rudely scorned. And when she finally gets the terrible knowledge that nothing can be done to save her life, she reels and snarls like a drunkard. Miss Hayward overacts.
>
> But for all that there comes a marked and respectable turning point when the heroine and her new husband—the physician who has tended her, of course—go off to the west of England to spend the last few months of her life.
>
> Suddenly, Miss Hayward is surrounded with sense and sincerity, with humanity and humility.
>
> And so her heroine is able to die simply and decently, and even the most hard-hearted skeptic is able to shed a genuine tear.

Genuine tears, perhaps, but not genuine dollars. *Stolen Hours* did not overwhelm the box office, and the scripts kept getting worse. "I read a script," Susan wrote friend and producer Martin Rackin, "it bores me and I send it back."

So Rackin himself tried. By return mail, he sent a script he hoped Susan would not find boring: trashy perhaps, but not boring. For whatever reason—continued restlessness, Rackin's persuasiveness, the need to earn some income—Susan accepted it . . . but it would prove to be yet another disaster; in fact, according to many, the worst so far.

The prospects for *Where Love Has Gone* didn't *seem* all that bad at first. The film was based on a hot Harold Robbins novel and Joseph E. Levine, who had just released Robbins's *The Carpetbaggers* to rock-bottom reviews and soaring box-office receipts, was prepared to score another financial coup with this new *roman à clef*, allegedly based on the Lana Turner–Cheryl Crane–Johnny Stompanato scandal of five years earlier.

In 1958, Lana Turner's lover, Johnny Stompanato had been found stabbed to death in her home, and Turner's fifteen-year-old daughter Cheryl Crane had been charged with the crime. Crane claimed she had done it because Stompanato had been beating her mother; others thought it was jealousy; still others wondered if maybe Turner hadn't done it herself, and Crane was covering up for her. Whatever the true story, Cheryl Crane was convicted and sent to a girl's correction home. In the Robbins version, the Turner character, Valerie Hayden, was played by Susan; and the daughter, Dani, by Joey Heatherton. His denouement: it *was* Dani who had wielded the knife—but she had been aiming for Val, and the two-timing lover had gotten in the way.

Pretty hot stuff for 1963. Further portents of success, Levine hoped, lay in the hiring of director Edward Dmytryk and scripter John Michael Hayes to repeat their *Carpetbaggers* chores. And to top it off, the studio expected an avalanche of publicity from casting Bette Davis and Susan Hayward in their first picture ever together—with Davis playing Hayward's mother.

That Susan had signed for the film after completing *Stolen Hours,* a remake of Davis's all-time favorite *Dark Victory* was reason enough to start sparks flying between the stars. The fact that Davis, just nine years Susan's senior, would be made up in platinum silver hair and inky eye make-up to look more like her grandmother added fuel to the impending fireworks.

At their first meeting, however—at a gala press luncheon held on December 5, 1963, by Paramount and Joseph E. Levine—the ladies acted extremely warm and cordial to one another. And, if, as some members of the press suspected, Davis was outraged when Susan appeared in a simple black suit, making her seem overdressed in a satin brocade cocktail dress, she concealed her feelings—then.

In 1970, though, when film historian Doug McClelland asked Davis about Susan, she replied: "It is with sadness I tell you Miss Hayward was utterly unkind to me on *Where Love Has Gone.* The title was prophetic. There was no one whose performance I admired more *up* to working with Miss Hayward. . . ."

Edward Dmytryk was caught in the middle.

In his book *It's a Hell of a Life but Not a Bad Living,* Dmytryk recalls:

> The first mistake was Susan. She had serious misgivings about playing a promiscuous woman. Yet Marty Rackin felt she was the only actress for the part, and he made a number of character concessions to win her agreement. The concessions improved the moral tone of the script, but diminished its dramatic possibilities. . . .
>
> Most female stars come on pretty strong—it comes with the territory—but Bette was undoubtedly the champ. . . . A diplomat she is not. It began when I had been shooting for some days, rewriting as I went along. Early one morning, I came on the set with a handful of new pages and found Miss Davis in her dressing room, ready for work. . . . I sat down with her and went over the proposed changes, with which she heartily concurred. Then, since Susan was still being made up, I went back to my office. Bette walked out on the set, where the crew was preparing our first setup, with her usual cheery greeting.
>
> "Hold everything, boys," she said. "We've just made a few changes in the scene."
>
> The "boys" were used to Bette, and didn't miss a beat, but the scuttlebutt factory went to work, and in a few minutes Susan heard that Bette Davis was rewriting her scenes. Unlike her opponent, Susan was an insecure actress, and suspicions immediately flooded her mind. Her agent was soon at the studio, and the three of us were in Rackin's office. We discovered that Susan's contract specified that she was bound only to the script she had originally read, and, good or bad—and even [John] Hayes admitted it lacked quality— that's all she was going to do. And that's all she did.

That's how Dmytryk saw it. When a reporter told Susan she "looked to have died for no special reason at the movie's end," she responded: "I agree with you. It wasn't written that way. Bette Davis was supposed to die until she suddenly insisted that she couldn't suicide in less than two pages of dialogue. So we flipped a coin. I lost, and won the death scene." Miss Davis saw the dispute in yet another way, explaining that there had been a "dispute about my interpretation. So I said to them: 'If the mother has to be shown as a monster, at least give me one scene being really monstrous to the daughter. So people will really believe it.' Unfortunately, Miss What's-her-name didn't see it that way and she did get top billing. So . . ."

It was a miserable experience for all concerned and no happier for the critics who were forced to sit through it. Bosley Crowther wrote indignantly: "Everything harsh and unflattering ever said about Hollywood films as vulgar entertainment might be said about the one that has been made from Harold Robbins's dexterously salacious and highly popular novel, *Where Love Has Gone*. It is cheap, gaudy, mawkish and artificial—offensive to intelligence and taste."

Newsweek was equally appalled: "One watches . . . in disbelief, wondering how in a movie from a major studio there could be such universal and serene ineptitude. Even the sets are ridiculous. . . . One must credit Hayward at least for slashing a terrible portrait of Bette to shreds."

Susan's career continued to slide. Stricken, she began to retire from the movie community, seeing fewer of her friends, rejecting all the scripts that came her way. Of course, the scripts that came her way these days were easy to reject. As things turned out, however, that winter she had things far more important to think about than bad reviews and bad scripts.

chapter 27

Susan's friends in Hollywood and Eaton's associates in Georgia
had continued to consider their marriage perfect. "That lucky
bastard," Harvey Hestor would say, "that guy can't lose!" In 1964,
his luck ran out.

His only son by his first marriage, Joseph, was killed. According to Timothy, "Joe's plane rammed into a mountainside in
West Virginia." Timothy, then nineteen, was left devastated by
the tragedy.

Outwardly at least, Eaton stoically accepted the loss. "It was
God's will," he said. Inwardly he was guilt-ridden for failing to be
the friend and father he should have been—he and Joe hadn't
really gotten along all that well, and now it was too late to do
anything about it. He was determined, however, not to show it.

His years as a file clerk at the FBI had taught Eaton Chalkley
everything he had to know about hiding things. His previous
wife—or wives, remembering Peggy Irwin's "twice-divorced"
slip—were never referred to (and he was supposed to be a
devout Catholic). He was able to shroud his business affairs in
secrecy; he never revealed the name of the law school he had
attended or his wartime activities. No one ever knew—not even
the FBI—which town in Virginia he had been born in. He merely
presented himself as a wealthy, healthy man.

He was neither.

The first indication that Eaton's health was not up to par
had come during 1958, when he had been stricken with a liver

infection. Susan had rushed to Georgia from the *Thunder in the Sun* location to be with him, but he had made a swift recovery and refused to harp on the illness, rumored to be hepatitis.

After Joseph's accident in 1964, however, there was a decided change in Eaton's appearance. He lost an alarming amount of weight, his jaundiced face became drawn, his eyes dead. He was in fact almost unrecognizable as the man Susan had married.

Throughout the early part of 1965, Eaton continued to have what his neighbors described as "sick spells." He seemed less interested in the estates in Carrollton and Heflin, preferring to spend his time at their home at 220 Nurmi Drive in Fort Lauderdale. The Chalkleys' three boats, the *Oh Susannah*, the *Old Susannah,* and the *Young Susannah,* were moored behind the property. Only when the two took off for a day's fishing did Eaton seem his old self again.

That spring, Joseph Mankiewicz sent Susan the script of *Anyone for Venice*, a modern comedy based loosely on the classic Ben Jonson play *Volpone.* She thought it funny, liked her part, and agreed to come out of semiretirement to work with him for the first time since the long-forgotten *House of Strangers.* Shooting was due to start in Italy in September. By then, however, she was seriously concerned about Eaton's physical condition. He seemed debilitated, lacking in enthusiasm—yet he insisted they make the trip to Rome. It would provide a much-needed lift, he said.

They checked into the new Hilton Hotel, and Eaton remained by the poolside, baking in the warm Roman sun, while Susan went to the Cinecitta Studios. Soon he came down with a bad cold, then a definite hepatitis attack. Susan's nerves went completely on edge. The strain of nursing Eaton in the early mornings and evenings while working all day at Cinecitta began to show on her face and affect her relationships with other members of the cast, though she did her best to be professional and cooperative.

Susan was working on a dream sequence, later eliminated from the film, when she consented to an interview with an American film-magazine reporter on a busman's holiday in Rome. The two were chatting in her dressing room during the lunch break, when Susan's private phone rang. The reporter recalled:

"Susan's youthful face suddenly aged with worry, and she turned ashen.

" 'My God, Eaton. I'll be right there. Don't worry.'

"She banged the phone down and mumbled with controlled anxiety, 'My husband has been taken seriously ill. I must get to the hotel immediately.' "

With her role in the film partially completed, she persuaded Mankiewicz to shoot around her for a couple of weeks so she could accompany Eaton back to Florida. Chalkley wanted his personal physician, feeling the treatment he had been receiving from the Italian doctors had only aggravated his condition. With Susan's help, he was able to descend the stairs and cross the Fort Lauderdale airfield, where a car was waiting to rush them to Holy Cross Hospital.

At the end of the week, Dr. Leonard Erdman told Susan she could return to Italy and finish the picture, but she had only just made it back there when she received a cable notifying her that Chalkley had become comatose. She was on the next plane back to the States.

Eaton emerged from the coma, but by now he had a premonition that death was imminent. After two weeks at Holy Cross, he asked to be taken home to die.

On January 9, 1966, at 7:55 A.M., Floyd Eaton Chalkley was gone. According to a later report by a friend of hers, Susan ran into the bathroom and let out a chilling series of screams. Finally pulling herself together, she emerged to call the physician and ask: "What do we do now?"

Dr. Erdman signed the official certificate of death. Eaton had died from hepatitis, an illness he had originally contracted in 1955, but which had flared up again in 1963 and stayed with him all this time. A contributing factor was cirrhosis of the liver —Eaton had been a heavy drinker.

Susan, seemingly composed, accompanied the body back to Carrollton the next day for a quiet burial, attended by some of Eaton's friends. The gravestone faced the home they shared.

Immediately afterward, Susan boarded the plane to return to Rome to finish work on *Anyone for Venice*, which was released in 1967 as *The Honey Pot*. The cast and director Joe Mankiewicz offered quiet condolences and watched with admiration as Susan calmly completed her remaining scenes. "I came back because

249

that's what my husband would have wanted me to do," she explained.

And then she collapsed.

Twenty-six months earlier, Jacqueline Kennedy had been eye-witness to her husband's assassination, and the public had expected her to play a black-clad, grieving martyr for the rest of her life. It wasn't her natural role, however, and, after an interval, she had resumed her social life, confounding their expectations.

After Eaton died, Hollywood too knew what it expected Susan to do. Her history of resiliency was so well known, her ability to overcome setbacks and emerge, smiling, on top again, that it predicted she would go through a decent period of mourning, then bounce back again, stronger than ever. But this time it was Susan's turn to confound. She did not bounce back. She entered a mourning that, to those around her, seemed extraordinary in its depth of feeling, and from which she did not emerge for years. It was almost as if she had set forth on a deliberate course of self-punishment.

Why? Did she see in Eaton's death an echo of the devastating death of her father—an event that she had learned about too late to even see his body—and from which Ellen Marrenner had so speedily recovered? Was she mourning the loss of the fantasy she had yearned for all her life—the gracious, easy marriage to the courtly Southern gentleman? Was she grieving over the sudden end of the one element of stability she thought she had had in a life increasingly filled with professional setbacks?

One thing is certain—she had buried the man in the red earth of Georgia, and there was one part she could yet play. Approaching forty-eight years of age, the perfect Southern wife became the perfect ante-bellum widow. Chalkley's faults had all faded with his death, and only his virtues remained. She mourned.

Only once did she let slip that there had been a flaw in the fantasy.

In an unguarded moment, she admitted to Wally, "If Eaton had lived a couple of years longer, I'd have gone bankrupt."

PART SIX

The Widow Chalkley
Fort Lauderdale, Florida
January 9, 1966 —
January 22, 1971

When you say ten years, it sounds like a long time. When you live it and are truly happy, it's only a moment.

MRS. SUSAN CHALKLEY

After her husband's death, she grieved like a Spanish widow. For years she couldn't look at anything she and Eaton had become involved in.

MARTIN RACKIN

chapter 28

HAVING NO ONE ELSE to turn to, Susan turned to God.

"I look to God for strength," she later told Martin Rackin. "I won't say when or how I found Him, but when I'm under pressure I rely on God."

On his deathbed, Chalkley had expressed concern for Susan's spirit. Many times during their years together she had considered embracing the Catholic faith—the faith her father had taken so lightly, and which, during his last days, her husband had clung to tenaciously. Now that she was alone and floundering, religion became an obsession with her.

Discussing it only with an old friend, Father Daniel J. Mc-Guire, she quietly began taking instructions for conversion. Father McGuire had first met Eaton in 1952, then Susan in 1958, in Rome, where he had been serving as an American secretary at the Jesuit headquarters. They'd stayed in touch over the years, establishing a warm friendship. Eventually, Father McGuire had become the pastor of St. Peter and Paul Roman Catholic Church in East Liberty, a suburb of Pittsburgh, Pennsylvania (he is now associated with Loyola College in Baltimore, Maryland).

He vividly remembers the furor that accompanied Susan Hayward's conversion to Catholicism and says sadly: "God bless her. I baptized her into the Church. Susan and I were good friends. I got calls from Hollywood and all over the place, and I said, 'I have nothing to say.'

"All this is sacred to me. I know at the time of the conversion, I called Susan and I mentioned to her I was getting all these calls. She just said to me, 'Do me one favor. Don't say a word. Please don't say a word.' That's what she said, and that's what I do.

"The girl is dead now, thank God—thank God in the sense that it is all over."

Father McGuire's reticence is understandable. Susan had taken great pains that her conversion not be turned into a Roman circus. On Wednesday, June 29, the day before her forty-ninth birthday, she left Fort Lauderdale incognito for East Liberty, Pennsylvania. She was baptized a Catholic the following morning and received her first Holy Communion at the mass. Contrary to written reports, though, the bishop of Pittsburgh was not present at that Holy Communion—Father McGuire did consent to correct that error, as well as the reports that it had been he who had given her the crucifix that she would keep with her for the rest of her life. The crucifix came from another.

Unfortunately, several persons at the services recognized Susan Hayward. Fans crowded around her, desecrating the beauty of the moment. One anonymous parishioner rushed to a nearby telephone to alert the press. Within a few hours, a bulletin about Susan Hayward's conversion had been teletyped to newspapers throughout the world.

Susan fled back to Fort Lauderdale and remained there in seclusion. She refused all interviews for several months, then, yielding to one persistent reporter, she broke down and discussed her reclusiveness. "There are times in your life when you jump into the stream and swim," she said. "There are other times when you jump out of the stream and watch it go by—until it comes time to jump in again."

Locked tight in her grief, she sold the ranch in Heflin, Alabama, "because a woman can't manage a cattle ranch alone— at least not this woman." She sold the Carrollton home as well.

She lost track of time. One day slipped into the next. With the help of prayer and Scotch, she endured her nights.

On fair afternoons, she'd wander down to the Fort Lauderdale dock and sail off for an afternoon of fishing, now her favorite occupation. Occasionally, she'd take in a movie, horrified at the prices being asked, though of course without admitting that salaries being paid to "bankable" stars were partially responsible.

"My idea of relaxing is just—doing nothing," she'd later say. "Stretching out and looking at the sky. I can do that for hours." And that's what she did. She visited almost no one. She discouraged people from coming to see her. Occasionally, she saw her sons. Greg was at Auburn University now, and Tim was studying cinematography at the University of Southern California prior to leaving for the army. Wally made it to Florida when he could.

Finally, sixteen months later, she decided to dip her toe into the stream again. Her dear friend director Mark Robson (*My Foolish Heart*) persuaded her to return to Twentieth Century-Fox to replace Judy Garland in the film adaptation of Jacqueline Susann's *Valley of the Dolls*, a tale of the rise and fall of three female stars and their drug problems. *Dolls* was already in production, but Garland's own pill problems had become so acute that, even after a week of shooting, Robson had not been able to obtain any usable film footage of Garland's scenes. Producer David Weisbart finally had to let her go before she jeopardized the whole picture. Although sympathetic to Garland's dismissal, Susan accepted Robson's offer:

"I'm doing it for you, Mark. The terms are secondary."

Her agent, however, did arrange a spectacular deal: fifty thousand dollars for two weeks' work, and a special framed billing at the end of the cast list: SUSAN HAYWARD AS HELEN LAWSON. The role consisted of only four scenes, but they were pivotal. She reported to work at her old "home studio" early on Monday, May 15.

Jack Bradford, then the "Rambling Reporter" columnist for a Hollywood trade paper, remembers catching up with Susan as she stepped down from her limousine onto the Twentieth lot to meet with David Weisbart, Mark Robson, and the cast. " 'It's great to be here again.' She smiled. 'As long as I know I can go home again.' "

And that's what she intended to do. *Valley of the Dolls* was not meant to be a comeback film, merely a tentative few steps into the world again. While there, she would do what was expected of her; when it was over, she would leave. She would not rule out the possibility of doing another film—"An actress should never say, 'never,'" she told Bradford; "she never knows when she'll get the urge"—but there were no plans for resuming her career in a more permanent way.

Though *Valley of the Dolls* was plagued by discord—each of the stars (Patty Duke, Sharon Tate, and Barbara Parkins) felt *she* should be the star of the film—Susan stayed above it all. Instinctively, she knew what Robson wanted from her and, in the process, her acting put the rest of them to shame. A prime example is in the movie's climactic scene, the ladies-room brawl between Lawson, an aging singer, loosely based, some said, on Ethel Merman, and the ambitious Neely O'Hara, portrayed by a badly miscast Patty Duke. Duke had won an Oscar as the young Helen Keller in 1962's *The Miracle Worker*, yet it is plain from the screen that she is simply unable to hold her own against Susan Hayward. The tussle ends with Neely pulling off Lawson's red wig, exposing the singer's white hair, then, laughing hysterically, throwing the wig into the toilet. When a sympathetic attendant asks Lawson if she'd like to leave from the back entrance, the latter, covering her disheveled hair with a scarf, replies, "I'll leave the way I came in—through the front door!" It is the film's most memorable moment.

During the shooting, Susan stayed at the Beverly Hills Hotel, where a bellman remembers she had few visitors and did little socializing. The studio picked up the bill. Upon completing her final take, Susan returned to Florida. She would not come back to Hollywood for a year.

Valley of the Dolls was released in December 1967 and received unanimous pans. The loudest came from Bosley Crowther, in the final month of his long career: "As bad as *Valley of the Dolls* is as a book, the movie Mark Robson has made from it is worse. It's an unbelievable, hackneyed and mawkish mishmash. . . ."

Only Susan escaped his barbs:

"Amid the cheap, shrill and maudlin histrionics of Patty Duke, Sharon Tate as a no-talent show-girl who gives up when she has to have a breast removed and Barbara Parkins as a little lump of New England maple sugar who goes astray in the wilds of Broadway, our old friend Susan Hayward stands out as if she were Katharine Cornell. Her aging musical comedy celebrity is the one remotely plausible character in the film."

Anticipating a box-office blockbuster regardless of the critical opinion, Twentieth arranged for an extravagant world premiere of *Valley of the Dolls* to be held aboard an empty 12,000-ton cruise ship called the *M.V. Princess,* anchored just off the Dodge Island seaport near Miami. Three hundred Dade County notables accepted invitations to "dine on sumptuous buffet, while being treated to a fashion show of $175,000 worth of dresses created for the film," plus the presence of Jacqueline Susann, Patty Duke, Sharon Tate, and Susan Hayward.

Ian Glass, covering the gaudy event for the *Miami News,* observed: "Considering how trying the evening was—with TV cameramen, bright lights, interviews and congratulations—it is remarkable the way the girls got through the whole thing without the aid of . . . a tranquilizer . . . or an amphetamine. . . . Miss Hayward who usually leaves her Fort Lauderdale home to fish . . . would obviously have preferred to be at sea."

Susan would have preferred to be *anywhere* else—after posing for a few photographs with Patty Duke, to show that the ladies harbored no hard feeling for one another in their private lives, she left early. Most of the others stayed to the end, however. After the screening, when a studio executive was cornered by a disgusted viewer who wondered why *Valley of the Dolls* had been given such an expensive launching, he smugly replied: "It just happens to be the biggest thing to hit the screen since *Peyton Place,* that's all. . . ."

Actually, he was wrong; it turned out to be much bigger: the highest-grossing movie Twentieth Century-Fox had produced in its history to that date.

The success of the film, and her own decent reviews, were not enough to draw Susan back to Hollywood, however. She returned to seclusion, and found excuses to turn down all the movie scripts sent her. "I crave anonymity," she insisted and did her best to attain it. Her dip in the stream had been just that—she was not yet ready to jump all the way in. That would come in a most surprising way nearly a year later.

In the interim, Susan made only one public appearance, in the spring of 1968, oddly enough, for the benefit of a man named Jack Frost, a nonprofessional organist who had been giving her private lessons. She had liked Frost so much that she had air-mailed one of his demo records to her agent with firm instruc-

257

tions: "Tell Joey Bishop Jack would be wonderful on his show." The late-night host had agreed to the booking, but with one catch: Susan had to introduce him to the audience. Other than an appearance on *Person to Person* in 1958, Susan had avoided talk shows, but she boarded a plane with Frost and his wife, showed up at the ABC studios and introduced her protégé cheerfully, saying: "You know he has to be great if I give up three days of fishing." But she was anxious to get back to Florida.

"I love Fort Lauderdale," she told local writer Bob Freund. "I haven't lived in Hollywood for any length of time for over ten years. I can never live there again. No, I couldn't . . . I say that with absolute conviction. I always fished on vacation, now it's a daily way of life.

"I just live like an ordinary human being."

In the interim too, Susan underwent an operation. In 1967, her gynecologist detected a small tumor and recommended she undergo a hysterectomy, which she did. The tumor was benign, and her recovery was rapid. She thought no more about it.

Then, in the summer of 1968, something happened that would throw her back into the stream with a vengeance. She got a call from her friend of nearly twenty-five years, Marty Rackin. An idea had been fermenting in Rackin's head. . . .

He remembered:

"I was one of the owners of Caesar's Palace then, and I phoned her in Florida. I didn't know how she would react, so I tried the old buddy approach. I'd always called her 'Hooligan'—with affection, of course, because of her early days in Brooklyn. I said, 'Hey, Hooligan, how long are you going to stay with the old folks in Sun City? How about coming to Vegas to do *Mame* for me?' I wasn't sure she wouldn't tell me to go jump in the river, but she said she'd think it over."

Mame? A musical? The only time Susan had ever appeared on stage was with Louella Parsons' Flying Stars, thirty years ago, and her sole professional singing experience had been in *I'll Cry Tomorrow*. How could she expect to survive the grueling demands of two performances a night with that background, and after the almost completely reclusive life she had led for over two years? Yet something was itching inside Susan. She'd been away for a long time, and even in her own eyes she had been the grieving widow for too long. It was time to get back to work.

258

And, besides, here was something *new*—what a fabulous way to recapture her audience.

Before signing, Susan told Rackin, "I'm doing this with my eyes wide open. There is a certain part of me that is nutty—I can't resist a challenge. And that's what it's all about, isn't it—how you meet the challenges."

chapter 29

IN EARLY SEPTEMBER 1968, outwardly bursting with optimism, inwardly apprehensive, Susan flew to New York for a week of conferences with the producers of *Mame,* during which they decided to present the show almost in its entirety rather than in the usual "tab" version of a Broadway musical popular in Vegas. The production, Susan was assured, would duplicate the high artistic standards of the original. In mid-October, Susan returned to New York, sublet Cyril Ritchard's Central Park West apartment, and went into training.

The company assembled around her included many excellent professionals: John Vivyan, TV's Mr. Lucky, as Beauregard Burnside; a talented off-Broadway actress named Loretta Swit (later famous as Hotlips Houlihan in *M*A*S*H*) as Agnes Gooch; Broadway veteran Betty McGuire as Sally Cato and Susan's understudy. Onna White, a celebrated choreographer, came in to stage the musical numbers and supervise the direction, following the Gene Saks original. Donald Pippin, who had met Susan briefly when she'd worked with his friend Charles Henderson on her songs for *I'll Cry Tomorrow,* and since become one of Broadway's leading musical directors and arrangers, was signed on to supervise the Caesar's Palace version. He'd also served in that capacity for the original Broadway production starring Angela Lansbury.

Pippin was reunited briefly with Susan in September. When she returned in October for rehearsals, he invited her out to dinner, hoping to establish a rapport for the weeks of grueling work that lay ahead of them.

"I've worked with many big lady stars, but Susan was more radiant, more beautiful even than she'd been on screen. Her personality and warmth and charm were infectious—and I'd been afraid that she might come on like the big movie star, the kind who won't give you the time of day when you're not working with her. Other than that, I can't remember anyone I'd looked forward to having dinner with as much," says Pippin.

During cocktails, he mentioned that he was from Georgia. "Well, I remember her face just lit up when I told her that. . . . She wanted to know how much time I'd spent in the South and eventually she began talking about her husband. I had known she had been widowed recently, but not much more, and I really didn't want to intrude upon her privacy. But I gathered she was finding it very difficult without him. . . . I got the impression, though, that she didn't want to lay her woes on anyone else. She wanted to fill her life with constructive things—getting busy and working. This was part of her reason for doing *Mame*.

"Maybe the timing was right, maybe the environment, possibly my background, but that evening she was completely open. I know only one thing, my heart went out to this woman. I was so taken with her."

After that evening at dinner, Pippin and Susan developed a totally relaxed working relationship.

"We rehearsed in my apartment," he remembers. "I worked with her on the dramatics and taught her the score. She was very nervous about making her theatrical debut. She told me, 'Oh my goodness, I'm so used to working with cameras, I don't know anything about stage values.'

"But she was so eager to learn. She was the most conscientious, hard-working professional . . . so intelligent . . . so at home. . . .

"When we worked on the score, she'd stand and lean over the piano and sing right to me; she had this wonderful, intimate way of working. We'd usually work late mornings—late mornings to me, in theater terms, usually means between noon and 3 P.M.—and there were some later afternoon sessions, because she had costume fittings. But she was always on time, always. One day I came flying back home—I'm kind of a fanatic about

261

being on time myself—and I was about one minute late; she was sitting in the lobby waiting for me. Many of the star ladies don't have that virtue . . . being on time is something they seem to ignore. Susan Hayward was not only punctual, but always ready to work.

"I find I don't usually like to drive a performer too much, and sometimes I would actually have to say, 'Look, Susan, let's just stop a minute and relax—let's not cover too much at one time.'

"But she was a workaholic. If she was having trouble with the modulation of the key, I would just get her to relax a minute. 'Look, let's get off it for a minute, then come back to it.' When we'd come back to it—she'd have it. It just seemed to sink in. So my memories of working with her were really of great, great pleasure."

In order for her to get through two shows a night, Don Pippin felt Susan needed vocal exercises to give her stamina. He suggested she work with Lehman Bick, who had been Lily Pons's mentor when the soprano was the toast of the Metropolitan Opera.

Maestro Bick too remembers: "Susan Hayward was the most studious student I ever had. That's what I respected so much about her. Though a big star, she never acted like one. I never knew anyone who worked as hard. And if things were correctly done, she was the easiest person in the world to get along with. She wanted people to know their job and not be afraid to execute it. But if they didn't . . .

"I remember her calling me one Saturday morning. She had hurt her toe and asked me to come up to her apartment for her lesson. I said, 'Susan, I don't like to teach outside my studio, but if this is an exception, I'll do so . . .'

"We worked alone for about forty-five minutes; then the accompanist joined us and we went over the songs for about another hour. Then I said, 'That's that.' She knew I was en route to the country and kept insisting the maid get me something to eat before I left the apartment. I told her that wasn't necessary, that I was behind schedule and had to get going. She threw her arms around me, kissed me and said, 'Thank you so much, darling, for coming up here. I appreciate it so.'

"Then . . . and this was the only time I ever saw her act THE STAR. She turned to the accompanist and in a spine-chilling

262

tone of voice demanded: 'Now *you* get back here by three o'clock sharp.'

"She could be the most adorable person in the world one minute and then turn into a shrew the next. Anyone she respected, she cooperated with a thousand percent. But with an underling, someone who felt intimidated by her name, she turned tough. I've never seen such a divided personality and it shocked me—completely."

It was at this time that Susan met Larry Ellis, a buoyant Broadway actor and singer who was also a student of Bick's. Her abrupt about-faces neither surprised nor shocked him.

"My lesson was at 11 A.M. after hers. It was arranged that way at my request so I could see her every day. That's how I got to know her.

"When Susan met someone for the first time, she was on her guard. She was polite enough, but she couldn't have cared less if you walked out the window after that. But once she liked you —she was a totally different person.

"You had to be on her level, though; you couldn't baby her. The minute someone seemed overly conscious of the fact that she was Susan Hayward and treated her like Susan Hayward, Movie Star, she played *that* role to the hilt. There's the answer to her personality changes.

"I remember the day we really became friends. She hadn't been absorbing a certain vocal exercise. I had been waiting outside for my session when Mr. Bick asked me to come in: 'Larry, come over here. Do this exercise.' Then, turning to Susan, he instructed, 'Now, Susan, I want you to walk around Larry and put your hand on his back and see how he's doing it.'

"Well, to tell you the truth, I was pretty thrilled, having her hand very low on my back, but I kept vocalizing, and suddenly she said, 'Oh my God, he's singing through his ass!' Mr. Bick laughed. 'Not quite, but you're getting the point. Now you do the exercise.'

"When she did it, I walked around her and put my hand low on her back, too, and she yelled, '*Hey, what are you doing*???'

" 'What do you mean, what am I doing?'

" 'What did you do to me?'

" 'I'm just trying to find out if you're doing it the right way. Isn't that how you found out I was doing it the right way?'

"She became thoughtful for a moment, then smiled. 'Oh, that's right. O.K., go ahead,' she said.

"That's how quickly she was able to change. As I said, though, you had to be on her level, and treat her like someone you liked for herself. Then she was wonderful."

On October 31, Lehman Bick held a surprise birthday party for Skip Redwine, a musical director and mutual friend of his and Ellis's. Among the guests were many of his students who were friends of Redwine's. A couple of days earlier, Bick had casually mentioned that he'd be very pleased to have Susan at the party.

"I'll be there," she promised.

"And she was," Maestro Bick says. "It was the first time I had ever seen her dressed up. She was always en route to rehearsals when she studied with me, looking neat and clean, of course, but very casual. The night she came to the party she had on a magnificent dress and was all decked out in her furs and jewelry, and she was breathtakingly beautiful.

"Now at my parties, I don't usually ask my students to sing. But that night, for some unknown reason I just felt like it. I asked Larry Ellis to start things going. In those days all you had to do was say, 'Larry, would you get up and . . . ,' and before you got the word 'sing' out, he'd be up there. . . . He sang and so did four or five of the other kids.

"Then I turned to Susan. 'Now you get up and sing some numbers from *Mame*.'

" 'Oh no, Maestro.'

"Well, she stalled. '*Susan, get up and sing*,' I ordered.

"And she got up there and sang every one of the numbers she had been rehearsing for Las Vegas.

"The next day, when she came for her lesson, she said: 'You know, I simply adore you, because no one would have done that except you.' "

"That's another thing we learned about Susan," observes Larry Ellis. "Her whole basic thing was that she didn't like weak or subservient men. She wanted men to grab her by the hair and tell her what to do. Professionally, anyway.

"Thanksgiving dinner was her own idea. When she learned that we had no specific plans for Thanksgiving Day, she invited the Maestro, Skip, and myself to her house. It was just the four of us. She fixed the dinner herself—the whole works—and it was just like a family affair. She didn't talk about her family, her children or late husband, though. [She didn't talk about Walter Wanger either, although he had died just a few days before.]

"We stayed away from shop talk too. She'd been working so hard on the show during rehearsals she just wanted to forget about it for a few hours. If she was tired, she didn't let on; but rehearsals can be more grueling than actual performances, and I knew from the rest of the cast that she never let up for a moment."

In early December, a charity group announced that Susan would do a benefit performance of *Mame* at the Winter Garden, and engraved tickets were printed with Susan's name on them.* The performance never came off, however. A columnist later noted that Susan had begged off, claiming a bad cold, then added acidly, "It probably settled in her feet." Maestro Bick, however, is not so sure Susan had ever agreed to do the performance in the first place. "I know that woman and she would never have agreed to do a single performance in New York under any circumstances. If she had contemplated it, I would have known."

He continues: "Just before she left for Vegas, I said to her, 'Susan, I know Las Vegas. Let me go out there with you for the first week to get you started.' If I had gone out there with her, I would have insisted to the producers that 'Miss Hayward is going to do certain rehearsals once to get balance and then that's it!' I could have foreseen warning of strain on her voice.

" 'Oh, Maestro, I've been in this business a long time. I know how to handle people,' she said.

"Her mind was made up. Fine. I didn't argue with her. Susan had the same lovely quality in her singing as she had in her acting —but frankly four weeks here wasn't enough to prepare her for two performances a night."

In Las Vegas, William S. Weinberger, president of Caesar's Palace, arranged for two previews prior to the gaudy premiere. He recalled: "Six hundred men from nearby Ellis Air Force Base were brought in for the first run-through with an audience at 11 A.M. in the morning. That evening was a $25-a-head social event—strictly local. I watched *both* rehearsals, the only two

---

* The invitations read: "You are invited to attend the run-through of Susan Hayward in *Mame*, Sunday, December 15—3 P.M., Winter Garden Theater. Contributions requested for Ben Irving Memorial." It is unclear who Ben Irving was.

shows I ever sat through, and Miss Hayward was fantastic. The boys stood and shouted. The evening crowd was one of those 'show me' audiences, and she certainly *showed* 'em. But she was one frightened girl."

Susan Hayward as *Mame* opened in the valley of the dice on December 27, 1968.

C. Robert Jennings flew in from Florida to interview Susan and review her performance for *Tropic,* a Sunday magazine supplement. "She lacked stage authority and her timing was terrible . . . but she was a curiously affecting Mame . . . danced passably and handled the vocals with an effective, low-key mezzo soprano. . . . Best of all, she was never boring. This *Mame* moved like Haley's Comet."

Jennings beat the crowd heading backstage to offer congratulations. When he asked if she was nervous, Susan replied, "*Oy gevalt!* You mean it didn't show? I was scared stiff the first fifteen minutes on that stage. . . . My hands may not have been shaking, but [indicating her stomach] I was shaking in here. I figured the worst they could do is fire me. Yet, it's fun. It's not exactly *easy* twice a night, but is anything worthwhile easy? After thirty years, I'm finally in the theater!"

When Onna White came into the dressing room, Susan happily credited her with her accomplishments that night, but Miss White insisted all the glory belonged to Susan: "I was really rooting for her with every nerve in my body. With no tryouts, it's quite amazing. She's a fantastic lady, a lady with a lot of guts, a very calm woman even when things are falling apart. A very *top* lady."

As for the critical reaction, a caustic San Francisco reviewer who had hated the show couldn't stay away from the dressing room—"I've always wanted to meet you," he told Susan—then went home to say patronizingly, "I'm glad it's Vegas and not New York, or even Los Angeles. It's like a charity turnout for Princess Margaret—they even applauded the costumes."

A piece in the January 11 issue of *Cash Box,* however, though hardly a rave, was fairer and more representative of the general critical view:

Susan Hayward opened a new window, traveled a new highway, and danced to a new rhythm. She made her stage debut in Vegas as the over-forty flapper in the Jerome

Lawrence-Robert E. Lee musical *Mame*. Having never sung nor danced, nor appeared on any stage before, there were, accountably, some thorny moments on opening night. Miss Hayward seemed unnerved and awed by the 1,000-seat Circus Maximus. Wooden at first—then overmannered. Thankfully the audience neither minded nor noticed. They applauded her every entrance, each new gown. By the time she had warbled her way into "We Need a Little Xmas," she was beginning to capture the audacious, unpredictable, last typhoon spirit of Mame Dennis. It didn't matter to most that she strayed from the melody and occasionally mangled the meter.

It's possible—even probable—that given a week or two to tame butterflies, she'll be charming the husk right off of everyone's corn. To us she's as endearing as ever—as enchanting as when she first lost Robert Young in *They Won't Believe Me*. The production is incidentally an occasion for lighting sparklers, crashing cymbals, and blowing bugles. It's all happening at Caesar's Palace, by the way. An open-end affair that could last into next June.

But it didn't last until June. By February, Susan was in serious trouble. First she was out with the flu, then with a twisted ankle, then her voice started giving out.

Maestro Bick remembers, "She woke me about 3 A.M. New York time. Her voice was barely more than a whisper. 'Maestro, I'm having a little voice trouble. Could you come out here and help me?'

"I replied, 'Let me see what I can do.'

"The next day, I sent her a wire. '*Find out I can leave immediately. My fee will be $2,500 a week, first class round trip transportation.*' I wasn't asking an outrageous amount. She was making ten times that much. I also specified that I wanted to stay at her home so that we could work in total privacy. That was essential. When anybody has trouble like this, you work with them, say, five or ten minutes at a time, then rest fifteen or twenty minutes. You can't work for any long periods of time without stopping.

"I didn't receive a reply. I waited three days and telephoned her.

"She was very friendly, but quite definite: 'Oh, Maestro.

Forget about it. I'm better, and I don't think it's necessary for you to come here.'

"So a few weeks later she had a chronic case of laryngitis, and that's when Celeste Holm was called in."

Don Pippin was fully aware of Susan's difficulties. "I had planned to go out for the opening night," he says—prior commitments had prevented him from going on to Vegas with the company—"but at the last minute I couldn't get anyone to cover me on Broadway. I spoke to her the next night, though, and she admitted, 'Oh God, this is hard. It's so very tiring and I get so dry.'

"That terrible dry air in the desert is the most horrendous thing. So I said: 'Now, Susan, you get a humidifier. Don't you dare go to sleep without one on, and get one for your dressing room too, and be sure to keep it on all the time. If you don't, you'll get "desert throat"—all the good singers do.'

"We spoke almost every other night when she was in Las Vegas. She told me the humidifier was a tremendous help, but she was still having problems. Part of that could have been fatigue and strain, but a great deal was emotional stress. With a singer using a voice, it becomes a treadmill of tension. She becomes worried that the voice is going, and that makes her even more tense.

"There was no way I could have been released from my Broadway commitment, but I wanted to get out there so badly when she told me she was having trouble. I wanted to be with her and take care of her. She brought that out of me. That woman had something . . .

"God, how I wished I could have been with her, maybe I could have prevented it from happening. I have a feeling she was beginning to push too hard, getting overtired and a little frantic. It becomes a squirrel cage.

"I was heartbroken when I heard they were planning to replace her with Celeste Holm. I know she was. I think that having to leave that show was much more important to her than just performing. It was an emotional thing. She was so sad inside because this was the one thing that had given her a feeling of identity. It was so important to her to be able to hold on to something. . . ."

And Susan fought to hold on. In a desperate attempt to

squelch the rumors, she protested, "I don't pretend to be a Barbra Streisand, but I think I'm a very good Mame. Nobody is replacing me. I don't cop out. I never have."

On February 17, 1969, however, Susan appeared at a hastily summoned press conference, where it was announced that, on the advice of three doctors, she was leaving the show. The strain on her vocal cords could cause severe damage, they said. Then, breaking down in tears, Susan whispered: "I've never copped out on anything in my life. That's why it is so hard to do this. . . ."

She didn't put the blame on the show or the producers or the desert air or anything.

Except herself.

She had one last gesture to perform, however. Before leaving, she held a party for the cast and crew, complete with orchestras and plenty of food and drink. In the middle of it, according to one report, she called over Celeste Holm, with whom some of the cast had worked before, and had apparently found trying, and said, "I want you to know that these are great people you're working with."

Miss Holm's response must have been less than wholehearted, because Susan's next words were:

"I don't think you heard me right. They're great people and if I ever hear of your abusing them, so help me, I'll come here and kick your ass back to Toledo, Ohio!"

chapter 30

Despite that last act, however, Susan Hayward had copped out, and she could not forgive the transgression. She had let down her dear Marty, her audiences, and perhaps, most importantly, she had let down herself.

The rubber ball of her father's optimistic saying, worn out by too many years of use and misuse, had failed to bounce back. Reluctantly, she faced up to the truth. The Vegas fiasco had been her own fault—brought on by a combination of avarice and pride.

Maestro Bick remembers: "When Susan refused my offer, to go to Vegas, Larry said, 'That's the end of you and Susan.' Well, shortly after she left *Mame,* she sent me a two-page typewritten letter, saying in essence that one of the biggest mistakes she had ever made in her life was not letting me come out there. She wondered why she had been so frugal when she hadn't had to be and I could have been such help. And if I had come out, she was convinced she would still have been in the show. Would I please forgive her and try to love her as she loved me?

"That letter is an indication of what a big person she was— to write and tell me what a mistake she had made. Not many people would do that."

Susan licked her wounds quietly and retreated into herself again. On a sudden impulse, she sold the Nurmi Drive house, and in April bought a lovely ninth-floor, two-bedroom condominium, with balcony, at 333 Sunset Drive in Fort Lauderdale.

Interestingly, it was an address very similar to the one she'd had in Carrollton, a fact that intrigued her.

At the same time, she gave away to a neighbor a collection of her films that Eaton had gathered together years ago as a gift. "I never showed them," she said. "They just took up space. You see, things like that, holding onto the past, would just bog me down. Not everyone, perhaps, but me, yes."

The condominium building, named The Four Seasons, included daily maid service in the maintenance charge, and the rooms were large and cheerful, but as with most apartments built in the 1960s and 1970s, they were not totally soundproof.

Susan lived directly above Dr. and Mrs. Russell Carson. Eleanor Carson vividly remembers the two years Susan was her neighbor. "She played her organ often—but it didn't bother us, because she didn't play it at an hour that would disturb us. My husband, who's a physician, is never here. He's always working.

"When she first moved into the building, she remained aloof from the tenants. You never saw her without big dark glasses, or a hood or a kerchief around her head. And she seemed terribly, terribly lonely. With that magnificent worldwide popularity, to be so lonely! Yet I think her loneliness stemmed from the fact that people were always after her for something other than just friendship.

"She was like a little teddy bear in life, not at all like in her movies—but who is, I guess. Just like a little teddy bear, she gave me the feeling of wanting to put my arms around her. And protect her.

"I'd often see her shopping, and we'd exchange hellos. In time, we established a rather neighborly relationship, but we were not close friends. She never discussed her late husband or any personal matters except her boys."

Tim was in the army then, serving with the Green Berets in Greece, Turkey, and Cambodia (but not Vietnam, as has been reported). Greg was finishing up his studies at Auburn University in Alabama, from which he graduated in June of 1969. Susan flew to Alabama to be on hand when he received his degree in veterinary medicine, and the next day returned home.

Eleanor Carson's nephew Ty French, a Manhattan artist and designer, recalls: "I saw Susan Hayward for the first time in our elevator [in Florida]. I recognized her instantly, in spite of the large fedora hat and dark glasses. She was frequently at the pool. There was always a great deal of socializing going on there— The Four Seasons had a fun ambiance—but Susan never joined in. Her neighbors discussed that. She was *always* by herself. I never saw her with a guest, never. After a while we struck up a casual acquaintance, just small talk. When she asked me to join her, we often sat in silent communication."

Eleanor Carson observes: "She was really not a very friendly person—except on a one-to-one basis. But I think she had a spiritual nature, and she seemed to be searching for this deeper thing within her. . . . I know that she was very active in the Broward County Heart Association, and there was a young man involved in it who squired her around. He was an escort for her for the affairs she chose to attend. . . ."

The young man was Ron Nelson, a dark-haired, bespectacled bachelor who would become head of the Broward County Heart Association. According to Tim Barker, Nelson began coming to the condominium on Sunset Drive in 1969, and eventually became a regular there.

Wally Marrenner, however, remembers that the relationship didn't take at first. When the two of them first met, sometime after Chalkley's death, "she used to tell me she didn't like him all that much. Then she had this lovely white dog that fell into the canal, and he went down and rescued the dog. From then on, Susan was friends with him." He paused. "I never cared too much for that association. . . ."

Neither, apparently, did Tim Barker. According to Barker today, in his own words, "The man moved himself into my mother's life because he needed something from her. She, in turn, needed something from him. My mother was vulnerable . . . what I'm trying to say is that he had his own ax to grind.

"When I met him, I said to my mother, 'What is *this*?'

" 'Oh, he's very big in the Heart Association. He takes me out socially.'

" 'Are you kidding? All these people you're seeing are from the Midwest. And you have nothing in common with them.' And after I'd met Nelson, I said to her, 'You have even less in common with him.' I used to kid my mother when she'd say, 'Hey, he's making advances at me.'

"I'd say, 'Come on, you know better than to believe *that!*' "

"My mother knew exactly where he was coming from. And she was cautious up to a point. . . . But I almost threw that man physically out of my house."

Exactly why Tim Barker is so angry at Ron Nelson is something he prefers not to spell out. Whatever Nelson may or may not have wanted from Susan, however, it is obvious what she wanted from him—companionship. She had made few friends, Tim was in the army, Greg—who was living in Jacksonville then —she saw only sporadically. She was a lonely woman.

On Christmas Day 1969, for instance, Eleanor Carson had a mild surprise: "We had an open house, and a few days earlier I'd timidly invited Susan to come down. I didn't think she would, but all the neighbors were invited, and I felt it would have been rude to exclude her.

"It really surprised me when she came through the door. Naturally I asked her if she would like a drink. And in that deep, throaty voice she said, 'I'll have a Bloody Mary.'

"At our Christmas parties it was a tradition to serve only eggnog . . . but we finally found the ingredients, and she went and sat right down in the middle of the living room floor. There were about twenty people in the apartment at that point. She just sat down on the floor and visited with everyone very casually . . . just in a very offish kind of way . . . not a close way. But she did sit on the floor, and I'll never forget it."

On Christmas Day, Susan had nothing else to turn to but a neighbor's casual invitation.

And it continued. The 1970s started badly for Susan. Early in the year, she broke an arm while trying to pull in a big one fishing in the Bahamas. It had just about healed when, restless and bored, she went on safari in Africa. Her vacation was ruined when she was felled by a mild case of pneumonia. She returned to Fort Lauderdale in April and suffered a broken ankle when her motorbike fell on her leg.

On May 11, 1970, she slipped quietly into Los Angeles to see what was going on. She wanted no part of the horror movies that aging glamour girls were now being misused in, nor was she interested in a guest-star shot in any of the current television series. She had too much pride to lower her sights and too much money to have to be forced to. Susan saw a few friends, then flew back to Florida, more depressed and as lonely as ever.

273

Eleanor Carson remembers: "Every so often during 1970 Susan was in our apartment with small groups. I never saw her drink a lot, but she seemed depressed to me; she wasn't alive. She was just sort of a recluse."

Although Eleanor Carson was unaware of it, Susan was drinking—heavily. Some time later, Susan would say to interviewer Robert Osborne, when asked if she had tried marijuana, "No. Evidently a lot of people do [smoke it], but knowing myself . . . well, I'm afraid I could become addicted because whatever I do, I always do intensely." And now she was beginning to drink intensely, not to the point of alcoholism—she could still *not* take a drink if she wanted to—but the Scotches and Beefeater martinis and Bloody Marys served as potent cures for her chronic attacks of insomnia.

On Friday night, January 21, 1971, they proved all too potent.

Alone and lonely, she had a few drinks and snuggled into an armchair. She was chain-smoking as usual while she read a news-magazine account of the sensational Charles Manson trial. Although she had had no scenes with Sharon Tate in *Valley of the Dolls* and had scarcely said more than a few words to the girl at the premiere, she had taken the brutal killings on August 9, 1969, almost personally. There was no mercy in her heart for Manson or his followers. She had told friends, "If somebody hurt anyone who was close to me or whom I loved and they weren't put to death for it, I'd kill them myself."

She lit a cigarette, unaware that the one she had been smoking had dropped into a crevice of her chair. Then, groggy, she went into the bedroom, put on a pair of blinkers, and fell into a deep sleep.

The next hours are etched into Eleanor Carson's memory: "We were getting up at six-thirty when we heard screams. We ran out on our balcony and saw smoke billowing from Susan's apartment. There she stood at the edge of the balcony screaming 'Fire, fire!'

"You wouldn't believe the smoke that was coming out of that apartment! We thought we had to do something to help that lady, so we pulled the sheets off our beds and began to tie them together into knots—but before we could throw them up to her, the firemen arrived. They had a terrible time getting through her door, because it was double-locked. You know, I'd always had visions that the fire department knocked down the door in situations like this—but they didn't. They just cut the lock out, and went in and rescued her through the smoke. At that point, my husband had gone up there too. I kept talking to her on the balcony to keep her calm, because we had the feeling she was going to jump. It was kind of frightening—she was so frightened. When the firemen opened the door, my husband brought her down here. She hadn't taken anything with her other than her crucifix and a picture of her first husband."

Did Mrs. Carson mean Susan's second husband Eaton Chalkley?

"No. No. I mean her first husband, the actor."

Reminded of the unpleasant divorce Susan went through twenty-three years before, Eleanor Carson impatiently exclaimed, "I know all about that. It was in all the newspapers, and the fan magazines I read in the beauty parlor were filled with it. I know what Jess Barker looked like. I've seen his movies on TV. The man in the *photograph* Susan rescued was *Jess Barker*. Take my word for it."

Jess Barker. It's an accepted phenomenon that, panicked by unexpected disasters—earthquakes, floods, or fires—people have a tendency to rescue strange possessions. What is remarkable here is not that Susan salvaged Barker's photograph—a secret Jess and their sons never found out, by the way—but *that she kept the photograph at all.*

Plainly, for all the bitterness and the blood and the intervening years, there was still something about Barker that she could not let go. He was the first man with whom she had been intimate, the father of her sons. She had invested an awful lot in the man —both love and hate. Perhaps, after all, she could not bring herself to throw away her memories.

Susan remained with the Carsons for the rest of the day and well into the evening. Meanwhile, a Fort Lauderdale staff writer, Patty Allen, got a tip that The Four Seasons fire had been in Susan Hayward's apartment. She managed to get a brief statement from Susan before the press descended en masse: "I'm fine, but the apartment is a wreck. Nothing valuable was lost, but it's a complete wreck. When I saw flames, the first thing I did was pick up the phone and call the fire department." Susan expressed her gratitude to the department.

Lt. Kenneth Nation of the department returned the compliment. "She went to the balcony, which was real good. She got outside the smoke and heat. She could have suffocated."

"I think," says Eleanor Carson, "that Susan was more in shock than frightened by this time. She told us when she had been awakened by the smell of smoke, she had had her blinders on her eyes and blackout curtains on her window, and she couldn't find her way out of anywhere.

"When my husband brought her downstairs, she was still in her night clothes, covered from head to toe with soot. It took about an hour to remove all that soot. Later, she sent my husband upstairs to look in the files for a dividend check for $45,000. Then she remembered her long mink coat and thought maybe that ought to come out too."

Dr. Carson suggested Susan have her lungs examined to be certain there was no smoke damage. Since Susan had her own physician in town, Carson drove her there. "By evening, Susan was very calm, amazingly so."

Eleanor Carson concludes: "People were terribly unkind. They practically knocked down my door after the fire. The phone was ringing right off the hook from fans and press who wanted her phone number or demanded to talk to her. I kept a record of how many calls we received, just for the fun of it.

"One photographer phoned and asked if he could come up to my apartment and take a picture. Susan refused. So he went across the canal and waited in somebody's backyard for I don't know how long. Susan and I went out on my balcony for a bit of fresh air—she was wearing a kerchief over her head—and in some flukey way that man got his picture.

"It was amazing to me. I didn't know that Susan still had that much of a press following. I wasn't aware of her magnificent popularity, I guess. But friends from all over the country and Europe sent me clippings."

That evening, Susan went to Jacksonville to stay with Greg and his new wife Susan.

"I was in Jacksonville a couple of weeks after the fire. Susan wasn't there, but I talked to Gregory about her and he assured me she was fine.

"That was that. I didn't hear anything from her after she left here. Not a word, not even a Christmas card. I guess I felt a bit hurt at the time, but that's how it goes."

Susan had survived trial by fire and then blocked it from her mind. The fire did have one beneficial effect, however. Perceiving the disaster as an omen, she was shaken out of her lethargy.

At fifty-four, she wanted to live again—as an actress.

She had no doubts that she could. The "angel on her shoulder" was still there.

Or so she thought.

PART SEVEN

Susan Hayward
Beverly Hills, California
September 1971 —
March 14, 1975 (2:25 P.M.)

I felt like a pianist who hadn't touched the piano for years. You wonder if you can still play, and you are terrified. Then you hit the first note, and it all comes back to you. The only thing I worried about was whether I had lost the ability to remember lines. Fortunately, my brain is in good shape.

SUSAN HAYWARD

chapter 31

WHILE SEEKING the stamina required for a comeback, Susan sold the condominium and spent the next several months idly traveling about. For brief periods, she stayed with her sons. In 1971, Tim, discharged from the army the year before, married a woman named Ilse Schenke and settled down in California, where he went to work for Susan's public relations agent Jay Bernstein. That year too Gregory made Susan a grandmother, which proved a somewhat difficult milestone for her. When asked later if she spent much time in Jacksonville with Gregory and her new grandson, she skirted the question with a curt:

"I see my grandson every few months. After all, he's not my son, he's my son's son, and I try not to be a smotherer. Anyway, with telephones and airplanes, we are never far apart. I can get on a plane and within hours get to wherever Greg and his family are."

Finally, Susan leased a house behind the Beverly Hills Hotel, and concentrated on reactivating her career. In early fall, she approached Norman Brokaw, a vice-president of the William Morris Agency.

"Look, I want to go back to work," she said. "And Norman, I still want to play the same rough, tough roles I did before. I want to play Tugboat Annie or somebody like that."

Brokaw recalls, "She had mellowed over the years. She was still very attractive, youthful-looking, and a pro. We didn't anticipate any problems getting her going again—not as Tugboat Annie, of course, but in a strong female role."

Before Brokaw could do anything specific, Marty Rackin called and asked, almost apologetically, if she'd care to do a cameo for him in the male-oriented *The Revengers,* starring William Holden and Ernest Borgnine. (The role was of an Irish woman Elizabeth Reilly, who nurses Holden back to health after he's been shot in a quarrel.) It was as good an opportunity as any to see if her technique was still there, and for her friend Marty, she was glad to do it. Perhaps too she felt guilty about *Mame.* She even refused to take more than the Screen Actors Guild minimum for the role, $487. She wasn't doing this for the money.

After a short location shoot in Mexico, her part in the film was done (it would be released in the fall of 1972), and she was relieved to find she still knew what to do. Meanwhile, Norman Brokaw had been reading scripts. Susan had turned down dozens of offers to make her TV debut, but now she conceded, "That's where the action is for women my age who aren't about to undress on the screen. I like these *Movies of the Week,* as they call them."

She got her first one through a twist of fate. *Fitzgerald and Pride,* the pilot for a projected series about a liberated woman lawyer (Barbara Stanwyck) and her young law partner (James Stacey), was in production when Stanwyck suddenly had to be rushed to the hospital for a kidney operation. "Ron Roth and Dick Berg were trying to figure out who could step into the role, and I suggested Susan Hayward," says Norman Brokaw. "But a name star like Susan Hayward would have wanted to have been offered the role first—correct? So in mid-November, I flew to Mexico City and met with her, with the script. I said, 'Susan, I'll tell you why I came down here to see you. Barbara Stanwyck took very ill, and she was in production for a TV movie that I think is a fabulous role. I'm sure that if Barbara had a choice of who she would want to replace her, it would be you. And from your standpoint, I felt that if you liked the role, you'd consider doing it.'

"She then ordered Brandy Alexanders for us, and she said, 'Norman, you sit down and relax. I'll start reading the script.' By the time I left the next day, she had agreed to do it . . . and did a helluva job."

Fitzgerald and Pride resumed shooting on December 6. While Susan was before the cameras, Brokaw feverishly worked to keep the momentum going—and was almost immediately successful. Aaron Spelling-Len Goldberg Productions liked the idea of Susan on television, and after negotiations, Brokaw secured a firm contract guaranteeing three *Movies of the Week*—each of which would serve as a pilot for a forthcoming series. It would be left to the American Broadcasting Company to decide which.

"If these TV movies are good enough for Helen Hayes, they're good enough for me," she laughed.

Don Taylor, who had played Lillian Roth's first husband in *I'll Cry Tomorrow*, and turned to directing in the midfifties, was behind the cameras on *Fitzgerald and Pride*. He recalls "working well with Susan during the filming, but no long-lost buddies type of thing." What remains foremost in his mind is the fate of its three stars. "Jim Stacey lost an arm and leg in a motorcycle accident, Lee J. Cobb had a heart attack a couple of years ago, and Susan . . . well, Fritz Weaver and I seem to be the only survivors."

Susan intended to be a survivor too. Having hired an aggressive press agent, Jay Bernstein, she made herself available for any important interviews he could get. She could no longer make the selection herself. The old guard were all gone now. Hedda Hopper was dead, others were in semiretirement writing books about the golden days, or, as in the case of Louella Parsons, vegetating in nursing homes. Rona Barrett was Number One now. Susan knew Barrett, but the other names and faces drew a blank. It was a totally new ball game with an entirely new team.

But she was still in control. In a *TV Guide* interview, she said, "I came back to work because the grief finally was all wrung out of me. . . . I looked around Fort Lauderdale and realized I was a freak in that society. I suddenly had an overwhelming desire to get back to Hollywood, where I could be just another freak among freaks."

When a woman reporter who had checked the files carefully reminded her she had once said she could never live in Hollywood again, she smiled and resorted to her trick of answering a question with a question: "Did I say that?" Then, remembering that new rules applied to the new game, she brought the woman up to date, sending her home with enough copy about her TV movie (and *The Revengers*) to almost assure additional audiences.

Jack Zink, entertainment editor of the *Fort Lauderdale News,* did a telephone interview with her in Hollywood. Sensing a juicy local story, he asked her about her remarks in the *TV Guide* piece.

"There's a lot of 'la-de-da' about life in Florida," she replied, "and while I can take some of it, I couldn't take it forever. The ocean and trips to the Bahamas kept me busy for a few years. But I had to start doing something again. I feel much more at home here in Hollywood. But," she added quickly, "if you print the story, I'd like you to send my love to all my dear friends in Fort Lauderdale."

Due primarily to Susan's presence, *Fitzgerald and Pride,* now more provocatively titled *Heat of Anger,* garnered a 23.2 rating and a respectable 37 percent audience share when it was telecast by CBS on Friday night, March 3, 1972. Kay Gardella's review in the *New York Daily News* summed up the attitude of critics and public alike. "Miss Hayward, still shapely and attractive, gave a very solid performance. It wasn't an easy story to move along and sustain viewer's interest, though, since there wasn't very much to it."

Her next movie—and, as it would turn out, her last—was *Say Goodbye, Maggie Cole,* the first of the three pilots she had contracted to do for Aaron Spelling. Directed by Jud Taylor, co-starring Darren McGavin, it was the story of a research doctor who breaks with her past after her husband dies of a heart attack, and takes a job with a Chicago slum clinic. Various plot turns had to do with a man with a brain tumor and a girl dying of leukemia, and, finally, Maggie's own realization that one can't run away from sorrow and heartbreak. Scheduled for September 1972, the critical reaction pretty much echoed the *Heat of Anger* verdicts: Hayward, yes; movie, no—though it too did decently in the ratings.

Maggie Cole had been filmed at Twentieth Century-Fox. Although Susan was reluctant to discuss the past, she had to admit that she "found it strange seeing all the new tall buildings where the old back lot used to be." The acreage that had once been the Africa of *Snows of Kilimanjaro* and *White Witch Doctor,* where Demetrius had fought the gladiators and David had slain Goliath, was now the mammoth Century City complex. Like Goliath, it was growing a little bigger every day. "But that's progress." She shrugged. "Either you move forward or backward. You can't stand still."

Willing to do anything to advance her reborn career, Susan did more than her share of prerelease publicity. "I love the pace of television," she exclaimed to the *Boston Sunday Herald-Traveler*. "It's a new challenge because it reaches to many millions of people. I'm excited and thrilled at the prospect of being seen by a whole new generation of young people."

When reminded that this whole new generation had been seeing her old films on television, and that *I Want to Live!* had practically been turned into a cult movie by then, she protested, "But they've chopped it up so badly. No one really gets to see the movie as it was made. I wish they would." Smiling, Susan added, "I still get one third of the profits."

Caught off guard by a more intimate question, she didn't hedge. "Marry again? It's a possibility, but not a probability. I have been a widow for nearly seven years. Of course, I have opportunities, but I think it's unfair to marry anyone unless I can completely love him and be willing to spend the rest of my life with him. So far, the gentlemen who have offered themselves and their fortunes—or misfortunes—to me have not been ones I could love deeply or live with the rest of my life.

"I have lived alone a long time now. I have accepted it; I'm used to it; and I've become more independent than I ever was. If God wants it, the right man will come along again. If not, so be it."

It was at this time, on August 18, 1972, that she agreed to see freelance writer Robert Osborne for yet one more interview on *Maggie Cole*. There was something different about this one, however. Susan was in a more somber mood, her answers more thoughtful, less flip than those she had been giving to others. It was almost as if she knew what would only become apparent much later: that this was the last interview she would ever do in her life.

Osborne remembers:

"It was done at 1301 Belfast, off Sunset Plaza Drive, in the Sunset Strip area, in her living room. Jay Bernstein was there, and I felt there was a great friendship-rapport between them of long standing. On the coffee table was a toy train and tracks, and a copy of *Hedda and Louella*. The house was nice, but cold

['I've no interest in homemaking, as you can see']; her body trim, face good but blotchy; she wore tinted glasses and answered the questions *to the point*, with conviction, and could only be described as being friendly in a cool way. She sat the whole time, gave total focus, and concentrated. At this vantage point, I can only say I have a strong suspicion she had no idea whatsoever of the affection with which the public held her. . . ."

Osborne recalls her sighing: "Everything that's worth telling about me has been said a thousand times. For that reason we decided to do something different. I tossed her a variety of words, asking her to say anything at all on the subject as it came up. My tape recorder was running; naturally I never erased that tape."

These are some of the highlights:

On ambition: "I feel sorry for anyone who doesn't have some drive and ambition. If you don't have it, you're nowhere—and going nowhere. You have to have a purpose in life, a reason for being. Otherwise, why be here?"

On her career: "If I were starting out in this day and age, I don't think I would choose an acting career. The motion picture industry has all changed so tremendously. I think I'd be much more attracted to a career in something like archaeology or geology. Acting, no."

On fans: "I don't think there are as many fans around now as there used to be; maybe for rock musicians, but not for actors, and that's good. People today are more sophisticated; they can accept a performer for what he does and not idolize him. I could never understand youngsters putting actors on a pedestal; it should be men and women who really contribute something to humanity. The man who makes a really fine law or does something in medicine—they're the ones who should have fans. Not actors."

On the star treatment: "I couldn't care less—and I never did care—about the A-Number One treatment. It's nice if you can have it, but it was never important to me. Some performers wouldn't work if their dressing room wasn't as posh as someone else's. Just externals, it means nothing. The only thing that's important is what you put on the film and what it does to your audience. Of course, now that I've said that, the next time I work they'll probably make me dress in a broom closet."

On her technique: "I had to learn to channel my energy very early in my career. In the old days of movie-making, when a director said, 'Action' and he meant for tears or laughter or whatever mood was needed, you had to be ready—or they'd get someone else to do the job. You couldn't take time to get 'in the mood'; you were paid to be in the mood. You have to have your emotions right on tap, to turn it on—snap! Like that. I got my early training with some very good directors—Gregory Ratoff, DeMille, William Wellman—and they weren't about to sit around and wait for me or anyone to get 'in the mood.' I didn't spend time between scenes joking with the crew or playing poker with the wardrobe women. I saved my energy so that when they said, 'Action,' I was ready. I learned it because it was part of my trade. And by the same token, I learned to turn the emotions off just as quickly."

On her sense of humor: "There's room for improvement. But I can laugh at myself, and that keeps it all straight; as long as you can laugh at your mistakes, you'll be all right."

On loneliness: "I know it well."

"I've been told," says Osborne, "that this was the last interview Susan Hayward did before she got word of her illness, after which she didn't grant any interviews. I remember her reply to my penultimate subject—Utopia. She said:

"The word should be struck from the dictionary. Do you know anybody who's ever found it? Anyone who's even visited or been there? I don't. The politicians all guarantee it, but I don't think there is any such thing; if there were, we'd probably all get very tired of it very fast. Life seems to be a constant battle with a few moments out now and then for relaxation. If there is a Utopia, you probably find it only when you're dead."

Four months later, Susan Hayward would discover that she herself was a dying woman.

chapter 32

How COULD SHE have failed to recognize the symptoms: the headaches, the dizziness, the blisters on her fingers from cigarette burns she didn't feel? She had had them all nine years earlier in the movie *Stolen Hours*. But that had been a *movie*. In real life, things like that simply didn't happen—at least not to you. So she chose to ignore them. She discussed the headaches with no one. She wore gloves to cover the suspicious burns, she refused to see a doctor and continued to talk optimistically about her plans for the future.

In December 1972, she was visiting friends in Georgetown in Washington, D.C., when she suffered a convulsive seizure. She was persuaded to check into Georgetown University Hospital for an extensive physical examination. Several brain specialists examined her and suggested she remain hospitalized for further tests and examinations over a period of time, but she was "feeling fine" and anxious to return to Hollywood. She blamed the headaches on nervous tension, the burns to carelessness.

Tim remembers, "She procrastinated a long time and by the time she found out what it was, it was too late."

She found out—when, early in March, she suffered another seizure at a party in Los Angeles. She left, pleading dizziness, but it was obvious that it was more than dizziness that evening.

Norman Brokaw recalls that he was in the process of negotiations for a series for Susan when he received a confidential call from Dr. Lee Siegel, who had been Susan's and Marilyn Monroe's physician when they were under contract to Twentieth. Both had retained his services after leaving the studio.

"Siegel," says Brokaw, "advised me not to accept any further offers for Susan's services. After giving a brief explanation of her illness and extracting a promise of secrecy, Lee sadly added, 'She is a dying woman.'"

Mr. Brokaw did not betray the confidence. When he spoke to Susan, he was his usual cheerful self. She, in turn, gave no indication that there was anything out of the ordinary happening in her life. She continued to be optimistic about her career. It was not possible that she was dying.

But a secret of this nature had to come out in time.

Later that month, Hollywood became aware that there was something terribly wrong with Susan Hayward's health.

Her entrance into Cedars of Labonon Hospital, under the name of Margaret Redding, and a terse "no comment" announcement concerning her condition set off a buzz of wild rumors. The corridor outside her room became crowded with reporters bent on finding out the mystery of her illness, and Susan had to be moved in the middle of the night to the quieter Century City Hospital.

It was Timothy who, under pressure, finally broke the story: Susan was suffering from multiple inoperable brain tumors. The doctors said she had only months to live. Tim added, "When I last saw my mother she was alert—but her condition fluctuates. She is a strong-willed woman, and she willed herself to accept her condition philosophically. However, I think she would like us to believe that the miracle will occur and that she will beat death as she has defeated so many things in her life. She is a fighter. She has a great conquering spirit, and everything that can be done is being done for her. Still her faith gives her the strength to face death without flinching. Don't forget, she's a Catholic. It's in the hands of God."

Susan, however, was determined to give God all the help she could. She would not die. *Would* not.

She was furious at Timothy for giving that interview; and even further upset when Tim was granted legal permission to take over her estate. "I hope people understand that I am doing this in my mother's interest. I hope they realize that her welfare is my concern—not greed or opportunism. It just had to be done," he explained.

And it did have to be done. "About $40,000 in unpaid bills had piled up because my mother was incapable of signing checks," he adds today. "Important bills such as insurance payments, things that couldn't be put off any longer."

Tim tried to explain that the courts had final jurisdiction over every check he signed, but it failed to pacify Susan. It wasn't the money so much as the *helplessness* she felt.

Susan returned home on the third weekend in June. "Mother looks absolutely marvelous," Tim said. "She's never been more beautiful. Naturally, she has a lot of continued rest and care ahead, but she'll be in familiar and comfortable surroundings and that means a lot to her and to us."

Tim told no one the greatest secret of Susan's confinement. Wally found out about it later: "When they transferred her to Century City Hospital, she was in the psycho ward. She went a little off her rocker. You can't blame her, because she was getting so much medicine and chemotherapy."

At that time, Wally was having his own problems. A bachelor until his mother had died, he'd finally married and settled down, but in 1973, his wife of fourteen years died. Then he was stricken by a heart attack—the first of two—and hospitalized.

Susan came to see him. "That's when I noticed Susan was sick. She had her nurse with her. After I got out of the hospital, we used to go to the Brown Derby for dinner and again we had the nurse with us. Susan had lost the strength in her fingers for cutting meat or lifting up a fork. The nurse—Carmen—had to cut the steak or whatever Susan ordered. Susan didn't talk about being sick. But I could see it was getting worse and worse."

Susan continued extensive chemotherapy treatments under the care of Dr. Siegel's nurse Opal Fauss, who came to the house to administer the injections. She continued to lose weight; she refused to lose hope, however. She was particularly happy when reading the cards and letters that poured in daily, filled with prayers, optimism, and good wishes.

One such letter came from a man with problems of his own. When President Richard Nixon, himself immersed in Watergate, learned about Susan's condition, he personally wrote a letter, very cheerful and upbeat, about how he and Mrs. Nixon were "delighted to learn her condition was so improved that she had been able to leave the hospital and return home to recuperate," reported columnist Dorothy Manners. "He saluted the gallant fight she had put up and expressed the wish she would soon be well enough that he and the family could welcome her to San Clemente. It was a warm and heartfelt letter, and it did wonders for Susan's spirits."

It was about this time that Larry Ellis reentered Susan's life. "I had just made the move to California," says Larry. "I had heard Susan had been ill, and I hesitated for a while before calling her. But Mr. Bick insisted upon it. He was worried about her and wanted me to tell him how she really was. He had given me a letter she had written him *after* the news first came out, and this will give you an idea of her frame of mind. The letter was typed on that script typewriter she had:

June 25, 1973

Dearest Maestro,

   It was so lovely to hear from you. As you know, I'm too stubborn to let anything happen to me. We're in there punching and ready to practice our la-la-la's. Outside of that, what else is new? With love and kisses and all good wishes. I hope Larry is hard at summer stock work. Say a prayer for me when you pass St. Patrick's.

Love, love, love—

"And then she wrote in her red pen—*Susan*—and drew in that little face with a smile that was such a fad in 1973."

After receiving Mr. Bick's letter, Larry called Susan and their friendship resumed as if it had never been interrupted, as if she were still well.

Larry Ellis says: "I remember one time when Susan said, 'Let's go to San Diego and make a day and night of it.' I offered to drive, but she protested, 'No, let's go in the big car and we'll have lots of leg room.'

"We were planning to be together from 10 A.M. until maybe two or three o'clock in the morning. . . . You know, I've read stories that said Susan hoarded her money. One said that she kept $400,000 in a paper bag in her safe-deposit box in Florida and would make trips to the bank to look at it and touch it. Who comes up with these things? That wasn't the Susan Hayward I knew.

"She was aware that I was a struggling actor and while we

291

were sitting in the living room waiting for the chauffeur, she put five $20 bills in my hand. 'Here, take this.'

" 'What's this?'

" 'Well, that's for the day. If you need more, let me know.'

"I said, 'Wait a minute, Susan, you're not paying for the day.'

" 'Then I'm not going. Look, don't act with me. You're not a big star actor; you don't make a lot of money.'

" 'That's true, but I have enough to take Susan Hayward out. Don't worry about it. I'll put it on my credit cards.'

" 'You're not going to pay interest charges on a hundred credit cards.'

"That was a nice thought, but I said, 'Oh, come on, Susan.'

" 'Now, Larry . . .' I could see the Irish flaring up. I kept throwing the money back at her and she kept throwing it back at me, and finally she said, 'If you throw that back at me one more time—go home!'

"Well, would you believe, after all that, we both decided all we wanted for lunch was a hamburger at Hamburger Hamlet!"

Ellis continues: "When we went visiting friends in San Diego and they asked, 'How do you feel?' she'd reply, 'I feel great. How do I look?'

" 'You look fabulous.'

" 'Well, that's how I feel.'

" 'How's the operation healing?'

" 'What operation?'

"And all the time I'd be looking at the hole in her head. The only way I'd spotted it in the first place was that I'd been behind her when we'd come out of the house, and the sun had been blazing right at the back of her head . . . She had on a wig, a gorgeous red Susan Hayward wig, and the hair was very thin back there to let the air circulate around the bandages. . . .

"She always wore a wig or a turban; kerchiefs really. I remember how shocked I was when one fell off. She looked the way Bette Davis had in *The Virgin Queen*, except Bette had had a little hair left. Susan was almost completely bald. It was heartbreaking. She had always been so proud of her beautiful hair. . . .

"But whatever misery she was feeling about that loss, she kept to herself. Only once do I remember her asking, 'How do I look, Larry?' It wasn't one of her good days, but I knew she didn't want any bull. 'Well, let's say I've seen you look better.' I think—I know—she appreciated the honesty.

"Whenever I came to the house, I always kissed her on both her cheeks. Once she said, 'Larry—what's with you? Why do you have to kiss me on both sides?' And I said, 'Well, it's double value.' She broke up laughing. She got such a kick out of the fact that someone would talk to her that way. That was my philosophy. The only way I could let her know I was not pitying her was to be flippant and stay away from gloom and doom.

"Susan would say I was the funniest guy she had ever met. That was an act, but I wouldn't let her know it was an act. Except for one time, I never saw her sad or feeling sorry for herself. There was an anger, of course—the kind of anger that made her fight back so hard, to say, in effect, 'I'm not going to let this happen to me'—but no self-pity."

There was that one time, however:

"We had a date for Sunday brunch. Carmen was off that day, the door had been left slightly ajar, and when I rang the bell she called, 'Come on in.'

"She was standing in the center of the room dressed in a white slack suit, no make-up: she looked absolutely beautiful. The stereo or radio was playing, and she went to turn it off. I would have done it for her, but she insisted upon doing certain things by herself; she hated even being helped into the car.

"She went over to the console, and squatted slightly, her legs in a 'V' position. Then suddenly she froze there.

" 'Larry, come here quick and help me. You're going to have to help me.' "

Larry hurried across the room to assist her. She was holding tightly to the set, trying not to fall. He put his arm around her waist and helped her to a chair in front of the fireplace.

"I was shaken. Now I was face to face with her illness. She started to cry. That was the first time she had ever given an indication of how deeply she was affected by it. 'Larry, what am I going to do? What am I going to do?' Then she added—as if it was important to me—'I can't go out to lunch today, I can't make it today.'

"I told her I would carry her to the car and we could go to a drive-in, but she replied, 'No, I can't.'

"I wanted to do something, anything, but she said, 'I think I want to be by myself now. If you would just help me to my bedroom and leave, I'll be fine.' I did as she asked. There were still tears in her eyes when I left."

In October 1973, Susan entered Massachusetts General Hospital for tests. The news was not good. And although she still refused to give in to the inevitable, she thought it wise to have a new will drawn up, and did so on December 6.

Declaring it to be her last will and testatment,* and with "the support and welfare of my brother, Walter Marrenner . . . one of my primary considerations," her sons being "gainfully employed," Susan set up two trusts: One was for $200,000 and was for Wally, "the said trustee [United California Bank] to pay the net income therefrom to my said brother, in monthly installments during his lifetime," with provisions for allowing Wally to dip into the principal should he come down with an illness requiring funds in excess of the income. Florence was nowhere mentioned.

The other trust was for the boys, consisting of the rest of her property, to be held for them "until they attain the age of 35," the two of them to share equally in the net income of that trust until they reached that age. With her usual sense of frugality, she added, "While both of my sons are self-supporting and successful, I request them to refrain from extravagance and from any substantial donations from the bequests I have made to each of them. It is my hope that each will save a very substantial part of the principal and use the income conservatively. The bequests to my sons will not be in a trust after they reach the age of 35, as both will be then more able to make their own judgments, but it will be helpful to them throughout their lives to have a reserve in event of need."

It was just such a reserve that Susan had always made sure she kept for herself—particularly when it came to the last person mentioned in her will: "My late husband, Floyd Eaton Chalkley, and I had no children. My former husband, Jess Barker, is not an heir at law and I bequeath him nothing. I request my two sons likewise to give him none of the funds that they receive from me. I do not believe that he has any claim upon me or my estate; we were divorced many years ago."

"*I request my two sons likewise to give him none of the funds that they receive from me.*" Not even a cup of coffee! That was

---

* The text is quoted in full in Appendix A.

the line that shocked both Gregory and Timothy. Says Tim: "My mother and father had had several rendezvous after she returned to Hollywood. This was an emotional decision on her part. I don't question her action, but as far as I was concerned, she could have taken it [the money] and lit a match to it. And I expressed that to her: 'Hey, don't hang this over my head. Take it out in the street and burn it.' My mother had very strong opinions . . . but I was floored by this."

When it was suggested to Tim that perhaps it had been his mother's way of controlling Jess Barker's destiny from the grave, he murmured quietly: *"That's it."*

It wasn't a cheerful Christmas. A large tumor growing on the left side of her brain had left the right side of her body paralyzed except for her arm. According to her doctor, the tumor would eventually spread to the right side of her brain as well, and leave her totally paralyzed. But still she refused to give in.

Early in 1974, she received an invitation to be a presenter at the forty-sixth annual presentation of the Academy Awards. The Academy was aware of her illness, but since it was customary to invite prior winners, they'd wanted to extend the courtesy anyway. Nobody expected her to accept—but there they were wrong. With her condition again in a state of temporary remission, Susan had every intention of going.

Oh, she hesitated for a while. First, she thought of accepting, then she changed her mind—but finally screwing up her determination, she decided she had to make one final spectacular appearance before her public. She owed herself that much.

Early the following week, she phoned designer Nolan Miller, and asked to see him about creating a gown for her appearance. Mr. Miller remembers: "I told her I'd do some sketches and she could pick the one she thought she'd look the most fabulous in. It was a labor of love.

"After I'd done about six sketches, Susan, accompanied by her nurse Carmen, came down to the shop. I showed her all of them. At first she liked a brown gown, but when I showed her the green, she really went mad for it. The gown was of chiffon completely covered with bottle-green piettes; high in front, with a dolman sleeve. I took her measurement—she couldn't have weighed more than eighty-five pounds by then, and I promised I'd have it completed well before Oscar night on April 2."

As Oscar night approached, however, she began having second thoughts about attending. By now, her brain seizures had become longer and more frequent. "What if I can't go through with it?" she asked Larry.

"Of course you can go through with it," he replied, and Nolan Miller echoed the sentiments when Susan came to him for a final fitting, even though more problems seemed to be presenting themselves. The dress was dazzling, but she needed more than a dress to complete the illusion.

"What should I do about covering my head?" she asked Miller.

"We're going out and getting you the goddamndest red Susan Hayward wig that anyone has ever seen," he said, and we got the wig and had it set in her old style and it looked fabulous.

"Suddenly it occurred to her that something was missing. 'Oh,' she moaned, 'I have no jewelry. It's all in the vault down south. What are we going to do about that?'

"I said, 'Well, let me see what I can do.' I picked up the phone and called Van Cleef on Wilshire Boulevard. Susan had been a very good customer there. I explained the situation, and Bill Rouser said, 'Bring her over and let her pick out anything she wants to wear.' So I went into the fitting room and said, 'Susan, forget about the dress for a few minutes. We're going over to Van Cleef and pick you up some jewelry.' By the time we got there, Bill had about six trays of necklaces, bracelets, and earrings out, and he said, 'Take whatever you want—and we'll have a messenger pick it up when you no longer need it.' It was fabulous!

"She picked out a diamond necklace and bracelet and earrings, then we returned to the shop and got her all together—just as a trial run, to see the way she looked. She was very pleased. Then she decided she would ask Frank Westmore if he'd come to her house and do her make-up before she had to leave for the Music Center telecast the following Monday."

Had she requested it, she could have been excused from attending the dress rehearsals on Sunday morning—but she didn't want to start any rumors about the possibility of her not making the show. Right now, it was the most important thing in her life.

Bob Osborne recalls: "I saw Susan at the rehearsals and she was a dynamo. She was dressed casually in a slacks outfit and wore no make-up, but that was par for the course at Oscar rehearsals, and one of the reasons the Academy kept the photographers away. I noticed she was limping slightly and seemed thinner than when I saw her last, but she was in a very 'up' mood, and to be truthful, I was beginning to wonder if all the gossip making the rounds had any basis in fact."

That's exactly what she wanted people to think . . . although she would confide in Nolan Miller, "This is the last time the public will ever see me."

The night after the rehearsals, Susan had dinner with Larry Ellis at an Italian restaurant on Santa Monica Boulevard. "It was her favorite place; they all knew her there, and they didn't treat her as if she were an invalid. She hated that kind of treatment.

"She talked about the way the dress rehearsal had gone and about how much she looked forward to the next evening and what a knockout her dress was. It was an early evening, because she wanted to get a good night's sleep. She didn't say it, but I sensed she knew that people were going to study her, to decide on their own if those death-watch stories were true. She really wanted to look gorgeous. I knew she would, though, because that face, even without make-up, was still lovely. And she could still walk on her own if she was on a level floor—if she had to go from a bare floor onto a rug or the reverse, she'd lose her equilibrium, but otherwise she was able to walk around without any noticeable trouble."

On the day of the ceremonies, Susan impulsively decided to add her magnificent sable coat to the gorgeous sequin gown and the jewelry she would be wearing that evening. She told Miller that she had worn the coat just once before, when she was in New York, and wanted to be photographed in it while she had the chance. It wasn't an admission that she was dying, just an acknowledgment that she was retiring from public life. She still wouldn't admit to anyone she was dying. She never mentioned the word—not even to her son Gregory, who came to visit periodically.

Miraculously, the illness, as Ellis said, had done little damage to her face. She was still remarkably pretty, even without make-up—but that wasn't enough, she told Miller: she wanted to look spectacular.

Frank Westmore remembers: "On the afternoon of the Oscar ceremony, Susan Hayward called and told me she was going to

be a presenter and wanted only a Westmore to do her make-up."
He went, of course. When he saw her, however, he was distressed
at her appearance: the rays of the cobalt treatment had destroyed
not only her hair, but her eyelashes and eyebrows as well. "I had
to reconstruct her as she had been thirty years before. I worked
feverishly for hours. . . . I was never more proud of my crafts-
manship."

Nolan Miller shared that sentiment. He prayed that nothing
would go wrong. Nothing did.

Immediately before she walked on stage, Dr. Siegel gave her a
massive dose of Dilantin, a drug used to ward off seizures. Moments later, she heard David Niven announce her name—"Miss
Susan Hayward"—and, shaking badly, she wavered a bit. Charlton Heston took her by the arm, murmured, "Easy, girl," and
together they walked out to the podium to a thunderous ovation—
and amazement: she looked so *good*. Surely she couldn't be dying,
as everyone had heard. Susan barely remembered what happened
next: the reading of the nominees for Best Actress, the announcement of the winner, Glenda Jackson. All she knew was that when
she made it backstage again, exhausted, she said to Carmen,
"Well, that's the last time I pull that off." Heston himself remembers: "That was the last time I saw her."

Leaving the Music Center afterward, Susan was drained; still
she insisted upon going on to a small party, promising to stay
"just a few minutes." She collapsed in a seizure later that evening.

As she had so many other times in the past year, though, she
recovered. "Susan phoned me the next morning," Nolan Miller
says. "She told me about Heston's supportive gesture and mentioned that she had caught a glimpse of me with Missy [Barbara]
Stanwyck at the awards. She said she'd spent the rest of the
evening trying to find us so she could be introduced to Missy.
Isn't that funny how one big star wants to meet another one?
However, there's a story behind this. When Susan was filming
on *Heat of Anger*, she was very concerned about Missy's
health. The minute I'd walk on the set, she'd ask, 'How is she?
Have you checked on her today?' She really kept tabs. Then
Susan started sending Missy little notes and flowers. Susan called
me and asked what Missy's favorite flower was and I said, 'Red
or pink roses.' Then she called Flower Fashions and ordered roses.
When Harry Finlay, the owner, asked how many she wanted to
send—one dozen, two—she said, 'No, I want to send *roses*, that

means at least twelve dozen.' The doctors wouldn't allow Missy to keep flowers in her room—she'd been getting so many—but when she saw Susan's arrangement she insisted on keeping it for awhile to really look at; they had to set up a table in the corner. It looked like a bush, it was so huge. And they hadn't even met. Then Susan got sick.

"Anyway, right after the Academy Awards, I mentioned to Susan that I was taking Missy to the Getty Museum—it hadn't opened yet and a friend of mine had arranged for me to take her on a private tour. As soon as I said it, Susan said she'd love to see it also, so she and Carmen joined us.

"It was so funny. When I introduced Missy and Susan, they were very formal about it. 'Hello, how are you,' in very elegant tones of voice. At the end of the afternoon, when we walked Susan and Carmen back to Susan's limousine, they were both hugging and kissing, with tears and the whole thing.

"Then the earlier situation reversed itself. Missy was calling me to ask, 'Did you speak to Susan? How is she?' She would write Susan little notes. But they never saw each other again. They'd talk about having dinner. A couple of times we'd be getting ready to pick Susan up when Carmen would call and say, 'I think you better not come, she's having a bad day.' "

Isn't it funny how one big movie star wants to meet another one?

Burt Reynolds too had wanted to meet Susan, as much as she had wanted to meet Stanwyck—"She had always been—no, still *is*—one of my favorite movie ladies"—but their careers had always crisscrossed. Reynolds's home, Jupiter, was only a short distance from Susan's Fort Lauderdale home, "but I just couldn't have rung her doorbell and said, 'Hi, I'm Burt Reynolds and I've always wanted to meet you,' could I?"

He could have if he had mentioned that he was a client of Dick Clayton—that same Dick Clayton with whom Susan had done "The Correct Thing" and who had come to the Charles Feldman Agency when Susan was a client there. Clayton had been a close friend of Ned Marin's, and there had been many encounters over the years.

Clayton promised Reynolds, "The next time I see her, I'll mention you want to meet her, and we'll get together for lunch. That was just before Susan was hospitalized." The next time Clayton saw her, Reynolds happened to be with him.

Reynolds remembers: "Dick and I were lunching at Scandia. I saw her first. I nudged my pal and said, 'Look, Susan Hayward's heading in our direction. O.K., buddy, keep your promise.'

"Dick rose, and when she got a little closer she recognized him and stopped at our table. Dick introduced us, and we said a few words. There was such a tremendous warmth and graciousness about her. I couldn't take my eyes off that lovely face. She had tinted glasses on, a scarf about her head, and she looked like a young girl. I never forgot that face. I'll lay it on you straight, I was thrilled."

"Burt was thrilled, all right," Clayton confirms. "He couldn't get his mind back on business. Burt has a tendency to be shy when he meets somebody he admires; he was like a schoolboy. The conversation was 'fan stuff' on both their parts. Susan, as honest as ever, admitted she hadn't seen any of Burt's films, but added he broke her up on the talk shows, Merv, Carson, whatever. Looking at them together, I thought, 'What an explosive team those two would have made if they had been of the same era. Though she usually steered clear of entanglements with leading men, I have a hunch she'd have gone for him personally.' " Of course, Reynolds is a Southerner too.

"It was just that one brief meeting," Clayton concludes, "but what an impression it left on him—particularly in light of what came afterward. . . ."

Stanwyck and Reynolds were not the only stars to want to meet Susan.

When she was feeling well enough to see visitors again after her Oscar-night collapse, Susan invited Larry Ellis to the house.

"She was so excited," Ellis remembers. " 'Oh Larry, Larry,' she said, 'you should have arrived a few minutes earlier. You'll never guess who was here. Katharine Hepburn. She just dropped by unexpectedly. Someone had told her I wasn't feeling well, and she told me that she was concerned about my eating correctly, so she brought a basket of food. Can you imagine that? Oh, I wish you were here so you could have met her!' "

Ironically, for all the years they had worked together in Hollywood, Hepburn and Hayward had met for the first time at the Oscar ceremonies that night. In fact, for all the emotional impact of Susan's appearance, Hepburn had unintentionally stolen some of her thunder when, earlier in the evening, she had appeared to present an honorary award to Lawrence Weingarten, a dear friend who had produced her films *Without Love, Adam's Rib,* and *Pat and Mike* as well as the Hayward starrers, *I'll Cry To-morrow* and *Ada.*

Though a three-time Oscar winner, Hepburn had never before (and has never since) appeared at the ceremonies, but she had done so this time because, as George Cukor notes, "Kate was one of the few people who knew that Weingarten was dying. It was her way of paying a final tribute to him—but the Academy had to promise that her appearance would be kept secret until she walked on stage."

The same spirit and admiration for courage that had moved her to pay tribute to Lawrence Weingarten now brought her to see Susan. In fact, all Hollywood, once so divided in its emotions toward Susan, was divided no longer. As one, they watched with empathy as she battled death.

Though Susan still refused to accept the fact that death was imminent, by July she did know she needed further treatment. Finally willing to undergo exploratory surgery, she made arrangements to fly east to Emory University in Atlanta. Larry Ellis stopped by for a visit the afternoon before she left. Carmen was packing Susan's things.

"Susan put on an awfully brave front for me," he remembers. "She told me she was returning south to get in some fishing and how much she was looking forward to getting back on the ocean again.

"Carmen was standing directly behind her and as Susan kept talking, Carmen just kept shaking her head, silently telling me that things were far more serious than Susan wanted me to know. I didn't let on that I thought there was anything unusual about the trip. I had read somewhere that Susan had always wanted to bag a black marlin, so I kidded her about that and told her to catch two and I'd stuff one and mount it above my fireplace. That day I may have given the best acting performance of my life."

In Atlanta, the doctor gave her his verdict. Ron Nelson later told Frank Greve of the *Miami Herald* that he had been with Susan when the doctor came in to deliver the report from pathology. According to Nelson, Susan said, "If he's gonna tell me what I think he's gonna tell me, you better leave."

Greve wrote: "He [Nelson] heard screams of disbelief, then silence, and went back in."

"Do you want to talk about it?" asked Nelson.

"Nothing to talk about, is there? I'm going home to Fort Lauderdale, and I'm going to act as if nothing happened."

Reverend Thomas Brew, a friend of Eaton Chalkley's from Carrollton, visited Susan in Fort Lauderdale, and at her request delivered communion. She made one more trip to Emory for a brain scan. On October 17, Dr. George Tindall informed the press that "Miss Hayward is quite ill." Shortly thereafter Susan went into a coma.

Four days later, she came out of it. A nurse admitted that her survival was nothing short of a miracle. "The woman simply refused to die."

chapter 33

*Her two-and-a-half-year struggle to keep herself alive
was absolutely extraordinary. It's amazing to stay alive
that long with this kind of illness. There is no other
case like it in medical literature.*

DR. LEE SIEGEL, BEVERLY HILLS

BY LATE OCTOBER, Susan was back in Los Angeles. The doctor
at Emory had warned her what to expect: she would lose the
power of speech, then her memory, then her swallowing reflexes.
At that point, unless she was fed intravenously, she would die.

Her will to live was stronger than the medical reality, however.
Her mind was as active as ever. She'd been home less than a week
when, going through her papers, she realized she had made a
glaring omission in her last testament. On November 7, she asked
her lawyers to draw up a codicil that would leave no doubt about
her intentions to disinherit Florence. Under no circumstances
did she want Florence or Florence's children to be beneficiary of
a single dollar.

With each day, her condition worsened, but she knew if she
gave in she would die. She did not wish to die, nor did she wish
to vegetate. She insisted on keeping in touch with those close to
her, but would allow only a handful of people to visit. She told
Marty Rackin, "If you come up here I'll never speak to you again."
However, she called Larry Ellis and invited him to lunch. Later,
Carmen Perugini called Larry: "I'm going to have to prepare you
for a shock. . . ."

"When Susan left here for Florida," Larry remembers, "she was still walking, still doing things for herself. When I saw her again, she was completely paralyzed. She could move nothing but her left arm. She could barely put a cigarette in her mouth. She tried, but Carmen would have to catch it and put it in her mouth for her.

"She was in a wheelchair—a special chair that converted to a type of cot. She was conscious of the fact that she wasn't looking very well. When she mentioned her appearance, I knew she wasn't fishing for phony compliments.

" 'Look, Susan, the last time I saw you, you looked better. Who knows, maybe the next time I come to see you you'll look better than you do now.'

"She laughed. 'Oh boy, you sure have a way with words.'

"She didn't look too well that afternoon. Her body had shriveled so. I think her weight was down to about eighty pounds. But even toward the very end she was still gorgeous. From her hairline to under the chin she was still the Susan Hayward who had won the Academy Award. That face never changed. There were no lines on it—just freckles and she never wore make-up. And the eyes— they were never half-closed. She still had those wonderful eyes.

"I used to tease her a lot, and she loved it. She couldn't help feeling everyone was pitying her so, and she hated *that*. When she said something incorrect, I'd just say, 'Oh come on, Susan, don't be so stupid.' She felt I was talking to her as if she had the energy to fight back, which pleased her."

Early in her illness Susan had gone to an astrologist to whom she had given her correct date and hour of birth—she'd been a lifelong believer in astrology. He'd assured her she would be alive in January 1975, and she was. "But," says Larry Ellis, "I knew by then she was going to die. One afternoon Carmen, who was usually very close-mouthed, confided, 'She is two years overdue dead.' "

Heartsick, Larry watched Susan slowly lose inches of ground. "And yet she never stopped fighting, never gave in, never gave up. It was unbelievable. She no longer dressed for the street, but the robes she wore could have been worn to a party—pink satin, pink lace, even the kerchief covering her hair was pink. But by now she had given up the wheelchair. She was totally bedridden."

Susan wasn't afraid to look at what lay ahead. And she no longer rejected the past. "Susan kept personal scrapbooks when she was a kid and a model, and Carmen would read all those things to her," Larry remembers. "Carmen was the only one there now. She was living with Susan morning, noon, and night. I'd come by; after I said goodnight to Susan, I'd sit down at the kitchen table with Carmen and look through those books with her. Everything was there—Susan's Holy Communion picture, her confirmation picture, things I'd never seen before."

Katharine Hepburn was a frequent visitor to the hilltop house, bringing baskets of food or freshly cut flowers. "She comes here," Susan told Larry Ellis, "and DEMANDS I get well. Not hopes. DEMANDS." Larry remembers what a big kick Susan got out of that.

"She rented a piano," Larry continues, "and Skip Redwine, my accompanist, would play and I'd sing all the songs she particularly liked. Her favorite, oddly enough, was *Happiness Is a Thing Called Joe*. Ethel Waters sang it originally, in *Cabin in the Sky* and it was one of Susan's numbers in *I'll Cry Tomorrow*. She couldn't get enough of it.

"She wanted to see some of her old movies again and hated the way they were edited for television out here. I had a movie projector and told her I was sure I could rent or get hold of some of her films. The one she paraticularly wanted to see was *Ada*, which made my mouth fall open. *Ada* was the last one I would have chosen. 'Why *Ada*?'

" 'Because that's the one I want to see.'

"Actually it was her second choice for the evening. The one she really wanted to see that night was *Rooster Cogburn*, with John Wayne and Katharine Hepburn. It hadn't been scored yet, but she wanted to see it anyway, and somebody had promised to send a print—not Hepburn: if she had told Hepburn to get it, it would have been gotten. Anyway, that movie didn't come, but she arranged for a giant screen, nine feet wide, to be placed in her bedroom, in front of her bed . . . and she watched *Ada*."

Ada was the story of a reformed prostitute who becomes acting governor of a Southern state. It didn't inspire her to talk about the South or her life there, though.

"Come to think of it," says Ellis, "she never talked about Chalkley or Jess Barker either. Just about her sons. She'd affectionately call them 'my angel' and 'my devil.'

"She mentioned that man she knew from Florida—Ron Nelson —but I don't think he got out here until the last week or two of her life. If he was here, I would have met him. I was at the house every day."

As Ellis watched in pain, he became aware that Susan was gradually losing control of her speech. "Yet, when she could hardly talk, she still tried to sing along with me. . . .

"I was singing the same old songs to her over and over again. Then I fell in love with a new song from *Mack and Mabel.* I told Susan, 'Hey, I learned a new song this week,' and I started to sing "Time Heals Everything." The first line in the song is the title—'Time heals everything'—and as I sang it, I suddenly realized that there she was, sitting there, six inches from me—and the song, which refers to a broken heart, suddenly took on a completely different meaning. I kept on singing in order not to let her know what I was thinking, and when it was over she said, 'Larry, you know what my favorite song is?'

" 'Yes, *Happiness Is Just a Thing Called Joe.*'

" 'Well, now *this* is my favorite song.'

"I had to sing it three more times for her. From then on, whenever I came over to see her, she said, 'I don't care how many songs you sing, Larry. Unless you sing "Time Heals Everything," I want you to leave.' "

Oddly enough, *Mame*'s Donald Pippin had been musical director of *Mack and Mabel,* and the man about whom the song was sung had been Robert Preston. Bob Preston—one of Paramount's Golden Circle in 1939—back when it had all begun for Susan Hayward. "Time Heals Eeverything" would be her last "favorite song." The circle was almost completed.

"Time Heals Everything." There was, of course, another meaning to the title. And time was closing in.

By the end of February, a new slate of Oscar nominees had been announced, and plans were being made for a new Oscar-night show. Unaware of the severity of Susan Hayward's condition, and remembering how spectacular her appearance in 1974 had been, the Academy wrote to say it wanted to present a special tribute in her honor: would Susan be able to come? She sent her regrets and requested they forget about the tribute.

By now, Dr. Lee Siegel was becoming alarmed. Susan was having trouble swallowing, and she had to be turned in bed, yet she refused to be hospitalized again. Siegel ordered an intravenous machine sent over.

On March 12, Susan asked Timothy to come to the house. She

306

had spoken to Gregory a few days earlier. Now she had some private things to say to her other twin. At the conclusion of their conversation, Tim remembers, "She said she loved me, then whimpered and collapsed."

Her condition worsened. Her lungs were beginning to fill with fluids, yet she kept struggling to stay alive with every ounce of strength left in her. Wally remembers seeing his sister for the last time on March 13. He recalls seeing a suction device on her chest and attached to a pump, meant to drain the fluid from her lungs. There had been a one-week accumulation.

"She was conscious at the time," Wally says. He stayed with her as long as he could. After he left, she had another seizure and went into coma. Even in coma, she put up a fight to cling to life.

At the end, it wasn't the cancer that caused her death. It was bronchial pneumonia, brought on by her weakened condition.

On Friday, March 14, 1975, Susan Hayward's eye flew open in a sightless stare. At that moment, Timothy knew his mother had gone.

At Dr. Siegel's request, an ambulance was called and Susan's body was transferred to Century City Hospital, where an autopsy was performed before she was sent on to the airport for the trip to Carrollton, Georgia.

No one knows who leaked the news to the press. The phone kept ringing, but Timothy wouldn't answer it. He was a publicity man by profession, but at that moment he deeply resented the invasion of his privacy. Later in the afternoon, he met with the reporters who had gathered outside the door of the house on the hill. He knew most of them, but his announcement was brief:

"My mother died at 2:25 this afternoon. I have nothing more to say."

That evening TV stations throughout the country broke the news of Susan Hayward's death. A great many showed film clips highlighting her career.

The clip usually screened last was from *I Want to Live!*

The majority of the newspapers began their stories: "Oscar-winner Susan Hayward. . . ."

Susan Hayward would have liked that. Edythe Marrenner would have too.

EPILOGUE

EDYTHE MARRENNER CHALKLEY had expressed a dying wish to her son Timothy that she be buried with simple dignity. The hoopla that a movie star's funeral attracted had always appalled her.

Tim did his best. He gave the Hollywood press an incorrect day of burial, so reporters would not descend on the small cemetery in Carrollton, and he tried to keep the news from Carrollton too, but he underestimated the fervor of the quiet people of that town. In a replay of the triumphal march they had given Susan and her Oscar seventeen years earlier, people lined the seven miles of highway from the Alton Funeral Home to the cemetery on Sunday, March 16, and watched as her body was driven by. Larry Ellis saw snapshots taken in Carrollton that weekend: "There were signs hanging on the windows of the stores shouting, *Welcome Home Susan.* When I saw those pictures, it almost destroyed me. *Welcome Home Susan*—God, how she would have hated that!"

She would have liked the eulogy, though. "She was a good woman who loved her family, her home, and her country, and I was proud to know her," the Reverend Thomas Brew told the five hundred mourners who had gathered in the tiny Our Lady of Perpetual Help Catholic Church. Three priests and a monsignor said the Requiem Mass.

Then, in a chilly drizzle, Timothy and Gregory helped carry their mother's rose-and-orchid covered coffin to the grave site, and, like her husband, Mrs. Eaton Chalkley was buried in the red clay of Georgia. The grave, located on the east side of the church, faced her home at 320 Sunset Boulevard.

It was exactly thirty-seven years to the day since her father had died.

Larry Ellis remembers how he first heard of Susan's death. He had not seen her for two weeks, and had made a tentative appointment to come to the house on Friday, March 14. On Wednesday, he called Carmen to find out if the date was still on. No one answered. For two days, no one answered. "On Friday, I decided to go up the hill to see if anything was wrong. I had to make a quick stop at a friend's house first. His television set faced the door, and, as he opened it, a still of Susan Hayward flashed on the television set. The sound was off. But I didn't need sound to tell me what had happened. I cried, 'My God, she's dead. She's dead.'

"This was a strong, lovely woman who loved life and was cheated out of many years—but when she was here, she gave it all she had. She was the most basically honest person Hollywood had to offer. Ambitious? *Yes*. Drive? *Yes*. But she was no con artist. If you were in her way, she wouldn't try to hurt you to get ahead; but if someone tried to hurt her, she was like a locomotive —and you'd better get out of her way.

"Susan wasn't scared of anyone. Nothing scared her. Nothing frightened her. Not even dying."

After the funeral, Wally and Timothy went back to California, Gregory to Florida. At sixty-eight, Wally lives in retirement now, playing golf and taking it easy. He had another heart attack a few years ago, but "I'm doing fine now," and has no plans to remarry. "I'm too old—who wants an old man?" He finds no fault in the way Susan set up his monthly payments in her will. "When Susan was getting very sick, she said, 'I took care of you, Wal, I took care of you.'" And she has.

Although he won't reveal her whereabouts, he admits he still sees Florence occasionally, the last time during the Christmas holidays of 1979. Her financial condition is still not good.

Florence Marrenner Dietrich is seventy now; her son Larry, thirty-six; her daughter Moira, twenty. A year after Susan's death, on March 19, 1976, Florence protested the codicil in her sister's will disinheriting her, and filed a claim against the estate for twenty thousand dollars. The court rejected the petition. At the time, she gave her address as 4555 North Figueroa, a seedy area of downtown Los Angeles.

Shortly after Susan's death, Dick Clayton remembers Florence's coming up to his office with Moira and asking if he could get her into pictures. "She was a beautiful kid," says Clayton. "Reminded me a little of Susan when I did that first modeling job with her. There was nothing I could do at that time and I didn't hear from them again." Soon thereafter, though, Moira was spotted by a Susan Hayward admirer on the location set of Peter Bogdanovich's movie *Nickelodeon*. The young man, startled by her resemblance to Susan, started a conversation with the pretty young red-haired teen-ager. "She told me that Susan Hayward was her aunt and that she wanted to be an actress as soon as she completed Catholic school. Then she wandered away. I wasn't sure whether she was an extra on the film or had just been watching the filming." As of this writing, there is no listing for Moira with the Screen Actors' Guild or the Screen Extras' Guild. Of Florence's other child, Larry, little is known.

According to the records of the County Clerk of Los Angeles, the last person to request the file on Edythe Marrenner Chalkley was named *Dietrich*.

Gregory Barker still makes his home in Jacksonville, Florida, with his wife Susan and their two children, and his veterinary hospital thrives. ("Oh God, is he successful!" exclaims Jess Barker proudly.)

Tim, associated with the Garrett Simes office as a publicist and personal manager, plans to break away on his own soon and concentrate on management of rock musicians. Asked about the three Chalkley siblings—unmentioned in Susan's will—he says tersely, "I'm not in contact with any of the relatives except my brother and my father."

Jess Barker had never considered the possibility of being mentioned in Susan's will in any way, "but," says Tim, "he was floored by that paragraph about him. *I* was floored." "*I request my two sons likewise to give him none of the funds that they receive from me.*" Barker accepted the edict "philosophically," yet says quietly, "That's why I couldn't get any presents from the boys."

He talks of his sons with great affection. Tim lives a few minutes away, and they have dinner together frequently. Tim and Ilse Barker have been divorced for several years, but Tim often takes his daughter Nadja to see her granddad. Jess goes to Jacksonville to visit Gregory and his two grandsons whenever possible.

The years have not been generous to Jess Barker. After returning to Hollywood in 1961, he worked for a while on television, and made his last film, *The Night Walker*, with Barbara Stanwyck and Robert Taylor, at Universal in 1968. After that, acting jobs were hard to come by. "I haven't worked in . . ." He'd rather not be reminded. But when he moved in 1977, he didn't bother to notify the Screen Actors' Guild of his change of address. Ironically, what may have contributed to Jess's inactivity in the 1970s was that a great many people thought Jess Barker was dead. In the 1950s, he was often confused with Lex Barker, Lana Turner's former husband. That Barker died of a sudden heart attack in 1974. In fact, one of Susan's Los Angeles obituaries noted "she had been divorced from the late Lex Barker."

Jess didn't come forth to correct it. Reporters who knew the difference and asked for interviews after Susan's death were all turned down. "I don't want a hatchet job on Susan." About restoring his own battered ego: "That's not important. All I want is to keep her in the same light she has always been." At age sixty-six, Jess has exorcised past demons. There's no rancor in his voice when he talks about Susan.

The twins claimed their inheritance in March of 1980, shortly after their thirty-fifth birthday. It is their money to do with as they choose. They love their father—they always have—and whether they will follow the terms of their mother's will remains to be seen. It will be a very private decision. They remain terribly loyal to their mother too. They loved her as well: "My mother was super," says Tim. "She taught us decency and honesty and gave us a true sense of morality."

There is one final postscript to the story of Susan Hayward. In June and July of 1979, the death of John Wayne from cancer released an ocean of eulogies and tributes to the star. In August, however, a different story appeared on the wires and in newspapers across the country. A journalist named Peter Brennan had become aware of some macabre facts: John Wayne had died of cancer. As had Susan Hayward. As had Agnes Moorehead in 1974 and Dick Powell in 1963. The one thing all four of them had had in common, besides the cause of their death . . . had been a film called *The Conqueror*, a movie made in the summer of 1954 in Saint George, Utah, a town fanned by radiation from eighty-seven above-ground atomic blasts in the adjacent Nevada desert during that period. One of the largest of those blasts had spawned a wind dubbed "Dirty Harry," which had swept across the desert in 1953, dropping radiation everywhere. In addition, according to Lee Van Cleef, the last surviving principal member of the cast, tons of contaminated earth had been shipped back to Hollywood for further shooting, thereby prolonging the actors' exposure.

And it did not end there. Ted de Corsia of *The Conqueror* cast had also died of cancer. Pedro Armendariz, had committed suicide in 1963 after learning that he had contracted lymph gland cancer. An unbilled actress, Barbara Gerson, was suffering from cancer of the skin, and many other members of the cast and crew had been similarly affected.

The Wayne family shrugged off the story as "coincidence," but in February of 1969, a study was released showing that children born in southern Utah in the 1950s died of leukemia at a rate two-and-a-half times greater than that of those born before the test. As a result, some seven hundred residents of Saint George are now filing suit against the federal government, claiming exposure to large doses of radiation without warning. The suits could run into the hundreds of millions of dollars if a connection between the tests and the cancer deaths is ever firmly established. With the furor of Three Mile Island and other nuclear "accidents," the government shudders at the publicity a proven *Conqueror* connection could set off. The lawsuits. The fears.

It is the final irony: it may have taken an atomic explosion to kill Susan.

A sign on Susan's resting place, put there probably by some Carrollton townsperson, reads, "Grave of Susan Hayward Chalkley," but the tombstone itself reads simply, "F. Eaton Chalkley, 1909–1966" and "Mrs. F. E. Chalkley, 1917–1975," with the inscription, "I am the resurrection and the life." No other epitaph than that.

Yet Susan herself may have voiced an appropriate one for herself in the course of her final conversation with Robert Osborne:

"When you're dead, you're dead. Nobody is going to remember me when I'm dead. Oh, maybe a few friends will remember me affectionately. Being remembered isn't the most important thing anyhow. It's what you do when you are here that's important."

"It's what you do when you are here that's important."

And it is for exactly that reason—for what she was and what she did—that she *is* remembered.

As a star. As a woman. And as a survivor.

313

APPENDIX A

LAST WILL AND TESTAMENT
OF
EDYTHE MARRENNER CHALKLEY

I, EDYTHE MARRENNER CHALKLEY, declare this to be my Last Will and Testament and I hereby revoke all prior wills and codicils to wills.

FIRST: I am presently a resident of the State of California but I intend to move to the State of Florida within a short time, and I intend to maintain my domicile there.

SECOND: I am not married. My husband, Floyd Eaton Chalkley, is deceased. My sons are Gregory Barker and Timothy Barker. I have a brother, Walter Marrenner.

THIRD: The support and welfare of my brother, Walter Marrenner, is one of my primary considerations. Both of my sons, Gregory Marrenner Barker, a resident of Florida, and Timothy Marrenner Barker, a resident of Los Angeles, are gainfully employed.

FOURTH: I give, devise and bequeath my furs to my friend, Carmen Perugini of Los Angeles.

FIFTH: All my other real and personal property (other than cash, bank accounts and stocks and bonds) I authorize my executor to sell, except such keepsakes my sons may wish to have.

SIXTH: I give, devise and bequeath to United California Bank, as trustee, for the benefit of my brother, Walter Marrenner, the sum of $200,000 and direct the said trustee to pay the net income therefrom to my said brother, in monthly installments during his lifetime. This trust shall be created when a preliminary or final distribution of my estate is made. Until the said trust for his benefit is established and provides a source from which to pay my brother Walter the monthly sum herein provided, the executor shall pay to him monthly $835 for his support. I believe that the annual income from said trust will produce a sufficient income for my brother's support who also has Social Security benefits for his further support. Should he have an illness requiring funds in excess of his income from the trust, such funds shall be paid from the $200,000 herein provided. The principal of the trust shall not otherwise be invaded. Upon my brother's demise, then the said principal sum of $200,000, together with any unexpended income remaining in said fund at the date of my brother's demise, I give, devise and bequeath to my trustee to be included in the trust referred to in Paragraph EIGHTH hereof if said trust is still in existence; otherwise, I give, devise and bequeath said sum to my two sons equally. Either the trustee or my sons shall make provisions for the reasonable funeral expenses of my brother.

SEVENTH: (a) I have invested in an annuity. Should any further payments therefrom become due and payable after my demise, I give, devise and bequeath such payments to my two sons equally.

(b) My jewelry has substantial value. I bequeath it to my sons to be divided, as equally as possible in value. An appraisal in my possession was made in 1967 and is a sufficient basis for the division of the jewelry.

EIGHTH: All the rest and remainder of my property, I give, devise and bequeath to my trustee above named, in trust for the benefit of my two sons, Gregory Marrenner Barker and Timothy Marrenner Barker, until they attain the age of 35. Until they attain that age, the trustee shall pay to them equally the net income of said trust. When my sons reach the age of 35, the assets of the trust shall be distributed to them equally and they shall receive the remainder of my property not otherwise disposed of herein, in equal shares.

NINTH: My late husband, Floyd Eaton Chalkley, and I had no children. My former husband, Jess Barker, is not an heir at law and I bequeath him nothing. I request my two sons likewise to give him none of the funds that they receive from me. I do not believe that he has any claims upon me or my estate; we were divorced many years ago.

TENTH: While both of my sons are self-supporting and successful, I request them to refrain from extravagance and from any substantial donations from the bequests I have made to each of them. It is my hope that each will save a very substantial part of the principal and use the income conservatively. The bequests to my sons will not be in a trust after they reach the age of 35, as both will be then more able to make their own judgments, but it will be helpful to them throughout their lives to have a reserve in event of need.

ELEVENTH: No interest in the principal or income of any trust created under this Will shall be anticipated, assigned, or encumbered, or subject to any creditor's claim or to legal process, prior to its actual receipt by the beneficiary.

TWELFTH: If either of my sons dies before the final distribution of my estate, and the trust herein created, then the remaining share of any such deceased son I give, devise and bequeath to my remaining son then living. If both of my sons shall die prior to such distribution, then I give, devise and bequeath the estate which my sons would have received had both or either survived, to the children of each son, one half to go to the children of Timothy and the other one half to the children of Gregory.

THIRTEENTH: If I am a resident of California at the date of my demise, I appoint my sons Gregory Barker and Timothy Barker as joint executors, and they shall serve without bond. If for any reason only one of them shall serve, he shall not be required to file a bond as such executor. If neither son survives or qualifies as an executor, I appoint United California Bank as executor, if I then reside in California. If I am a resident of Florida at the time of my demise, then I hereby appoint the Everglades Bank of Fort Lauderdale, Florida, as my executor.

FOURTEENTH: I desire to be buried at Carrollton, Georgia. I shall leave funeral instructions with my sons or with others, as they need not be set forth in this will.

Executed at Beverly Hills, California, this 6 day of December, 1973.

EDYTHE MARRENNER CHALKLEY

On the date written below, EDYTHE MARRENNER CHALKLEY declared to us, the undersigned, that this instrument, consisting of four (4) pages, including this page on which this attestation clause is concluded, was her Last Will and Testament and requested us to act as witnesses to it. She thereupon signed this will in our presence, all of us being present at the same time. We now, at her request, in her presence and in the presence of each other, subscribe our names as witnesses.

We declare under penalty of perjury that the foregoing is true and correct.

Executed on December 6th, 1973, at Beverly Hills, California.

JOHN E. HOFFMAN
Residing at Los Angeles
California

L. MCLAUGHLIN
Residing at Hermosa Beach
California

APPENDIX B

FILMOGRAPHY

NOTE: *All dates are based on the New York openings. The director's name appears in italics after these dates. Susan made several short subjects. These are indicated by an asterisk before the title.*

* CAMPUS CINDERELLA. Warner Brothers, 1938. *Noel Smith.* Johnnie Davis, Penny Singleton, Anthony Averill, Peggy Moran, Oscar O'Shea, Wright Kramer, Janet Shaw, Rosella Towne, Dorothy Comingore. 13 minutes.

GIRLS ON PROBATION. Warner Brothers, October 27, 1938. *William McGann.* Jane Bryan, Ronald Reagan, Henry O'Neill, Elizabeth Risdon, Esther Dale, Sig Rumann, Sheila Bromley, Joseph Crehan, Anthony Averill, Dorothy Peterson, Emory Parnell, Ed Stanley, Vera Lewis. 63 minutes.

BEAU GESTE. Paramount, August 2, 1939. *William A. Wellman.* Gary Cooper, Ray Milland, Robert Preston, Brian Donlevy, J. Carrol Nash, Broderick Crawford, Albert Dekker, James Stephenson, Donald O'Connor, Harold Huber, Ann Gillis, Heather Thatcher, Billy Cook, David Holt, Martin Spellman, Charles Barton, George P. Huntley, Harry Woods, James Burke, Henry Brandon, George Chandler. 120 minutes.

OUR LEADING CITIZEN. Paramount, August 23, 1939. *Alfred Santell.* Bob Burns, Joseph Allen, Jr., Elizabeth Patterson, Gene Lockhart, Kathleen Lockhart, Charles Bickford, Clarence Kolb, Paul Guilfoyle, Fay Helm, Otto Hoffman. 87 minutes.

$1,000 A TOUCHDOWN. Paramount, October 4, 1939. *James Hogan.* Martha Raye, Joe E. Brown, Eric Blore, John Hartley, Syd Saylor, Don Wilson, Joyce Mathews, Tom Dugan. 71 minutes.

ADAM HAD FOUR SONS. Columbia, March 27, 1941. *Gregory Ratoff.* Ingrid Bergman, Warner Baxter, Richard Denning, Fay Wray, Johnny Downs, Helen Westley, June Lockhart. 80 minutes.

SIS HOPKINS. Republic, April 30, 1941. *Joseph Santley.* Judy Canova, Charles Butterworth, Bob Crosby and Orchestra with the Bobcats, Katherine Alexander, Jerry Colonna, Elvia Allman. 97 minutes.

AMONG THE LIVING. Paramount, December 12, 1941. *Stuart Heisler.* Albert Dekker, Harry Carey, Frances Farmer, Maude Eburne, Jean Phillips, Gordon Jones, Archie Twitchell, Dorothy Sebastian, Harlan Briggs, Ernest Whitman, Frank M. Thomas, Rod Cameron, Catherine Craig, Richard Webb. 68 minutes.

REAP THE WILD WIND. Paramount, March 26, 1942. *Cecil B. DeMille.* Paulette Goddard, Ray Milland. John Wayne, Robert Preston, Raymond Massey, Lynne Overman, Charles Bickford, Louise Beavers, Martha O'Driscoll, Janet Beecher, Elizabeth Risdon, Barbara Britton, Hedda Hopper, Victor Kilian, Walter Hampden, Milburn Stone, Byron Foulger, James Flavin, Julia Faye, Maurice Costello, narrated by Cecil B. DeMille. 124 minutes.

THE FOREST RANGERS. Paramount, October 21, 1942. *George Marshall.* Fred MacMurray, Paulette Goddard, Albert Dekker, Lynne Overman, Eugene Pallette, Regis Toomey, James Brown, Clem Bevans, Rod Cameron, Chester Clute. 87 minutes.

I MARRIED A WITCH. United Artists, November 19, 1942. *Rene Clair.* Fredric March, Veronica Lake, Robert Benchley, Cecil Kellaway, Elizabeth Patterson, Robert Warwick, Mary Field, Eily Malyon, Emma Dunn, Monte Blue, Robert Homans, Reed Hadley. 82 minutes.

* A LETTER FROM BATAAN. Paramount, 1942. *William H. Pine.* Richard Arlen, Janet Beecher, Jimmy Lydon, Joe Sawyer, Keith Richards, Esther Dale, Will Wright. 15 minutes.

STAR SPANGLED RHYTHM. Paramount, December 30, 1942. *George Marshall.* Walter Abel, Eddie (Rochester) Anderson, William Bendix, Karin Booth, Eddie Bracken, Virginia Brissac, Rod Cameron, Macdonald Carey, Jerry Colonna, Bing Crosby, Gary Crosby, Cass Daley, Albert Dekker, Cecil B. DeMille, Dona Drake, Ellen Drew, Tom Dugan, Katherine Dunham, Frank Faylen, Susanna Foster, Eva Gabor, Frances Gifford, Paulette Goddard, William Haade, Sterling Holloway, Bob Hope, Jack Hope, Betty Hutton, Johnnie Johnston, Cecil Kellaway, Alan Ladd, Veronica Lake, Gil Lamb, Dorothy Lamour, Arthur Loft, Richard Loo, Jimmy Lydon, Diana Lynn, Fred MacMurray, Marion Martin, Mary Martin, Ray Milland, Victor Moore, Lynne Overman, Mabel Paige, Barbara Pepper, Dick Powell, Robert Preston, Anne Revere, Marjorie Reynolds, Betty Jane Rhodes, Preston Sturges, Franchot Tone, Arthur Treacher, Ernest Truex, Vera Zorina. 99 minutes.

YOUNG AND WILLING. United Artists, February 5, 1943. *Edward H. Griffith.* William Holden, Eddie Bracken, Barbara Britton, Robert Benchley, Martha O'Driscoll, Mabel Paige, Florence MacMichael, James Brown, Jay Fassett, Paul Hurst, Olin Howland, Billy Bevan, Cheryl Walker. 82 minutes.

HIT PARADE OF 1943. Republic, April 15, 1943. *Albert S. Rogell.* John Carroll, Eve Arden, Gail Patrick, Walter Catlett, Melville Cooper, Mary Treen, Astrid Allwyn, Tim Ryan, Tom Kennedy, Grandon Rhodes, Dorothy Dandridge, Wally Vernon, Count Basie and Orchestra, Ray McKinley and Orchestra. 90 minutes.

JACK LONDON. United Artists, March 2, 1944. *Alfred Santell.* Michael O'Shea, Osa Massen, Virginia Mayo, Harry Davenport, Frank Craven, Ralph Morgan, Louise Beavers, Regis Toomey, Hobart Cavanaugh, Morgan Conway, Jonathan Hale, Olin Howland, Paul Hurst, Pierre Watkin, Richard Loo, Sarah Padden, Leonard Strong, Dick Curtis. 92 minutes.

* SKIRMISH ON THE HOME FRONT. Paramount, for U.S. Government Office of War Information, 1944. Alan Ladd, Betty Hutton, William Bendix. 13 minutes.

THE FIGHTING SEABEES. Republic, March 19, 1944. *Howard Lydecker and Edward Ludwig.* John Wayne, Dennis O'Keefe, William Frawley, Leonid Kinskey, Grant Withers, J. M. Kerrigan, Paul Fix, Addison Richards, Duncan Renaldo, Ben Welden, William Forrest, Jay Norris, Ernest Golm, Adele Mara. 100 minutes.

THE HAIRY APE. United Artists, July 2, 1944. *Alfred Santell.* William Bendix, John Loder, Dorothy Comingore, Roman Bohnen, Alan Napier, Tom Fadden, Raphael Storm. 92 minutes.

AND NOW TOMORROW. Paramount, November 22, 1944. *Irving Pichel.* Alan Ladd, Loretta Young, Barry Sullivan, Beulah Bondi, Cecil Kellaway, Grant Mitchell, Helen Mack, Darryl Hickman, Anthony Caruso, Jonathan Hale. 84 minutes.

DEADLINE AT DAWN. RKO, April 3, 1946. *Harold Clurman.* Bill Williams, Paul Lukas, Joseph Calleia, Osa Massen, Lola Lane, Jerome Cowan, Marvin Miller, Roman Bohnen, Joe Sawyer, Constance Worth, Steven Geray, Joseph Crehan, William Challee, Jason Robards, Sr. 83 minutes.

CANYON PASSAGE. Universal, August 7, 1946. *Jacques Tourneur.* Dana Andrews, Brian Donlevy, Hoagy Carmichael, Patricia Roc, Ward Bond, Rose Hobart, Lloyd Bridges, Andy Devine, Tad and Denny Devine, Stanley Ridges, Fay Holden, Victor Cutler, Dorothy Peterson, Onslow Stevens, Halliwell Hobbes, James Cardwell, Peter Whitney. 90 minutes.

SMASH-UP, THE STORY OF A WOMAN. Universal-International, April 10, 1947. *Stuart Heisler.* Lee Bowman, Eddie Albert, Marsha Hunt, Carl Esmond, Carleton Young, Charles D. Brown, Sharyn Payne, Robert Shayne, Janet Murdoch, Tom Chatterton, George Meeker, Larry Blake, Bess Flowers. 113 minutes.

THEY WON'T BELIEVE ME. RKO, July 16, 1947. *Irving Pichel.* Robert Young, Jane Greer, Rita Johnson, Tom Powers, George Tyne, Don Beddoe, Frank Ferguson, Harry Harvey, Janet Shaw, Anthony Caruso, Milton Parsons. 95 minutes.

THE LOST MOMENT. Universal-International, November 21, 1947. *Martin Gabel.* Robert Cummings, Agnes Moorehead, Joan Lorring, John Archer, Minerva Urecal, Eduardo Ciannelli, Frank Puglia. 89 minutes.

TAP ROOTS. Universal-International, August 25, 1948. *George Marshall.* Van Heflin, Ward Bond, Boris Karloff, Julie London, Whitfield Connor, Richard Long, Arthur Shields, Griff Barnett, Sondra Rogers, Ruby Dandridge. 109 minutes.

THE SAXON CHARM. Universal-International, September 29, 1948. *Claude Binyon.* Robert Montgomery, John Payne, Audrey Totter, Henry (Harry) Morgan, Harry Von Zell, Heather Angel, Cara Williams, Chill Wills, John Baragrey, Addison Richards. 88 minutes.

TULSA. Eagle-Lion, May 26, 1949. *Stuart Heisler.* Robert Preston, Pedro Armendariz, Chill Wills, Lloyd Gough, Paul E. Burns, Ed Begley, Lola Albright, Harry Shannon, Jimmy Conlin, Roland Jack, Pierre Watkin, Dick Wessel, Tom Dugan, John Dehner, Charles D. Brown, Selmer Jackson. 88 minutes.

HOUSE OF STRANGERS. Twentieth Century-Fox, July 1, 1949. *Joseph L. Mankiewicz.* Edward G. Robinson, Richard Conte, Luther

Adler, Efrem Zimbalist, Jr., Esther Minciotti, Debra Paget, Hope Emerson, Paul Valentine, Diana Douglas. 101 minutes.

My Foolish Heart. Goldwyn-RKO, January 19, 1950. *Mark Robson.* Dana Andrews, Kent Smith, Robert Keith, Jessie Royce Landis, Lois Wheeler, Gigi Perreau, Karin Booth, Martha Mears, Edna Holland, Philip Pine, Barbara Woodell. 98 minutes.

Rawhide. Twentieth Century-Fox, March 25, 1951. *Henry Hathaway.* Tyrone Power, Hugh Marlowe, Dean Jagger, Jack Elam, Edgar Buchanan, George Tobias, Jeff Corey, James Millican, Louis Jean Heydt, Ken Tobey. 86 minutes.

I Can Get It for You Wholesale. Twentieth Century-Fox, April 4, 1951. *Michael Gordon.* Dan Dailey, George Sanders, Sam Jaffe, Vicki Cummings, Barbara Whiting, Randy Stuart, Mary Phillips, Marvin Kaplan, Harry Von Zell, Richard Lane, Steven Geray, Charles Lane, Marion Marshall, Marjorie Hoshelle. 91 minutes.

I'd Climb the Highest Mountain. Twentieth Century-Fox, May 10, 1951. *Henry King.* William Lundigan, Rory Calhoun, Barbara Bates, Alexander Knox, Lynn Bari, Gene Lockhart, Ruth Donnelly, Jean Inness, Kathleen Lockhart. 88 minutes.

David and Bathsheba. Twentieth Century-Fox, August 14, 1951. *Henry King.* Gregory Peck, Raymond Massey, Jayne Meadows, Kieron Moore, James Robertson Justice, John Sutton, Francis X. Bushman, Paula Morgan, Teddy Infuhr, Gwyneth (Gwen) Verdon. 153 minutes.

With a Song in My Heart. Twentieth Century-Fox, April 5, 1952. *Walter Lang.* David Wayne, Rory Calhoun, Thelma Ritter, Robert Wagner, Helen Westcott, Una Merkel, Lyle Talbot, Max Showalter, Robert Easton, Leif Erickson, Richard Allan, Carlos Molina, Nestor Paiva; the singing voice of Jane Froman. 117 minutes.

The Snows of Kilimanjaro. Twentieth Century-Fox, September 18, 1952. *Henry King.* Gregory Peck, Ava Gardner, Hildegarde Neff, Leo G. Carroll, Torin Thatcher, Ava Norring, Helene Stanley, Marcel Dalio, Richard Allan, Lisa Ferraday, Ivan Lebedeff. 114 minutes.

The Lusty Men. RKO, October 24, 1952. *Nicholas Ray.* Robert Mitchum, Arthur Kennedy, Arthur Hunnicutt, Frank Faylen,

Walter Coy, Carol Nugent, Lorna Thayer, Maria Hart, Karen King, Eleanor Todd, Jimmy Dodd, Burt Mustin, Sam Flint, Riley Hill, Robert Bray, Sheb Wooley. 112 minutes.

THE PRESIDENT'S LADY. Twentieth Century-Fox, May 21, 1953. *Henry Levin.* Charlton Heston, Fay Bainter, John McIntire, Margaret Wycherly, Carl Betz, Whitfield Connor, Trudy Marshall, Gladys Hurlbut, Nina Varela, Charles Dingle, James Best, Willis Bouchey, Jim Davis. 96 minutes.

WHITE WITCH DOCTOR. Twentieth Century-Fox, July 1, 1953. *Henry Hathaway.* Robert Mitchum, Walter Slezak, Mashood Ajala, Joseph C. Narcisse, Michael Ansara, Timothy Carey. 95 minutes.

DEMETRIUS AND THE GLADIATORS. Twentieth Century-Fox, June 18, 1954. *Delmer Daves.* Victor Mature, Michael Rennie, Debra Paget, Anne Bancroft, Jay Robinson, Richard Egan, Ernest Borgnine, Barry Jones, William Marshall, Charles Evans, Jeff York, Carmen de Lavallade, Selmer Jackson, Dayton Lummis, Woody Strode, Paul Richards. 101 minutes.

GARDEN OF EVIL. Twentieth Century-Fox, July 9, 1954. *Henry Hathaway.* Gary Cooper, Richard Widmark, Hugh Marlowe, Cameron Mitchell, Rita Moreno. 100 minutes.

UNTAMED. Twentieth Century-Fox, March 11, 1955. *Henry King.* Tyrone Power, Richard Egan, Agnes Moorehead, Rita Moreno, John Justin, Hope Emerson, Brad Dexter, Henry O'Neill, Kevin and Brian Corcoran, Philip Van Zandt. 111 minutes.

SOLDIER OF FORTUNE. Twentieth Century-Fox, May 27, 1955. *Edward Dmytryk.* Clark Gable, Gene Barry, Michael Rennie, Anna Sten, Tom Tully, Jack Kruschen, Alex D'Arcy, Russell Collins, Richard Loo. 96 minutes.

I'LL CRY TOMORROW. MGM, January 12, 1956. *Daniel Mann.* Jo Van Fleet, Richard Conte, Eddie Albert, Don Taylor, Margo, Virginia Gregg, Don Barry, Carole Ann Campbell, Ruth Storey (Conte), Peter Leeds, David Kasday, Veda Ann Borg, Tol Avery, Nora Marlowe. 117 minutes.

THE CONQUEROR. RKO, March 30, 1956. *Dick Powell.* John Wayne, Agnes Moorehead, Pedro Armendariz, Thomas Gomez, John Hoyt, William Conrad, Ted de Corsia, Richard Loo, Lee Van Cleef, Peter Mamakos, Leslie Bradley, Sylvia Lewis, Jarma Lewis, Fred Graham, George E. Stone, Jeanne Gerson, Leo Gordon. 111 minutes.

TOP SECRET AFFAIR. Warner Brothers, January 30, 1957. *H. C. Potter.* Kirk Douglas, Paul Stewart, Jim Backus, Roland Winters, John Cromwell, Charles Lane. 100 minutes.

I WANT TO LIVE! United Artists, November 18, 1958. *Robert Wise.* Simon Oakland, Virginia Vincent, Theodore Bikel, Alice Backes, Wesley Lau, Dabbs Greer, Philip Coolidge, Gage Clark, Russell Thorson, James Philbrook, Lou Krugman, Joe DeSantis, Raymond Bailey, Marion Marshall, Peter Breck, Brett Halsey, Jack Weston. 120 minutes.

THUNDER IN THE SUN. Paramount, April 8, 1959. *Russell Rouse.* Jeff Chandler, Jacques Bergerac, Blanche Yurka, Carl Esmond, Fortunio Bonanova, Bertrand Castelli, Felix Locher, Veda Ann Borg, Pedro De Cordoba, Jr. 81 minutes.

WOMAN OBSESSED. Twentieth Century-Fox, May 27, 1959. *Henry Hathaway.* Stephen Boyd, Theodore Bikel, Dennis Holmes, Barbara Nichols, Florence MacMichael, Ken Scott, James Philbrook, Arthur Franz. 103 minutes.

THE MARRIAGE-GO-ROUND. Twentieth Century-Fox, January 6, 1961. *Walter Lang.* James Mason, Julie Newmar, Robert Paige, June Clayworth, Joe Kirkwood, Jr. 98 minutes.

ADA. MGM, August 25, 1961. *Daniel Mann.* Dean Martin, Wilfrid Hyde-White, Ralph Meeker, Martin Balsam, Frank Maxwell, Connie Sawyer, Larry Gates, Ford Rainey, Charles Watts, Robert F. Simon, William Zuckert, Richard Benedict, Kathryn Card, Robert Burton, Helen Beverly. 109 minutes.

BACK STREET. Universal-International, October 12, 1961. *David Miller.* John Gavin, Vera Miles, Virginia Grey, Reginald Gardiner, Charles Drake, Natalie Schafer, Tammy Marihugh, Robert Eyer, Dick Kallman, Joyce Meadows, Alex Gerry, Hayden Rorke. 107 minutes.

I THANK A FOOL. MGM, September 14, 1962. *Robert Stevens.* Peter Finch, Diane Cilento, Cyril Cusack, Kieron Moore, Athene Seyler, Richard Wattis, Laurence Naismith, Brenda de Banzie. 100 minutes.

STOLEN HOURS. United Artists, October 16, 1963. *Daniel Petrie.* Michael Craig, Edward Judd, Diane Baker, Paul Rogers, Robert Bacon, Joan Newell, Peter Madden, Gwen Nelson. 97 minutes.

WHERE LOVE HAS GONE. Embassy-Paramount, November 2, 1964. *Edward Dmytryk*. Bette Davis, Michael Connors, Joey Heatherton, Jane Greer, Anne Seymour, DeForest Kelley, George Macready, Ann Doran, Willis Bouchey, Anthony Caruso, Whit Bissell. 114 minutes.

THE HONEY POT. United Artists, May 22, 1967. *Joseph L. Mankiewicz*. Rex Harrison, Maggie Smith, Cliff Robertson, Edie Adams, Capucine, Adolfo Celi, Luigi Scavran. 131 minutes.

VALLEY OF THE DOLLS. Twentieth Century-Fox, December 15, 1967. *Mark Robson*. Barbara Parkins, Patty Duke, Sharon Tate, Paul Burke, Tony Scotti, Lee Grant, Martin Milner, Charles Drake, Alex Davion, Naomi Stevens, Robert H. Harris, Robert Viharo, Richard Angarola, Jeanne Gerson. 123 minutes.

HEAT OF ANGER. New CBS Friday Night Movies/Stonehenge Productions-Metromedia Producers Corp., 1972. *Don Taylor*. James Stacey, Lee J. Cobb, Fritz Weaver, Bettye Ackerman, Jennifer Penny, Mills Watson, Ray Simms, Tyne Daly. 75 minutes.

THE REVENGERS. National General Pictures, 1972. *Daniel Mann*. William Holden, Ernest Borgnine, Woody Strode, Arthur Hunnicutt, Roger Hanin, Scott Holden. 110 minutes.

SAY GOODBYE, MAGGIE COLE. ABC Wednesday Movie of the Week/ Spelling-Goldberg Production, 1972. *Jud Taylor*. Darren McGavin, Beverly Garland, Dane Clark, Michael Constantine, Jeanette Nolan, Michele Nichols, Maidie Norman, Richard Anderson. 75 minutes.

NOTE

Susan Hayward also appeared in seven "Lux Radio Theater" broadcasts: *Hold Back the Dawn*, Nov. 10, 1941 (with Paulette Goddard); *Petrified Forest*, Apr. 23, 1945 (with Ronald Colman); and recreations of her original roles with her film co-stars in *Tap Roots* (Sept. 1948); *My Foolish Heart* (Aug. 28, 1950); *I'd Climb the Highest Mountain* (Oct. 29, 1951); *I Can Get It for You Wholesale* (Mar. 31, 1952); *With a Song in My Heart* (Feb. 9, 1953).

She was also seen on television in a cameo role in Louella Parsons's 1956 *The Gay Illiterate* telecast; *Person to Person* with Edward R. Murrow in 1958; and the *Joey Bishop Show* in 1968.

ACKNOWLEDGMENTS

AFTER the immediate family and co-stars, who does one thank first for the time, effort, and other contributions that go into creating a biography? So many helped. . . .

My appreciation goes to Norman Brokaw, vice-president of the William Morris Agency, Susan's final Hollywood agent, and my current one, both for his remembrances of Susan and the encouragement he gave me with this project; to Helen Barrett, also of William Morris, my New York literary agent whose practical and emotional assistance got me through some very difficult moments. And of course my gratitude to my editor Neil Nyren, who was always available above and beyond the call of duty and who turned what could have been an ordeal into a challenging pleasure.

I am beholden to director George Cukor for finally setting the record straight as to the *exact* circumstances that led to Susan's initial trip to Hollywood and for telling me for the *first time* the true story that invalidates every other myth printed about Susan's Scarlett O'Hara screen tests.

I spoke with Lillian Roth, whose life Susan portrayed. Miss Roth, Dick Clayton, Burt Reynolds, Peggy Moran Koster, actress Lurene Tuttle, *I Want to Live!* co-star Virginia Vincent, Irene Selznick, and Jane Greer unhesitatingly answered my persistent questions. Don (Red) Barry, involved in that unfortunate, headlined episode with Susan, shared his happier memories of her with warmth and affection. I caught up with John Carroll just prior to his death. His recollections added a bit of spice—since few remember his short-lived engagement to Susan. Ben Medford remembers it and much more about early Susan Hayward. As her first agent, Mr. Medford supplied information I couldn't have gotten elsewhere—and did not pull his punches.

Donald Pippin, today executive musical director of the new Radio City Music Hall Entertainment Center and one of Broadway's most respected musical figures, spent three months preparing Susan for *Mame*. He spent precious free time rehearsal breaks in order to supply details of a period in Susan's life never before fully documented.

Maestro Lehman Bick, Susan's vocal coach during *Mame* rehearsals, provided additional details, as did Larry Ellis, a Broadway singer-actor, who met Susan at this time, and then reentered her life as it was slowly ebbing away. It was as painful for him to talk about those final days as it was for me to record them. But Larry's recollections, as shattering as they may be, inspired my title—*Portrait of a Survivor*—as did Nolan Miller's heartbreaking experience: designing the dazzling green sequin dress Susan wore for what she knew would be her last public appearance. Larry and Nolan told their stories exclusively to me. How do I find the words with which to thank them?

I am equally beholden to my dear friend Robert Osborne, who taped the last interview Susan gave and generously donated his valuable material for me to use in whatever way I felt fit. Jack Bradford, who often interviewed Susan Hayward, also put his exclusive material at my disposal.

Another good friend, editor-reporter Douglas McClelland, presented me with his extensive Hayward archives, personal correspondence, and rare photographs. His encouragement was also invaluable. Eduardo Moreno, the owner of the most extensive photograph collection of Susan Hayward in existence, was equally generous. Fox publicists, John Campbell, and Sonia Wolfson, whom Susan adored, were able to provide insights on the star.

New York Daily News reporter Donald Flynn, and retired magazine editor Henry Malgreen, were also of great help, as were Richard Webb and Saul Goodman, who were there when . . .

The recollections of Darryl F. Zanuck, Walter Wanger, Martin Rackin, Mark Robson, George Marshall, Lee Bowman, Jane Froman, Maxwell Arnow, Hedda Hopper, Adele Fletcher, and Stuart Heisler; and of the very alive, well, and active Danny Mann, Bob Wise, Frank Westmore, and Edward Dmytryk, were essential to my efforts to create a definitive portrait of this private woman.

I'd be remiss to ignore the contribution made by Eleanor Carson, Susan's neighbor in Fort Lauderdale. Dr. and Mrs. Russell Carson were eyewitnesses to the 1971 fire that almost cost Susan her life. Eleanor Carson related the story in its entirety, as well as other anecdotes about Susan's lonely life in Fort Lauderdale. Thanks too to Mrs. Carson's nephew Ty French.

I am particularly indebted to three highly respected physicians, Dr. Morton Marks of New York University Medical Center, Dr. Jerome J. Hoffman of Fort Lauderdale, and Dr. Donald Rubell of Beth Israel and Lenox Hill hospitals in New York City, for the assistance they gave me with my very difficult medical research. These experts in their diversified fields would not accept a fee for their help. Donations will be made to Cancer Care in their names.

Reverend Daniel McGuire, the priest who converted Susan Hayward to Catholicism, and Carmen Perugini, Susan's nurse and companion during the final years of her life, were both contacted. Although each adamantly refused to violate Susan's confidences in any way, they generously corrected glaring errors that had previously been printed and accepted as gospel. For this, I both thank and respect them.

Acknowledgments

Rebecca Boyd Stern was as always my "lucky charm"; Harry Kroft was another. My appreciation extends to Allan Maybee, who did my Southern research, and the indomitable Joan O'Brien who, as before, did most of my California legwork. Barbara Grether interviewed Susan's former make-up woman, Molly Briggs. Requesting anonymity are the various men and women at the Court of Records in New York and Los Angeles and the FBI, OSS, and CIA headquarters in Washington who searched for and found legal and public documents that supplied accurate information contradicting a myriad of previously published fallacies.

Jay Bobker spent sleepless nights typing certain sections of this manuscript I would not allow out of my home.

But I could never have made deadlines without the help of my cousin Arlene Bobker, the only person other than Mr. Nyren privy to the entire manuscript. Arlene lent an ear when I needed a confidante, a pair of sharp eyes to keep my tenses straight, and a giant-sized dictionary to correct my spelling. Arlene also kept me well-supplied with hamburgers, which I needed, and cigarettes, which no one needs. But she wouldn't do windows! I am in her debt for helping me through this writing experience.

B. L.

INDEX

Abbott and Costello comedies, 91, 93
Academy of Motion Picture Arts and
    Sciences, 92
    Academy Awards, vii, 3, 105–106,
        111, 135, 136, 204–205, 228–231,
        295–298
Acosta, Donald Barry de, 195–200, 203
Actors' Equity, 26
Ada, 238, 305, 324
Adam Had Four Sons, 57–62, 81, 319
Adam's Rib, 301
Albert, Eddie, 193
Algiers, 92
All About Eve, 60
Allen, Betty, 218
Allen, Dick, 125
Allen, Hadley, 218
Allen, Jane, 189
Allen, Joseph, Jr., 48
Allen, Patty, 275
Allure, 80
American Academy of Dramatic Art,
    27
American Broadcasting Company
    (ABC), 283
"American Medley," 120
Among the Living, 65, 319
Anastasia, 208, 229
And Now Tomorrow, 74, 80, 91, 320
Andrews, Dana, 109, 130–132
Angelica, 95
Anyone for Venice, 248, 249
Aparico, Julio, 139
Archerd, Army, 198
Armendariz, Pedro, 313
Arnow, Max, 41, 42
Artists and Models, 122
Aspern Papers, The (James), 100
Atlanta Constitution, 241
Atom bomb tests, Nevada (1953), 179,
    312–313
Auburn University, 255
Auntie Mame, 228
Autry, Gene, 61
Awful Truth, The, 58

Babes in Arms, 50
Bacall, Lauren, 210
Back Street, 237, 238, 324
Backes, Alice, 222
Bacon, James, 230
Ball, Lucille, 229
Bankhead, Tallulah, 324
Barker, Gregory Marrenner, 242, 273,
    297, 307, 309–312
    birth of, 90

Barker (*continued*)
    childhood of, 91, 104–105, 123, 136,
        146, 152, 157, 172, 174, 176, 188,
        197, 204–206
    education of, 212, 237, 241, 271
    and last will of S. H., 294–295, 315–
        317
    marriage of, 276
Barker, Ilse Schenke, 281, 311
Barker, Jess, 189–190, 204, 242, 275
    acting career of, 76–79, 111–112,
        129, 137
    divorce trial testimony, 158–177
    and last will of S. H., 294–295, 311,
        316
    marriage to S. H., 77, 93–95, 99,
        102–103, 112–113, 128–131, 136–
        141, 146–151, 153–156
Barker, Lex, 312
Barker, Nadja, 311
Barker, Susan (Gregory's wife), 276
Barker, Timothy Marrenner, ix, 5, 42,
    214, 236, 242, 271–273, 288–290,
    306, 307, 309–312
    birth of, 90
    childhood of, 104–105, 123, 136,
        146, 152, 157, 172, 174, 176, 188,
        197, 204–206
    education of, 212, 237, 241
    and last will of S. H., 294–295, 315–
        317
    marriage of, 281
Barker, Winnie, 80, 84
Barnes, Howard, 65, 100
Barrett, Judith, 48, 54
Barrett, Robert, 78
Barrett, Rona, 283
Barry, Don. *See* Acosta, Donald
    Barry de
Barrymore, John, 11
Barstow, James S., 114
Bathsheba, 116
Baxter, Warner, 50, 58, 61, 62
Beau Brummel, 11
Beau Geste, 48, 49, 134, 318
Beckley, Paul V., 226, 232
Beckwith, Frank, 41, 43, 44, 45, 89
Belser, Emily, 193
Bendix, William, 75
Bennett, Joan, 91, 95, 220
Berg, Dick, 282
Bergman, Ingrid, 58–62, 106, 207, 208,
    229, 230
Bernhardt, Sarah, 24
Bernstein, Jay, 281, 283, 285
Best Years of Our Lives, The, 110

Beverly Hills Hotel, vii
Beverly Hilton Hotel, vii
Bey, Turhan, 88
Bick, Lehman, 262–267, 270, 291
Bikel, Theodore, 222
Bird of Paradise, 155
Bishop, Joey, 258
Black Book, The, 111
Blair, Betsy, 139
Blondie Goes Latin, 58
Bogart, Humphrey, 210
Bogeaus, Benedict, 80
Boles, John, 237
Booth, Shirley, 136, 139
Borgnine, Ernest, 282
Boston Sunday Herald-Tribune, 285
Bower, Helen, 125
Bowman, Helene, 98
Bowman, Lee, 95, 97, 98 and *n.*, 100
Box Office magazine, 133
Boy Meets Girl, 26
Boyd, Stephen, viii
Boyer, Charles, 61, 235, 237
Bracken, Eddie, 67, 69
Brackett, Charles, 145–146
Bradford, Jack, 255, 256
Bradna, Olympe, 47
Brand, Harry, 128
Brando, Marlon, 135
Brew, Reverend Thomas, 302, 309
Briggs, Mollie, 93, 94, 328
Britton, Barbara, 67
Brokaw, Norman, 281–283, 288, 289
Broken Arrow, 154
Brophy, Frank, 213
Brother Rat, 44, 45
Brown, James, 67
Brown, Joe E., 49
Brown, John Mason, 234
Brown, Kay, 34
Buck Benny Rides Again, 53–54
Burn, John, 120 and *n.*, 124
Burns, Bob, 49
Burton, Richard, 110, 136
Butterworth, Charles, 61

Cabin in the Sky, 305
Caesar and Cleopatra, 234
Caesar's Palace, 258, 260, 265
Calhoun, Rory, 120, 124, 130
Cameron, Kate, 202
Campbell, Louise, 48
Campus Cinderella, 42, 318
Cannes film festival, 205, 206
Canova, Judy, 61
Canyon Passage, 92, 93, 109, 321
Capra, Frank, 58
Carnovsky, Morris, 52
Carol, Martine, 207
Carpetbaggers, The, 243
Carrington, Guy, 241
Carroll, Harrison, 155
Carroll, John, 68–72, 79, 98
Carroll, Nancy, 47
Carrollton, Georgia, 217–218, 309
Carruth, Milton, 96
Carson, Eleanor, 271–276
Carson, Johnny, 300
Carson, Russell, 271, 275, 276
Cash Box, 266
Cat and the Canary, The, 49

Cat on a Hot Tin Roof, 228
Cavett, Frank, 100
Century City Hospital, 289, 290, 307
Chalkley, Alma, 219
Chalkley, Floyd Eaton, 203–211, 225,
   227, 228, 247
   death of, 249–250
   finances of, 236–237, 247
   health of, 247–249
   marriage to S. H., 212–219, 231, 235,
   236–238, 242
Chalkley, Joseph, 242, 247, 248
Chalkmar (ranch), 238, 241
Chandler (Dorothy) Pavilion, 3
Chandler, Jeff, viii, 19, 154, 155, 158,
   232
   death of, 240
Chandler, Marjorie, 154
Chaney, Lon, Jr., 11
Chaplin, Charlie, 49, 50
Chatterton, Ruth, 47
Chicago Tribune Syndicate, 128
Christian, Linda, 114
Cinecitta Studios, 248
CinemaScope, 138, 143, 144, 146, 156
Clair, Rene, 67
Clayton, Dick, 27, 299, 300, 310
Clayton, Jan, 83
Cobb, Lee J., 283
Cohn, Harry, 58, 59, 62, 78, 81
Colbert, Claudette, 47, 56, 72, 234, 235
Colman, Ronald, 48, 90
Colonna, Jerry, 61
Columbia Pictures, 58, 76, 78, 81
Confidential magazine, 239
Congo Maisie, 69
Connolly, Mike, 200, 211, 212
Conqueror, The, 157, 177, 179, 204,
   312–313, 323
Conte, Richard, 108, 193
Cook, Johnny, 145
Cooper, Gary, 47, 48, 134, 146, 155,
   156
Cooper, Merian C., 40
Cooper, Rocky, 156
Cork Film Festival, 208
Corsica, Ted de, 313
Cotten, Joseph, 53
Count Basie band, 69
Cover Girl, 78, 81
Cramer, Stuart W., III, 157, 183
Crane, Cheryl, 244
Crane, Steve, 88
Crawford, Joan, 106, 197
Crosby, Bing, 47, 56, 95
Crosby, Bob, 61
Crowther, Bosley, 63, 125, 142, 145,
   202, 226, 232, 238, 243, 246, 256
Cukor, George, 34, 35, 39, 40, 41, 43,
   44, 98, 301

Dailey, Dan, 115
Dallas Morning News, 63
Dancing Co-Ed, 50
Daniel, Billy, 121
Daniels, Chick, 197
Dark Victory, 242
Dark Waters, 80
Darnell, Linda, 126
Darvi, Bella, 145
Daves, Delmar, 144

Index

David and Bathsheba, 117–118, 124, 322
David de Donatello Award, 232
Davis, Bette, 4, 60, 76, 90, 235, 242, 243, 244, 245, 292
Dead End, 26
Deadline at Dawn, 90, 91, 321
"Deep in the Heart of Texas," 120
de Havilland, Olivia, 61, 78, 111, 138
Dekker, Albert, 65
Delacorte, Albert, 104
Demetrius and the Gladiators, viii, 145, 180, 323
DeMille, Cecil B., 65, 234, 287
Denis, Paul, 231
Denning, Richard, 4, 58
Depression, Great, 21, 26, 28
DeSylva, Buddy, 61, 74, 75, 80, 92
Deval, Jacques, 116
Dickinson, Angie, 27
Dietrich, Florence Marrenner. *See* Marrenner, Florence
Dietrich, John, 239
Dietrich, Marlene, 47, 200
Dietrich, Moira, 240, 310–311
Dixon, Eddie, 25
Dmitri, Ivan, 32, 33, 35
Dmytryk, Edward, 244–246
Donlevy, Brian, 48
Dorothy Vernon of Haddon Hall, 11
Dorsen, Mr. and Mrs., 170, 171
Dougherty, Yvonne, 211
Douglas, Kirk, viii, 210
Dove, Billie, 138
Dowling, Eddie, 78
Downs, Johnny, 58
Dr. Jekyll and Mr. Hyde, 62
Dragonfly Squadron, 150 *n.*
Dramatic School, 49
Drew, Ellen, 48, 53
Duke, Patty, 256, 257
Duna, Steffi, 68, 98
Dunne, Irene, 237
Dunne, Philip, 116, 144
Durbin, Deanna, 91

Eckhardt, Emmy, 235
Eddy, Nelson, 69
Egan, Richard, 180
Ellis, Larry, 263, 264, 270, 291–310
"Embraceable You," 122
Emory University, 301, 302, 303
Emslie, Mrs. Robert, 10, 15
End of Summer, 26
Epstein, Julius J., 109
Epstein, Philip G., 109
Erdman, Leonard, 249
Executive Suite, 222

Fabian, Max, 60
Fairbanks, Douglas, 11
Faris, Barry, 73
Farmer, Frances, 47, 53, 65
Farmer's Daughter, The, 106
Fauss, Opal, 290
Feagin Drama School, 27, 82
Feldman, Charles, 81, 88
Feldman (Charles) Agency, 299
Field, Betty, 48, 53
Fields, W. C., 47
Fighting Seabees, The, 75

Finch, Peter, 241
Fitzgerald and Pride, 282, 283, 284
Flaherty, Vincent X., 204, 213, 228, 231
Fleming, Victor, 98
Fletcher, Adele, 236
Fletcher, Margie, 235
Flying Tigers, 69
Foch, Nina, 79, 82
Fogler, Gertrude, 43
Follow Thru, 21
Fonda, Henry, 50
Fonda, Jane, 27
Foreign Correspondent, 92
Foreign Press Association, 135, 229
Forest Rangers, The, 66, 319
Fort Lauderdale News, 284
Four Daughters, 45
Four Seasons, The (condominium), 271–280
Fox-Movietone News, 182
Frank, Gerold, viii
Frankenstein, 91
Franzero, Carlo Maria, 234
Freeman, Y. Frank, 56–57
French, Ty, 271–272
Freulich, Roman, 225
Freund, Bob, 258
Frings, Ketti, 60
Frisco Sal, 91
Froman, Jane, 120 and *n.,* 121–124
Frost, Jack, 257, 258

Gaal, Franciska, 47
Gable, Clark, 69, 83, 181
Gang, Martin, 158, 238
Garbo, Greta, 92
Gardella, Kay, 284
Garden of Evil, 148, 156, 158, 323
Gardner, Ava, 138
Garland, Judy, 180, 255
Gaynor, Mitzi, 212
Gentlemen Prefer Blondes, 126, 145
Gentleman's Agreement, 106, 117
Georgia Military Academy, 237
Gerson, Barbara, 313
Gidding, Nelson, 222
Ginsberg, Henry, 37
Girls' Commercial High, 23, 25
Girls on Probation, 45, 318
Glass, Ian, 257
Glenwood Theater, 24
Goddard, Paulette, 49–50, 56, 58, 61, 65, 66, 67, 72, 74, 75, 81
Goldberg, Len, 283
Golden Boy, 53
Golden Globe Awards (Foreign Press Association), 229
Goldwyn, Samuel, 108, 109, 110
Gomez, Thomas, 178
Gone With the Wind (film), 34, 35, 49, 98, 182
Gone With the Wind (Mitchell), 34
Good Luck Mr. Yates, 78
Gordon, Michael, 114
Government Girl, 78
Governor's Ball, vii, 229, 231
Grable, Betty, 134
Graham, Barbara (Bloody Babs), 222, 225, 226

Graham, Sheilah, 147, 148, 154, 180, 205, 206, 212
Grant, Cary, 35, 229
Grauman's Chinese Theater, 124, 154
Greatest Show on Earth, The, 135
Green, Johnny, 191, 192
Greer, Jane, 102
Greve, Frank, 301
Griffin, Merv, 124, 300
Griffin, Mr. and Mrs. T. R., 218
Grossel, Ira, 19–20. *See also* Chandler, Jeff
Grossel, Mrs., 20
Group Theater, 26, 52, 53
Guernsey, Otis L., Jr., 75
Guinele, Jorge, 209, 210
Gunfighter, The, 117
Gussow, Mel, 145

Hahn, S. S. (Sammy), 158–159, 199
Hairy Ape, The, 75, 76, 320
Hale, Wanda, 70
Haley, Jack, 21
Halls of Montezuma, The, 122
Hammack, William, 241
Hampshire House, 115
Hanna, David, 124
"Happiness Is a Thing Called Joe," 192, 305, 306
Harpbrite, Margaret C., 155
Harvard *Lampoon*, 238
Hathaway, Henry, 113, 156
Hayes, Hal, 198, 200–204
Hayes, Helen, 283
Hayes, John Michael, 244, 245
Hayward, Brooke, 41
Hayward, Leland, 41, 77
Hayward, Susan:
  Academy Award nominations, 105–106, 111, 204–205, 228–231
  awards given to, 116, 134, 135, 208, 228, 229, 232, 238
  birth of, 15
  and cancer, 3, 288–307
  in car accident, 9–10, 16, 17, 18
  childhood of, 9–22
  conversion to Catholicism, 253, 254
  death of, 307–310
  divorce trial testimony, 159–177
  education of, 22–25
  home in Carrollton, Georgia, 217–218
  last will and testament of, 294–295, 303, 315–317
  marriage to Barker, 5, 77, 93–95, 99, 102–103, 112–113, 128–131, 136–141, 146–151, 153–156
  marriage to Chalkley, 5, 212–219, 231, 235, 236–238, 242
  modeling career of, 30–34, 130–131
  named Susan Hayward, 41
  singing of, 191–192, 262–267
  sleeping pill overdose, 187–191
Hayworth, Rita, 74, 78, 98
He Who Gets Slapped, 11
Heat of Anger, 284, 325
Heatherton, Joey, 244
Hecht, Ben, 59, 60, 226
Hedda and Louella, 285
Heflin, Van, 53, 69, 101
Heiress, The, 111

Heisler, Stuart, 96, 97, 98, 100, 106
Henderson, Charles, 191, 192, 260
"Henrietta" award, 135
Henry, William, 48
Hepburn, Katharine, 35, 47, 52, 53, 138, 300, 305
Heston, Charlton, viii, 3, 4, 133, 142, 298
Hestor, Harvey, 203, 204, 205, 217, 218, 219
Hi Gaucho, 68
Hickman, Sgt. Carl, 73
High Noon, 134, 135
Hill, Virginia, 69
His Weird and Wanton Ways: The Secret Life of Howard Hughes, 157
Hit Parade of 1943, 67–72, 320
Hodges, Joy, 50
Hold Back the Dawn, 60
Holden, William, 48, 67, 282
Holiday, 85
Hollywood Canteen, 78
Hollywood Reporter, 124, 142, 200
Holm, Celeste, 268, 269
Honey, Pot, The, 249, 325
Hope, Bob, 47, 49, 56, 61
Hopkins, Miriam, 47
Hopper, Hedda, 59, 127–130, 148, 154, 198, 236, 283
House of Strangers, 108, 321
Houser, Marvin, 46
How to Marry a Millionaire, 145
Hughes, Howard, 126, 127, 137, 138, 152–157, 175, 177, 178, 182, 183, 239
Hunter, Ross, 237
Hurst, Fannie, 237
Hutton, Betty, 74
Hyams, Joe, 231

I Can Get It for You Wholesale, 114, 115, 116, 120, 322
I Married a Witch, 67, 319
I Met Him in Paris, 98
I Thank a Fool, 241, 324
I Want to Live!, 4, 221, 225, 307, 324
I Wanted Wings, 57
I'd Climb the Highest Mountain, 114, 117, 119, 120, 322
Idiot's Delight, 26
I'll Cry Tomorrow, vii, 188, 191–197, 201–208, 323
"I'm Sittin' on Top of the World," 192
Immerman, Stanley, 188, 189
Intermezzo, 58, 60
International News Service, 73, 193
Interrupted Melody, 205
Irvine (Theodora) School for the Theater, 80
Irwin, Peggy, 203, 247
It Happened One Night, 58
It's a Hell of a Life but Not a Bad Living (Dmytryk), 245
Ivanhoe, 135

Jack London, 75, 320
Jackson, Andrew, 142
Jackson, Glenda, ix, 4, 298
Jackson, Rachel Donelson, 142
Jacobson, Arthur, 46

Jam Session, 78
James, Henry, 100
Jane Froman Story, The. See *With a Song in My Heart*
Jarmyn, Jil, 198, 199
Jellinek, Elvin, M., 97
Jennings, C. Robert, 266
Jim Thorpe—All American, 204
"Jim's Toasted Peanuts," 120
Joan of Arc, 106
Johnson, Erskine, 147, 154
Jones, Jennifer, 204
Jonson, Ben, 248
Jordan, Dorothy, 40
Jourdan, Louis, 229
Jungle Captive, 91
Justin, Sidney, 88

Kane, Mr. and Mrs. Joseph, 218, 219
Karp, Maurice, 103
Kazan, Elia, 52
Keep Your Powder Dry, 89
Kelly, Kerry, 139
Kelly, Gene, 98, 139
Kelly, Grace, 181, 208
Kennedy, Arthur, 127
Kennedy, Jacqueline, 250
Kentucky Rifles, 189
Kerr, Deborah, 228
Keyes, Evelyn, 48
Kidnapped, 50
Kilgallen, Dorothy, 158, 198, 201
Kimball, Stanley, 214
King, Bruce, 221
King, Henry, 117, 118, 119
King Features Syndicate, 73
King Kong, 40
Kings County Hospital, 10
Korvin, Charles, 91
Koster, Henry, 42
Koster, Peggy Moran, 42

Labotta, John, 33
Ladd, Alan, 69, 78, 80
LaFaye, Emma, 71
LaFaye, Julian, 68
LaFuente, Señor, 139
Lake, Veronica, 57, 61, 67, 72
Lamarr, Hedy, 92
Landis, Carole, 42
Lane, Priscilla, 45
Lang, Jennings, 220
Lang, Walter, 121–125, 236
Lansbury, Angela, 260
Lawrence, Jerome, 266–267
Lawson, John Howard, 100
Lee, Dixie, 95
Lee, Robert E., 267
Leigh, Vivien, 49, 234
LeMaire, Charles, 144, 210, 212, 235
Leontovich, Eugenie, 60
Letter from Bataan, A, 319
Levine. Joseph E., 243, 244
Lewis, Diana, 42
Life and Times of Cleopatra (Franzero), 234
Life magazine, 90, 100, 134, 201, 202
Lind, Cris, 58
Little, Martha, 143, 147, 160, 162, 163, 166, 183
Little, Sara, 12, 23, 28, 143, 218

Logan, Janice, 48
Lombard, Carole, 47
Lone Wolf Strikes Back, The, 58
Look magazine, 90, 124, 201, 202
Los Angeles Times, 202
Los Angeles Music Center, 3
Lost Horizon, 58
Lost Moment, The, 100, 179, 321
Lost Weekend, The, 98, 99
Louis, Jean, 237
Love Is a Many Splendored Thing, 205
Lupino, Ida, 138
Lusty Men, The, 127, 137, 322
Lyons, Leonard, 73

Mack and Mabel, 306
MacLaine, Shirley, 228
MacMichael, Florence, 67
MacMurray, Fred, 47, 66, 74, 75
McCarthy, Neil, 213
McClelland, Doug, 66, 244
McGavin, Darren, 284
McGuire, Betty, 260
McGuire, Father Daniel J., 253, 254
McGuire, Dorothy, 106
McKinley, Ray, band of, 69
Magic, 78
Magnani, Anna, vii, 202, 205
Mame, 258–269
Man in Half Moon Street, The, 74
Mankiewicz, Don. 222
Mankiewicz, Joseph L., 108, 248, 249
Mann, Danny, 191–195, 238
Manners, Dorothy, 291
Manson, Charles, 274
Mapes, Jacques, 237
March, Frederic, 4–5, 67, 112
Marin, Ned, 137, 154, 299
Marlowe, Hugh, 156
Marquand, John, 210
Marrenner, Edythe. *See* Hayward, Susan
Marrenner, Ellen, 10–24, 41, 43, 44, 64, 72, 82–84, 123, 175, 187, 188, 212, 236
   death of, 224
   marriage of, 13–14
Marrenner, Florence, 11–12, 16–24, 35, 44, 62, 64, 65, 82, 84, 94, 141, 187, 239–240, 310
   birth of, 14
   dancing career of, 20–22
   and last will of S. H., 303, 310
Marrenner, Joseph, 12, 14
Marrenner, Kate Harrigan, 11–12, 14
Marrenner, Wally (Walter, Jr.), ix, 12–24, 64, 71, 72, 147, 163, 188, 212, 236, 250, 254, 272, 290
   birth of, 15
   marriage of, 290
   and last will of S. H., 294, 307, 310, 315–316
Marrenner, Walter, ix, 10–28, 187
   death of, 43, 44
   illness of, 33, 35, 41
   marriage of, 13–14
Marriage-Go-Round, The, 234, 235, 237, 324
Marry Me Again, 150n
Marshall, Alan, 40
Marshall, George, 66, 101

Martin, Charlie, 73, 74
Martin, Dean, 238
Martin, Freddy, band of, 69
Martin, Mildred, 182
Marty, 205
"M*A*S*H," 260
Mason, James, viii, 116, 235
Mason, Pamela, 116
Massachusetts General Hospital, 294
Massey, Raymond, 66, 117
Matheson, Richard, 157
Mathews, Joyce, 48
Mature, Victor, 144
May, David, 87
Mayer, Louis B., 62, 69
Medford, Ben, 37, 41, 43, 44, 46, 57,
    58, 60, 62, 71, 72, 75, 79, 81, 83
Melville Goodwin, U.S.A., 210
Mercury Theater Company, 26
Meriwether, Lillian, 11
Meriwether, Walter Scott, 11
Merman, Ethel, 256
Metro-Goldwyn-Mayer (MGM), 43, 49,
    101, 191
Metropolitan Hospital, Welfare Island,
    33
Meyer, Dr. Frederick, 210
Miami Herald, 301
Miami News, 257
Milland, Ray, 47, 48, 65, 66, 98, 99
Miller, Nolan, 295, 296, 297, 298
Miracle Worker, The, 256
Mirisch Films, Ltd., 242
Mississippi Sun, 11
Mitchell, Cameron, 155
Mitchell, Margaret, 34
Mitchum, Robert, viii, 127, 131, 133,
    145
Modern Screen, 103, 104, 134, 239
Monahan, Mabel, 220–221, 222
Monroe, Marilyn, 126, 134–135, 143,
    145, 207, 288
Monsieur Beaucaire, 11
Montgomery, Ed, 221
Montgomery, George, 43
Montgomery, Robert, 106
"Montparnasse," 120
Moorehead, Agnes, 4, 179
    death of, 312
Morris (William) Agency, 281
Morrison, Patricia, 48
Motion Picture Herald, 69, 133
Motion Picture magazine, 11, 104, 112,
    137
Motion Picture Photographers' Associa-
    tion, 116
Moulin Rouge, 135
Mourning Becomes Electra, 106
Movieland, 104
Movies of the Week, 282, 283
Mowrer, Roy, 66
Mr. Deeds Goes to Town, 58
Mr. Smith Goes to Washington, 58
M. V. Princess (ship), 257
My Cousin Rachel, 135
My Foolish Heart, 108, 109, 110, 111,
    322

Nation, Lt. Kenneth, 276
Neal, Patricia, 156
Nelson, Ron, 272, 273, 301, 305–306

New Moon, 21
New York Capitol, 62
New York Daily News, 27, 52, 70, 202,
    231, 284
New York Daily Mirror, 73, 75
New York Film Critics' Society, 111
    awards, 136, 202, 228
New York Herald Tribune, 65, 75, 100,
    114, 226, 232
New York Post, 65, 115
New York Sunday News, 63
New York Times, The, 63, 70, 75, 113,
    114, 118, 125, 142, 145, 202, 220,
    226, 235, 238
New Yorker, The, 109
Newmar, Julie, 235
Newsweek, 90, 102, 118, 246
Niagara, 135
Night Music, 52, 53
Night Walker, The, 311
Niven, David, 3, 228, 229, 298
Nixon, Richard M., 290–291
Nothing but the Truth, 61
Novak, Kim, 207, 208

Oakland, Simon, 222
Oberon, Merle, 80, 91
Odets, Clifford, 52
O'Grady, Florence, 23
O'Keefe, Dennis, 68–69
Olivier, Sir Laurence, 229
$1,000 a Touchdown, 49, 318
O'Neill, Carlotta Monterey, 75
O'Neill, Eugene, 75
O'Neill, Zelma, 21
Osborne, Robert, 274, 285, 286, 287,
    296, 313
Our Leading Citizen, 49, 318
Out of the Frying Pan, 67

Paget, Debra, 152
Pantages Theater, Hollywood, vii, 4,
    111, 205
Papote, Jean, 138, 139, 140
Paramount Pictures, 46, 47, 67, 72, 232
    Golden Circle, 48, 53
Parker, A. B., 218
Parker, Dorothy, 100
Parker, Eleanor, 205
Parkins, Barbara, 256
Parsons, Louella, viii, 50, 51, 52, 59,
    71, 75, 88–89, 92, 136, 148–151,
    153, 154, 156, 158, 191, 197, 200,
    205, 208, 210, 212, 232, 237, 283
Parsons' Flying Stars, 50, 258
Pasadena Playhouse, 48
Pat and Mike, 301
Pearson, Ellen F. *See* Marrenner, Ellen
Peck, Gregory, 6, 117, 118, 130
Perkins, Emmett, 221
Person to Person, 258
Perugini, Carmen, 4, 295, 301, 303,
    304, 305, 310
    mentioned in last will, 315
Peters, Jean, 126, 138, 153, 157, 183
Petrified Forest, The, 90
Pettebone, Jean, 84
Peyton Place, 257
Philadelphia Inquirer, 182
Philadelphia Story, The, 52
"Phillip Morris Playhouse," 73

Photoplay magazine, viii, 11, 103, 121, 134, 155
Pickford, Mary, 11
Pink, W. T., 15
Pippin, Donald, 192, 260, 261, 262, 268, 306
Playwrights' Company, 26
Pons, Lily, 262
Popenoe, Dr. Paul, 103
Porgy and Bess, 26
Possessed, 106
Pot of Gold, 58
Powell, William (Dick), 42, 178, 179
    death of, 312
Powell, Eleanor, 21
Powell, Jane, 134
Power, Tyrone, 113, 114, 117, 180, 182
Powers, John Robert, 29
Powers, Stephen R., Jr., 199
Preisser, Cherry, 51
Preisser, June, 50, 51
President's Lady, The, 133, 142, 323
Preston, Robert, 48, 66, 106, 306
Prospect Heights High, 25
Pryor, Thomas, 70, 113, 114

Queen Christina, 92
Quiet Man, The, 135
Quinn, Anthony, 136

Rackin, Martin, 45, 243, 245, 251, 253, 258, 259, 282, 303
Radio City Music Hall, 62, 111, 201
Rage in Heaven, 62
Rappaport, Charlotte, 19
Ratoff, Gregory, 6, 58, 60, 77, 78, 81, 287
Rawhide, 113, 114, 116, 120, 322
Raye, Martha, 49
Reagan, Ronald, 50, 51, 52
Reap the Wild Wind, 65, 319
Redbook, 203
Redwine, Skip, 264, 305
Republic Studios, 61, 62, 69, 70, 73, 75
Revengers, The, 282, 283, 325
Reynolds, Burt, 27, 299–300
Richmond News-Leader, 63
Riot in Cell Block 11, 220
Ritter, Thelma, 124
RKO, 50, 78, 90, 106, 127, 179
Road to Singapore, 54
Robbins, Harold, 243
Robe, The, 123, 143, 144, 154
Robinson, Edward G., 108
Robinson, Pat, 73
Robson, Mark, 110, 255
Rogers, Ginger, 207
Rogers, Henry, 84
Rogers, Roy, 61
Rooster Cogburn, 305
Rose Tattoo, The, 202, 205
Ross, Frank, 144
Rossellini, Roberto, 207
Roth, Lillian, viii, 188, 192, 193, 194, 201
Roth, Ron, 282
Rudin, Milton, 158, 238
Russell, Jane, 126
Russell, Rosalind, 105, 106, 228, 229
Ruth, Morgana, 211
Rutherford, Ann, 87

Saks, Gene, 260
Salinger, J. D., 109
San Francisco Examiner, 221
Santley, Joseph, 62
Santo, Jack, 221
Saturday Evening Post, 32, 33, 34, 48–49
Saxon Charm, The, 106, 321
Say Goodbye, Maggie Cole, 284, 285, 325
Schallert, Edward, 202
Schenck, Joseph, 133
Schenke, Ilse, 281
Schmidt, Lars, 229
Schulberg, Mrs. B. P., 78
Screen Actors Guild (SAG), 282
Selznick, David O., 34, 40, 58, 59, 92
Selznick, Irene, 34–35
Selznick International Studios, 35, 39, 40
Separate Tables, 228
Seven Men from Now, 198
Seventeen, 53
Shadow, The, 58
Shady Lady, 91
Shapiro, Harold, 182
Shaw, George Bernard, 234
Shaw, Robert, 58
Sheridan, Ann, 111
Shipp, Cameron, 61
Sidney, Sylvia, 47
Siegel, Bugsy, 69
Siegel, Dr. Lee, 288, 289, 290, 298, 303, 306, 307
Silver Screen, 104
Simmons, Edna, 17
"Sing You Sinners," 192
Sis Hopkins, 61, 319
Skirmish on the Home Front, 320
Skolsky, Sidney, 134, 154, 197, 200, 211
Smash-Up, The Story of a Woman, 95, 97, 98, 99, 100, 101, 103, 202, 217, 321
Smith, Roland H., 120n
Snake Pit, The, 11
Snows of Kilimanjaro, 133, 322
So Proudly We Hail, 72, 81
Soldier of Fortune, 180, 181, 323
Some Came Running, 228
Somebody Up There Likes Me, 222
Sound of Music, The, 222
South Pacific, 212
Spreckels, Kay, 181
Spelling, Aaron, 283, 284
Stacey, James, 282
Stage Coach, 92
Standing Room Only, 74, 75
Stanwyck, Barbara, 23–24, 282, 298–299, 311
Star Is Born, A, 112, 180
Star Spangled Rhythm, 319
Stella, 111
Stevens, Robert, 241
Stevens, Ruby. *See* Stanwyck, Barbara
Stock market crash (1929), 21
Stolen Hours, 242, 243, 324
Stompanato, Johnny, 244
Stone, Irving, 142
Story of Demetrius, The, 143, 144, 145
Street, James, 100

Streetcar Named Desire, A, 135
Sturges, Preston, 61
Sullavan, Margaret, 41, 237
Sullivan, Ed, 72
Sullivan's Travels, 61
Summertime, 204
Susann Jacqueline, 255, 257
Swain, Dodee Hazel, 167
Swit, Loretta, 260

Take One False Step, 111
Talmadge, Herman, 119
Tap Roots, 100, 101, 321
Tate, Sharon, 256, 257, 274
Taylor, Don, viii, 283
Taylor, Elizabeth, 110, 228, 234
Taylor, Jud, 284
Taylor, Robert, 311
Technicolor, 156
Theater Guild, 26
They Won't Believe Me, 102, 267, 321
Thief of Bagdad, The, 11
This Gun for Hire, 78
This Love of Ours, 91
This Man Is Mine, 126, 127
Thornton, Walter, 29, 31, 32, 35, 36, 53, 158
Thornton (Walter) Agency, 29
Three Faces of Eve, 208
Thunder in the Sun, 232, 324
Thunder Rock, 53
Tierney, Gene, 126
Tierney, Lawrence, 90
"Time Heals Everything," 306
Time magazine, 75, 90, 91, 106, 118, 142, 182, 202, 235
Time of Their Lives, The, 93
Tindall, Dr. George, 302
Titus, Deacon, 11
To Each His Own, 111
Tobias, George, 114
Todd, Richard, 207
Tomlinson, Virginia, 95
Top Secret Affair, 210, 324
Totter, Audrey, 106
Touch of Class, A, 4
Trail of the Lonesome Pine, The, 77
Trevor, Claire, 78
Tropic, 266
Trotti, Lamar, 120, 125
Tucker, Bobby, 212
Tufts, Sonny, viii, 78
Tulsa, 106, 321
Tunberg, Karl, 241
Turner, Lana, 42, 74, 88, 89, 136, 138, 244, 312
Tuttle, Lurene, 201
Tuttle, Tommy, 235
TV Guide, 283, 284
Twelve O'Clock High, 117
Twentieth Century-Fox, 58, 81, 106, 116, 119, 126, 133, 143, 209, 229, 232, 234, 255, 257
Twinkle in God's Eye, A, 198
Two Flags West, 154
Typhoon, 54

"Uncle Wiggily in Connecticut," 109
United Artists, 58, 67, 75, 80
Universal, 90, 91, 106

University of Southern California, 255
Untamed, 54, 181, 323

Vagabond King, 192
Valentino, Rudolph, 11
Valery, Bernard, 207
Valley of the Dolls, 255, 256, 257, 274, 325
Van Cleef, Lee, 312
Variety, 65, 98, 99, 100, 124, 182, 198
Victoria Regina, 26
Vincent, Virginia, 223, 224, 225
V.I.P.'s, The, 110
Virgin Queen, The, 292
Vitaphone, 31
Viva Zapata!, 135
Vivyan, John, 260
Volpone, 248

Wagner, Robert, viii, 122, 123, 125, 217
Wald, Jerry, 126
Walgreens drug store, 26
Walker, Clint, 240
Walker, Helen, 74
Walker, Judge Herbert Y., 159, 180
Wallace, Sylvia, 134
Wanger, Walter, 42, 77, 92, 93, 94, 95, 98, 100, 102, 106, 107, 219, 220, 224–226, 229, 230, 234
  death of, 265
Warner, Jack, 45, 158, 210
Warner Brothers, 37, 41, 43, 46, 89, 210
Waters, Ethel, 305
Way of all Flesh, The, 54
Wayburn, Ned, 20, 21
Wayne, David, 120
Wayne, John, viii, 61, 65, 66, 69, 75, 178, 179
  death of, 312, 313
Weaver, Fritz, 283
Webb, Richard, 54–55, 56
Weidman, Jerome, 114
Weiler, A. H., 118
Weinberger, William S., 265
Weingarten, Lawrence, 192, 300, 301
Weisbart, David, 255
Wellman, William, 48, 287
West, Mae, 47
West Side Story, 222
Westmore, Frank, 296, 297
Whelan, Arleen, 50, 51
"When the Red, Red Robin Comes Bob, Bob, Bobbin' Along," 192
Where Love Has Gone, 243, 244, 245–246, 325
Whitcomb, Jon, 32
White, Gordon, 208, 210
White, Onna, 260, 266
White Witch Doctor, viii, 145, 172, 323
Widmark, Richard, 122, 155
Wilkerson, G. W., 188
Williams, John, 201
Wills, Chill, 189
Wilson, Earl, 201
Winchell, Walter, 152–153
Winterset, 26
Wise, Robert, 222, 223, 224, 225
With a Song in My Heart, 4, 118–126, 134, 135, 322
Without Love, 301

Index

Wolfson, Sonia, 130, 131, 235
Woman Obsessed, A, 229, 232, 324
Women, The, 49
Wood, Yvonne, 101, 102
Woodward, Joanne, 208
World's Favorite Screen Star of 1952, 175
Wright, Cobina, 201
Wyman, Jane, 50, 51, 52

Yates, Herbert, 71
Yawger, Dorothy, 23
You Can't Take It With You, 58, 114
Young, Loretta, 74, 106
Young, Robert, 267

Young, Roland, 75
Young and Willing, 67, 320
Young Mr. Lincoln, 50
Youngblood Hawke, 98

Zaenglin, Florence. *See* Marrenner, Florence
Zaenglin, Larry, 82, 238, 310, 311
Zaenglin, Udo, 65, 82, 238
Zanuck, Darryl, 50, 106, 107, 108, 111, 113, 116–119, 122, 126, 131, 134, 135, 137, 138, 143, 144, 145, 148, 154
Zink, Jack, 284

BEVERLY LINET has known Hollywood as a writer, editor, reviewer and publicist for over thirty years; first as a columnist for *Modern Screen,* then *Photoplay,* then as editor of *Who's Who in Hollywood* and *Who's Who in TV.* She is also the author of *Ladd: The Life, the Legend, the Legacy of Alan Ladd.* Born in Brooklyn, as was Susan Hayward, Beverly Linet was a professional acquaintance of the star. She now lives in New York City.